Cultural Heritage, Transnational Narratives and Museum Franchising in Abu Dhabi

This publication contributes to new understandings of how heritage operates as a global phenomenon and the transnational heritage discourses that emerge from this process. Taking such a view sees autochthonous and franchised heritage not as separate or opposing elements but as part of the same process of contemporary globalised identity-making, which contributes to the development of newly emergent cosmopolitan identities. The book critically examines the processes that are involved in the franchising of heritage and its cultural effects. It does so by examining the connections and tensions that emerge from combining autochthonous and franchised heritage in the United Arab Emirates, providing a unique window into the process of creating hybrid heritage in non-Western contexts. It develops new ideas about how this global phenomenon works, how it might be characterised and how it influences and is itself affected by local forms of heritage. By exploring how autochthonous and franchised heritage is produced in Abu Dhabi it becomes clear that Western-dominated practices are often challenged and, perhaps more importantly, that new ways of understanding, producing and living with heritage are being articulated in these previously marginal locations.

The book offers innovative insights into heritage as a transnational process, exploring how it operates within local, national and international identity concerns and debates. It will appeal to scholars and students interested in critical heritage studies, museums, tourism, cultural studies and Middle Eastern studies.

Sarina Wakefield is Lecturer in Museum Studies and Programme Director Museum Studies (Distance Learning) in the School of Museum Studies at the University of Leicester. She is also the Founder and Director of the Museums in Arabia conference series. Previously, she has lectured at College of Arts and Creative Enterprises, Zayed University, Dubai, UAE, and UCL Qatar on the MA in Museum and Gallery Practice. Also, she has worked on museum and heritage projects in the UK and Bahrain. Her primary research focuses on critical heritage studies and museology of the

Gulf. More broadly, she is interested in transnational identity, globalisation, universal museums, franchise museums, the global art market, heritage and migrant identity, and the relationships between heritage and sports. She has published around these subjects in international journals and books, and is editor of the forthcoming volume *Museums of the Arabian Peninsula: Historical Developments and Contemporary Discourses* (Routledge). She is also the co-editor for the Routledge book series *Cultural Heritage, Art and Museums in the Middle East*. She received her BSc in Archaeology and her MA in Museum Studies from the University of Leicester (UK) and her PhD in History from the Open University (UK).

Cultural Heritage, Transnational Narratives and Museum Franchising in Abu Dhabi

Sarina Wakefield

Routledge
Taylor & Francis Group

LONDON AND NEW YORK

First published 2021
by Routledge
2 Park Square, Milton Park, Abingdon, Oxon OX14 4RN

and by Routledge
52 Vanderbilt Avenue, New York, NY 10017

Routledge is an imprint of the Taylor & Francis Group, an informa business

British Library Cataloguing-in-Publication Data
A catalogue record for this book is available from the British Library

Library of Congress Cataloging-in-Publication Data
A catalog record has been requested for this book

ISBN: 978-1-138-08822-1 (hbk)
ISBN: 978-1-315-11003-5 (ebk)

Typeset in Times New Roman
by codeMantra

To Tracey

Contents

Illustrations

Figures

Tables

Acknowledgements

I am grateful to the generous individuals and organisations that contributed to this body of work. I am particularly grateful to all the cultural heritage practitioners and Emirati residents that met with me for coffee or lunch, or invited me to their offices and homes to share their views with me. Thank you for placing your faith in my research and for giving up your valuable time to contribute. Particular thanks need to go to the following organisations: Department of Culture and Tourism – Abu Dhabi (previously the Abu Dhabi Authority for Culture and Heritage and the Tourism Development Investment Corporation), Sharjah Museums Department, Louvre Abu Dhabi, Guggenheim Abu Dhabi, Zayed National Museum and the British Museum. In addition, I would like to thank fellow researcher Jillian Schedneck, who accompanied me on numerous research trips to Abu Dhabi, for our discussions and enjoyment along the way.

Thank you to my thesis advisors Rodney Harrison, David Vincent and Kevin Hetherington for providing me with advice, encouragement and support through my PhD studies and beyond. The initial research for this book would not have materialised without your ongoing enthusiasm for the topic and your faith in me. I would like to thank both Jessica Hughes and Steve Watson for agreeing to be my thesis examiners. Steve Watson sadly passed away shortly after this, and his kind words and enthusiasm will remain with me always. I would also like to acknowledge the financial support I received during my fieldwork through the award of an Open University Fellowship and all of the administrative staff in both the Faculty of Arts and the Research Degrees Center who have facilitated numerous requests over the years. In particular, special mention goes to Anne Ford.

I have gained a great deal from discussing my works at various conferences and events. Thanks especially to those that have become both colleagues and friends along the way; these include: Mark Beech, Laila Prager, Sabrina DeTurk, Anjana Reddy, Victoria Penziner-Hightower, Rodney Harrison and Jessica Hughes. Special thanks need to go to Simon Knell, Divya Tolia-Kelly and Emma Waterton for their time and input on this book project. You all continue to inspire me.

I would like to give enormous thanks to my family, especially my parents, Richard and Beryl, and my best friends, Tracey and Adam, for your support and faith in me always. Tracey was taken from us too soon and this book is dedicated to her, and all the special memories we have shared.

Preface

Cultural Heritage, Transnational Narratives and Museum Franchising in Abu Dhabi examines both the rationale and the mixed consequences of adopting a global heritage discourse to narrate and present transnational and cosmopolitan identities. It seeks to explore the particular nuances of heritage and its relationship both to nation building and to the development of transnational tourist economies in the Gulf states. At its most basic, heritage is a process that applies certain standards and protocols to aspects of the past (both tangible and intangible), which are then used to construct particular identities for people in the past and the present (Smith 2006; Harrison 2013). At the time of this study Abu Dhabi in the United Arab Emirates (UAE) was in the process of actively developing and formalising, through the development of new procedures and practices, a new heritage industry, which included both autochthonous[1] and franchised formations of heritage; as such it was possible to analyse and trace the early heritage developments in the city.

In particular, a large-scale Cultural District was being developed on Saadiyat Island, which will result in the establishment of five large-scale cultural institutions. The planned developments include two cultural heritage franchises – the Louvre Abu Dhabi and the Guggenheim Abu Dhabi – and three large-scale autochthonous institutions – the Zayed National Museum, the Maritime Museum and the Performing Arts Centre. Alongside these activities, Abu Dhabi is actively documenting and preserving autochthonous heritage – tangible and intangible. This has led to an increased focus on heritage conservation and preservation. In particular, the preservation of buildings in Abu Dhabi city, the most notable being Qasr Al Hosn fort, which was the first permanent structure in the city. Qasr Al Hosn fort has become a national symbol and has been linked to the development of the city and the nation's history. As such, the site has been through a period of preservation and reinterpretation, which has resulted in the fort being reopened as a heritage museum and its importance as iconic heritage symbol being further enhanced. Furthermore, since Abu Dhabi has developed from a predominantly oral-based society the intangible past is a significant source of heritage, and as such events and performances are also significant elements of national heritage practice (see, for example, Prager 2015).

My approach is positioned within the interdisciplinary field of critical heritage studies: more specifically I take the view that heritage is an emergent and active 'process'. This book examines for the first time how autochthonous heritage and franchised heritage processes are being used to develop a transnational heritage industry in the Emirate of Abu Dhabi. While these aspects are analysed as separate formations of heritage based on different processes, scales and interpretations, I see them both as embedded dialectical processes that operate within the same system of heritage, which is being used to craft and support Abu Dhabi's contemporary identity. In doing so, I suggest that hybridity and cosmopolitanism serve as key issues within the contemporary transnational heritage economy, arguing that examining heritage as a hybrid practice enables us to challenge the traditional boundaries that have been dominant within Eurocentric interpretations of heritage, which has served to reinforce the 'canonisation' of heritage (Harrison 2010a). Instead, I attempt to take a broad view of heritage production, and in doing so I argue for a hybrid heritage that recognises and interrogates the multi-vocalised processes that are inherent within cross-border collaborative practice. This book explores some of the issues that emerge from the parallel construction of autochthonous and franchised heritage in Abu Dhabi. Yet this parallel construction is not read as autochthonous vs franchised, Western vs non-Western, East vs West. Rather, through my analysis, I provide a way to move past these dichotomies to understand how heritage is emerging as an institutionalised and political project in Abu Dhabi, using varying scales of heritage.

The emergence of a new heritage industry in Abu Dhabi offered a unique opportunity to explore the process of heritage-making by investigating the development of new museums and heritage organisations, and the development of new procedures and protocols that were being used to govern the ways in which heritage is managed and presented. This book explores how heritage, franchised and autochthonous, has been used to develop Abu Dhabi's transnational identity, and the meanings and values that were being attached to that heritage – locally, nationally and internationally. The book draws on my experience of living and researching in the Gulf for over a decade. Primarily, the data was collected during two years of detailed ethnographic research in Abu Dhabi between November 2010 and January 2012. Further empirical data has been gathered since this period as part of my ongoing research in Abu Dhabi (2013–2019). My continuing analyses have enabled me to offer further critical reflection on the developments that have happened since this time, in particular the opening of the Louvre Abu Dhabi Museum in November 2017.

This book explores how and why heritage is developed in certain ways, and the multiple meanings and attitudes that emerge from this within Abu Dhabi. In doing so, I was able to map out and analyse the socio-cultural processes that were shaping heritage in Abu Dhabi. Due to the level of activity in Abu Dhabi, heritage developments were (and still are) occurring at varying scales and locations. In order to understand these developments I took a multi-sited ethnographic approach. The book presents together the perspectives of individuals who were involved in the process of producing heritage and opinions from residents who were responding to these developments. It does so by drawing on data collected from semi-structured interviews, participant observations and documentary and visual data, which allowed me to access and analyse the attitudes, meanings and experiences that are attached to heritage in Abu Dhabi.

Interviews were used to engage with a broad range of heritage practitioners and residents in Abu Dhabi. In total seventy-one semi-structured interviews were carried out with heritage practitioners, professionals based outside the sector but involved through governmental positions and members of the local community.[2] The interviews that I conducted can be classified into two types: official and unofficial. Official interviews were used to gain an understanding of the processes at work within the production of state-sanctioned heritage within Abu Dhabi and the motivations for producing particular types of official heritage. It enabled me to draw on their roles, insights and attitudes towards heritage practices in order to gain insight into the practicalities and challenges of working with heritage in Abu Dhabi. Unofficial interviews were used to explore how Emirati residents were engaging with official and unofficial heritage in Abu Dhabi. Interviewing members of the local community enabled me to consider the gap between policy and practice. It also allowed me to ask questions about local attitudes towards heritage that may challenge the ways in which official heritage is presented.

In addition to semi-structured interviewing, I compiled and set up an online questionnaire using Surveymonkey.com.[3] This allowed me to reach younger Emirati respondents who were less prominent within my interviews.[4] I felt that it was important to capture the opinions of both the younger and the older generations of Emiratis since they have different experiences and memories of the UAE due to the rapid socio-cultural changes that have occurred within the Emirates since the discovery of oil. Observations and site visits allowed me to see first-hand how heritage was being presented and engaged with. These physical sites were chosen because they were open and accessible, and because exhibitions, events, discussions and activities were being staged there.[5] I spent considerable time visiting, on multiple occasions, museums and heritage sites in Abu Dhabi and the broader UAE. These visits allowed me to experience, observe and document both my own experiences and thoughts, and those of my fellow visitors.

Finally, the use of written source material allowed me to explore how heritage is being presented to the public by examining media reports, official government documents, promotional materials and so on. I utilised published material that was available from the government, such as *Plan Abu Dhabi 2030*; heritage organisations, such as the vision and mission statements for the existing and planned heritage sites (the Louvre Abu Dhabi, the Guggenheim Abu Dhabi, the Zayed National Museum, the Maritime Museum, the Performing Arts Centre, the Abu Dhabi Heritage Village and the Al Ain National Museum); promotional material from heritage sites, such as leaflets, brochures, catalogues, and so on; and the analysis of ethnographic, local historical and newspaper sources. These documents held important information that shed light on how heritage is produced and engaged with in Abu Dhabi. Specifically planning and legislative materials provided a snapshot of a particular time when societies' values were such that legislation was enacted to encapsulate them (see Soderland 2009). Media sources, such as newspapers, were valuable for exploring how the government communicates about heritage – locally, regionally and internationally, presenting an important commentary on the present and the heritage and identity issues that Emiratis face. In particular, articles in *The National* and *The Gulf News* were insightful for keeping track of the heritage developments and the debates they engender.

This book explores contemporary developments in relation to both franchised and autochthonous heritage within the city of Abu Dhabi, allowing me to examine heritage as a hybrid process in a non-Western context. In doing so, it provides an analysis of the processes of cultural heritage franchising and its cultural effects. The key questions posed by this book are: what happens when heritage is franchised, and what happens to the places that accept these franchises? These questions are particularly important because the phenomena of franchising heritage and its cultural affects have received limited attention within academic studies. This book is significant in that it develops new ideas about how cultural heritage franchising works as global phenomena, how it might be characterised and how it influences and is influenced by autochthonous forms of heritage. It therefore seeks to consider how heritage operates as a hybrid process by exploring the heritage processes that are being used to develop and present heritage in Abu Dhabi.

Chapter one situates Abu Dhabi's cultural heritage industry within the development of the Emirates and the emergence of the cultural industries within the Gulf States. Chapter two illustrates how the emergence of globalisation and the development of transnational heritage agendas and practices are linked to contemporary nation building. It explores how globalisation has impacted the way in which heritage operates as a material and social process and the resultant transnational formations of heritage that that have emerged. I argue that heritage is being used as a hybrid global process and that this is leading to the development of global cosmopolitan heritage discourses, which need to be critically explored in order to enhance our understanding of transnational heritage processes. Chapter three examines the processes that surround the development and operation of cultural heritage franchises; how they are formed, how they operate and how they are connected to the transnational heritage sector. In doing so, I argue that cultural heritage franchising is explicitly connected to the development of newly emerging cosmopolitan identities in non-Western nations. Chapter four explores how cultural heritage franchises are implicated within the politics of heritage by examining their role in bilateral relations. I argue that cultural heritage franchising in Abu Dhabi is an overtly political process, which is linked to the development of transnational heritage infrastructures and bi-lateral relations.

Chapters five through seven provide a framework from which to exam-ine the interconnections and tensions that emerge from the processes that are involved in the creation of cultural heritage franchise institutions. Chapter five identifies and analyses the way in which cultural heritage franchises are connected to capacity development and knowledge develop-ment. It discusses how cultural heritage franchises are implicated within the translation of heritage practices and processes, and how they connect to the complex legacies that relate to the historical development of cultural heritage development in the West and the dominance that it has held, and continues to hold, in the global cultural arena. Chapter six interrogates the issues that are associated with the translation of cultural heritage franchises across borders. In particular, it pays attention to the specific details that emerge from translating cultural heritage in non-Western nations through an examination of the Louvre Abu Dhabi and the Guggenheim Abu Dhabi's pre-opening exhibitions and events. Chapter seven considers how heritage is understood as a concept and how this relates to the 'official' production of heritage in Abu Dhabi. It also examines how Emirati residents are engaging with and responding to the cultural heritage developments in Abu Dhabi.

Chapter eight investigates how the Louvre Abu Dhabi museum has been shaped by the cultural heritage franchise relationship between the UAE and France. It explores how universalism and cosmopolitanism have been re-imagined and re-produced in the museum, and how this has impacted the museum's exhibitionary practices in Abu Dhabi. Chapter nine concludes by analysing how autochthonous and franchise heritage dynamics have changed over time and how this relates to power, authority and knowledge development.

Ultimately, this book contributes to our understanding of heritage as a trans-national process by exploring how heritage operates within local, national and international identity concerns and debates. This is important because heritage has always been seen to be specific to particular societies and cultures, and as such the way in which heritage has been put to use to negotiate cross-border relationships has received less attention. In doing so, I argue that heritage gains what I term 'transnational currency' through the legitimation and political po-sitioning of contemporary heritage methods and procedures, which is attached to Western European-dominated interpretations. I therefore problematise and critique the process of cultural heritage franchising, which is ultimately re-shaped, challenged and resisted when translated across borders.

Notes

1 I use the term 'autochthonous' heritage to describe the context-specific cultural process of developing cultural heritage, tangible and intangible in the place where it occurs. The term 'autochthonous' generally refers to something 'formed or originating in the place where found' ('Autochthonous' n.d.).

2 Interviewees consisted of forty-four heritage practitioners, seven professionals and twenty Emirati residents. To compile comparative data, and due to the fact that not all heritage practitioners were permanently based within Abu Dhabi, I also conducted interviews in the Emirates of Dubai, Sharjah, Ajman and Qatar. All interviews, with the exception of one, were conducted in English and in person.

3 I used both closed and open-ended questions so that I could generate basic details such as age, gender and nationality before going on to ask open-ended questions to gather data about the attitudes and understandings of heritage in Abu Dhabi. I posted a link to my online questionnaire on my Twitter feed and culturally focussed groups on Facebook to promote my survey. In addition, I sent the survey link to my interview respondents and to contacts at universities in the UAE for further dissemination. The online survey generated an additional data set from forty-nine respondents.

4 Eighty per cent of the forty-nine survey respondents were between the ages of eighteen and twenty-nine, which demonstrates that the survey was particularly effective at capturing the views of younger Emiratis, who were less prominent within my interviews.

5 I conducted participant observations at exhibitions and temporary events organised by the cultural authority in Abu Dhabi, the Louvre Abu Dhabi, the Guggenheim Abu Dhabi and the Zayed National Museum. In addition, observations were carried out at cultural events in Al Ain, Dubai, Ras al Khaimah and Sharjah.

1 Cultural heritage development in Abu Dhabi

The development of large-scale transnational museums in the Gulf has often served to overshadow the history of museums in the Gulf States, however, the genealogy of museum development in the Arabian Peninsula can be traced back to the 1950s (Hirst 2012; see also Erskine-Loftus 2010, 2013b; Bouchenaki 2011; Al-Ali 2013; Al-Ragam 2014; Bouchenaki and Kreps 2016) (Table 1.1). The development of museums in the region is complex and multi-faceted and has varied depending upon the different social, political and economic influences of each nation (Wakefield Forthcoming). The initial museological trend in the region was to turn historic forts into national museums (Prager 2015) using ethnographic representations.[1] Key themes focused on pearling (Penziner-Hightower 2014; Thabiti-Willis 2016), Bedouinity (Prager 2015) and the role and legitimacy of the ruling elite in national development and economic transformation. The region's early museums played a key role in the production of national symbolism and identity (on Qatar see Al-Mulla 2014 and on the UAE see Penziner-Hightower 2014; Simpson 2014; Prager 2015). Arguably, it was through the process of nation building that 'traditions' were 'invented' (Hobsbawm and Ranger 2010) and put on display within these early museums. In the process, the emergent museographic landscape sought to create 'imagined communities' in the service of the state (Anderson 2006). Yet these early museums were often developed in consultation with international museum and heritage practitioners (Exell and Wakefield 2016: 2) and as such drew on the principles and practices of Western European museological traditions (Bouchenaki and Kreps 2016: xv). Although, these early museums were overtly connected to a national past, they explicitly connected with global models of museums and transnational museum practices, which is often overlooked within examinations of national, or the broader autochthonous, museum and heritage formations.

Private museums have also played an important role in the museological landscape of the Arabian Peninsula (Hirst 2012). For example, Exell has argued, using the Sheikh Fasial bin Qassem Al-Thani Museum in Qatar as a case study, that private collecting is a direct manifestation of Qatari socio-cultural dynamics, which offers a counter-discourse to state-sanctioned

Table 1.1 Museum developments in the Arabian Peninsula

Institution	City and state	Date
Kuwait Museum	Kuwait City	1957
Failaka Museum	Failaka Island, Kuwait	1964
Fujairah Museum	Fujairah, UAE	1970
Dubai Museum	Dubai, UAE	1971
Al Ain National Museum	Al Ain, Abu Dhabi, UAE	1971
Qatar National Museum	Doha, Qatar	1975–2004
Museum of Archaeology and Ethnography	Muscat, Oman	1978–1999
Oman National Museum	Muscat, Oman	1978
Museum of Islamic Art	Doha, Qatar	2008
Mathaf	Doha, Qatar	2010
Oman National Museum	Muscat, Oman	2016
Etihad Museum	Dubai, UAE	2017
Louvre Abu Dhabi	Abu Dhabi, UAE	2017
King Abdulla Aziz Center (*Ithra*)	Dharan, KSA	2017
Jameel Art Centre	Dubai, UAE	2018
Qasr Al Hosn	Abu Dhabi, UAE	2018
Sheikh Abdulla Al Salem Cultural Centre	Kuwait City, Kuwait	2018
Qatar National Museum	Doha, Qatar	2019

Source: Table compiled by the author.

heritage narratives (Exell 2013a, 2014). However, her analyses fail to account for the elitist nature of the collection and Sheikh Faisel's position as a member of the ruling elite. Aubry in his examination of traditional costume collections in the Arabian Peninsula offers a more nuanced interpretation of private collecting. Arguing that the role of the private collector and their choices regarding what to collect is fundamental to understanding their broader role within the cultural heritage landscape of the Gulf States (Aubry 2014). Kelly (2016), in her analyses of Kuwait, suggests that private museums provide evidence of a more community-centred 'holistic' approach to collecting and audience engagement. Due to the scope of this book and limited access to private collections in the UAE the current analysis does not include a discussion of private collecting or private museums in the UAE.

Since the early 2000s, large-scale, state-led museum projects such as the Louvre Abu Dhabi, the Guggenheim Abu Dhabi and the National Museum of Qatar (to name but a few) has attracted large-scale media interest, locally, nationally and internationally. It is no exaggeration to say that the last two decades have witnessed a 'museum-boom' in the Gulf States. As a result large-scale museum projects have been completed in Kuwait, Oman, Qatar, UAE (Table 1.2) and Saudi Arabia, which demonstrate the sheer speed and scale at which museum developments are happening in the Gulf States. As a result, interest in academic studies on the region has also grown. In particular, a number of edited works have attempted to fill gaps in the literature by providing a case-study analyses of museum and heritage

Table 1.2 Timeline of cultural heritage developments in the United Arab Emirates

Date	Institution	Emirate
1968	National Center for Documentation and Research	Abu Dhabi
1969	Al Ain National Museum (currently under renovation)	Al Ain
1971	Dubai Museum	Dubai
1981	Abu Dhabi Cultural Foundation	Abu Dhabi
1981	The National Library	Abu Dhabi
1987	Sharjah Museum of Islamic Civilization	Sharjah
1987	Ras al-Khaimah National Museum	Ras al-Khaimah
1991	Ajman Museum	Ajman
1991	Fujairah Museum	Fujairah
1993	Emirates Heritage Club	Abu Dhabi
1993	Sharjah Archaeology Museum	Sharjah
1995	Bait Al Naboodah	Sharjah
1996	Sharjah Science Museum	Sharjah
1997	Sharjah Art Museum	Sharjah
1997	Sharjah Natural History Museum and Desert Park	Sharjah
1997	Al Hisn Fort Museum	Sharjah
1997	Naif Museum	Dubai
1999	Bait Sheikh Saeed bin Hamad Al Qasimi (closed for restoration)	Sharjah
2000	Umm al Quwain Museum	Umm al Quwain
2005	Sharjah Heritage Museum (established; renovated in 2012 as part of the heart of Sharjah project)	Sharjah
2008	Sharjah Classic Cars Museum (first opened; re-opened in 2013/currently under renovation)	Sharjah
2009	Classical Cars Museum (2013 relocated to Ain Al Fida)	Abu Dhabi
2010	Sharjah Heritage Museum	Sharjah
2017	Louvre Abu Dhabi	Abu Dhabi
2017	Etihad Museum	Dubai
2018	Qasr Al Hosn Museum	Abu Dhabi
2019	Al Shindiga Museum (Phase one)	Dubai
2019	Qasr Al Watan	Abu Dhabi

Source: Table compiled by the author.

developments in the Gulf. Two edited volumes by Erskine-Loftus (2013a, 2014) take a predominantly practice-based approach by examining professional practice in the context of museum development and newly emergent collecting policies and practices. While Exell and Rico (2014) engage with some of the ways in which cultural heritage discourses are constructed and put to use in the region. Mejcher-Atassi and Schwartz (2012) provide an analysis of the methods and processes that have been applied to collecting, specifically in archives and museums in the region. The edited volume by Erskine-Loftus, Penziner-Hightower and Al-Mulla (2016) addresses various issues relating to national identity and museums in the Arabian Peninsula, whereas, the edited volume by Exell and Wakefield (2016) provides an examination of museum and heritage practices across the region by linking scales of development, local, regional and global, to regional and transnational processes. Finally, the forthcoming volume, *Museums of the Arabian Peninsula: Historical Developments and Contemporary Discourses* examines the historical and contemporary emergence of museums in the Arabian Peninsula as a discursive and interconnected process (Wakefield Forthcoming).

What is clear is that each state has focused on museum and heritage development in varying ways depending on their cultural heritage policies and priorities. In the UAE for example, each Emirate has taken its own approach to cultural heritage development, which has been shaped by the strategic direction of the rulers, the Emirate specific cultural authorities and the availability of economic resources. More specifically, Pianese (2018) has argued that Abu Dhabi is taking a 'globalized approach' prioritising tourism and events; Sharjah a 'localized approach' and Dubai a 'global creative approach'. Architectural analyses have focused on the emergence of new urban centres (see Elsheshtawy 2004, 2013; Alraouf 2016a) and the challenges of conservation and revitalisation (on Bahrain see Alraouf 2010, 2014; on Doha Scharfenort 2014; Alraouf 2016b and Al-Mulla 2016; on Kuwait Nakib 2016; and on the UAE Elsheshtawy 2019). Exell (2016a) explores the relationship between museum developments and modernity in the Gulf States. However, the analysis relies heavily on the Qatari museums landscape where the author is currently based as well as limited analysis of Bahrain and the UAE (for more detailed analysis on Bahrain see earlier work by Fibiger (2011) and on Abu Dhabi see earlier work by Wakefield (2011, 2012, 2013, 2014) on cosmopolitanism and universalism and Prager (2015) on heritage festivals and national identity in the UAE).

In general, the study of museum development has been split into two oppositional frameworks, which are assumed to be either 'traditional' or 'modern' (Abu-Lughord 1998; Erskine-Loftus 2013b). Other dichotomies have also been applied to the museum and heritage developments in the Gulf: Western or non-Western, tribal or modern, national or transnational. These dichotomies draw on essentialised notions of identity and orientalist discourses (Exell and Rico 2013), the West is viewed as predominantly modern and material and the Arabian Peninsula is seen as traditional and predominantly immaterial. A limited number of authors have attempted to consider heritage in a framework that considers both local and global processes (Fox, Moutada-Sabbah and Al-Mutawa 2006c; Fibiger 2011; Al-Ragam 2014; Wakefield 2015). This book contributes and builds on these debates, especially my earlier work on franchising, cosmopolitanism and universalism (Wakefield 2011, 2012, 2013, 2014) by providing an in-depth and critical discussion of the emerging cultural heritage landscape in Abu Dhabi. My analysis seeks to go beyond works that have discussed museum developments as a response to modernisation either as a reactionary force against the perceived threatening forces of globalisation or as part of a process of modernity and modernisation. This book serves to challenge these binary notions by providing an analysis that explores the parallel construction of both autochthonous and franchised heritage.

I argue that heritage development in Abu Dhabi is not a question of dialectical opposites. Instead, I posit that autochthonous and global aspects of heritage are used within a framework of transnational identity construction. In doing so, my work contributes to contemporary debates within the critical museums and heritage studies by suggesting a new framework for analysing heritage developments. My approach is particularly pertinent to understanding heritage in places where museums and heritage institutions are emerging as new institutional processes.

Geographical context and historical development

As I mentioned in the previous section, early nation building in the UAE focused on the development of museums in historic forts. This was largely in response to three key societal changes: the British withdrawing from the UAE, the discovery of oil and the foundation of the Federation. The first state-sanctioned museum to be established in the UAE was the Al Ain Museum, which was developed at the request of the late ruler Sheikh Zayed bin Sultan Al Nahyan (Sheikh Zayed I). Through the 'invention of tradition' (Hobsbawm 2010) the nation was put on display using ethnographic and archaeological materials. In addition to these collections the museum also featured a video installation that historicised the Emirates development from the discovery of oil. As such, developing a strong sense of national identity has been on the official agenda since the early formation of the nation state. More recently, increasing focus has been devoted to transnational identity formation, which is the focus of this book.

Geographically the UAE is situated on the shores of the Arabian (or Persian) Gulf (Figure 1.1). Abu Dhabi is the largest of the seven emirates. Prior to the UAE becoming an independent Federation it was referred to by various names such as the 'Trucial Coast, Trucial Oman' (Blau 1995) or 'the Pirate Coast' (Al-Fahim 1995). The area at this time was turbulent as rivalries and piracy were a common threat to maritime trade (Onley 2009; Penziner-Hightower 2011). This paved the way for a partnership to develop between the British, who provided protection, and the Trucial Sheikhdoms, who agreed to give the British exclusive territorial control of the coastal waters.[2] When the British withdraw their protection from the region Sheikh Zayed bin Sultan Al Nahyan the Emîr[3] of Abu Dhabi at the time, supported by the then Emîr of Dubai Sheikh Rashid bin Saeed Al Maktoum suggested a union. The union resulted in the formation of

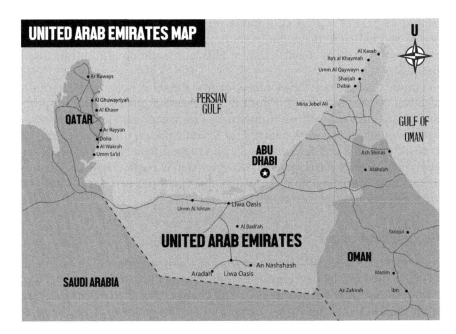

Figure 1.1 Map of the United Arab Emirates.
Source: Downloaded from Vecteezy.com 6 May 2019. https://www.vecteezy.com Vector Design by Vecteezy.com

the Federation on February 27, 1968, which included: Abu Dhabi, Ajman, Bahrain, Dubai, Fujairah, Qatar, Sharjah and Umm al-Quwain.[4] However, Bahrain and Qatar later decided to remain autonomous states. It was not until December 2, 1971 that the Federation of the UAE was officially established and only later in 1972 that Ras Al Khaimah joined (National Center for Documentation and Research n.d.[b]). Today the UAE consists of seven Emirates: Abu Dhabi, Ajman, Dubai, Fujairah, Ras Al Khaimah, Sharjah and Umm Al-Quwain. Sheikh Zayed I became the first President of the newly formed Federation ruling until his death in 2004, and Sheikh Rashid became the Vice-President and Prime Minister of the UAE. Khalaf has noted that 'the *al-ittihad* (union) of the seven Emirates is arguably one of the most significant events in the history of the UAE' (2002: 35). The formation of the Federation is the focus of the Etihad Museum in Dubai.

As I noted at the beginning of this chapter, nationalism has played a central role within the production of heritage in the Western world. In the Gulf States tribal politics were concerned with authority over people, not over territories with boundaries (Heard-Bey 2004). As such Partrick (2009) argues that UAE tribal structure is used to produce an authorised national identity by linking history, lineage and development within the state's official discourse.

He suggests, drawing on the work of Bassam Tibi, that group tribal solidarity (*asabiyya*) remains an important aspect of contemporary Arab relations, which is now based on the authority of the ruling sheikh over the nation (*ibid.*: 9). Tribal relations are significant as they not only remain important aspects of contemporary societal structure in Abu Dhabi, but they also affect the ways in which heritage is produced and presented. The UAE's federal and social structure is not the only unique quality, Islam plays a significant role as the dominant religion of the UAE. This means that legislation and national identity are intimately connected to Islam and the practice of the Muslim faith (Findlow 2000: 46).

Economic growth and multiculturalism has had a significant impact on Abu Dhabi. The discovery of oil in 1958 dramatically affected Abu Dhabi and the UAE as a whole. The result is that Abu Dhabi has transformed its economy from a nomadic subsistence economy to be one of the world's wealthiest oil producing nations (Ansari 1987; Khalaf 2006: 245; Davidson 2009, 2010). The discovery of oil in the 1960s impacted the economic, political and social dimensions of life within the UAE. According to Davidson 'the UAE controls around ten percent of the world's known oil reserves and of this ninety percent comes from Abu Dhabi' (2007: 37). The significant changes from pre-oil to post-oil Abu Dhabi led to the introduction of a new urban layout. Emirati historian Mohammed Al-Fahim described from first-hand observations the development of 'public works', which included the development of new 'houses, roads, governmental buildings, an airport, and so on' (1995: 267). The pace and scale of change within Abu Dhabi in such a short period of time cannot be overestimated. The development of new industries and new patterns of life brought with it a need for skilled workers, which resulted in an influx of migrant workers, which led to a demographic imbalance where international workers far outnumber the Emirati population (*ibid.*: 251; Davidson 2007). Oil wealth had a significant impact on the UAE, its federal structure, and tribalism by providing the financial impetus for change. In addition, these developments led to a renewed need for heritage apparatuses that supported the state and the emergent nation-building narrative.

Alongside these socio-economic shifts came a significant change in leadership with the succession of key rulers, from Abu Dhabi and Dubai, to the two highest positions of power within the federation. This political change has had a significant effect on heritage investment in the twenty-first century. In 2004, Sheikh Khalifa bin Zayed al Nahyan became the president of the UAE and the ruler of the Emirate of Abu Dhabi after the death of his father Sheikh Zayed I.[5] The UAE Vice-President and Prime Minister is Sheikh Mohammed bin Rashid Al Maktum who became the Ruler of the Emirate of Dubai in 2006. The allocation of power within the Federal government correlates to the political power and economic position of the individual Emirates. The change in leadership had a significant impact on state planning, which resulted in a new phase of development (Elsheshtawy 2008: 274). This new phase of development required a different strategic plan, which resulted in the development of the Urban Structure Framework Plan, *Plan Abu Dhabi 2030* (Abu Dhabi Urban Planning Council 2007). The plan set out to illustrate how Abu Dhabi planned to develop and its projected growth up until the year 2030. The main strategic aim of the plan was to position Abu Dhabi as a global city using three key priority areas as its focus:

1   Environmental – Protect and enhance the natural resources and cultural heritage of Abu Dhabi
2   Social – Integrate nature and humanity
3   Economic – Foster economic development and leverage financial resources in a thoughtful and prudent manner

(*ibid.*: 31)

Protecting and enhancing cultural heritage is a key aim within the future development plans for Abu Dhabi. However, it is Abu Dhabi's plans for several large-scale international and national heritage institutions that are taking centre stage in shaping Abu Dhabi's cultural identity and international heritage practices. These changes have arguably had a significant impact on the way in which heritage has come to be viewed and presented within the UAE.

Cultural policy and creativity

Abu Dhabi is continuing a long tradition of national investment in heritage and cultural centres. The ruling elite have continued to shape society in Abu Dhabi, in particular the current ruler, Sheikh Khalifa bin Zayed Al Nahyan, has focused his attentions towards the development of cultural heritage institutions. National governments therefore play a fundamental role in shaping cultural developments, which is culturally specific and policy driven. Abu Dhabi's Cultural District project was based on an economic plan that draws on models of successful high-profile cultural projects such as the Guggenheim Museum Bilbao. Creative cities have therefore been linked to several activities, which include one off-mega projects, large-scale flagship developments, and cultural traditions and practices (Pratt 2010: 18). In western European cities:

> prestigious cultural projects acted as symbols of rebirth…in declining cities such as Glasgow, Sheffield and Bilbao…newly acquired cosmopolitanism [and competition] in wealthier cities like Frankfurt…modernity and innovations [through the development of new cultural industries such as fashion, crafts and design] in cities like Montpellier, Nimes, Grenoble, Rennes, Hamburg, Cologne, Barcelona and Bologna… and …reconciliation in cities like Berlin and Derry, with high potential for social conflict.
>
> (Bianchini 1993a: 15–16)

However, the actual measurable 'impact' is abstract and hard to substantiate and often lead to frictions between 'internationalisation strategies and the need to protect and develop indigenous local and regional identities' (*ibid.*: 2; 19). In Abu Dhabi, Saadiyat Island dominates the city rhetoric as the flagship development for the city.

Through the development of new cultural projects Abu Dhabi is creating linkages between city development and creativity. Discussions of creative cities have been heavily influenced by the work of Richard Florida (2004). Florida argues that creativity is the primary driver of contemporary developed economies. He bases his proposition on his analysis of the creative sector, which he argues is made up of creative professionals who now use knowledge and creativity' to control the economy instead of 'natural resources and the efficiency of physical labor' (Florida 2004: 1; 3–4; 49). However, Pratt has criticised the direct linking of the creative economy to economic development, which ultimately serves to benefit the elite and/or distinguish one city from another (2010: 13). He suggests that one example of this would be the way that artists are marginalised from new elite contemporary art centres. For example, in Dubai contemporary art space Alserkel has been criticised locally for being elitist even though it is aimed at being a community focused space. Markusen has gone further to suggest that there is not enough evidence to prove the link between creativity and economic success (2006: 1921). Furthermore, there is no proven link between creativity and economic development. Similarly Hall argues that studies linking creativity and cities have tended to generalise trends rather than critically consider quantifiable correlations between creativity and specific places (2000: 642). Generalisations are further problematic as they do not allow for a consideration of the diverse cultural contexts in which developments happen (*ibid.*) or for historical instances of creativity and cosmopolitanism (Hall 1998). Hall, using various examples, such as fifth-century Athens, fourteenth-century Florence and twentieth-century Berlin, suggests that these cities demonstrate periods of transition where an influx of international workers and rapid economic and social transformation led to the emergence of new social relations, which resulted in conflict (2000: 646). According to Pratt analyses therefore need to focus on, 'the subtleties of historical and locally specific practices of cultural and creative activities' (2010: 13). This is particularly important for analyses of cultural heritage developments within the Gulf as a reading of new developments would set contemporary museum construction purely as an act of modernity. However, as mentioned earlier, the development of museums and heritage across the region is far more nuanced and historically embedded than such readings would account for.

What is clear, is that the role of national governments in the development of the heritage sector is culturally specific. City developments are heterogenous with significant 'differences in their ideological backgrounds, levels of financial resources and powers, and in the nature of relations between the public, private and voluntary sectors' and that there is not one 'definition of "culture" adopted by national and city governments' (Bianchini 1993a: 1). Within this book I use the term 'culture' to refer to 'shared meanings' (Hall 2013: xvii). Regardless, the linkage between city development and creativity has taken hold and the rhetoric has been applied to new emerging urban centres, such as Abu Dhabi.

Saadiyat Island: the creation of a cultural zone

The Abu Dhabi Tourism Authority (ADTA) initially established the Tourism Development Investment Corporation (TDIC) to oversee the planning and implementation of the Saadiyat Island project. The Cultural District on Saadiyat Island was being developed by the TDIC at an estimated cost of $27bn (Abu Dhabi Authority for Culture and Heritage n.d.[a]). The Abu Dhabi Authority for Culture and Heritage (ADACH), established in 2005, on the other hand was primarily responsible for the preservation and conservation of cultural heritage of Abu Dhabi (Abu Dhabi Authority for Culture and Heritage n.d.[b]). This meant that the large-scale developments on Saadiyat Island were originally being managed as future tourism assets under the umbrella of a commercial tourism company, whereas ADACH controlled heritage assets that were primarily considered to be related to national identity concerns, which included:

> both tangible and intangible aspects of Emirati heritage including and not limited to: archaeological, architectural, oral narratives, folklore, customs and beliefs, music, poetry, sports and dance, and traditional skills such as dhow building, pearl diving.
>
> (Abu Dhabi Authority for Culture and Heritage n.d.[a])

UNESCO's global discourse also had an impact upon the way that Abu Dhabi has developed its cultural heritage industry. It was stated on ADACH's website in 2011 that:

> The creation of ADACH was a direct result of the implementation of the Abu Dhabi Cultural Heritage Management Strategy, a five-year strategy prepared by a UNESCO-led team working closely with local experts. The Strategy identified the principal issues affecting the development of Abu Dhabi's culture and heritage and laid down goals for its activities.
>
> (*ibid.*)

This is perhaps not surprising given the influence that international organisations have had within the region. For example, UNESCO was involved in developing the proposals for the Bahrain National Museum, Kuwait National Museum, Qatar Museum and the Saudi Museum (Hirst 2012).

ADACH was also responsible for developing Abu Dhabi's Qasr Al Hosn, a historic fort that is closely linked to the national story, along with other national sites. Qasr Al Hosn is one of the oldest stone buildings remaining in Abu Dhabi. It was originally built as a watchtower and later it became home to the royal family before being converted in to a cultural centre and museum (Al-Fahim 1995). The importance of this site is reflected in the site's development and conservation, which I will discuss in chapter six. In 2012, the tourism department, TDIC, merged with the cultural department, ADACH. Throughout this book, with the exception of chapters eight and nine, I discuss the TDIC and the ADACH as separate entities. I do so because the research reflected in this book predominantly relates to developments that took place whilst they were separate entities.

The way in which cultural heritage is structured and institutionalised is also suggestive of the power relations that underpin the development of heritage. The UAE is an autocratic society, and this has an enormous impact on when, how and by whom heritage is produced and presented. This also has important implications in the way that heritage is managed and governed. The approach that is taken towards heritage development in the UAE is essentially top-down and state-driven, which means that the organisations who are responsible for heritage are also state driven. This is not unusual as many nations have their heritage regulated by their governments and/or monarchies. What is different in Abu Dhabi, and the UAE, is the level of control that the leaders actively assert within state affairs such as heritage production (Fox, Moutada-Sabbah and Al-Mutawa 2006b; Davidson 2009). As Ponzini notes 'Abu Dhabi's urban development is based on a narrow oligarchic system. Large-scale projects are discussed and decided by the royal family and cohesive network of relatives, publicly funded agencies and development corporations' (2011: 254). For example, the board of directors for both the TDIC and ADACH were chaired by Sheikh Sultan bin Tahnoun Al Nahyan. As well as being a member of the royal family Sheikh Sultan also held a number of further strategic positions within Abu Dhabi.[6] Sheikh Sultan has played a central role in the development of the cultural heritage sector and the efforts to establish Abu Dhabi as a global cultural centre. For example, his close relationship with the French Republic was evident when he was made a *Commander of the Ordre des Arts et des Lettres*, in recognition of his contribution to French and international cultural developments (Tourism Development Investment Corporation 2013).

Abu Dhabi is continuing the trend of developing of cultural centres. However, what is different in Abu Dhabi is how cultural heritage franchises and autochthonous aspects of heritage are drawn together within the strategic plan, *Plan Abu Dhabi 2030*, to help deliver the vision of turning Abu Dhabi into a global cultural centre (Abu Dhabi Urban Planning Council 2007). As such, all of the proposed cultural institutions on Saadiyat Island have a common agenda and that is to position themselves as 'world-class' global institutions.

Saadiyat Island: the Cultural District and its museums

In 2004 the plans for the Saadiyat Island development were announced by the Abu Dhabi Government. Saadiyat Island, which means 'isle of happiness' when translated from Arabic to English is 'located 500m off the coast of Abu Dhabi' and 'occupies 27 square kilometres of land' (Tourism Development Investment Corporation n.d.[a]). The island when complete will contain seven Districts (Table 1.3) featuring 'residential housing, leisure and tourism facilities, civic and cultural institutions' (Tourism Development Investment Corporation n.d.[b]). Ponzini has been critical of the master plan arguing that the development is 'exclusive and exclusionary' (2011: 257).

The economic potential of heritage is an important aspect of the developing cultural heritage industry in Abu Dhabi and is linked to the Emirates broader diversification plans. Positioned between Asia and Europe, Abu Dhabi is ideally located to develop its tourism industry. Kirshenblatt-Gimblett has noted that cultural heritage tourism is so significant that 'the World Bank now factors culture into economic development and investment' (2007: 163). More recently the World Bank has focused on supporting cultural diversity, sustainability and heritage preservation (Ijjasz-Vasquez and Licciardi 2016). This focus was further cemented when the World Bank and UNESCO signed a Memorandum of Understanding on July 13, 2017 focused on furthering both parties' sustainable development agenda (World Bank 2017).

The significance of the growing tourism industry in Abu Dhabi can be observed from the estimated tourism growth in *Plan Abu Dhabi 2030*, which provides projections of '4.9 million visitors by 2020; and 7.9 million visitors by 2030' (Abu Dhabi Urban Planning Council 2007: 45). In 2017 Abu Dhabi's tourism figures stood at 4.875 million (Abu Dhabi Chamber 2018: 5), which suggested that the Emirate is not only on-track for the 2020 target but was likely to exceed the projections. However, due to the effects of Covid-19 on the global travel industry in 2020 these figures were expected to reduce significantly.

Table 1.3 The seven Districts of Saadiyat Island

Saadiyat Island Districts
Saadiyat Cultural District
Saadiyat Beach District
Saadiyat Marina District
Saadiyat Reserve District
Saadiyat Promenade
Saadiyat Lagoons District
Saadiyat Retreat District

Source: Table compiled by the author.

The Saadiyat Island museums

The Cultural District area of Saadiyat Island is being developed specifically to house the planned cultural institutions. The District is being developed with a clear transnational focus. The TDIC stated on its website that the 'aim is for Saadiyat Cultural District to become an international cultural platform that will act as a beacon for artistic experience, change and education' (Tourism Development Investment Corporation n.d.[c]). The TDIC describes the cultural institutions as 'strategic components of the Abu Dhabi Government's vision for the Emirates' (Tourism Development Investment Corporation n.d.[b]). The planned cultural heritage institutions all feature a distinct global identity through the commissioning of five internationally acclaimed Pritzker Prize winning architects. This adds further status to the project as it 'will be the only place in the world' to do so (Tourism Development Investment Corporation n.d.[c]). As such the '[s]tar architects were supposed to grant identity to the city and to link their fame and style to Saadiyat Island' (Ponzini 2011: 256). Saadiyat Cultural District will include four of the five proposed cultural institutions: the Louvre Abu Dhabi, the Guggenheim Abu Dhabi, the Zayed National Museum and the Performing Arts Centre. The fifth, the Maritime Museum, will be located in the Saadiyat Marina District.

The Louvre Abu Dhabi

On March 6, 2007 the president of Abu Dhabi's tourism authority, Sheikh Sultan bin Tahnoon al-Nahayan and French Culture Minister, Renaud Donnedieu de Varbres signed an agreement to develop the Louvre Abu Dhabi (see Louvre n.d.[a]; Riding 2007a: 1–2). The Louvre Abu Dhabi was the first cultural institution to be completed as part of the Saadiyat Island masterplan. After more than a decade in development the Louvre Abu Dhabi opened to the public on November 11, 2017 (Figure 1.2).[7] The partnership allows the museum to use the Louvre name for thirty years and six months and in return France would be paid €164 million over the partnership period (Poncelet 2007). As part of the agreement France set up an agency to oversee the Louvre Abu Dhabi's development, Agence France-Muséums, to provide a series loans, which will decrease in number as the museum's permanent collection grows and will provide four temporary exhibitions a year for fifteen years (*ibid.*). Notably, this is the first time that the Louvre has franchised its name outside of France, a move that has generated both national and international controversy (Cachin Clair and Recht 2006; Riding 2007a, 2007b, 2007c). The debates regarding the Louvre Abu Dhabi will be unpacked further in chapter three in my discussion of cultural heritage franchising. However, suffice to say that the debates' implicit orientalist undertones critiqued the projects based on their commercial imperatives and the erroneous assumption that Abu Dhabi had no priori cultural heritage.

Figure 1.2 The Louvre Abu Dhabi.
Credit: Photograph by the author.

The completed museum was designed by Pritzker Prize winning architect Jean Nouvel. Nouvel describes the Louvre Abu Dhabi museum as an 'island on an island' (Tourism Development Investment Corporation n.d.[d]). When the museum opened in 2017 it had over six-hundred artworks in its permanent collection and three-hundred loans from French institutions.[8] The museum's collection draws on French museology and is presented 'chronologically' with 'different civilisations in parallel as the visitor moves forwards on a journey through time' (Tourism Development Investment Corporation n.d.[e]). The museum began hosting temporary exhibitions at the beginning of 2018, which I will discuss in more depth in chapter 8.

The Guggenheim Abu Dhabi

The Guggenheim Abu Dhabi museum will be developed through a partnership between the Solomon R. Guggenheim Foundation (Guggenheim Foundation) and the Abu Dhabi Government (Solomon R. Guggenheim Foundation 2007). The original, 2006, partnership agreement was led by the former director and chief artistic officer of the Guggenheim Museum, Thomas Krens. At the time of writing the project had been pushed back and there was no confirmed opening date for the museum.[9] As part of the Louvre Abu Dhabi's first year anniversary the museum organised a symposium during which Mohamed Khalifa Al-Mubarak suggested that the Guggenheim Abu Dhabi was in the final stages of design (Al-Mubarak 2018). In 2019 Richard Armstrong, the director of the Guggenheim Foundation and the Guggenheim Museum in

New York, suggested that the construction for the building, which would take three to four years, would begin shortly (Euronews 2019).

The design for the Guggenheim Abu Dhabi by Pritzker Prize winning architect Frank Gehry features a series of cones that are representative of 'the region's ancient wind-towers, which both ventilate and shade the museum's exterior courtyards in a fitting blend of Arabian tradition and modern sustainable design' (Tourism Development Investment Corporation n.d.[f]). The museum is planned to have galleries on four different levels within the museum, which will be positioned around a central atrium, a workshop space and a theatre (Tourism Development Investment Corporation n.d.[g]). The museum is set to contain '13,000 square metres of gallery space in the monumental piles of gallery boxes, and eleven iconic cone-like structures providing a further 18,000 square metres of exhibition space' (Tourism Development Investment Corporation n.d.[h]), making it the largest of the planned institutions on Saadiyat Island.

Since his departure from the Guggenheim Foundation Thomas Krens has been publicly critical of the project in Abu Dhabi. Speaking on the podcast *In Other Words* Kren's reflected on the political landscape in Abu Dhabi suggesting that 'the world financial crisis and the Arab Spring has changed the equation radically' and that 'it may not be such a good idea these days to have an American museum…with a Jewish name in a country [that doesn't recognise Israel] in such a prominent location, at such a big scale' (Krens 2017). In response to Kren's criticism the Guggenheim issued a statement to *The Art Newspaper* reaffirming the museum's commitment:

> At a time when greater understanding among peoples and cultures is especially urgent, the Guggenheim Foundation remains committed to the Guggenheim Abu Dhabi and its transformative potential as a catalyst for exchange and for expanding the narratives of art history.
>
> (Cited in Ruiz 2017)

At the time of writing few details had been released regarding the plans for the Guggenheim Abu Dhabi's collection. It is expected that the Guggenheim Abu Dhabi's activities will focus on developing the museum's 'permanent collection, organise exhibitions, generate scholarship and undertake educational programmes' (Tourism Development Investment Corporation n.d.[g]). According to Richard Armstrong, director of the Guggenheim Foundation and the Guggenheim Museum in New York, the museum's collection is expected to focus on global art from 1965 onwards and highlight 'a variety of perspectives' from all over the world (Euronews 2019). Like the Louvre Abu Dhabi, the Guggenheim Abu Dhabi has begun developing a programme of pre-opening exhibitions to engage with the public, which I will discuss in detail in chapter seven. The Guggenheim Abu Dhabi is predicted to present a transnational view of contemporary art (Tourism Development Investment

Corporation n.d.[g]); this differs from the Louvre Abu Dhabi's approach, which is focused on universalism.

The Zayed National Museum

The Zayed National Museum will not be a franchise like the Louvre Abu Dhabi and the Guggenheim Abu Dhabi. Instead, the Abu Dhabi Government initially drew on the expertise of the British Museum through a high-profile consultancy agreement. The consultancy came to an end in 2017 with the authority retaining many of the British Museum team who were recruited for the project. The Zayed National Museum is aimed at examining the history of the UAE by focusing on the life of Sheikh Zayed I (Zayed National Museum n.d.[a]). The museum is being designed by Pritzker Prize-winning architect Lord Norman Foster and his firm Foster + Partners. Originally, the Zayed National Museum was due to open in 2013, however at the time of writing, the project had been pushed back and there was no confirmed opening date. Again, Al-Mubarak stated at the 2018 Louvre Abu Dhabi Symposium that the Zayed National Museum was being actively worked on (Al-Mubarak 2018). As the national museum, the Zayed National Museum is playing a prominent role within the Saadiyat Island development, which is reflected in the museum's central position within the Cultural District. National symbolism is evident within the museum's architecture. The museum's design features three distinctive towers that are influenced by the wings of a falcon, which links the project to the heritage of falconry in the UAE and the national symbolism of the falcon (Wakefield 2012). When complete the Zayed National Museum will house both permanent and temporary gallery spaces (Zayed National Museum n.d.[b]). Again, in a similar way to the Louvre Abu Dhabi and the Guggenheim Abu Dhabi, the Zayed National Museum has begun a series of pre-opening events to engage with the public.

The Maritime Museum

The Maritime Museum, as I noted in the previous section, will be the only one of the cultural institutions to be built outside of the Cultural District. Instead the museum will be positioned on the shoreline of Saadiyat Island's Marina District (Tourism Development Investment Corporation n.d.[i]). The details surrounding the Maritime Museum's development were limited at the time of writing due to the museum being part of the second phase of development. According to the TDIC the Maritime Museum is expected to explore the 'region's seafaring history' (Tourism Development Investment Corporation n.d.[j]). The museum is being designed by Pritzker Prize-winner Tadao Ando. The website suggests that Tadao Ando's design was inspired by the 'nature, landscape and maritime traditions' of the UAE and as such takes 'the form of a sail full of wind, carved out from a simple volume'

(Tourism Development Investment Corporation n.d.[i]). The museum, like the Zayed National Museum, will be nationally and regionally focused. From the available evidence the museum is set to explore how dhow-making and pearl diving were essential livelihoods, and how this contributed to Abu Dhabi's position as a trading hub in the past (*ibid.*). No details were available during the period of research regarding who will be responsible for the development of the museum and its collections.

The Performing Arts Centre

As with the Maritime Museum, there were few details available regarding the development of the Performing Arts Centre, which will also be part of the second phase of Saadiyat Island's Cultural District (Tourism Development Investment Corporation n.d.[k]). The remit of the Performing Arts Centre is distinctly transnational in scope. According to the TDIC's website the centre will bring 'world-class performers of opera, dance, drama and music from across the globe' to Abu Dhabi (Tourism Development Investment Corporation n.d.[l]). The Performing Arts Centre was being designed by Zaha Hadid's architectural firm. The website goes on to suggest that Hadid's design was inspired by 'forms encountered in the natural world' (Tourism Development Investment Corporation n.d.[m]). The TDIC quotes the late Hadid who describes her design as 'embedded like pearls and exposed at the same time, emerging out of the structure, like fruits of a plant, facing the sea' (*ibid.*). The Performing Arts Centre is expected to consist of 'a music hall, concert hall, opera house, drama theatre, an experimental performance space' (Tourism Development Investment Corporation n.d.[l]) as well as an Academy of Performing Arts aimed at developing the performing arts locally and regionally (Tourism Development Investment Corporation n.d.[m]), which indicates a desire to nurture a home-grown culture of performing arts.

The plans for the Cultural District suggest that Abu Dhabi has recognised the potential of cultural heritage for developing the Emirate's global identity and cultural tourism. The trend for cultural districts is not exclusive to Abu Dhabi. For example, the West Kowloon Cultural District in Hong Kong, when complete, will include several large-scale cultural projects based on Foster + Partners' *City Park* concept. The District will include the: Xiqu Centre, Hong Kong Palace Museum, M+ Museum, Lyric Theatre Complex, Freespace, M+ Pavilion and The Art Park (West Kowloon Cultural District Authority 2018a). The rhetoric that surrounds the development of the West Kowloon Cultural District is similar to the rhetoric that surrounds Abu Dhabi's Cultural District, which is distinctly transnational and competitive in scope. For example, on the West Kowloon Cultural District website it states that the District 'is one of the largest cultural projects in the world' (*ibid.*), which will provide 'world-class exhibitions, performances and arts and cultural events' (West Kowloon Cultural District Authority 2018b). One of the key objectives of the district is to 'facilitate the long-term development of Hong Kong as an international arts and cultural metropolis' and to become 'a cultural gateway to the Pearl River Delta' (West Kowloon Cultural District Authority 2018c). In addition, the Development Plan describes how the West Kowloon Cultural District will incorporate 'local and traditional as well as international and modern elements' (*ibid.*). For example, the design of the 'Xiqu Centre draws together the traditional and contemporary, taking familiar Chinese concepts like the gateway and courtyard and reinventing them for Hong Kong's modern urban environment' (West Kowloon Cultural District Authority 2018d). Again, this is similar to the Saadiyat Island project. Suggesting that cultural development is as much about competition as it is about political and economic development.

The cultural heritage franchise

A significant shift within the transnational heritage economy has been the increase in the franchising of particular cultural heritage brands. Rather surprisingly there has been little discussion of how cultural heritage franchising is defined and put to use. It is important to note that the very process of defining a museum as a cultural heritage franchise is far more complicated than mere terminology. By using the term cultural heritage franchise, the museum is explicitly connected to financial motives and market strategies drawn from the business sector. This forces us to think about museums and culture in a similar way that we think about well-known franchises such as McDonald's. Ritzer 2010 has suggested that the McDonald's franchise model set the tone for future franchises by establishing a series of independent franchisees across the United States (and later internationally) who paid a fee for the right to use the business model and brand (2010). It was the franchisee who took on the financial risks at these new locations while developing the brand for the McDonald's corporation.

Similar trends can now be observed within the cultural industry, most notably through the activities of the Guggenheim Foundation which was the first organisation to produce a cultural franchise. The foundation's first Museum, the Guggenheim Museum, was established in New York in 1937 (Solomon R. Guggenheim Foundation n.d.[a]). In 1949, the Guggenheim Foundation began expanding its operations overseas with its first branch in Venice, Italy. In 1997 the Guggenheim Foundation established its second branch the Deutsche Guggenheim Berlin in Germany and then in 1997 the Guggenheim Museum Bilbao in Spain. It was the Guggenheim Museum Bilbao 1997 that really established cultural heritage franchising as a significant transnational phenomenon. Alvarez Sainz has suggested that the increase in tourism and the international visibility that the GMB brought to the Basque region contributed to an increased interest in cultural heritage franchising and the use of Pritzker Prize winning architects within new museum projects (2012: 101). The significance of the Bilbao partnership and the SRGF's franchise model is that it provided a framework for international museum branding and cultural heritage franchising. It is the SRGF's franchise model that is providing the basis for the design and development of the planned Guggenheim Abu Dhabi and the newly opened Louvre Abu Dhabi.

At a purely economic level, the term 'franchise' is used to describe the process of granting a license 'for the sale of (goods) or the operation of (a service)' (Oxford Dictionaries 2014: 'Franchised'). I use the term 'cultural heritage franchising' at its most basic to describe the way in which the brand name of a museum and its operational processes are sold and distributed. In the case of this book, I explore the way in which franchised heritage processes are used within a transnational context. This is problematic for the cultural industry as the substantial revenues that cultural heritage franchising brings challenge the long-held view that museums and heritage institutions should operate as purely non-profit institutions. The International Council of Museums (ICOM) for example defines the museum as:

> A non-profit making, permanent institution in the service of society and its development, open to the public, which acquires, conserves, researches, communicates and exhibits the tangible and intangible heritage of humanity and its environment for the purposes of education, study and enjoyment.
>
> (ICOM 2007)

In 2019, ICOM proposed a revised, and arguably more inclusive, definition for museums:

> Museums are democratising, inclusive and polyphonic spaces for critical dialogue about the pasts and the futures. Acknowledging and addressing the conflicts and challenges of the present, they hold artefacts and specimens in trust for society, safeguard diverse memories for future generations and guarantee equal rights and equal access to heritage for all people. Museums are not for profit. They are participatory and transparent, and work in active partnership with and for diverse communities to collect, preserve, research, interpret, exhibit, and enhance understandings of the world, aiming to contribute to human dignity and social justice, global equality and planetary wellbeing.
>
> (ICOM 2019)

However, the new definition was the subject of detailed debate at the 25th General Assembly of the International Council of Museums (ICOM) in Kyoto Japan. As such, ICOM postponed the vote to adopt the new definition. The 2007 definition therefore still stands.

The profit-driven nature of cultural heritage franchising conflicts with this idea. The globalisation of cultural heritage through the process of franchising has led to concerns about cultural homogeneity and the financial motivations of these institutions (Bradley 1997; Lowry 2004; Ostling 2007). This has led to the development of the term 'McGuggenheim', which is used as a negative label to emphasise the profit-driven motives of franchises (Zulaika 1997: 90). What these critiques overlook is the broader global motivations for cultural heritage franchising and its cultural effects. This book aims to address this gap by exploring the cultural effects that franchising has in Abu Dhabi.

The choice to use the term 'cultural heritage franchise' rather than 'museum franchising' was a conscious one. I use the term 'cultural heritage franchising' because it is better able to capture the broader social and cultural dynamics that are involved in the production of these institutions. It acknowledges that the processes that are involved in the production of museums as franchise institutions connect to cultural heritage processes that are drawn from diverse cross-cultural settings with deeply historicized and often contested pasts. Many of these cultural heritage processes and traditions are operating outside the preserve of the museum. In addition to this the terminology draws our attention to the fact that franchise museums do not operate in a vacuum. Instead they are part of cultural heritage traditions that have developed in the nations from which they were first developed, and the nation in which the new institution is becoming developed. Since this book is concerned with exploring the hybrid processes of heritage production it was more appropriate to adopt the term 'cultural heritage franchise'.

The terminology therefore reflects a conscious acknowledgment and engagement with the recognition that the 'franchise' is the product of the exchange and co-production of diverse heritage traditions across national borders. By taking this broader view of the process of cultural heritage franchising it allows an engagement with how different actors are implicated in the processes of cultural heritage development, which results in the production of a new museum institution as the end product. Most importantly it asks: what happens when heritage is franchised, and what happens to places that accept these franchises? Ultimately then this book explores the way in which franchised heritage processes are used within Abu Dhabi and the resultant hybrid heritage processes that emerge from this process of conscious exchange and co-production.

I use the term autochthonous to describe heritage that is produced and preserved in Abu Dhabi and the UAE. Whilst connected, there are very important distinctions between the terms 'indigenous' and 'autochthonous'. The term 'indigenous' is generally used to describe that which is 'produced, living, or existing naturally in a particular region or environment' (Merriam Webster n.d.: indigenous). Sokolovskiy draws a distinction between the terms 'autochthonous' and 'indigenous' by suggesting that '[a]utochthonous is a broader or more inclusive in terms of population groups (groups with homelands within the state borders), and indigenous is a narrower legal concept (autochthonous groups who practice subsistence economy)' (2013: 207–8). Gausset, Kenrick and Gibb (2011) suggest that the term has strong links to the displacement and marginalisation of peoples living in regions previously untouched by settlers. Since Abu Dhabi, and the broader UAE, is not a region that has seen the displacement of its population, I therefore felt that it was inappropriate to use the term 'indigenous' within the context of this book. I specifically employ 'autochthonous' to describe both the process of producing cultural heritage and the resultant formations (tangible and intangible) that this takes within Abu Dhabi. I therefore define 'autochthonous' heritage as a context-specific cultural process, which results in the production of 'tangible' and 'intangible' cultural heritage in the place where it was found. In this book then, autochthonous heritage is used to define heritage processes that are developed and utilised in situ.

Hybridity and heritage

The parallel construction of autochthonous and franchised heritage in Abu Dhabi offered a unique opportunity to analyse to examine hybrid processes in action. As such, I was able to analyse how these heritage formations enmesh to produce what is arguably a hybridised heritage process in Abu Dhabi. I do not position these processes in opposition but rather seek to explore how these processes of heritage, which have emerged from specific cultural traditions, are understood and utilised within this hybrid process that is ultimately seeking to establish new ways of understanding and valuing heritage in Abu Dhabi. Hybridity has had, and continues to have, various meanings and applications. It is therefore important to set out my own reading and interpretation of hybridity and its use within this book.

Early discussions of hybridity focused predominately on the biological aspects of hybridity (Coombes and Brah 2000: 3), which were used to support essentialist discourses in museums in the nineteenth and twentieth centuries' in western Europe (Bennett 1995). Alternative readings have included the concepts of 'creolisation', '*mestizaje*' and 'syncretism'. Creolisation, has been used to the analyse and describe the process of cross-cultural mixing that occurred between indigenous, African and European people involved in the slave trade in the New World and its effects on language and culture (Garcia Canclini 2005: xxxiii). The importance of creolisation lies in its recognition of the emergence of new forms of culture as a result of cross-cultural interaction, voluntary and forced interaction. *Mestizaje* is a Latin American term that refers to '*mestizo*', which highlights the 'mixed and in be-tween' (Nederveen Pieterse 2009: 78). It relates specifically to the histories of the New World (Garcia Canclini 2005). and 'has served as an elite ideology', which refers to the 'whitening or Europeanization' of Latin America (Kraidy 2005: 76). Whereas syncretism refers to the fusion of different religious beliefs and practices (Kraidy 2005; Nederveen Pieterse 2009); hybridity, on the other hand, focuses on the way in which cultural processes and practices are affected by instances of hybrid interaction. Bhabha (2010) has used his interpretation of hybridity to theorise processes of cross-cultural interaction and decolonisation, while Clifford (1997) has been concerned with the hybrid intersections of cross-border travel and, perhaps most importantly for this analysis, the interaction of cultures in museums, which I will discuss in more detail in chapter two.

However, hybridity should not be used to suggest a process of smooth integration and fusion of cultures as this runs the risk of obscuring the power relations that run through such processes of hybridisation (Bhabha 2010; Garcia Canclini 2005). Garcia Canclini (2005) argues that we need to move from a descriptive understanding of hybridity. Drawing on the work of Cornejo Polar (1997: 180), who suggests that hybridity can be joined and left in the same way that modernity can, Garcia Canclini makes an important observation:

> If we speak of hybridization as a process to which one can gain access and which one can abandon, from which one can be excluded, or to which we can be subordinated, it is possible to understand the various subject positions implicated in cross-cultural relations.
>
> (2005: xxxi)

In other words, if we see the process of hybrid heritage production as a social process we can begin to interrogate and unpack the power relations that are involved in the complex interactions that occur during the exchange and co-production of heritage at a transnational level.

My view draws most closely from the work of Garcia Canclini who defines hybridity as the 'Sociocultural processes in which discrete structures or practices, previously existing in separate form, are combined to generate new structures, objects, and practices' (*ibid.*: xxv). He goes on to argue 'that the so-called discrete structures were a result of prior hybridisations and therefore cannot be considered pure forms of origin' (*ibid.*). Throughout this book, as previously mentioned, I see heritage as a socially constructed process. I also suggest that the heritage processes employed in Abu Dhabi are hybrid. In my engagement with the concept of hybridity I take the view that hybridity, like Garcia Canclini suggests, is not merely the fusion of separate entities (tangible or intangible) (*ibid.*: xxvii), instead I see it is a 'process', one that is intimately connected to the transnationalisation of the heritage sector and the cosmopolitan agendas of nation states. It is also a highly charged and political process.

This book is concerned with exploring how the process of hybridisation creates new cultural interactions, institutions and ways of valuing and preserving the past. It is therefore the conscious hybrid production of heritage that I am interested in and the heritage practices and products that ensue from the development of complex hybrid interactions. Ultimately, I take the view that the heritage developments in Abu Dhabi are part of a conscious process of cultural hybridisation.

A transnational approach

This book seeks to explore the significant differences between the way in which heritage is developed in the Gulf States and the more traditional models of the development of heritage in the eighteenth, nineteenth and twentieth centuries in western Europe. In doing so I suggest that this analysis will contribute to new understandings of how heritage operates as a global phenomenon and the transnational heritage discourses that emerge from this process. Taking such a view sees autochthonous and franchised heritage not as separate, or opposing elements, but as part of the same process of contemporary globalised identity making, which contributes to the development of newly emergent cosmopolitan identities.

I use the term transnational throughout this book to describe how heritage increasingly reaches across national borders. Hannerz suggests that the term transnational describes global 'phenomena which can be of quite variable scale and distribution, even when they do share the characteristic of not being contained within the state' (1996: 6). I suggest that transnational does not necessarily lead to the disappearance and loss of state power but instead that transnationalisation is making it increasingly impossible to separate heritage that operates within national boundaries and heritage that operates across national boundaries. This is an important aspect of the transnationalisation of heritage, and it is part of how it can be distinguished from the dominant national heritage discourses of the nineteenth and twentieth centuries.

The transnationalisation of heritage not only raises questions about the role of heritage in relation to globalisation, but also about how relevant those traditional models of heritage and nation building (which were largely developed through the exploration of processes which had occurred during nineteenth and twentieth centuries in Western, industrialising and post-industrialising contexts) are in understanding the role of heritage in contemporary non-Western contexts. Early academic heritage studies have been primarily interested in analysing the ways in which heritage has been implicated within the production of identities at a local, national and regional scale (Graham, Ashworth and Tunbridge 2000). Harrison has suggested that heritage has been used to '[p]roduce a set of common origins for a homogenous set of cultural values (often associated with the origin myths of particular ethnic groups) with which the conditions of citizenship are associated' (2013: 87). Hobsbawm and Ranger (2010) have argued how these ideas reflect particular historical trajectories relating to western Europe and North America in the late eighteenth, nineteenth and twentieth centuries. The extent to which these particular models continue to be relevant in light of contemporary shifts in global economies and geopolitics has recently begun to be questioned (Winter and Daly 2011) but have not been examined in detail.

In the twenty-first century museums are no longer bound to the areas in which they were developed. They have as Kratz and Karp argue become 'portable social technology' (2007: 4). One of the ways in which this is made possible is through the franchising of particular museums and galleries. I have suggested that 'a key contemporary phenomenon relating to the transnationalisation of heritage is the franchising of particular museums and galleries, developed within particular socio-cultural contexts, as global heritage institutions, as in the case of the Guggenheim and the Louvre Museums for example' (Wakefield 2011).

More specifically, the extent to which they are relevant to the very different historical, economic and political trajectories of the Gulf States has previously not been considered. This book recognises that many of the heritage processes that are being employed globally are based on a particularism that is still powerful enough to present itself as universal. By exploring how autochthonous and franchised heritage is produced in the Gulf States it becomes clear that many of these Western-dominated practices have been challenged, and perhaps more importantly, that new ways of understanding, producing and living with heritage are being articulated in these previously marginal locations.

Notes

1 At the time of writing, several of the UAE's early fort museums were in the process of being renovated such as the Al Ain National Museum and the Dubai Museum.
2 See the website of the National Center for Documentation and Research (n.d.[a]) for further historical details regarding the withdrawal of the British.
3 *Emir* is a title given to Muslim rulers in Islamic nations.
4 See the website of the National Center for Documentation and Research (n.d.[b]) for further details regarding the formation of the Federation.
5 See the website for the Zayed National Museum (n.d.[a]) for further details.
6 Sheikh Sultan bin Tahnoon Al Nahyan is Chairman of the: Abu Dhabi Tourism & Culture Authority; Tourism Development & Investment Company; Abu Dhabi National Exhibitions Company; Al Ain Wildlife Park & Resort; Eastern Region Development Committee, member of the Executive Council of Abu Dhabi Emirate and the Managing Director of the Emirates Foundation for Philanthropy (Tourism Development Investment Corporation 2013).
7 The Louvre Abu Dhabi was originally scheduled to be completed by 2012. A budgetary review of Abu Dhabi's development projects in 2012 resulted in a reassessment of the Emirate's plans and the organisation of the sector as a whole. One of the results of this was a revised timeline for the planned cultural heritage institutions on Saadiyat Island. The Louvre Abu Dhabi's revised opening date was then predicted to be the 2 December 2015, which would have coincided with the UAE's National Day (see Tourism Development Investment Corporation n.d.[n]). Further delays then saw the museum opening pushed back again to November 11, 2017.
8 Loans from several of France's cultural institutions were included in the 2007 inter-governmental agreement. Institutions involved include in the initial loans exchanged at the time of the museum's opening included: Louvre Museum; Centre Pompidou; Orsay and Orangery Museums; National Library of France; National Museum of Asian Arts - Guimet; Quai Branly Museum - Jacques Chirac; Palace, Château, Castle, Museum and National Domain of Versailles; Rodin Museum; Cluny Museum – National Museum of the Middle Ages; City of Ceramics – Sèvres & Limoges; Museum of Decorative Arts; National Archaeological Museum of Saint-Germain-en-Laye; Fountainbleu castle. For details of the contract see Balkany (2007).
9 The Guggenheim Abu Dhabi was originally due to open in 2013. The opening date was then pushed back to 2017 during Abu Dhabi's 2012 project reviews.

2 Transnational heritage

The emergence of heritage studies as an academic field has led to a focus on how heritage has been used to produce identities (these heritage developments have been explored in depth elsewhere see, for example, Smith 2006, 2012; Harrison 2013; Dicks 2015; Waterton and Watson 2015a, 2015b). Early writers on heritage such as Raphael Samuel (1994) and David Lowenthal (1998) identified conservation as an integral element within the development of heritage in the United Kingdom during the 1980s and 1990s. Samuel (1994), in particular, suggested that through the conservation process individuals joined forces to preserve and engage with the past in what he describes as a 'democratic process'. Robert Hewison (1987) has been more critical, suggesting that during periods of social disruption and decline, the past is idealised through nostalgic representations that are used to make the past seem better than it actually was. These formations and processes of heritage have been explored by considering how heritage is implicated in the production of heritage locally, regionally and nationally (Graham, Ashworth and Tunbridge 2000; Smith 2006; Harrison 2013), and how this is related to the study of the rise of nationalism and modern nation states (Hall 2008; Harrison 2010b, 2013). Hobsbawm and Ranger (2010) note how these ideas emerged in the late eighteenth, nineteenth and twentieth centuries as institutions such as museums were created, which coincided with the age of imperialism and the expansion of European nation states. Heritage has therefore been employed as a system of representation to define and represent national identity, drawing on political, economic and social circumstances. Crucially this system draws on processes of categorising and listing using established criteria and values (Carmen 2005; Harrison 2010a, 2013), which creates what Smith (2006) terms an 'authorized heritage discourse' on a global scale.

This chapter interrogates how the contemporary transnational heritage economy draws on cosmopolitan and universal frames of reference, which I term cosmo-universal, to produce globally translatable heritages. Although universal discourses have been widely challenged and disputed (see O'Neill 2004; Fiskesjö 2010 and Curtis 2005, 2006), they continue to operate and have significant implications, particularly as they relate to power knowledge networks (see Harrison 2010b, 2013; Meskell and Brumann 2015). This chapter examines how universalism has been framed as a cosmopolitan project to challenge anti-universal discourses and legitimise transnational representational practices. The chapter then goes on to link these developments to postmodernity and cross-border heritage practices, which is contextualised within a theoretical approach grounded in cultural hybridity.

Global categorisation and authentication

The United Nations Educational, Scientific and Cultural Organization (UNESCO) has played a fundamental role in the globalising and universalising narratives that have been institutionalised as 'global heritage' through the development of legal frameworks and the listing and categorisation of aspects of heritage, tangible and intangible (Harrison 2010b, 2013; Meskell and Brumann 2015). The foundations for UNESCO were set by the League of Nations[1] and the International Committee on Intellectual Co-operation, which operated between 1936 and 1946.[2] Meskell and Brumann note that 'the universalist aspirations for global governance envisaged by the League of Nations' set the foundations for the establishment of UNESCO with its focus on 'peace, humanitarianism, and intercultural understanding' (2015: 24; see also Donnachie 2010). However the League of Nations remained a politically laden and exclusive network.[3] The League of Nations, and the International Committee on Intellectual Co-operation, served to institutionalise the role of the 'expert' in governing heritage on a global scale. Next came the Athens Charter that developed out of the First International Congress of Architects and Technicians of Historic Monuments in 1931 (ICOMOS 2019). The Charter led to the development of 'a code of ethics and principles that were applied internationally for preservation of heritage through the restoration and preservation of ancient buildings', which were used to shape and embed a global heritage ideology based on prescribed 'values' of preservation (Donnachie 2010: 117). The Charter was significant as it set the basis for the establishment of a global cultural heritage framework. In doing so, these early charters were fundamental in shaping the global preservationist ethos.

It was not until November 16, 1945, at a UN Conference in London, led by France and the UK, attended by representatives from forty-four countries, that UNESCO was established.[4] UNESCO's initial aim was post-war rebuilding after World War II and in particular the 'preservation and rescue of historic sites' in Europe (Donnachie 2010: 118; Meskell and Brumann 2015). However as Di Giovine (2015) observes these early initiatives by UNESCO were not based on the same 'universal' and 'ethical' values that we can observe in contemporary practices. In the same year, the International Council of Museums (ICOM) was established to focus on the transnational role of museums in education, conservation and restoration. However, it was not until 1977 when it established its own *Code of Ethics* and policies relating to museums that ICOM began to expand its international activities beyond western European nations (ICOM n.d.).

Cultural heritage became further governed by the ratification of the Venice Charter in 1964 during the Second Congress of Architects and Specialists of Historic Buildings in Venice (ICOMOS 2015). The Charter set out a series of standards and procedures for the conservation and preservation of historical sites. As Donnachie has noted the Charter specifically linked 'authenticity' to 'the historical and physical context of the site' (2010: 120), which emphasised the materiality of the past. During the same meeting, the International Council on Monuments and Sites (ICOMOS) was proposed by UNESCO. ICOMOS (2015) was officially formed in 1965 based on a network of expert members who evaluated sites for nomination to the World Heritage List and as such 'became a key player in the World Heritage selection and designation process' (Donnachie 2010: 121). The World Heritage Convention developed from concerns for conserving both cultural and natural (UNESCO 1972; Harrison 2010b; UNESCO n.d.[b]). UNESCO has been highly successful in establishing a global heritage system through the World Heritage Convention and the Listing process, which ultimately operates as a system of global governance (Byrne 1991; Kirshenblatt-Gimblett 2007; Harrison 2010a, 2010b, 2013; Donnachie 2010). Considerable attention has been paid to the 'process' of World Heritage Listing and the categorisations applied to this 'bureaucratic' method of monitoring and controlling heritage across national borders (Carmen 2005; Smith 2006: 99–100; Harrison 2010a, 2013). More broadly, UNESCO's remit draws on cosmopolitan discourses that present an ethical framework. This framework stresses the role of cultural heritage in promoting 'peace and harmony' between nations (Donnachie 2010: 118).

In 2020, there were '1121 inscribed properties (or sites) from 167 state parties on UNESCO's World Heritage List', which included: '869 cultural sites, 213 natural sites and 39 mixed sites combining cultural and natural heritage, 39 transboundary sites' (UNESCO n.d.[c]). The sheer number of listings serve to illustrate how popular the World Heritage Listing process has become. A key issue that emerged regarding World Heritage Listing was that heritage was predominantly listed using tangible criteria, which resulted in the list being heavily biased towards western European nations (see Byrne 1991; Smith 2006; Kirshenblatt-Gimblett 2007; Harrison 2010b, 2013; Waterton, Watson and Silverman 2017). However, recent years have seen considerable growth in nominations from non-Western nations. This continued interest in World Heritage Listing demonstrates that the idea of global heritage has settled into the international discourse.

Due to the political nature of heritage and its use within nation building these expressions of heritage have often not been in-line with local culture (Smith 2006; Harrison 2013; Basu and Modest 2015; Meskell and Brumann 2015). This exclusionary practice disempowers as it serves to prioritise the preservation of certain segments of society, while alternative segments are marginalised in the management process. Hall suggested that heritage is based on 'a process of selective canonisation, which focuses selectively on the nations' high points and memorable moments' (2008: 221; Harrison 2010b: 2). Harrison (2010b) has developed this idea further arguing that these lists can be considered forms of a 'heritage canon'. Whereas Waterton, Watson and Silverman have argued that global heritage is 'embedded in Herzfeld's (2004) "Global hierarchy of value" and as such is a hegemonic process' (2017: 5).

Due to selective processes that are involved in categorising and placing value onto aspects of the past heritage is often 'predatory' (Harrison 2013), which can result in the production of 'heritage victims' (Gonzalez-Ruibal 2009). The result is that 'official' heritage narratives often serve to exclude and disempower individual members of society through the selective preservation and presentation of the past. In 1994 the development of the Global Strategy to heritage created to 'promote a global strategy for a more balanced, representative and credible World Heritage List' by the World Heritage Center (Donnachie 2010). UNESCO began addressing this issue by lobbying nations that were under-represented. However, the lobbying process also served a political purpose as it served to promote and reinforce the benefits of the World Heritage List and as such the hegemonic power structures of UNESCO.

The selective nature of the listing process was evident in UNESCO's early World Heritage List, which failed to acknowledge and recognise intangible forms of heritage as global. In 2003, UNESCO responded to this criticism by expanding the categorisation process to include intangible heritage (Harrison 2010a, 2010b). According to Article 2 of the *2003 Convention for the Safeguarding of Intangible Cultural Heritage*, intangible aspects of heritage can be categorised as follows:

> The practices, representations, expressions, knowledge, skills – as well as the instruments, objects, artefacts and cultural spaces associated therewith – that communities, groups and, in some cases, individuals recognise as part of their cultural heritage. This intangible cultural heritage, transmitted from generation to generation, is constantly recreated by communities and groups in response to their environment, their interaction with nature and their history, and provides them with a sense of identity and continuity, thus promoting respect for cultural diversity and human creativity.
>
> (UNESCO 2003a)

Following this definition, intangible cultural heritage is further designated by UNESCO into one of the following categories:

- Oral traditions and expressions, including language as a vehicle of the intangible cultural heritage.
- Performing arts.
- Social practices, rituals and festive events.

- Knowledge and practices concerning nature and the universe.
- Traditional craftsmanship.

(ibid.)

Kirshenblatt-Gimblett has argued that the processes of categorising intangible cultural heritage through the World Heritage List imply a process whereby individuals '[a]re not only cultural carriers and transmitters but also agents in the heritage enterprise itself' (2007: 179). However, she goes on to argue that this process of formalising and categorising cultural practices alters not only how they practised and understood but it also affects who is involved in the performative act of heritage.

Importantly, Harrison has argued that 'a representative heritage place or object derives its values from the extent to which it can act as an exemplar of the class of place or type of object' (2010b: 26). The idea here is that heritage practitioners preserve things or places that can act as representative samples of the past, which are then considered necessary now and for the future *(ibid.)*. However, the issue of 'value' and 'power' remains implicit within the construction of 'representative' heritage. Furthermore, 'the open-ended nature of ICH means it is often the most endangered component in World Heritage due to globalisation and the relative lack of interest among the young, language being the prime example' (Donnachie 2010: 134). Leading to heritage being performed by actors who may have no links to the cultural heritage performance or practice. In Abu Dhabi, non-Emirati actors are often employed to perform individual heritage acts at festivals (see Prager 2015). Transnational heritage is playing an increasingly significant role within the development of Abu Dhabi's autochthonous heritage, which can be evidenced within Abu Dhabi's growing number of World Heritage List applications.

'World Heritage' in Abu Dhabi

In Abu Dhabi the World Heritage Listing process is being used to further develop the UAE's national and international profile. Rather than being opposed to the global discourses that surround the development of the cultural heritage franchises on Saadiyat Island, autochthonous heritage is used to support and further develop Abu Dhabi's global identity. For example the Cultural Sites of Al Ain (Hafit, Hili, Bidaa Bint Saud and Oases Areas) were first nominated to the World Heritage List in 2007 based on their 'universal value':

> The serial property of The Cultural Sites of Al Ain, with its various component parts and the regional context in which it is situated, provides testimony to ancient sedentary human occupation in a desert region. Occupied continuously since the Neolithic, the region presents vestiges of numerous prehistoric cultures, notably from the Bronze Age and the Iron Age.
>
> (UNESCO n.d.[d])

This resulted in the Sites inscription to the tentative List of World Heritage Sites in 2008 and their final listing in 2010 (UNESCO n.d.[e]). Beech suggests that awareness of heritage in the UAE had grown as a direct result of the development of global heritage initiatives such as those by UNESCO in Abu Dhabi (2011: Interview). World Heritage Listing was clearly playing a significant role within the developing heritage tourism sector. Importantly, until recently, autochthonous heritage has predominantly been interpreted as intangible. Therefore in Abu Dhabi we can see that tangible forms of heritage have been marginalised as interpretations have been based on intangible understandings of heritage. This has led to the view that tangible aspects of the past are less 'valued', which I discuss further in chapter seven.

The emphasis on intangible heritage has led to the UAE receiving several inscriptions on the *Representative List of the Intangible Heritage of Humanity* (UNESCO n.d.[e]). The intangible inscriptions resulted from both single nation (UAE) and transnational applications (Table 2.1). Falconry as an overarching practice has been inscribed on UNESCO's Intangible Heritage of Humanity list. I have noted elsewhere that falconry has been used to communicate the UAE's sporting heritage locally, nationally and internationally as part of the Emirates' transnational vision (see Wakefield 2012). Transnational World Heritage nominations are different from other World Heritage nominations listings and to a certain extent undermine the critique of the States' control of the World Heritage nomination process for ideological purposes.

There is also a clear parallel between the process of transnational heritage listing and cultural heritage franchising in the sense in which these transnational listings are also framed as cosmopolitan actions. They do this because they operate across and within co-operation with other nations. For example, the inscription of falconry on the Intangible Heritage of Humanity list was achieved in conjunction with eighteen other nations.[5] Notably, falconry was inscribed as a living human heritage on UNESCO's Representative List of Intangible Cultural Heritage of Humanity in 2010 as a result of a bid led by the UAE. These transnational listings also allow nations to develop links, which are often strategic, to other nations through co-produced nominations.

The imbalanced nature of UNESCO's listing is an essential issue as it undermines the power and universal credentials of the World Heritage List. UNESCO's core weakness then, is that the organisation's power is reliant upon the 'buy-in' of diverse nations around the world. It was reported in September 2009 by *The National* newspaper that there was a 'geographical imbalance' in the applications received by UNESCO for inclusion on the *Representative List of Intangible Cultural Heritage of Humanity* (Morris 2009). Francoise Riviere, representing the director-general of UNESCO, is quoted as having said at a meeting in Abu Dhabi that, 'Africa and [the] Arab States are far behind other regions' and that, 'out of a total of 280 applications…only two Arab countries, the UAE and Oman, have submitted nominations' (*ibid.*).

Table 2.1 List of intangible cultural heritage inscriptions for the United Arab Emirates

2011	**List of intangible cultural heritage in need of urgent safeguarding**
United Arab Emirates	Al Sadu, traditional weaving skills in the United Arab Emirates
2012	**Representative list of the intangible cultural heritage of humanity**
United Arab Emirates – Oman	Al-Taghrooda, traditional Bedouin chanted poetry in the United Arab Emirates and the Sultanate of Oman
2014	**Representative list of the intangible cultural heritage of humanity**
Oman – United Arab Emirates	Al-Ayyala, a traditional performing art of the Sultanate of Oman and the United Arab Emirates
2015	**Representative list of the intangible cultural heritage of humanity**
United Arab Emirates – Oman	Al-Razfa, a traditional performing art
United Arab Emirates – Saudi Arabia – Oman – Qatar	Arabic coffee, a symbol of generosity
United Arab Emirates – Saudi Arabia – Oman – Qatar	Majlis, a cultural and social space
2016	**Representative list of the intangible cultural heritage of humanity**
Germany – Saudi Arabia – Austria – Belgium – United Arab Emirates – Spain – France – Hungary – Italy – Kazakhstan – Morocco – Mongolia – Pakistan – Portugal – Qatar – Syrian Arab Republic – Republic of Korea – Czechia	Falconry, a living human heritage
2017	**List of intangible cultural heritage in need of urgent safeguarding**
United Arab Emirates	Al Azi, art of performing praise, pride and fortitude poetry

Table adapted from the UNESCO Lists of Intangible Cultural Heritage and the Register of Good Safeguarding Practices (UNESCO n.d.[c]).

This not only illustrates how the Arab world has been marginalised but also illustrates how UNESCO encourages 'buy-in' to the dominant discourses by suggesting that nations are somehow behind for not having aspects of their heritage, tangible and intangible, designated as World Heritage, which serves to illustrate the problematic power relations that underpin transnational heritage listing.

World Heritage branding

In order for UNESCO's World Heritage List to work, it needs to offer nations some form of return. It is here that relationship branding becomes essential. Ryan and Silvanto (2011) have argued that the process of World Heritage Listing has become an essential method for nations to develop their brand and tourism potential. Wallace provides a useful definition of branding through her discussion of museum branding. She argues that '[a] brand is a distinctive identity that engenders loyalty' and that as such the process of 'branding consists of creating and maintaining a body of programs and attitudes that convey an explicit promise, encourage familiarity, and generate on-going support' (Wallace 2006: 1). This definition is useful for both the analysis of World Heritage Listing and for my discussion of cultural heritage franchises. Ryan and Silvanto have argued that 'the World Heritage designation represents a promise of value and differentiation' that creates an expectation of what the visitor can expect from a World Heritage Site visit, it therefore operates as a brand (2011: 308). In this sense, the association that a brand name brings allows a nation to be seen as possessing heritage that is valued through the 'authorized heritage discourse' (Smith 2006), and this valuing enables the developing nation to establish its reputation and consequently its tourism value through an association with the World Heritage brand (Harrison 2010b; Ryan and Silvanto 2011; Meskell and Brumann 2015).

Since the early 2000s, Abu Dhabi has actively been developing cultural heritage sites for tourism.[6] Parts of the Hili archaeological site in Al Ain, which is an element of the World Heritage designated Cultural Sites of Al Ain, have been incorporated into the Hili Archaeological Park. Hili Archaeological Park is a landscaped garden specifically designed and developed to make the heritage site more accessible to the public (Abu Dhabi Government n.d.). Finds from the site are also on display at Al Ain Museum, which at the time of writing was closed for renovation.[7] However, sites such as Hili have been criticised by local archaeologists for their limited interpretation and community engagement (Beech 2011: Interview) and their lack of 'visual' appeal (Hellyer 2011: Interview). These statements are suggestive of a perception that World Heritage Sites should be 'monumental' and large-scale to attract tourists. Indicating that issues relating to values of 'scale' and 'monumentality' continue to persist (Harrison, 2013). However, due to the increasing diversity of the World Heritage List, we have witnessed the inscription of sites that are less visually stunning, though of no-lesser value. In addition, the lack of awareness of archaeological sites further suggests that tangible sites have up until recently been marginalised within the heritage landscape of Abu Dhabi.

I suggest that the development of the cultural heritage franchise brand works in a similar way to World Heritage Site branding. For example the Guggenheim Foundation through the process of cultural heritage franchising, has developed its brand identity globally (Table 2.2). Obtaining and developing a 'branded' museum, such as a Guggenheim or a Louvre, is a

Table 2.2 Guggenheim museums – proposed, existing and closed

Guggenheim Museums	Location	Proposed	Opened	Closed	Expected opening	Cancelled
Solomon R. Guggenheim Museum	New York, United States		1959			
Peggy Guggenheim Collection	Venice, Italy		1929			
Guggenheim Museum Bilbao	Bilbao, Spain		1997			
Guggenheim Abu Dhabi	Abu Dhabi, United Arab Emirates				Delayed (no available date)	
Deutsche Guggenheim	Berlin, Germany		1997	2012		
Guggenheim SoHo	New York, United States		1992	2001		
Guggenheim Las Vegas	Las Vegas, United States		2001	2002		
Guggenheim Hermitage Museum	Las Vegas, United States		2001	2008		
Guggenheim Guadalajara	Guadalajara, Jalisco, Mexico	2005				2009
Vilnius Guggenheim Hermitage Museum	Vilnius, Lithuania	2008			2013 (originally 2011)	2010
Guggenheim Helsinki	Helsinki, Finland	2011				2012
Guggenheim Helsinki	Helsinki, Finland	2013 (second bid)				2016
Salzburg Guggenheim	Monchsberg, Salzburg, Austria	1990				1991
Tokyo Guggenheim	Odasiba Island, Tokyo, Japan	1990				2004
Rio de Janeiro	Rio de Janeiro, Brazil	2000				2003
Taichung	Taichung, Taiwan	2003				2004
Hong Kong Guggenheim	Hong Kong	2005				2006
Manhattan Guggenheim	Manhattan, New York, United States	2000				2002

Source: Table compiled by the author.

means of communicating the power and prestige of the nation on a global scale. One of the benefits of museum franchising is that it enables the 'home' museum to expand its audience (Caldwell 2000: 29–30). However, it should be remembered that franchise brands, like World Heritage Sites, are often globally recognised but not necessarily directly experienced (Ryan and Silvanto 2011). The Guggenheim Museum Bilbao, for example, is a franchise that many people are aware of but have never physically visited.

Cultural heritage franchising, much like World Heritage listing, creates a global grouping whose membership signifies the distinctiveness of the nation and its heritage. The result, to borrow from Gell, is that cultural heritage franchises are 'made more or less desirable by the role they play in a symbolic system' (1986: 110). Arguably, big tourist pulling brands are the most popular franchises to have due to their established global identity in the market. This process is far from value free and as such is just as likely to bring varied forms of exclusion as it is inclusion. In fact, the process is exclusionary as it marginalises poorer nations who do not have the vast financial means to fulfil the requirements for membership (see Adie 2017 for a discussion of World Heritage Sites as franchises). The discourse of universalism is therefore used to mask the global hegemonic processes that are used to define heritage as 'global'.

Global listings and global groupings essentially set a universal agenda that allows for the formation of organisations and institutions that lay claim, through the development of standards and agendas, to the rights to talk about all cultures and all cultural property (tangible and intangible). This hegemonic system serves to reinforce the power and global reach of heritage institutions, which is predominantly led by western European nations.

This discussion of UNESCO World Heritage nominations from the UAE has shown that the way in which global heritage is negotiated through the nomination process is not based purely on a hegemonic process. On the contrary, national governments are active in the process of negotiating nominations and their transnational heritage identities. The procedure of designating heritage as global through the World Heritage nomination process can, therefore, be seen as a hybrid heritage process. However, the dominant power remains with UNESCO as the governing institution. In this sense, global heritage is co-produced through the listing process. UNESCO designation offers Abu Dhabi the potential to further develop both its global identity and awareness of its autochthonous heritage at home. In this way autochthonous and franchised heritage is not opposed but is being directed towards a similar goal, that goal being the development of a transnational, cosmopolitan identity.

Heritage, ownership and universal museums

Global heritage governance has attracted criticism and resistance due to its hegemonic approach, which ultimately serves to take ownership of individual nations' cultural property (tangible and intangible). Appiah (2009) in his discussion of Nigeria's terra-cotta Nok sculptures, has observed how the process of global categorisation and listing brings up the issue of ownership. He suggests that when heritage is categorised as World Heritage, a tension emerges between the attachment to the World Heritage List (and brand) and the attachment that individuals have to those aspects of the past that are characterised as national heritage (*ibid.*). This issue is perhaps most apparent in the way that universalism has been used within cultural policies such as the *Declaration on the Importance and Value of Universal Museums* as a response to repatriation debates.

In 2002, the *Declaration on the Importance and Value of Universal Museums* was signed by a group of museums from Europe and North America in response to calls for the repatriation of artefacts and human remains (Schuster 2004: 4). O'Neill argues that the Declaration suggests that the aim of universal museums is 'to represent world cultures in accordance with its "universal" mission for the sake of mankind' (2004: 190; see also Flessas 2013). He goes on to cite the then director of the British Museum, Neil Macgregor, who wrote an article for *The Guardian* newspaper in which he suggests that the British Museum is a 'Universal Museum'. In his article, MacGregor maintains that 'the quality and diversity of the museum's collection means it is able to explore and represent the world as a whole' (O'Neill 2004: 190). The debates around universalism and repatriation are often linked historically to the British Museum and early debates regarding the Parthenon Marbles (Cuno 2008). According to Flessas this process produces a 'value hierarchy privileging an imaginary West' who through the museum 'enjoy immense social prestige, which remains their most precious capital' (2013: 10). Furthermore, those museums holding items of questionable provenance see the objects as part of their identity and 'the nations which house them' (Curtis 2005; Fiskesjö 2010). However, O'Neill criticised MacGregor arguing that the Declaration's 'credibility is undermined through its use as a defence against repatriation claims'. He cites Geoffrey Lewis's criticism that appeared in an ICOM bulletin in which he suggests '[t]he Declaration is a statement of self-interest, made by a group representing some of the world's richest museums; they do not, as they imply, speak for the "international museum community"' (Lewis 2004: 3 cited in O'Neill 2004: 191). Furthermore, the debates surrounding the Declaration are framed within Western terms of reference (Curtis 2005: 6). The issue of ownership is essential and has implications for cultural heritage franchising. The Louvre Museum in Paris, for example, contains works from around the world, which may be contested by other countries through similar calls for repatriation.

Early universal museums were vital agents in the nineteenth-century imperial and colonial project of Europe. During the late eighteenth and early nineteenth centuries universalism was used in the context of national rivalry to highlight national identity and illustrate differences between lesser-developed nations. The museum played an essential role in shaping and defining national identity in European nations at this time; key players were the British Museum, the National Gallery and the Louvre Museum.

As the first universal museum, the Louvre Museum was central to the development of universal and colonial discourses at the time. The French Revolution witnessed a significant political shift from ruling monarchies to the Republic state. The Louvre Museum in Paris, founded in 1793 CE, played a strategic political role in this shift.[8] Before the establishment of the French Revolution, royal collections were private elite status symbols that 'functioned as reception rooms, providing sumptuous settings for official ceremonies and framing the figure of the prince' (Duncan 1995: 22). The transition to the public museum sought to materialise the links between the newly established nation state and the public. The Louvre Museum served as the flagship symbol of the new national identity. The national identity discourses moved away from a national identity channelled through the king, to one that was focused on the state, and as such the Louvre Museum sought to use architecture, collections and the introduction and control of public cultural space to position France as a dominant force in cultural production (Duncan and Wallach 1980: 454).

Early museums operated as elite spaces for the reproduction of bourgeois ideologies and aristocratic identity (*ibid.*: 452; see also Ajana 2015: 320). This process was distinctly political as these early museums developed their power as symbols of national identity. Alongside this came the 'civilising role' of the museum (Duncan 1995). Bennett's seminal study of nineteenth-century museums highlighted the role that knowledge and power have played in the development of museums and the categorisation of the past, which he defined as the 'exhibitionary complex' (1995: 73). The museum was used to not only educate the public about art, a public without education in art; it was also used to civilise people through institutionalised behaviour. The institutionalisation of museum behaviour meant that new rules needed to be introduced and monitored (*ibid.*: 27). With the establishment of the Louvre Museum came a shift in display and the role of collections, particularly as an 'educative apparatus of the state' (Harrison 2013) in defining national identity and citizenship in the nineteenth century.

Originally a product of the Enlightenment the Universal Museum has been repackaged and repositioned within the Gulf States through the newly opened Louvre Abu Dhabi. The Louvre Abu Dhabi has been explicitly positioned as a universal museum. While the postcolonial collecting processes and approach to developing collections in Abu Dhabi is markedly different to the colonial approach taken by the Louvre Museum in the past, issues relating to the sale, ownership and location of cultural property remain contentious issues in contemporary museums and heritage practice. However, due to the authoritarian nature of UAE society issues relating to provenance and ownership have remained largely uncritiqued. Furthermore, the ideological inheritance of 'universalist' practices remains omni-present in the re-imagined museum in Abu Dhabi. Ownership and exclusivity remain critical issues in the Louvre Abu Dhabi. Perhaps most concerning is whether this new universalism, packaged up within a purportedly postmodern museology, will serve to perpetuate the power relations of the past.

As Sayyid notes the geographies of universal claims are significant because when something is defined as universal, it is also often associated with the West (2000: 264). Sayyid's ideas are highly relevant to how 'universal' ideas and practices are applied to cultural heritage. Tuhiwai Smith argues that:

> the collective memory of imperialism (which is intimately linked to the notion of universal) has been perpetuated through the ways in which knowledge about the indigenous peoples was collected, classified and then represented in various ways back to the West, and then, through the eyes of the West, back to those who have been colonised.
>
> (2012: 2)

Within the heritage sector, universalism and the associated production of global heritage has been used to position the West as the centre of knowledge. The West has benefitted from the increase in museum developments in new territories, especially in non-Western nations through the dissemination of a 'Western typology of museums and the art and artifact display paradigms it characteristically deploys' (Phillips 2007: 18; see also Boast 2011: 65). Universalism is necessary for cultural heritage franchising since it relies on a standardised museum model, that includes the museum's branding, operational structure, collecting and educational strategies, which can be translated across borders. The branding and saleability of the cultural heritage franchise is based upon the way in which universalism is attached to the processes of international museum development and the idea that museums can be developed and sold as universal institutions.

In addition, cosmopolitanism is used to depoliticise the project by positioning the process of cultural heritage franchising as a shared and iterative process. Bennett (2017) has argued that the politics of museums has shifted through time and within different cultural contexts such as Britain, Australia, the USA, France and Japan. The universal museum was originally used as a tool of enlightenment, whereas, the discourse surrounding the Louvre Abu Dhabi has been used to emphasise a 'transversal' approach that emphasises 'commonality' and 'universal elements' between cultures. Contemporary interpretations of universalism have therefore shifted as heritage takes on increasingly globalised forms. The contemporary iteration of the universal museum has drawn on the humanising and ethical mandates of cosmopolitanism, which I will explore in depth in the following section. This discourse is strategically used to reposition universalism as a cosmopolitan and inclusive project, which I define as 'cosmo-universalism'.

The processes that museums and heritage institutions have employed have emerged mainly from the way in which states officially sanction heritage to tell specific stories about the past (Smith 2006; Harrison 2010b, 2013;

Bennett 2013, 2017). As such, these processes are inevitably connected to contemporary concerns. These debates are significant because they draw attention to the importance of exploring how heritage operates at an ideological level to construct narratives of the past and how it operates at a practical level to materialise the past through the production of tangible and intangible forms of heritage.

Heritage, cosmopolitanism and global ethics

Over time the interpretations and meanings that have been attached to cosmopolitanism have changed and expanded. As a result, cosmopolitanism remains a highly contested term with no set definition (Beck and Sznaider 2010: 382). Cosmopolitanism has been traced back to Greek antiquity to the Cynics and the Stoics (see discussions by Appiah 2007; Meskell 2009; Bielsa 2016). Appiah notes the term 'cynic' refers to scepticism of customs and traditions situated within national ideologies, which led to the emergence of cosmopolitanism, 'citizen of the cosmos', during the fourth century BCE with the Cynics.

> A citizen – a *politès* – belonged to a particular *polis,* a city to which he or she owed loyalty. The cosmos referred to the world, not in the sense of the earth, but in the sense of the universe. Talk of cosmopolitanism originally signalled, then, a rejection of the *conventional view that every civilized person belonged to a community among communities.*
>
> (Appiah 2007: xii)

In the third century BCE the Stoics further developed the cosmopolitan idea. For example, Diognese (412–323 BCE) declared, 'I am a citizen of the world (*kosmopolitês*)' when asked where he was from (*ibid.*: xii). However early cosmopolitanism displayed a duality, Diognese claims to be a member of the global community, yet, at the same time, he 'was socially displaced, stigmatized and disempowered' (Schiller and Irving 2017: 1).

Cosmopolitanism has frequently been linked to Enlightenment philosophy and the work of Immanuel Kant who proposed that all human belong to a single community (Appiah 2007; Nashashibi 2007: 124; Starkey 2012). Beck and Sznaider suggest that Kant's cosmopolitanism is linked to economic and political developments in Europe, which resulted in 'relatively closed societies' moving into 'universal eras' (2010: 389) and the emergence of notions of '*universal* humanity' (Starkey 2012: 25) and 'world citizenship' (Abdelhalim 2010: 64). Yet, as Abdelhalim notes, cosmopolitanism is not a purely Western notion and can be found in numerous non-Western contexts, such as in the work of 'Indian poet Tagore' and within 'the Islamic concept of the '*Umma*' (*ibid.*: 64; see also Schiller and Irving 2017: 1). Furthermore, as Mignolo observes, the cosmopolitan project has been 'linked to coloniality and the emergence of the modern/colonial world' in both religious and secular campaigns during moments of modernity (2002: 158). Mignolo draws our attention here to the political and power undercurrents of cosmopolitanism.

Contemporary cosmopolitanisms

More recently contemporary cosmopolitanism has most generally come to be 'characterized by the globally-held moral tenant that human beings – and not ethnic communities, nations or states – are the ultimate units of concern' (Abdelhalim 2010: 64). As Isin and Turner suggest '[h]uman rights underpin the notion that cosmopolitanism involves both recognition and respect for other people' (2010: 173). I discussed in the proceeding section cosmopolitan values and the celebration of difference through the promotion of shared heritage, which is often referred to (or branded) as global, universal or transnational, is playing a significant role within global identity making (see also Wakefield 2011, 2013). Global heritage discourses draw on cosmopolitan ideologies to suggest that people have an ethical obligation to contribute to world heritage. Universal cultural heritage practices operate as a double-edged process, which serves to promote an ethics of respect and tolerance but at the same time operates as a hegemonic force through the institutionalisation of heritage. In doing so, the transnational heritage economy through its selective use of cosmopolitanism, based on a presumed global ethic, gains 'currency' and 'legitimacy' at an ideational level, in effect it colonises.

The ethical dimensions of cosmopolitanism are evident in Appiah's work where he suggests the existence of two strands of cosmopolitanism:

> One is the idea that we have obligations to others, obligations that stretch beyond those to whom we are related by the ties of kith and kind, or even the more formal ties of a shared citizenship. The other is that we take seriously the value not just of human life but of particular human lives, which means taking an interest in the practices and beliefs that lend them significance.
>
> (2007: xiii)

If we consider Appiah's cosmopolitism in relation to the Universal Declaration on Cultural Diversity we can potentially see his two strands of cosmopolitanism at work:

> Culture takes diverse forms across time and space. This diversity is embodied in the uniqueness and plurality of the identities of the groups and societies making up humankind. As a source of exchange, innovation and creativity, cultural diversity is as necessary for humankind as biodiversity for nature. In this sense, it is the common heritage of

humanity and should be recognized and affirmed for the benefit of present and future generations.

(UNESCO 2001)

The declaration first suggests that there is an obligation to recognise global 'cultural diversity'. This then allows for the second strand of cosmopolitanism, where the declaration goes on to draw attention to the value that is placed on diversity by working to preserve the 'heritage of humanity'. Abu Dhabi's role as facilitator of cross-cultural exchange was set out on ADACH's website where it states:

> Internationally it [Abu Dhabi] is contributing to the strengthening of intercultural dialogue and the appreciation of different cultures by developing projects that encourage the strengthening of cultural traditions and experiences.
>
> (Abu Dhabi Authority for Culture and Heritage n.d.[c])

Cosmopolitan references can be observed in this statement, which emphasises Abu Dhabi's obligation to 'others', the obligation of recognition, and the value of other cultural traditions and experiences. What we see here is a 'cosmopolitan outlook' in which Abu Dhabi presents the nation as 'simultaneously as part of the threatened world and as part of their local situations and histories' (Beck 1999: 391). Yet, as Beck and Sznaider argue later, rarely do individuals think or act in such binary terms (2010).

In terms of world heritage Kirshenblatt-Gimblett has argued that it serves as 'a vehicle for envisaging and constituting a global polity within the conceptual space of a global cultural commons' (2007: 161). In this sense, nations use global heritage processes to define their identities and their membership of humanity. Whereas Bennett has argued that museums have been rethought as 'differencing machines'. He suggests that there has been a new iteration of the museum that has resulted in them working to become 'committed to the promotion of cross-cultural understanding' (Bennett 2017: 46). The mobilities of heritage things, ideas and processes are therefore often presented as an obligation that is bound up within global and cosmopolitan frames of reference.

As I noted in the previous section, for the Louvre Museum, the partnership with Abu Dhabi offered an opportunity to reposition its contemporary identity within cosmopolitan terms. I have argued elsewhere that central to the museum's self-professed global discourse are claims to 'universal themes and common influences', which are used to 'illustrate similarities arising from shared human experience transcending geography, nationality and history' (Wakefield 2014: 105). In this sense, a 'cosmo-universal' discourse is used to re-position universalism as a cosmopolitan and inclusive project (Wakefield 2012, 2013, 2014). Global aspirations are also present within the rhetoric behind the Guggenheim Abu Dhabi:

The Guggenheim Abu Dhabi will move beyond a definition of global art on geography by focusing on the international dynamics of local, regional and international art centres as well as their diverse historical contexts and sources of creative inspiration. In realizing this endeavour, the museum will acknowledge and celebrate the specific identity derived from the cultural traditions of Abu Dhabi and the United Arab Emirates, as well as other countries comprising the Middle East, even as it pioneers a novel, visionary model that will redefine the art-historical canon.

> (Solomon R. Guggenheim Foundation n.d.[b]).

The heritage project in Abu Dhabi serves as a symbol of Abu Dhabi's place within the global system by positioning the Emirate's cultural identity, both past and present, within transnational and universal terms.

Furthermore, Abu Dhabi is proclaiming through its attachment to Western museographic traditions is proclaiming itself as a global cultural centre through its attachment to Western. This is evident in official statements regarding the Louvre Abu Dhabi:

Abu Dhabi has put its hand on its heart and said that the Louvre Abu Dhabi's messages are ones that it wants to send to the rest of the world: messages of unity, acceptance, connectivity and tolerance. These were messages that were important 1,000 years ago but are even more important today. Abu Dhabi is the beacon that will broadcast these messages to the Arab world and to the rest of the world.

> (Mohamed Khalifa Al-Mubarak, chairman, Abu Dhabi Tourism & Culture Authority cited in Leech 2017a)

In doing so, Abu Dhabi is not only making statements about its power to operate within the global economy but also its power to reframe Western heritage in Abu Dhabi. In this sense, Abu Dhabi challenges the neo-colonial power of the West by asserting its role in creating new frames of reference in the non-Western world. This illustrates how the cultural heritage franchise uses international collaborations and interconnections, real and imagined, to present and communicate in cosmopolitan terms.

National identity and cosmopolitanism

The processes of globalisation and the new frames of international cultural relations that it produces have been critiqued for their perceived role in weakening the nation state (Hobsbawm 2010; Nash 2009). National identity is considered to be natural and cosmopolitan and global identity to be an artificial construct (Beck and Sznaider 2010: 388). As such cosmopolitanism can be challenged and resisted as it is seen as a threat to nationalism and national identity (Starkey 2012: 25). However cosmopolitanism and nationalism are not mutually exclusive (Beck and Sznaider 2010: 388) and as such transnationals 'remain rooted in their nations of origin' (Robbins 1998). Meskell has argued that 'rooted cosmopolitanism acknowledges attachments to place and particular social networks, resources and cultural experiences that inhabit that space' (2009: 3–4). The reference to roots here is important when considering cross-cultural interactions as it emphasises the socio-cultural dynamics that are present when cultures come into contact through partnership and exchange. However, this interpretation of 'rootedness' does not account for moments of uprooting and movement, nor does it distinguish between historic roots and contemporaneous roots.

Arguably, cosmopolitanism 'has retained a direct link with the idea of the "nation states" (Abdelhalim 2010: 64). In Abu Dhabi the rhetoric behind the planned museums on Saadiyat Island suggests that the projects are being used to position Abu Dhabi's transnational and cosmopolitan credentials (see also Wakefield 2013, 2014, 2017b). The Louvre Abu Dhabi for example claims that it serves:

> To translate exactingly and instinctively the spirit of openness and dialogue demonstrated by a young Arab nation. Abu Dhabi is a multicultural city between Asia and the West where the North South relations are condensed, and where cosmopolitanism is a fact of life. It thus provides a natural invitation to take part in a dialogue and share experiences.
>
> (Louvre n.d.[a])

In doing so, this statement reveals the museum's attachment to the UAE and national identity. Cosmopolitanism in this sense operates at both national and international levels. One way that this occurs is by promoting transnational heritage as a:

> Dialectical process in which the universal and particular, the similar and the dissimilar, the global and the local are to be conceived, not as cultural polarities but as interconnected and reciprocally interpenetrating principles.
>
> (Beck 2006: 72–73)

Taking such an approach emphasises the role of both global and local actors, which is particularly important to this analysis. Heritage works in this way to establish Abu Dhabi's national identity and cosmopolitan credentials globally. I therefore use the term transnational to highlight both the global and national imagining that occurs within the global realm of heritage. Furthermore, transnationalism stresses the hybrid inter-relations between the national and the transnational. Cosmopolitanism in this sense plays a significant role in the way that the modern nation state imagines and represents itself through the transnational heritage industry.

Un-cosmopolitan heritages

The production of cosmopolitan heritage identities does not neutralise difference; on the contrary, it draws on difference to promote cosmopolitanism as the natural way forward. This is achieved by taking aspects of the past that link to other cultures and nations and using them to construct an identity that is referenced in both national and transnational terms. However, there is a fundamental problem with this cosmo-universal positioning as it suggests that there is only one cosmopolitanism, which represents an elite form of cosmopolitanism (Nussbaum 1996: 4). However Robbins argues that 'like nations, cosmopolitanisms are now plural and particular. Like nations, they are both European and non-European and they are weak and underdeveloped as well as strong and privileged' (1998: 2). Nashashibi has challenged the perception that cosmopolitanism is associated with the elite and explores 'ghetto cosmopolitanism' through his analysis of the Blackstones street gang and their engagement with the Islamic faith in Chicago (2007: 123). As such there are both 'powerful cosmopolitans' and 'disempowered cosmopolitans' (Gonzalez-Ruibal 2009: 117).

In Abu Dhabi cosmopolitanism is being used to develop heritage that could be considered 'high culture', as such, predominantly the heritage that is being presented is based on elite versions of the past. In Abu Dhabi, the heritage narratives that are being produced exclude the huge numbers of labourers who are largely invisible in daily life. The heritage that is getting remembered is that of the elites or ruling classes, the right kind of cosmopolitan image, the elite kind. Heritage in this view serves to reinforce national identity and demarcate non-Emiratis from Emiratis.

In Abu Dhabi, the cosmopolitan image that is presented does not account for the varied roles and influences that international actors have played within the development of the Emirates industry and culture. This issue is further compounded by the urban planning process, which sets out to create distinct spaces for UAE nationals, migrant workers and expatriates, which has resulted in the creation of elite and exclusionary spaces (Elsheshtawy 2008, 2011: Interview). The Central Market District was populated by small informal shops run by low-income migrant workers, which Elsheshtawy (2008) argues did not fit Abu Dhabi's desired image. Therefore the Central Market District was demolished to make way for the new *souq*.[9] As such transnational networks generate 'status systems and cultural relationships founded on "uncosmopolitan" values such as cultural appropriation and status-based social exclusion' (Kendall, Skrbis, and Woodward 2008).

Furthermore, cosmopolitanism ignores the abuses that migrant workers suffer. Reports by Human Rights Watch have argued that labourers on Saadiyat Island are being subjected to abuses, which have included acts such as passport confiscation, unlawful changes to contracts and the charging of huge recruitment fees (Human Rights Watch 2012a), which can lead to workers being forced in to 'conditions of forced labour' (Human Rights Watch 2012b). The Saadiyat Island museum projects have also faced scrutiny related to the treatment of migrant construction workers in the Gulf by the Gulf Labor Artist Coalition who have been involved in a series of protests and artist boycotts aimed at promoting fair working conditions for labourers on the Island (Gulf Labor Artist Coalition 2019). Cosmopolitan approaches to heritage must then be seen within the 'struggles and friction' (Tsing 2005) that emerge in culturally specific hybrid global heritage contexts. At the same time recognising that there is not one cosmopolitanism but varying cosmopolitanisms (Schiller and Irving 2017: 1). This is a particularly useful approach as it allows us to also explore the multiple cosmopolitanisms that emerge on the ground: the grass-roots cosmopolitanisms.

Hybridity and heritage

As I noted in chapter one, I take the view that hybridity is a 'process' which I specifically interrogate in relationship to the construction of transnational heritage identities in Abu Dhabi. As such, I reject the oppositional positioning of the local and the global. Robertson (1995) has used the term 'glocalization' to unpack the ways in which local and the global forces interact and enmesh to produce qualitatively new forms. In this sense when thinking about heritage, global and autochthonous heritage processes would combine and enmesh to produce unique heritage formations. At the same time recognising the myth of essentialised pure origins and existing historical hybridisations (Garcia Canclini 2005: xxv). Importantly, this 'enmeshment' occurs across varying scale of heritage – local, regional, transnational – and as such should not be considered new forms of binary opposites. Meethan argues that, 'the influences which are realised in specific localities are not only the result of outside changes, but also due in part to internal pressures for change' (2001: 167). The binary positioning of East and West, and global and local, has been an issue within the Gulf States, which 'fail[s] to capture the actual complexities of the contemporary world' (Turner and Khonder 2010: 5). Fibiger builds on this work suggesting that Islamic critiques of globalisation in the Gulf have focused on the argument that modernisation, globalisation and Westernisation are seen as a threat to Islamic values and local traditions. He argues that such views 'fail to acknowledge the global role that Islam plays as a world religion and a globalised practice' (Fibiger 2011: 194). In a similar vein Kapoor argues that '...reading the world in binary terms (First/Third World, developed/underdeveloped), ignores the existence of Third Worlds in the First ... and

First Worlds in the Third' (2003: 574–575). Moreover, these distinctions create further tensions in terms of insider and outsider identity politics.

Similarly, debates within the heritage literature have up until recently tended to position the development of localism as a defence against the threat of globalisation. In particular, Harvey (1989) has discussed how heritage is used to define and defend local identity. Global forces in this sense are seen as a threat to the state and officially sanctioned heritage discourses (Harrison 2010a). Within the Gulf, this has manifested itself in the way in which the establishment and growth of heritage in the UAE is used as an attempt to define and reinforce local and national identities in response to rapid economic development, large numbers of migrant workers and the transnational flow of goods and services from abroad (Khalaf 2000, 2002). Khalaf has suggested using Dubai's Heritage Village as a case study that heritage preservation in the Gulf has emerged as a direct response to the threat of globalisation (2002: 13). He also argues in relation to camel racing in the UAE that, 'preserving UAE heritage, and maintaining national identity in the context of the threatening forces of modernization, constitute the dynamics of inventing this tradition' (Khalaf 2000: 7). Seen in this way the development of new traditions are 'important symptoms and therefore indicators of problems' (Hobsbawm 2010: 12).

Schofield and Szymanski (2011) call for a recognition of how local people value and view their local environment and how they are preserved through global heritage which illustrates that global versus local dichotomies do not work, as neither the global nor the local works in isolation. Rather as Robertson argues 'what is often referred to as the local is essentially included within the global', which 'also involves the "invention" of locality' (1992: 35). The implication of this for heritage is that it points to the role that cultural heritage plays in the production of identity, and how these ideas are used to reinforce and reproduce ideas about national identity, which are used within the context of global heritage discourses. Appadurai suggests that:

> The new global cultural economy has to be seen as a complex, overlapping, disjunctive order that cannot any longer be understood in terms of existing center-periphery models (even those that might account for multiple centers and peripheries).
>
> (1990: 6)

When considering the processes that surround the production of cultural heritage franchises it is essential to consider the way that both the local and the global enmesh. By focusing on heritage as a hybrid co-produced process it is possible to challenge the dominant binaries that have dominated debates within heritage. This book serves to challenge this essentialist divide and suggest an alternative reading of the heritage landscape in Abu Dhabi, which focuses on the dialectical processes of heritage that operate across and within varying categorisations of heritages.

Hybrid heritage: politics and power

Hybridity has a long history, which can be traced to its emergence during the eighteenth century within the natural sciences – to categorise the mixing of plant or animal species – and during the nineteenth century, which was based on the belief that humans belonged to different categories that were used to reinforce and perpetuate colonial and imperial power (Coombes and Brah 2000: 3). This appropriation of hybridity by the Victorian extreme right was used as the scientific basis for racial categorisation based on 'species distinctions among humans' (Young 1991: 10; Coombes and Brah 2000: 3). Racialised ideology was translated into European museums in the nineteenth and twentieth centuries as the museum sought to categorise and present evolutionary categories using objects and artworks to display the 'progress' of the Western world against the 'primitiveness' of the 'Other' (Bennett 1995, 2004). These now outdated and racist evolutionary categories demonstrate that hybridity has been present within the discourses of display since the establishment of the earliest museums in Western Europe. Past hybrids have therefore 'served ideologies of integration and control – not pluralism and empowerment' (Kraidy 2005: vii) as it is often championed today. Rather hybridity has been charged with 'ignoring [and reinforcing] cultural and social discrimination' (Burke 2009: 7). Significantly, these early examples highlight the political and contested nature and the ways in which the hybrid has been appropriated for national and political purposes under the guise of culture.

Orientalism refers to the ways in which the West produced a hegemonic discourse that was used to reproduce and control the Orient, which became embedded within 'institutions, vocabulary, scholarship, imagery, doctrines, even colonial bureaucracies and colonial styles' (Said 1978: 2). Tuhiwai Smith argues, drawing on the work of Said, that:

> The globalization of knowledge and Western culture constantly reaffirms the West's view of itself as the centre of legitimate knowledge the arbitrator of what counts as knowledge and the source of 'civilized' knowledge. This form of knowledge is generally referred to as 'universal' knowledge, available to all and not really 'owned' by anyone, that is, until non-Western scholars make a claim to it. When claims like that are made history is revised (again) so that the story of civilization remains the story of the West.
>
> (2012: 66)

Yet, Said's Orientalism provides no space for resistance and agency, instead, postcolonial theorists such as Bhabha have argued for hybridity (2010: 73). Postcolonial understandings have sought to break down essentialist understandings of binary opposites in favour of messy, transient and multifaceted connections that are continually in-flux and subject to negotiation and renegotiation.

The concept of 'third space' was developed by Bhabha who suggests that this space is where different cultures have come into contact and engaged with each other, and where colonialism was challenged as new hybrid formations emerged from colonial encounters (*ibid.*: 53–56). Drawing on literary and cultural theory he argues that the translation of colonial discourses and practices aimed at producing a singular universal system, based on a Western essentialised cultural model that served to master the 'Other', were challenged and circumvented. As such, Bhabha argues that something new emerges from the interactions between the coloniser and the colonised and that 'all forms of culture are continually in a process of hybridity' (Rutherford 1990). However, when talking of the transnational Bhabha acknowledges that this 'is not a smooth passage of transition and transcendence' (*ibid.*: 8). For Bhabha an 'ambivalence' emerges through attempts of enforced translation. Bhabha therefore argues for an analysis of the 'in-between' or 'the "parts" of difference' (*ibid.*). Bhabha's conceptualisation of the 'third space' therefore provides space for questioning the binary categorisations of cultural heritage and in doing so suggests new possibilities where alternative modes of 'articulation' and 'negotiation' are possible (*ibid.*: 53–56). However, Bhabha has been criticised for failing to fully analyse the historical and political conditions (Parry 1996; Mitchell 1997).

Clifford has conceptualised the museum as 'contact zones' where different cultures connect and encounter each other in his discussion of hybridity (1997: 192–193). Clifford's interpretation draws on the work of Mary Louise Pratt who defined the 'contact zone' as 'the space of colonial encounters, the space in which peoples geographically and historically separated come in to contact with each other and establish ongoing relations, usually involving conditions of coercion, radical inequality, and intractable conflict' (Pratt 1992: 6–7 cited in Clifford 1997: 192). Clifford argues that museums need to be based on 'active collaboration and a sharing of authority' (1997: 210). in order for the marginalised to be included as collaborators. However, Clifford fails to acknowledge the power dynamics of collaborative action (Boast 2011) and in doing so he fails to recognise that exchange may have varied meanings and may be experienced differently by diverse groups and individuals. Furthermore, by setting hybridity into spaces and 'zones' Clifford suggests that they can be separated and recognised as distinct from other spaces of cultural interaction. In doing so, any linkages to elsewhere are excluded from the collaborative project. In the case of cultural heritage developments in the UAE the hybrid heritage context involves both local and international actors working inside and outside of the physical boundaries of the nation state. In this sense, the hybrid context is transnational, multi-layered and multi-vocal.

Garcia Canclini sees hybridity as rooted in both the past and the present, which can be seen as a process of 'cultural reconversion' where the global versus local divide is challenged, resisted and restructured (2005: 172). The hybrid process of co-producing heritage then is subject to different interpretations and re-interpretations by individuals and groups at different times in different contexts. This is particularly important for understanding how hybrid heritage operates as a process. Seeing hybridity in this way enables an exploration of the political, social and economic circumstances that brought it in to play. Bhabha argues that through 'iteration…something may look the same, but in its enunciation, in the moment of its instantiation, in the thing that makes it specific, it reveals that difference of the same' (Mitchell 1995). Here Bhabha is referring to his discussion of 'mimic men' who he describes as those that are 'almost the same, but not quite', which operate as forms of resistance (2010: 121). Bhabha's concept of hybridity illuminates the power relations that are embedded within cultural translations. Statements made by the French president François Hollande, are suggestive of the hybrid power relations behind cultural heritage franchising in Abu Dhabi. Hollande stated that France, through the Louvre Abu Dhabi partnership, 'will never overstep its role, will never impose…we don't tell them what to do, but explain what we would do in a similar situation' (cited in Jones 2014).

It is within the liminal in-betweenness of cultural translation where binaries such as East/West are resisted and where hierarchies and knowledge networks are challenged and re-made (Bhabha 2010, 1996). I examine the development of cultural heritage in Abu Dhabi in the context of varying power relations within and between, practitioners and Emirati residents and what this tells us about the experience of difference and hybrid heritage identities. In doing so, I examine the negotiations and formations that emerge within the hybrid heritage landscape in Abu Dhabi. In particular, I raise questions about the power relations that operate within hybrid heritage, how they are resisted and circumvented in often subtle and unacknowledged ways.

Global governance has clearly impacted the way that heritage, as a material and social process, has developed on a transnational scale. A process that has continued to gain momentum as globalisation continues to influence the preservation and display of heritage on a global scale. I have argued that the dominant hegemonic national agenda of museums and heritage organisations is being replaced with transnational agendas and protocols as global power shifts. This process is problematic as the power relations that are inherent within the global categorisation and listing process are masked through the cosmopolitan positioning of heritage. Cosmopolitanism is shaping the ways in which objects; settings and spaces are used within the development of museums and heritage places within the emirate of Abu Dhabi. What results from this are specific hybrid heritage processes that are co-produced across borders. The development of hybrid heritage processes is not an equal process because the control and movement of heritage is in the hands of the elite and not all nations have access to the same economic and political powers. Therefore, cosmopolitanism, like universalism, is exclusionary as well as inclusionary.

I expand on these debates and argue that cultural heritage is produced and reproduced in cross-cultural hybrid contexts that create dialectical relationships occurring within and between perceived boundaries, which have traditionally been seen to be operating at varying scales – local vs global, West vs East, intangible vs tangible. In the transnational setting heritage is opened up to the possibility of hybrid enmeshed encounters. Heritage in this sense is a hybrid process that involves a processes of negotiation, translation and resistance. This process is acutely political when processes and procedures are introduced into regions where ideas relating to the interpretation and construction of heritage may be drastically different and may be in the process of emergence. This book contributes to debates regarding the methods, values and procedures that are applied to cultural heritage production in transnational hybridised contexts, which further elucidates our understanding of the politics of transnational heritage.

Notes

1 The Covenant of the League, established in 1920, was included in the Treaty of Versailles, which ended the war between Germany and the Allied Powers. The League was established after World War I as a peacekeeping organisation. However it was unsuccessful in preventing the outbreak of World War II. For further discussion of the league see UNOG (n.d.[a]).
2 The International Committee on Intellectual Co-operation was established in 1922 to advise the League on activities to promote intellectual co-operation (UNOG n.d.[b]).
3 See discussion in Donnachie on the United States refusal to join the League (2010: 117).
4 The UN and UNESCO both established headquarters in Paris (see UNESCO n.d.[a] on the development of UNESCO's mission).
5 Eleven nations were included in the original World Heritage bid: United Arab Emirates – Belgium – Czechia – France – Republic of Korea – Mongolia – Morocco – Qatar – Saudi Arabia – Spain – Syrian Arab Republic. In 2012, Austria and Hungary were added to the inscription bringing the total to thirteen State Parties. Then in 2016, the designation was re-examined again, which resulted in Germany – Italy – Kazakhstan – Pakistan – Portugal being added to the inscription bringing the total to eighteen State Parties (UNESCO n.d.[f]).
6 However, as noted in chapter one, Abu Dhabi has been developing museums and heritage sites since the late 1960s (see Bouchenaki 2011; Hirst 2012).
7 Artefacts from the Umm al-Nar excavations are also on display at the Al Ain Museum, the Heritage Village in Abu Dhabi and the Ras Al Khaimah National Museum in Ras Al Khaimah.
8 See discussions regarding the development of the Louvre Museum by Duncan and Wallace (1980) and Duncan (1995). For further discussions of the links between the Louvre Museum and the Louvre Abu Dhabi see Skluzacek (2010) and Ajana (2015).
9 *Souq* is an Arabic term used to describe a market in Middle Eastern cities.

3   Cultural heritage franchising

There is a range of literature that considers the legal and practical frameworks of franchising (for an overview of the key franchising literature see Elango and Fried 1997; Verbieren, Cools and Van den Abbeele 2008). This literature has focused primarily on commercial franchising in the United States. Verbieren, Cools and Abbeele (2008) have identified three broad themes within the franchising literature. These themes focus on the relationship between the development of franchises and the societies in which they are placed, the creation and duplication of franchise relationships, and the control and operation of franchise systems. However, what is missing from these definitions is a consideration of cultural heritage franchises: how they are formed, why they work in particular ways and in whose interest they operate.

There have been several studies that have explored the development of the Guggenheim Museum Bilbao and the Bilbao Effect (see key studies by Giovanni 2001, Gomez and Gonzalez 2001, Azua 2005, Plaza 2007, and Alvarez Sainz 2012). Cultural heritage franchising has been linked to city development by the high-profile redevelopment of the city of Bilbao, Spain, and the role that the development of the Guggenheim Museum Bilbao played within this. The success of the Guggenheim Museum Bilbao and the way in which the media has linked the museum's development to its role in the regeneration of the city of Bilbao led to the emergence of the terms 'Bilbao Effect' (Giovanni 2001; Gomez and Gonzalez 2001; Azua 2005; Plaza 2007; Alvarez Sainz 2012) and 'Guggenheim Effect' (Plaza, Tironic and Haarichd 2009). The Bilbao Effect generally refers to how cultural institutions such as museums or art galleries are strategically developed as global institutions to facilitate economic and residential development and tourism (Giovanni 2001; Gomez and Gonzalez 2001; Azua 2005; Plaza 2007; Alvarez Sainz 2012). Evans (2005), for example, has argued that Bilbao's development was based on using culture to regenerate the area and that the Guggenheim Museum Bilbao was developed as the flagship development for Bilbao. As discussed in chapter one, this model is based on the concept of using creativity and culture to shape city development, a creative city model (Bianchini 1993a, 1993b; Florida 2004; Markusen 2006).

Alvarez Sainz has noted that 'in the 10 years since the Guggenheim Museum Bilbao opened more than 10 million people have visited' (2012: 101). She goes on to suggest that it was the development of the Guggenheim Museum Bilbao and its global positioning that ultimately established the Guggenheim as a global brand. However, Zulaika (1997) argues that visitors to the Guggenheim Museum Bilbao go to Bilbao purely for the museum. Plaza, Tironic and Haarichd (2009), on the other hand, argue that the Guggenheim Museum Bilbao did not develop in a vacuum and that the revitalisation of Bilbao needs to be considered within the broader framework of city development that was occurring at the time. For example, they cite the development of the transportation network as a central aspect of making the city more accessible and attractive for tourists and residents (*ibid.*). This illustrates that while the Guggenheim Museum Bilbao may have contributed to the regeneration of Bilbao that it was only one aspect of the city's overall strategic plan. In this sense high-profile museum development and any associated Bilbao Effect needs to be considered within the broader political, economic and social circumstances from which they emerge to get a fuller understanding of how they work within a development framework.

In addition to this, not all cultural heritage franchises are successful. Some franchises, as Thornley (2002) has noted, become loss-making institutions, for example, the Guggenheim Las Vegas and the Guggenheim Soho both shut down after brief periods of operation. Nyadzayo, Matanda and Ewing note in relation to commercial franchising that it is commonly assumed that the brand will automatically 'sell itself' (2011: 1108; see also Adie 2017: 49). These failing cultural heritage franchises illustrate the need to look at the specifics of these partnerships and in particular question their relevance locally and internationally. More research needs to be done to explore what makes cultural heritage franchises unsuccessful as well as successful. This will mean not only exploring cultural heritage franchising in terms of design and characteristics but also studying in-depth how they emerge and operate in specific cultural settings. The longevity of franchise partnerships is also an issue. What happens when a cultural franchise agreement comes to an end? In the case of the Deutsche Guggenheim, it meant that the partnership contract was not renewed. The Deutsche Guggenheim was developed in 1997 within the headquarters of the Deutsche Bank as part of a 15-year agreement. During the partnership, the Deutsche Guggenheim museum staged '57 exhibitions and attracted 1.8 million visitors. It also commissioned 17 artists – among them John Baldessari, Anish Kapoor, Gerhard Richter and James Rosenquist – to create new works that were first shown at Deutsche Guggenheim' (Vogel 2009). When the ending of the partnership between the Solomon R. Guggenheim and the Deutsche museum was announced in January 2012, no official announcement was made as to why. Some sources speculated that it was the result of the European economic crisis. However, a statement by Richard Armstrong that appeared in the *New York Times* is more suggestive of a reflection that perhaps the partnership was no longer needed: 'Berlin today is a very different city from what it was when we began. We feel the time is right now to step back and re-examine our collaboration to see how it might evolve' (*ibid.*). This suggests that perhaps one of the benefits of cultural franchising is that they do not need to go on indefinitely. However, I do believe that both the financial crisis and the increased awareness of the Guggenheim brand will have had a significant impact on the renewal of the contract. More recently, Plaza, Tironic and Haarichd (2009) have explored the impact of the Guggenheim Effect on Bilbao's art scene, and Baniotopoulou (2000) has analysed the museum from a curatorial viewpoint.

There remains a lack of alternative critical interpretations of cultural heritage franchising and an in-depth understanding of how they operate beyond the Bilbao precedent. In particular, very little has been said about how cultural heritage franchising affects and is affected by the cultures in which they are developed. This chapter seeks to ask alternative questions to facilitate a better understanding of how cultural heritage franchising operates as a transnational process and how as globalised heritage they interact with and respond to the places in which they are developed.

Defining the cultural heritage franchise

As I noted in chapter one, the cultural heritage franchise has been the subject of limited analysis and has remained surprisingly undefined. Blair and Lafontaine suggest that franchises are '[M]ost often understood as a contractual arrangement between two legally dependent firms in which one firm, the franchisee, pays the franchisor the right to sell the franchisor's product and/or the right to use its trademarks and business format in a given location for a specified period of time' (2005: 3). The *Merriam Webster Online Dictionary and Thesaurus* provide a legal definition of a franchise, which also alludes to the rules and procedures that are applied to franchise agreements. This definition states that a franchise is '[a] right or license that is granted to an individual or group to market a company's goods or services in a particular territory under the company's trademark, trade name, or service mark'. The franchise is then developed and run using a guiding framework in return for an agreed-upon fee (Merriam Webster n.d.: 'Franchise'). However, it is worth noting that cultural heritage franchise agreements are not necessarily based on a partnership between two legally independent firms, which I will discuss in more detail shortly. Since there is no specific definition for cultural heritage franchises, it is useful to consider how cultural heritage franchises are defined and put to use in Abu Dhabi.

Cultural heritage franchising and authenticity

One of the critical questions surrounding globalisation, which is of particular significance to the development of heritage within Abu Dhabi, is whether the processes of globalisation end in homogeneity and a loss of authenticity (Featherstone 1990). The concept of authenticity has been the subject of much discussion by heritage practitioners and academics alike (see Harrison 2010b; Byrne 2011; Waterton, Watson and Silverman 2017). Due to the disparate views on the interpretation and practical application of authenticity in the field, there is no hard or fast definition of the term. Tveit notes that 'the word authenticity is derived from the Greek *"authentes"* and has the double meaning of authority and original' (2007: 293–294). Authenticity then is connected to the idea that:

> Heritage is something that can be passed from one generation to the next, something that can be conserved or inherited, and something that has historic or cultural value. Heritage might be understood to be a physical 'object'; a piece of property, a building or a place that is able to be 'owned' and 'passed on' to someone else.
>
> (Harrison 2010b: 9)

However, defining authenticity in this way is problematic for the way in which cultural heritage is defined and produced. However the main issue is not if or how authenticity is proven, but rather, how authenticity is used, why it is needed, and in whose interest it works? (Bendix 1997) This ties into the political nature of heritage, which is arguably as much about political and economic imperatives as it is about preserving the past. In other words, the authenticity of cultural heritage is prescribed by a set of ideas and values that are applied to the categorisation of heritage (Harrison 2010a). Crucially how heritage is ascribed meaning and value vary.

One of the most commonly referred to examples of the way that culture has become homogenised is through the process of franchising. McDonald's has acted as the standard model from which other franchises have developed their brand reach and operational practices. Ritzer argues that the McDonald's model operates, 'through four main strategies – efficiency, predictability, calculability and control', which work to create a familiar and standardised product that customers can easily recognise (2010: 4). This process has been defined as 'McDonaldization' because of these links to the fast-food industry and in particular the McDonald's model (*ibid.*: 6). Pine and Gilmore suggest that authenticity in museums is based on two aspects. The first is 'being true to one's own self' and the second is 'being what you say you are to others' (1999: 79). The first point relates to staying true to the museum brand, identifying what you are and sticking to it. The second relates to the connection between what the museum says it is and the way the public experiences it. Pine and Gilmore argue that by 'doing something that is antithetical to what you really are' that museum's run the risk of being fake or inauthentic (*ibid.*: 79). The process of developing cultural heritage franchises offers the ultimate threat to the proponents of 'authentic' heritage. The Louvre Abu Dhabi catalogue states that the museum is not a replica, 'a little Louvre in Abu Dhabi'. Instead, the catalogue emphasises the museum's 'own unique identity' by reiterating the museum's role as 'a universal museum' attempting to go 'beyond the restrictions of time and place' (Al-Mubarak and Martinez 2017: 5). The resistance to the use of the term 'franchise' by cultural workers seems to be connected to the negative connotations that are associated with the term and its linkages to economic gain, duplication and inauthenticity.

Cultural heritage franchising challenges the dominant belief that museums are developed as non-profit institutions to serve the public good, which is often connected to the needs and identities of 'local' and 'national' publics. The development of the franchise model by the Guggenheim Foundation led to the museum being nicknamed the 'McGuggenheim' by *Forbes* magazine. In France, the Louvre Abu Dhabi has been the subject of similar name calling with the nickname '*le Louvre des sables*' (the Louvre in the Sands) (Jones 2014: 51). *Forbes* liken Thomas Krens to 'a Disney executive who uses business buzz words such as "economies of scale", "brand awareness" and "levering our expertise" to describe the operations of the Guggenheim' (Klebnikov 2001). It is Kren's overt business approach which is associated negatively with the commercialisation of cultural heritage institutions (Honigsbaum 2001). In this sense, the translation of cultural heritage through the process of franchising tends to produce stereotypes that are seen as a threat to the original museum. Hybridity in this sense 'signals the threat of "contamination" to those who espouse an essentialist notion of pure and authentic origins' (Coombes and Brah 2000: 1). The association of the cultural heritage franchise with money and re-production is the ultimate challenge to the essentialist notion of authenticity.

The announcement of the partnership between the Abu Dhabi government and the French government to develop the Louvre Abu Dhabi generated criticism from the international media, the museums' sector, and the French (Riding 2007b; Riding 2007c; Kluijver 2013). Cachin, Clair and Recht's (2006) criticism, has been a common feature of international media accounts, which has been used to fuel heated debates about the projects (see also critiques by Riding 2007a, 2007b; Rykner 2007). Riding (2007b) notes that 'Françoise Cachin, former director of French museums; Jean Clair, former director of the Picasso Museum; and Roland Recht, a leading art historian' wrote a critique of the Louvre Abu Dhabi partnership in *Le Monde* magazine. Cachin, Clair and Recht argue that 'from a moral point of view one can only be shocked by the commercial and promotional use of masterpieces of our national heritage' (cited in Riding 2007b). The notion of cultural heritage franchising goes against the perception that museums are not-for-profit institutions in the service of the communities they serve, which was further picked up by Clair (2007) who argued against the commercial use of the Louvre name, which he suggests weakens French museology and identity.

Following Cachin, Clair and Recht's critique came an article by the French art website *La Tribune de l'Art* that called for individuals to sign a petition against the Louvre Abu Dhabi partnership (Rykner 2006). Individuals were asked to sign the petition by quoting the following statement either by email or by postal mail:

> I fully share the views expressed by Françoise Cachin, Jean Clair and Roland Recht in the article entitled: 'Museums are not for sale', published in Le Monde on 13 December 2006 and I hope that we maintain the integrity of collections of French museums.
>
> (*ibid*)

Duncan (1995) has discussed the controversies that surrounded the early development of the Met Museum's collection, which was built by wealthy American patrons and focused on the masterpieces of European art. The project was highly critical at the time as they were building collections, and arguably American national identity, based on European art rather than American art. The Western led orientalist critiques, therefore, tend to overlook the parallels with early collecting in the West. Critiques have also focused on the adverse effects that could be felt in France such as visitors to French museums being deprived of crucial masterpieces for sustained periods of time and the harmful effects of franchising France's cultural heritage (Cachin, Clair and Recht 2006). Counterarguments have focused on the small number of artworks being loaned to France out of the museums' total collection. Cerisier-ben Guiga (2007) stated during a parliamentary discussion in 2007 'that the number of works of art that will be loaned to the Abu Dhabi Museum remains limited, of the order of 300 per year in the early years, in comparison with some 30,000 works of art that France lends each year' and that 'that the practice of counterparties in the exchange of works of art is not a new phenomenon'. In addition, examples from the past were drawn on to legitimise the project and countercritiques:

> This controversy is not unlike the controversy aroused in 1962 by the loan of the Mona Lisa to the United States. André Malraux, Minister of Culture, had, at the time, faced the opposition of the conservators of the Louvre Museum and he had to obtain the agreement of General de Gaulle for this operation.
>
> (*ibid*)

Part of the reactionary nature of the debates was the late consultation of parliamentary members. As Herlory notes 'the French Parliament was not involved in the Louvre Abu Dhabi project until September 2007, six months after the intergovernmental agreement which paves the way for the establishment of the Louvre Abu Dhabi had been signed' (2008: 67).

The protests against the Louvre Abu Dhabi are set within a distinctly national discourse, which sees cultural heritage in France as connected primarily to the national discourse, and therefore the old models of heritage as bounded by borders as I noted in the previous chapter. Utilising cultural heritage in transnational settings is emerging more prominently, and these arguments fail to acknowledge how these new relationships are reproducing and developing France's national identity elsewhere. Cultural heritage franchising is equated with commercialisation and inauthentic replication. However, this overlooks the complexity and nuances that are present within the processes of developing cultural heritage franchises.

The dominant heritage discourses that have emerged from Western-Europe have through their emphasis on preserving physical objects intact led to a very narrow view of authenticity (see Harrison 2010a, 2013; Byrne 2011). I noted in chapter two that UNESCO's global policies have been challenged, which has led to the development of new systems of global classification. This recognition of the short comings of UNESCO's policies led to the development of alternative global systems of classification for heritage such as the 1994 Nara Document on Authenticity, which recognises non-Western conservation processes and values (Logan 2001 cited in Askew 2010: 27). The production of alterative global classifications highlights the inherent flaw within UNESCO's system and points to the underlying economic, political and cultural power relations that underpin global heritage processes. This recognises that global classificatory systems need to incorporate non-Western conservation processes and values (*ibid.*). Byrne suggests that:

> When you look at the Thai way of building and restoring temples, it suggests an acceptance of impermanence. The traditional way of restoring stupas, for instance, simply encases the old object inside another much bigger one. The original in this sense is consumed by the restoration.
>
> (2011: 146)

These examples illustrate how restoration and authenticity are based on the value judgements of museological methods that have primarily emerged from the West. In addition, as MacCannell (2013) notes in relation to heritage tourism, authenticity is interpreted differently by different people. This calls in to question the assumption that branded museums are copies of the original.

Cultural heritage franchises should be considered in relation to their distinct cultural settings and their responsiveness to their audiences – local, national and international. Staiff and Bushell have suggested that translation is not about producing an authentic copy. Instead, they argue that the process of translation 'is always a cultural, social and political intervention by the translator', therefore, 'who undertakes the translation and how it is

undertaken are therefore critical issues' (2003: 117). It would be overly sim-
plistic to assume that heritage organisations wanted to recreate heir images
in precisely the same way in a different region. These are issues that I will
pick up within my discussion of the data in chapters five and seven in relation to the processes that surround the development of cultural heritage
franchise institutions.

The way the Guggenheim has presented its cultural heritage franchises
in the past has been less overtly political. However, the bilateral nature of
the partnership is still stressed. The Guggeheim Foundation is a privately
funded arts institution, not a government institution like the Louvre, and as
such there are essential differences between these partnerships. The Guggenheim Abu Dhabi partnership is between the Guggenheim Foundation
and the Abu Dhabi Government, whereas the Louvre Abu Dhabi partnership is between the French government and the Abu Dhabi Government.
This can be observed within other heritage franchise partnerships such as
that of the Guggenheim Museum Bilbao, which is also based on an agreement between the Basque Government and the Guggenheim Foundation.
The Guggenheim Abu Dhabi is the preserve of Abu Dhabi as a nation and its
political motivations and objectives, and the Guggenheim Foundation with
its institutional politics and motivations. The Louvre Abu Dhabi, on the
other hand, is arguably more politically loaded. The Louvre Abu Dhabi is
the preserve of both the Abu Dhabi government and the French government
and is subject to the political motivations and objectives of both nations.
This is not unusual as Blair and Lafontaine note, drawing on the example
of TV cable franchising in the United States, that 'governments still grant
franchises to certain industries' (2015: 4). What this suggests is that the governments have an interest in the franchising of particular industries. The
motivations for franchising may be based on economic, political or social
imperatives. Their desire to maintain control of these sectors through franchising and how they shape and promote these partnerships are essential for
the understanding of cultural heritage franchising as a global and hybrid
process. The critical point is that cultural heritage franchises have different
political motivations that affect the way that transnational partnerships are
agreed to, and the resultant forms that they take. In Abu Dhabi, the dominant discourses that surround the franchising of cultural heritage are linked
to cross-cultural co-operation, exchange and understanding. The process
of exchange and relationship building that is undertaken is therefore positioned as a 'cosmopolitanism act', which is used to transmit the nation's
role (both in the originating nation and in the accepting nation) as a global
cultural actor.

Contracting cultural heritage

I noted earlier that there has been no working definition of cultural heritage
franchising. Similarly, there is no standard protocol for cultural heritage

franchise agreements. The cultural heritage franchise contract plays a vital role in the way that the partnerships are agreed upon and enacted. These agreements may not be the most appealing or exciting aspects of heritage research for some, but they contain relevant data regarding the mechanisms of complex cross-border exchanges and the power relations that underpin them. They are also important indicators of the bureaucratisation of heritage. It is essential to understand each of these processes and their implications in order to gain a broader understanding of how cultural franchising works in practice. One way to do this is to explore the terms of the agreement between the Abu Dhabi Government and the French Government, and the Abu Dhabi government and the Guggenheim Foundation.

In general, written franchise contracts are legally binding agreements that set out the conditions under which a franchise is to be developed and operated, and the rights and obligations of both parties. These agreements generally have a limited and specific life span. The agreement for the Louvre Abu Dhabi is set out in a 30 years and six months contract between the Abu Dhabi government and the French government whereas the agreement for the Guggenheim Abu Dhabi is based on a 20 years and six months contract between the Abu Dhabi government and the Guggenheim Foundation. These contracts set out both the financial and non-financial obligations between the parties involved, and as such, contain a wealth of information that can be used to interrogate the process of developing cultural heritage franchises. Elango and Fried (1997) have noted, drawing on information from the US Department of Commerce, that there are two distinct types of franchising models (see also Bradach 1998; Blair and Lafontaine 2005). 'Product/trade name' franchising 'is used to describe a franchise partnership 'between the supplier and the dealer in which the dealer agrees to acquire some of the identity of the supplier in order to become the preferred source of the supplier's goods'. 'Business format' franchising, on the other hand, 'is an on-going relationship between the franchisor/franchisee that not only includes product, service and trademark, but also the entire concept of the business' (*ibid.*: 68).

The cultural heritage franchises in Abu Dhabi are being developed based on a business format model – based on an agreement that includes contract fees, brand rights, royalties and the Guggenheim and Louvre Museums business model. This is because the Abu Dhabi government is drawing on the franchisor's, the Louvre Museum and the Guggenheim, brand name, professional practices and collections. Arguably an essential benefit of cultural heritage franchising is the access to the franchisor's collections and professional practices that may otherwise not be available. Perhaps most significantly for Abu Dhabi franchising is particularly useful when there are no pre-existing industries and business models (Quinn 1999). The franchise in this sense serves as both an exchange of knowledge and processes.

Cultural heritage franchise agreements contain monetary and non-monetary contract clauses. Monetary contract clauses include statements about the cost of building and operating the Museum (Bradley 1997). It also sets out the agreed fee that the franchisee agrees to pay to the franchisor (Elango and Fried 1997; Blair and Lafontaine 2005). The agreement between the French and the UAE authorities breaks down the payment of fees, which includes the payment for the brand rights and the ongoing service costs (Poncelet 2007). In addition to paying a set franchise fee the Abu Dhabi Government the agreement also covers the on-going costs for acquisitions, recruitment and the curatorial and administrative services provided by both the Guggenheim Foundation, and the Louvre Abu Dhabi. During the cultural heritage franchise agreements, Abu Dhabi can use the name Louvre (for thirty years and six months) and Guggenheim (for twenty years) (*ibid.*). Agence France-Muséums was established to advise on aspects of the Louvre Abu Dhabi's operations, management and curatorial strategies (Agence France-Muséums n.d.[a]). In other words, the agency is charged with delivering the partnership agreement.

Created in 2007, as part of the intergovernmental agreement between France and the UAE, Agence France-Muséums has provided:

> assistance and expertise to the authorities of the United Arab Emirates in the following areas: definition of the scientific and cultural programme, assistance in project management for architecture including museography, signage and multimedia projects, coordination of the loans from French collections and organization of temporary exhibitions, guidance with the creation of a permanent collection, and support with the museum's policy on visitors.
>
> (*ibid.*)

The agency operates through both a governing body and a scientific committee. It is particularly interesting to consider the backgrounds of key board members on the governing body, for example, Sandra Lagumina who chairs the Board of Directors of Agence France-Muséums is the chief operating officer asset management at Meridiam (Agence France-Muséums n.d.[b]). Meridiam (2017) is a global investment and asset management company based in Paris that focuses on 'developing, financing and managing long-term public infrastructure projects'. The appointment of a Meridiam representative as the head of the board was clearly a strategic decision. Also serving on the Board of Directors is Christian Giacomotto, Chairman of the Board of Managing Partners of Gimar Finance and Anne Mény-Horn, the chief executive officer is a cultural lawyer (Agence France-Muséums n.d.[b]). The fact that the agency is overseen by a commercially focused representative is telling of the commercial and legal imperatives of the partnerships.

The political dimensions of the partnership are further apparent through connection with the nation state. Like many nations around the world, the French government regulates the museum sector in France.

However, the French museums' sector has always been intimately tied to the politics of the nation, as I will discuss in-depth in chapter four. Interestingly, this structure has been translated to Abu Dhabi with key members of the ruling elite playing strategic roles on the board. The French state is represented on the Board of Directors for the agency and the scientific committee. The three representatives on the Board of Directors at the time of writing included: Jean Guéguinou, French Ambassador; Philippe Barbat, Director of Heritage (appointed by the Minister for Culture) and Laurence Auer, Director of Culture, Education, Research and Network (appointed by the Minister for Foreign and European Affairs) (*ibid.*).

The cultural institutions represented on the Board of Directors at the agency include a select number of government-owned museums represented by their directors[1]: Louvre Museum; Orsay and Orangery Museum; National Library of France; National Museums and Grand Palace; Pompidou Center; National Museum of Asian Arts – Guimet and the Quai Branly Museum – Jacques Chirac (Agence France-Muséums n.d.[b]). The Scientific Council is the consultative body of Agence France-Museums which was set up to deliver the museological obligations of the partnership (Agence France-Muséums n.d.[c]), in other words, to deliver the benefits of the partnership in Abu Dhabi.[2] As Balkany notes the Louvre Museum is certainly prominent within the Governing Body and the Scientific Committee, however, it does not have overall control of the board with three votes out of eleven on the board and three votes out of nine on the committee (2007; see also Herlory 2008). The Louvre Museum's power becomes apparent within the practical administration of the partnership through the delivery of the benefits. Agence France-Muséums through the delivery of the scientific project (administered by the Scientific Committee) is responsible for training Emirati museum professionals, coordinating loans from French museums for a period of ten-years and organising temporary exhibitions for a period of fifteen-years throughout the agreement (Agence France-Muséums n.d.[a]). French collections and expertise, therefore, play a central role in the agreement. It is the development of collections and the circulation of loaned works that are unique to cultural heritage franchising. Within commercial franchising, the aim is to develop brand awareness and meet sales targets. With cultural heritage franchising, the aim is to develop collections and to increase the circulation of objects and artworks from the parent organisation.

The commercial franchising literature is also suggestive of non-monetary contractual obligations and the role of expertise within the commercial sector (Blair and Lafontaine 2005: 79; Elango and Fried 1997). A key non-monetary element of cultural heritage franchising is heritage expertise, which distinguishes cultural franchising from commercial franchising due to the specialised nature of the heritage sector. According to the agency's website, its purpose is to fulfil its service obligations to the Abu Dhabi Government through:

• Definition of the scientific and cultural project
• Assistance to the project management
• Loans from French collections and the organisation of temporary exhibitions
• The creation of a permanent collection
• The museography, the signage, and the multimedia projects
• The museum's policy on visitors

(Agence France-Muséums n.d.[a])

The website goes on to state that the agency is responsible for:

• The Scientific and Cultural Project
• The Development Strategy
• The Management Team and Skilled-Staff Training
• Organisational Support, Museum Concept and Construction Supervision
• Loans from French Public Collections Over a 10-year Period from the Museum's Opening
• Advice and Assistance on the Museum's permanent collection and acquisition strategy
• A 15 Year Temporary-Exhibition Programme

The agency is financed entirely by the government of the UAE. This agreement provides further insight into how the Louvre Abu Dhabi is developed and supported by the French partner organisations.

Bradley has noted the service obligations for the Guggenheim Museum Bilbao from his analysis of the museum's 1991 Development and Programming Services Agreement, which he summarises as:

• Develop an initial four-year plan (including detailed operating budget)
• Direct and manage the acquisitions program
• Provide collection management services
• Develop an educational program in museum management, curatorial research and programming, and advice on the hiring personnel

(1997: 52)

The exact details for the Guggenheim Abu Dhabi partnership were not available as the Guggenheim Foundation is not legally required to publish its contracts like the Louvre Museum in France. I requested this information from both the Guggenheim Foundation and the TDIC, but neither organisation could share this information with me due to the legal restrictions that surround the partnerships. However, I was able to find a press announcement on the Guggenheim Museums' website detailing the operational framework for the Guggenheim Abu Dhabi.

According to the Guggenheim Foundation 'the operating agreement has been established for fifteen years – following five years for design development and construction – and may be renewed in 2027' (Solomon R. Guggenheim Foundation 2007). Principal elements of the agreement include:

- Joint Administrative and Programme Entity for the Guggenheim Abu Dhabi Project
- Establishment of Guggenheim Abu Dhabi museum staff
- Training and Mentorship
- Acquisitions and Commissioning Programme
- Collections, Acquisitions and Commissioning Committee for the Guggenheim Abu Dhabi
- Special Exhibitions Programme
- Educational program for UAE schools and universities
- Guggenheim Abu Dhabi office in New York City

(*ibid*)

Practical components of the Louvre Abu Dhabi and Guggenheim Abu Dhabi partnerships include the following:

- Develop an initial four-year plan and an operating budget
- Direct and manage the acquisitions program
- Provide collection management services
- Develop an educational program in museum management, curatorial research and programming
- Provide advice on hiring personnel
- Provide loans throughout the course of the agreement

Newspaper sources, based on official statements about the agreements from the TDIC and the Louvre Abu Dhabi, suggest that temporary exhibitions and object and artwork loans will form part of the service commitments to Abu Dhabi (Riding 2007b). As I noted earlier, Agence France-Muséums are contracted to arrange loans and temporary exhibitions to the Louvre Abu Dhabi for ten and fifteen years (Agence France-Muséums n.d.[a]). These aspects of the agreements are essentially value-added benefits that cannot be obtained elsewhere; as such, they are vital elements within cultural heritage franchising. Within cultural heritage franchising non-monetary obligations and expertise are crucial aspects of the partnership agreements.

The process of cultural heritage franchising brings up important issues that relate to how cultural heritage is translated and defined in cross-cultural contexts. As I noted in chapter two, the way that cultural heritage franchise partnerships are developed and managed has implications for the values that are attached to them in non-Western contexts. Importantly cultural heritage franchise agreements act as 'authorizing institutions of heritage' (Smith 2006: 87), defining what the museum is, what it should look like, how it should be operated, what it should include and who should be its visitors. Also, it puts a value on the cultural heritage franchise through the exchange of money for this authorising process. The institutionalisation of heritage through the process of cultural heritage franchising, therefore, contributes to the unequal distribution of power (Smith 2006; Harrison 2013), which at the outset seems to imply a one-way power exchange from the franchiser to the franchisee. This suggests that these exchanges are embedded within economic, cultural and political motivations. As Appadurai suggests, 'exchange is the source value for such goods, and thus the value resides in social relations and is subject to the complexities that such relations themselves entail' (1986: 9). Franchising then is a 'shared and iterative culture' (Johnson 2013: 8). Power is also tied up to the business relationship as set out by the definitions of the contract. As I will discuss in chapter five, the role of expertise in these shared activities is complex and nuanced in transnational heritage settings.

The elements of cultural heritage franchising

I suggest that cultural heritage franchising generally consist of the following common elements:

- *Brand name* – the loan of the brand name for an agreed period.
- *Curatorial services* – provide collections care, research on existing and future collections, exhibition development, public engagement, work with the community.
- *Collections development* – direct and manage acquisitions programmes to develop permanent collections for the museum.
- *Cross-site loans* – objects and artworks are loaned across museum sites for an agreed period. Loans may also include the touring of pre-designed exhibitions.
- *Education and knowledge transfer* – develop an educational programme in museum operation and management, advise on hiring personnel, provide on the job training, conduct outreach in schools, at career fairs, operate exchange programmes.
- *Operation and management of the museum* – develop an initial museum plan and operating budget.

This list is indicative of the role that cultural heritage franchising plays in establishing standardised practices and processes that are applied to the development of new global museums. Cultural heritage franchising incorporates aspects of existing transnational practice. The primary aim is to develop local capacity and audiences for the museum. A cultural heritage franchise can, therefore, be seen as a more holistic process of exchange as the partnership is used to develop a full suite of heritage processes and skills development (through training and education) that can be taken forward by the franchisee at the end of the agreement.

Finance plays a significant role in the establishment of the partnership but ultimately, the terms of the agreement come through a negotiated process. How effectively it does, this depends upon the relationship between the franchisee and the franchisor. Bradach's research into corporate franchising found that the 'metaphor of marriage is often used by commercial business managers to describe the franchise relationship' (1998: 35). The usefulness of this for my analysis of cultural heritage franchising is that it illustrates the level of fit and commitment that goes into the process of franchising cultural heritage. Kopytoff argues that 'the production of commodities is also a cultural and cognitive process' (1986: 64). Therefore, the process of franchising cultural heritage can be seen as a hybrid process, which is based on negotiating and establishing the terms under which both parties gain from the relationship and perhaps most importantly how new forms of cultural heritage are produced. However, this process of producing cultural heritage franchises is far from neutral. The value systems that the cultural heritage franchise is developed from are predominantly based on systems of valuing and preserving heritage that emerged from within western European nations. This raises questions about who is given the power to present, what is presented and in whose interests. These issues will be explored in more depth in chapter five through an examination of the role of capacity building in cultural heritage franchising. In sum, the process of cultural heritage franchising is profoundly political and culturally embedded. The cultural role of the cultural heritage franchise and its local effects is an essential aspect of contemporary global heritage practice.

The Zayed National Museum will not be a cultural heritage franchise like the Louvre Abu Dhabi and the Guggenheim Abu Dhabi. Instead, as I noted in chapter one, the museum was originally being developed with the advice and expertise from the British Museum based on a consultancy contract. Interestingly there are apparent similarities between the cultural heritage franchise agreements and the consultancy agreements concerning the services offered. Media announcements made by the British Museum shed light on the details of the partnership. Rosenbaum posted a copy of the initial press announcement on her blog, which she received from the PR firm Ruder Fin. In the press release, it states that:

> The British Museum will serve as a consulting partner to Zayed National Museum's operating body and will advise on a full range of issues, from design, construction and museography to educational and curatorial programming as well as training.
>
> (Rosenbawm 2009)

The critical difference between the Zayed National Museum project and the cultural heritage franchise is ownership of the national story and the authority of the State in constructing those narratives. Instead, 'creating a museum with a strong national identity is paramount for the Zayed National Museum project' (British Museum Representative 2011: Interview). Technical expertise was prioritised in the case of the Zayed National Museum, rather than specialist knowledge and name recognition.

Loan of a brand name, through the cultural heritage franchising process, is not necessarily appropriate when developing national heritage institutions with the help of international heritage professionals. However, branding is still an essential element. The importance of the British Museum brand is evident within the press release, which announced the partnership. In the release Sheikh Sultan bin Tahnoon Al Nahyan, Chairman of TDIC and ADACH, refers to the British Museum as a 'great and historic institution, known for its unsurpassed expertise in every field and its profound respect for every culture' (Rosenbaum 2009). This illustrates that linking the Zayed National Museum to the British Museum's brand reputation as well as gaining their expertise was a measured move, and of great importance in terms of profile building. The use of internationally renowned architects Foster + Partners also plays a significant role in the branding of the museum. The ultimate aim is to create not just a museum but an iconic symbol for the nation.

The partnership also contains a distinctly political dimension. Zaki Anwar Nusseibeh, vice chairman of ADACH and advisor to the Ministry of Presidential Affairs, explained from his knowledge and personal involvement in the planning and development of the Zayed National Museum that the rulers want the museum to be at the centre of the cultural heritage developments. The idea is that the visitor will 'start [their visit] with the national story' through a visit to the Zayed National Museum and then they will go on to visit the other museums on Saadiyat Island (Nusseibeh 2011: Interview). This reflects a conscious shaping of the physical space within the Cultural District. The location of the proposed museums in the heart of the Saadiyat development is therefore essential spatially and symbolically. Politically it serves to position Abu Dhabi within the centre of the cosmopolitan heritage project. The partnership may not be based on the direct loan of a brand name, but brand transference is still an essential element that is being used to strengthen the global and cosmopolitan image of Abu Dhabi further. However, the Zayed National Museum is being developed along similar lines to the cultural heritage franchises as it places primacy on Western-style heritage processes. The power relations at play within the project, which seek to set the Zayed National Museum at the heart of the project, are undermined by the dominant approach of the British Museum as a consultant. As a result, consultancy relationships are subject to similar political issues to that of cultural heritage franchising.

Universal dialogue: the changing face of the Louvre

In a similar way to the Guggenheim Abu Dhabi, the Louvre Abu Dhabi is presented in a way that emphasises how the Louvre museum is reimagining itself as a global institution. In the process, it has sought to position the new museum in Abu Dhabi as the 'first universal museum to be constructed outside the Western world',[3] which I will discuss in more depth in chapter seven. The Louvre Abu Dhabi, according to the Louvre Museum's website 'will express the universalism of its time, that of a globalised and interdependent world' (Louvre n.d.[a]). Furthermore, it goes on to suggest that the 'Museum's universal themes and common influences will be highlighted to illustrate similarities arising from shared human experience transcending geography, nationality and history'. Since the museum's opening, this global rhetoric has been used in virtually every speech, presentation or public article. The museum's tagline states *See humanity in a new light*. The Louvre is still very much bound up with the nation and the French notion of patrimony, but it has expanded its interpretation of its audiences to one that is more globally focused.

The curatorial concept for the Louvre Abu Dhabi is related to the legacy that the museum has with the Louvre Museum in Paris and its connection to nineteenth-century Enlightenment traditions. Analysis of the Louvre Museum's website and interviews with members of the Louvre Abu Dhabi project team suggest that the Louvre is re-applying and re-framing this idea within the contemporary project in Abu Dhabi, which I have suggested is based on a new form of 'cosmo-universalism'. The Louvre website states that 'in true enlightenment style, visitors will be invited to study for themselves, compare them, and delight in their unique qualities and meanings' (*ibid.*). The website goes on to suggest that the museum's displays will follow a 'traditional chronological form' and that:

> The journey proceeds chronologically with different civilizations developing in parallel as the visitor moves forwards on a journey through time. The display features four major periods: archaeology and the birth of civilization; medieval days and the birth of Islam; the classical period from humanism to enlightenment; and modern and contemporary starting at the end of the 18th century.

A more recent review of the Louvre Museum's website revealed that this text is no longer on the site. However, at the time of writing the same wording appeared on the Louvre Abu Dhabi page of the rebranded Department of Culture and Tourism (Department of Culture and Tourism 2018). The Louvre Abu Dhabi section of the Saadiyat Island website also provided further evidence of this chronological approach. It stated that the Louvre Abu Dhabi museum would provide a timeline that provides '[v]isitors with the beginnings they need to understand how art developed in each civilization (the

West, Arabic and Muslim world, and Asia, as well as Africa, the Americas and Australasia)' (Tourism Development Investment Corporation n.d.[u]). In this sense, the development of the Louvre Abu Dhabi provides evidence to suggest that the museum still subscribes to the idea that the development of global collections automatically leads to universal understanding. Suggesting that the visitor to the Louvre Abu Dhabi, like the nineteenth-century visitor to the Louvre museum, is expected to understand and engage with what they have presented automatically, which is predominantly visual and object-based.

The Louvre suggests on its website that the organisation has 'adapted through time to societies' changing needs through the ages' (Louvre n.d.[a]). Yet it is still using methods of representation that are fundamentally flawed in the context of cross-cultural translation. Erskine-Loftus has argued that 'unquestioned assumptions about how museums communicate and how visitors understand have been built on Western cultural and social understandings, which are not universal' (Erskine-Loftus 2013b: 471). What is missing is an active engagement with audiences in Abu Dhabi. Translatability is therefore not a given in Abu Dhabi. This suggests that the Louvre Abu Dhabi and the Guggenheim Abu Dhabi are drawing on old European notions of Culture and Civilisation and showing how Islamic cultural heritage and arts can be displayed according to those models. In doing so, it could be argued that it is actually exhibiting western European museum practices as artefacts in and of themselves.

It states on the Louvre Abu Dhabi's website that 'Louvre Abu Dhabi is a new cultural beacon, bringing different cultures together to shine fresh light on the shared stories of humanity' (Louvre n.d.[a]). It is essentially a grand attempt to challenge the established art historical 'canon' and at the same time, rewrite the history of humanity. Albeit a very Franco-phone version of humanity seen through a 'cosmo-universal' lens. This shows how the Louvre museum is using the development of the museum in Abu Dhabi to move away from its past image, which is based on an exclusive nationalist outlook. Instead, it has now begun to adopt a more transnational approach as an evolving but established global institution. In order to continue to maintain its position in the emerging global heritage market, the Louvre museum needs to reposition itself as a global institution by doing, so it reinforces the power of the French nation at home and abroad.

Sherman (2004) has suggested that the approach to display that emerged during the Enlightenment was predominantly based on French ethnography. This had a significant impact on the establishment of the Louvre museum in Paris and the way it subsequently developed its collections and exhibitionary practices through time. Central to the Louvre museum's exhibitionary practise was the belief that objects and artworks could be displayed and compared next to each other in order to represent different peoples' and their relationships between them (*ibid.*). Official statements suggest that the

Louvre Abu Dhabi's curatorial concept is being developed and related to the legacy that the museum has with the Enlightenment traditions of the Louvre Museum. The contemporary project is also being positioned within such a view, as the Louvre Abu Dhabi website states that, 'in true enlightenment style, visitors will be invited to study for themselves, compare them, and delight in their unique qualities and meanings' (Louvre n.d.[a]). A senior member of the Louvre Abu Dhabi project team explicitly linked the values and identity of the proposed Louvre Abu Dhabi to the enlightenment values of the Louvre museum.

> The Louvre Abu Dhabi's values and identity are based on discovery, exchange and education. The ultimate aim of the museum is to allow visitors to discover for themselves how art developed in different cultures and civilizations around the world. For all these reasons, the Louvre Abu Dhabi will make the museum truly universal. Its unique museological approach – displaying objects together and arts of a same period but from geographical origins – will create a dialogue between artworks, sculptures and objects: visitors will discover shared influences and connections between different cultures around the globe – giving insight into the history of humankind since the beginning of time.
>
> (Louvre Abu Dhabi Representative 2011: Interview)

Furthermore, in the newly opened Louvre Abu Dhabi's exhibition catalogue, it states that the Louvre Abu Dhabi '...represents the advent of the very concept of the museum, as invented in Enlightenment Europe, into the Arab world for the first time' (Al-Mubarak and Martinez 'Foreword': 4–5). Yet these ideas have been mainly discredited within critical heritage studies and museological discourse as outdated and inappropriate ways of engaging with diverse cultures and global audiences. It takes for granted, as I noted in chapter two, that this approach is translatable within non-Western contexts. This is a significant critique as museums are still a relatively new concept in Abu Dhabi and the UAE.

Reciprocity and dialogue

What is particularly interesting about cultural heritage franchise partnerships is reciprocity of the relationship. As mentioned earlier, the museum partners and the cultural authority in Abu Dhabi stress the bilateral and strategic nature of the partnerships. This illustrates how the partnerships are being presented within a discourse that draws explicitly on 'cosmo-universalism' to suggest that reciprocal exchange can only occur when nations enter into a global cultural dialogue. Cultural heritage organisations and heritage practitioners are recognising the potential of thinking and working transnationally through cross-border partnerships. For example, the Louvre Museum refers to its shifting global outlook on its website where the former director of the Louvre Museum is quoted as having said: '[w]e have a duty to enhance our international action and come up with new forms of co-operation' (Loyrette n.d.). In a further example, former director of the British Museum, Neil MacGregor, stated in 2011 in a panel discussion[4] at Manarat al Saadiyat that:

> The 19th Century notion of a national museum rests on the assumption that people in one city are the same. Now people of the world inhabit cities. National museums have to explore the culture of international peoples, diverse peoples and that is what is new.

These examples are indicative of the museum institutions' awareness of increasing global opportunities and markets.

Cross-cultural exchange featured heavily in a pre-opening exhibition held at Emirates Palace entitled *The Cultural District*. The exhibition provided an introductory section, which explained the purpose and plan for Saadiyat Island and the Cultural District. The exhibition was the first to present details of the cultural project to the public in detail, providing architectural plans and models for each of the five museums. The Guggenheim Abu Dhabi section of the exhibition featured a panel display that set out the strategic vision for the planned museum. The following extract was taken from this panel:

> The commitment to international communication and global cultural exchange-through the development of museums, collections, and programs– is a superior position because of its inclusive, democratic, and is both respectful of difference and excited by it.

The importance of this statement is that it promotes the Guggenheim Museum's potential for global reach in terms of both attracting visitors and developing a global brand for Abu Dhabi. This vision is clearly set within cosmopolitan terms by drawing on words such as 'inclusive', 'democratic', 'respectful', 'interconnected' and 'interdependent'.[5] The text is phrased within World Heritage rhetoric as advocated by UNESCO, which places emphasis on words such as 'mankind [sic]', 'dialogue', 'common identities' and 'shared histories' (UNESCO 2011). This is similar to Fibiger's (2011) observations of Bahrain's global heritage discourse, which I discussed in chapter three. It also serves as further evidence of the strategic, communicative and symbolic role of the cultural heritage franchise. This was also observed within the approach taken towards autochthonous heritage before the TDIC and ADACH merged. In 2010, ADACH's website stated that by being involved in the exchange of cultural heritage Abu Dhabi was '... contributing to the strengthening of intercultural dialogue and the appreciation of different cultures' (Abu Dhabi Authority for Culture and Heritage n.d.[b]). The rhetoric that surrounds the development of cultural heritage franchising in Abu Dhabi, therefore, suggests that cosmopolitan ideologies are bound up within the heritage discourse. This rhetoric has continued to gain traction since the establishment of one cohesive heritage authority, which I will discuss in chapter nine. However, the cultural heritage projects exclude alternative or marginalised communities.

Transnational heritage presents heritage as a reciprocal project in which nations develop their cosmopolitan identities in order to be included in the global representations of heritage. By drawing on the ideological stance of cosmopolitanism, the cultural heritage franchise is distanced from the more negative aspects of the exchange through the pursuit of the common good. This connects with the discussion from chapter two, in which I illustrated how transnational heritage formations are part of a much broader shift from a view of heritage as bounded by local and national identities towards a more globally focused way of producing heritage. It is through global 'collective collaboration' (Appiah 2007) that transnational heritage is produced and presented. The Cultural District on Saadiyat Island is not just about developing culture it is also about developing a global dialogue and a transnational identity. The cultural heritage franchise is involved in more complex cultural processes than debates concerning the commodification and exchange allow for.

The goal of the contemporary project in Abu Dhabi, and arguably elsewhere, is focused on what I suggest is a form of 'cosmopolitan essentialism'. By this, I mean that dominant nations are using cosmopolitan ideology to create global heritage processes, the problem with this as I argued earlier, is that this is a selective neo-colonial process. It is through this global process of importing cultural heritage that dominant nations can trade in elitist tourism-focused heritage products. Instead, it serves the new class of international heritage consumer-elites who through their dominant positions can define and shape the production of official versions of the past that are then used within the production of global heritage discourses.

Notes

1 At the time of writing the following individuals serving on the Board of Directors at Agence France-Muséums included: Jean-Luc Martinez, President-director of the Louvre Museum; Maxence Langlois-Berthelot, Managing Director of the Louvre Museum; Alberto Vial, Diplomatic Advisor, Louvre Museum; Laurence des Cars; President of the Orsay and Orangery Museums; Laurence Engel, President of the National Library of France; Chris Dercon, President of the National Museums and Grand Palace Serge Lasvignes, President of the Centre Pompidou; Sophie Makariou, president of the National Museum of Asian Arts - Guimet; Stéphane Martin, President of the Quai Branly Museum – Jacques Chirac (Agence France-Muséums n.d.[b]).

2 Jean-Luc Martinez chairs the Scientific Council and is also the chairman-director of the Louvre Museum (Agence France-Muséums n.d.[c]).

3 Observation at the Saadiyat Story Exhibition, Manarat Al Saadiyat: December 1, 2010.

4 The panel discussion: *The National Museum: A Symbolic Identity* took place at Manarat al Saadiyat on April 27, 2011. Speakers on the panel included: Neil MacGregor, director of the British Museum; Henri Loyrette, director of the Louvre Museum; Shobita Punja, CEO of the National Cultural Fund, Ministry of Culture and Government of India; and Wafaa El Saddik, president of Children's Alliance for Traditions and Social Engagement.

5 Observation at *The Cultural District* exhibition, Emirates Palace, Abu Dhabi, November 29, 2011.

4 Globalisation and bilateral heritage

In chapters two and three, I illustrated how changes in global processes have led to the development of new forms of transnational heritage, observing how heritage has come to operate globally using cosmopolitan narratives to express both national and transnational identities. In order to understand the process of franchising as it relates to cultural heritage it is necessary to explore the broader issues that surround globalisation and the co-production of heritage. The rise of late capitalist economies and modernity has had a profound impact on the Emirate of Abu Dhabi and consequently the way that heritage is being developed and presented. This chapter considers how heritage works within and alongside the processes of globalisation and the power relations that underpin transnational heritage processes. It examines how transnational cultural heritage emerges and operates within specific politico-economic circumstances that often remain undiscussed. Arguing that cultural policy and international interests are increasingly shaping the way that heritage is presented globally, which is directly related to the development of bilateral relations, trade and tourism. The development of heritage is therefore embedded within Abu Dhabi's broader political landscape.

Globalisation and heritage

It is important to first note that globalisation is not a purely modern phenomenon. For example, the development of museums during the nineteenth century was part of the process of colonisation which was itself a globalising practice (Long and Labadi 2010: 2). Like the terms, cosmopolitanism and hybridity, the term globalisation has been subject to various interpretations and definitions. Giddens (1990) suggests that the processes of globalisation have intensified, which has resulted in an increase in the speed at which globalisation is felt and operates. Castells (2009) has argued that one of the reasons for this is because new technologies such as the internet have led to increasing connection, which he defined the 'networked society'. However more recent studies of the 'network society' have offered more critical approaches challenging the 'ethnocentric universal claims' and interrogating networks as 'space of places' (Chi 2013). I take the view that globalisation is about more than the movement of global processes and the impacts that they have in diverse localities around the world. I consider globalisation, like I do heritage, as a cultural 'process'. Robertson argues that globalisation involves 'both to a compression of the world and the intensification of consciousness of the world as a whole' (1992: 8). In this sense globalisation is both an ideological and a practical process. One of the ways in which this connects to global heritage is that it employs established processes of producing and presenting heritage, and it also, as I suggested in chapter two, serves to promote and reinforce cosmopolitan ideology. I therefore take the view in this book, drawing on Steger's discussion of globalisation, that heritage should be considered as part of the 'process of globalization' that is based on 'a set of social processes of intensifying global interdependence' and 'globalism', which is the 'ideologies that endow the concept of globalization with particular values and meanings' (2009: 99). Taking such a view acknowledges that people do not just accept the forces of globalisation but are actively involved in the production of global processes and exchanges across borders.

The dynamics of global cultural heritage production are therefore important. Tomlinson suggests that globalisation is shaped by cultural processes; and conversely that cultural processes are affected by globalisation (2007: 1). This is particularly significant for heritage as it places emphasis on the ways in which local and global heritage processes interact and enmesh, which is at the heart of this study. Appadurai has suggested that, 'the production and consumption of particular goods across cultures is the major process by which the other is experienced' (1986: 27). He goes on to argue that globalisation is linked to 'economy, culture and politics', which can be explored by focusing on 'the relationship among five dimensions of global cultural flows that can be termed "scapes" (a) ethnoscapes, (b) technoscapes, (c) financescapes, (d) mediascapes and (e) ideoscapes' (Appadurai 1996: 33). Suggesting that these 'scapes', due to their 'fluid and irregular shape', challenge the idea of globalisation as a homogenous process (*ibid.*: 33). This is important for heritage as transnational forms are created and re-produced through a series of global processes that are based on connections between people, places and aspects of the past (tangible and intangible aspects). Furthermore, certain heritage forms and formations are more desirable and therefore more globally mobile than others.

Transnational heritage charters and agreements

International agreements and charters have played an important role in establishing international power structures. The 1944 United Nations Monetary and Financial Conference, also known as the Bretton Woods Conference, led to the development of a number of new global financial institutions, such as the International Monetary Fund, the World Bank and the General Agreement on Tariffs and Trade (which later developed in to the World Trade Organization) (Steger 2009: 38–39). Global museum and heritage development emerged through the policies of the World Commission on Culture and Development, which influenced the World Bank's involvement in the conservation and development of cultural heritage, particularly in non-Western nations (Nardella and Mallinson 2015: 193). Long and Labadi have suggested that institutions of global governance were particularly important in promoting cross-cultural understanding as well as encouraging global systems of economic and political co-operation (2010: 3). Perhaps most significantly, the introduction of this hegemonic system of global governance gave power and legitimacy to a select group of nations (Steger 2009). Similarly, as noted in chapter two the articles and statues of UNESCO employ hegemonic global processes and legitimisation tactics. As such, nationalism remains a key structure that 'continues to shape the way countries interact with global processes and with global institutions such as the World Bank and, in particular, the United Nations' (Long and Labadi 2010: 5). Askew (2010) has also suggested that UNESCO's global nomination process and the way in which it promotes heritage as a universal often serves national agendas. These heritage organisations are therefore politically charged and connected to global power.

The UNESCO system of heritage is based on the development of a global heritage ideology, devised and led by globally powerful nation states, that encourages other nation states to be part of the UNESCO system of categorisation. It also means that through their acceptance on the World Heritage List that nations accept the rules of governance and conservation that UNESCO sets out (Harrison 2013: 64), which is predominantly based on Western systems (Kirshenblatt-Gimblett 2007; Askew 2010; Byrne 2011: 147). In a similar way, the process of cultural heritage franchising is made possible through a system of exchange that draws on the political power and wealth of selected nations. Kratz and Karp have argued that it is crucial to explore the geographical dimensions of global heritage production. They note that:

> When the Guggenheim museum for example describes itself as 'global', for example, the use of the term conceals the fact that the museum limits its expansion of programming to relatively wealthy parts of the world and has no plans for whole continents that have their own museum traditions.
>
> (2007: 36–37)

They go on to suggest that what is needed is a more critical analysis of the geographical processes surrounding global heritage, which can account for the origins, direction, and political dimensions of globalised heritage processes (*ibid.*: 37). Global power therefore shifts within and alongside the processes of globalisation (Friedman 2002: 33) and as such transnational heritage can reinforce, reproduce and alter global power relations.

The dynamics of the world economy are shifting. The implication for the Gulf is that it has opened up the potential for the global power relations in Pacific Asia (Davidson 2009; Ulrichsen 2010). In particular, Davidson notes that relations between the UAE and China are playing a significant role within these developments, linking the 'Gulf's rich energy resources and Pacific Asia's massive energy needs' (2010: 1). In 2011, *The National* newspaper published an article discussing the UAE's oil links with China and that the Abu Dhabi National Oil Company was developing its focus on emerging markets. In particular it noted that Abu Dhabi was 'doubling its oil exports to China from just under 100,000 barrels per day (bpd) to 200,000 bpd starting in 2014' (Yee 2011: 7). Simpfendorfer suggests that economic developments between the Gulf and Asia are part of the opening up of a new twenty-first-century 'Silk Road' (2009: 1).

In cultural terms the cultural heritage developments in Abu Dhabi are arguably contributing to the development of South Asian tourism in the region. Somers Cocks (2017) noted in an article in *The National* newspaper reporting on the opening of the Louvre Abu Dhabi that France's president, Macron suggested that the Louvre Abu Dhabi serves as a meeting point between East and West, which has challenged the once dominant global axis towards Europe and the United States. Once complete the Saadiyat Island institutions will offer Asian tourists the opportunity to go to the Louvre and the Guggenheim without having to undertake lengthy travel. This is significant as South Asian workers traditionally have limited vacation time (Bardsley 2011: 7). In addition to the focus on tourism, the UAE is also putting increasing efforts in to its bilateral relationships with other nations. Of particular note to this book is the deepening strategic partnership between the UAE and France based on political, economic and cultural relations.

Politics, power and cultural heritage

Global heritage processes are intimately linked to global power relations. Nye differentiates between two types of power, 'hard power' and 'soft power' (2004, 2011). 'Hard power' operates as a coercive force, which is often linked to economic, military and/or political actions by one nation against another. Hard power is used to force 'others to act in ways that are contrary to their initial preferences and strategies' (Nye 2011: 11). Conversely, 'soft power' is non-coercive as it uses a nation's culture and values 'to achieve goals through attraction rather than coercion' following this line of thought others are encouraged 'to want the outcomes that you want' (Nye 2004: 5–6). Therefore 'other countries - admiring its values, emulating its example, aspiring to its level of prosperity and openness want to follow it' (*ibid.*: 5).

Nye's 'soft power' is significant for our understanding of the politics of heritage as it works at a nation state level to encourage states to 'buy in' to the global business of heritage. In the case of UNESCO's World Heritage, soft power is used to persuade nations to join the process of global listing. Long and Labadi have suggested that, 'nations use World Heritage Listing as a form of soft power, a means of communicating their cultural credentials to the world' (2010: 6). When heritage is re-packaged as 'universal' it gains currency as a process that carries the potential for facilitating connections across borders that can be utilised within bilateral relations and cultural diplomacy initiatives. I argued in chapter two that universal ideologies have been overtly used within the cultural partnership between the UAE and France from the outset, for example, Jacques Chirac, then President of France (1997–2007), in his message to the President of the UAE Sheikh Khalifa stressed the Louvre's role in universalising discourses:

> By choosing the Louvre, the emirate of Abu Dhabi did not just want to enter into partnership with the world's most visited and well-known museum. It chose one whose mission, from the outset, has been to attain the universal, i.e. the essence of mankind, through contemplation of works of art.
>
> Created from ancient French royal collections and constantly en-riched over more than two centuries, the Louvre has from its inception firmly believed that art conveys universality.
>
> (Chirac 2007)

Further bilateral activity has occurred within the military field in the form of the of transnational security arrangements such as the development of a French Navy Base, in Abu Dhabi (Cody 2009), which represents a form of 'hard power' (Nye 2004). Notably this is 'France's first new military base outside of its territory in 50 years' (Habboush 2009a). The development of the Navy Base is important as it provides France with a strategic position in the Gulf and provides the UAE with increased protection in the region (Stracke 2008; Cody 2009). Economic relations have been further enhanced through the UAE's purchase of '40 Airbus 380 aircraft and has brought about $10.4 billion worth of armaments from France during the last decade' (Riding 2007a: 1).

The ways in which cultural heritage operates within the global realm of politics and international relations is therefore highly significant as it is ac-tively used as a tool of cultural diplomacy. According to Ang, Isar and Mar suggest that cultural diplomacy is a strategic 'governmental practice' that is carried out by '[g]*overnmental* agents and envoys' to achieve a nation's identity aims, which may be connected to local, national or international concerns (2015: 365). The bilateral role of culture is often made explicit, for example, Sheikh Sultan bin Tahnoon, chairman of ADACH stated that the Louvre Abu Dhabi agreement was 'an additional pillar of our bilateral re-lations. This agreement will open new horizons for cultural tourism and scientific co-operation' (Khaleej Times 2007).

As part of the 2007 intergovernmental agreement further provisions were made for the restoration of certain museum and heritage sites in Paris, including a wing of the Louvre - the Pavilion de Flore and the Palace of Fontainebleau (Poncelet 2007; see also Ajana 2015: 323; McClellan 2012: 277) and the establishment of the Paris-Sorbonne University Abu Dhabi. These activities add further evidence of strategic policy led cultural activities, which operate as forms of 'soft power'. The UAE funded the restoration of the nineteenth-century theatre inside the Palace of Fontainebleau in France. The Palace served as a royal residence for eight centuries (Château de Fontainebleau n.d.[a]). The Palace and Park of Fontainebleau was listed on UNESCO's World Heritage List as a Site of Universal Value in 1981 (UNESCO n.d.[g]). The theatre, which was built between 1853 and 1856 by Hector Lefuel for Napoléon III (Château de Fontainebleau n.d.[b]), re-opened in June 2019 after being closed for over a century and a half. The theatre will continue to receive support from the UAE government through a reported annual grant of €5 million (Leech 2014a). In return for its support the UAE receives brand name recognition: *The Imperial Theatre - Sheikh Khalifa bin Zayed Al Nahyan Theatre* (Department of Culture and Tourism 2017). It was reported by the Emirates News Agency that Mohamed Khalifa Al Mubarak, Chairman of DCT Abu Dhabi, stated that:

> The inauguration of the Sheikh Khalifa Bin Zayed Al Nahyan Theatre at the Chateau Fontainebleau presents yet another cultural achievement resulting from the close ties between France and the UAE, further emphasising the crucial role cultural diplomacy plays in the preservation of the world's cultural heritage not only in times of peril, but also of peace.
>
> (Salman 2019)

However, the restoration of a wing of the Louvre the Pavilion de Flore did not happen as originally planned. Media reports in 2013 suggested that €25m that the UAE had given to France had not been used to renovate the floor of its *Pavillon de Flore* housing the *Centre de Recherche et de Restauration des Musées de France*. The original plan was to re-open the gallery and to rename it the Sheikh Zayed bin Sultan Al Nahyan Gallery (Somers Cocks 2013). Instead, in 2017, the Sheikh Zayed bin Sultan Al Nahyan Centre, which presents an overview of the history of the museum, opened in the Louvre's *Pavilion de l'Horologe* (Leech 2017b). International cultural partnerships therefore gain currency as tools of bilateral tools.

Similar cultural partnerships have been established between the UAE and other nations, particularly the UK. As I mentioned in chapter one, the UAE has been working in partnership with the British Museum who were employed as consultants for the planned Zayed National Museum project. As part of the original agreement the British Museum contributed to the delivery of three pre-opening exhibitions at Manarat Al Saadiyat,[1] which I will discuss in more detail in chapter seven. In 2018, the partnership was renewed and it was announced that the British Museum would be renaming Gallery 51, the Sheikh Zayed bin Sultan Al Nahyan Gallery for Europe and the Middle East (Dennehy 2018a).[2] In return, the British Museum would loan objects to Abu Dhabi to be exhibited in the planned Zayed National Museum. A statement from Mohamed Khalifa Al Mubarak, chairman of the DCT illustrates the strategic aims of this international partnership '[w]e are delighted to build on our long history of collaboration with the British Museum as part of DCT Abu Dhabi's mission to establish lasting cultural partnerships with leading institutions worldwide' (*ibid.*).[3] The decision to sponsor Gallery 51 was decisive with press coverage focusing on the gallery's focus on global patterns emerging from the Middle East region. For example the following extract appeared in *The National* newspaper: 'this gallery shows the impact of the introduction of farming in the Middle East and its spread to Europe, thereby shaping the modern world' (Harris 2018). I argue that cultural heritage is being strategically employed using cultural policy objectives to fulfil, in part, the international cultural strategies of the UAE and France. Cultural heritage in this sense is actively employed as a strategic bilateral process.

The willingness of Emirati authorities to work with authorities in France and the UK suggests a clear strategy to employ soft power to develop Abu Dhabi's influence and power internationally. It was Emirati authorities who initiated the partnership and who wield the power of wealth within the relationship. The French and the British partners bring their brands and consequently their cultural legacies through their connections to western European values and collections, which are inherently connected to the difficult and charged histories of colonialism. Abu Dhabi is not only gaining a foothold in the international political sphere by wielding its 'power' but is also becoming, through brand association, connected to the biggest cultural players in the game and their colonial histories.

Qasr Al Watan: bilateral symbolism

In March 2019, Qasr Al Watan, which means Palace of the Nation, opened to the public inside the Presidential Palace in Ras Al Akhdar, Abu Dhabi. The palace also contains the offices of the President, the Vice President and Crown Prince of Abu Dhabi. The Presidential Palace is the official meeting place for the UAE Cabinet and the Federal Supreme Council – the highest constitutional authority in the UAE. The decision to open up the palace to visitors 'came from the President Sheikh Khalifa in a bid to boost cultural understanding of the UAE' (Duncan 2019). Qasr Al Watan consists of seven key zones that focus on aspects of the palace's function and its role in Emirati governance and culture. The zones include:

- A Memory from the Palace
- The Great Hall
- Presidential Gifts

- Spirit of Collaboration
- The Presidential Banquet
- House of Knowledge
- Qasr Al Watan Library

On display in the zone aptly named 'Presidential Gifts' are a range of diplomatic gifts received by the UAE such as 'carpets from Turkmenistan, an ornate sword and shield from Kazakhstan, armour from Japan and a khanjar from Oman'. As such, the room has a distinctly political role to play in the Qasr Al Watan's narrative. As Herlory notes the 'tradition of rulers exchanging gifts of arts is primarily motivated by the question of Prestige' (2008: 36). The zone is '[d]esigned as a vibrant showcase of cultural exchange and international diplomacy' (Qasr Al Watan n.d.[a]). Similarly, the 'spirit of collaboration' room was designed to host summits of the Federal Supreme Council, Arab League and Gulf Cooperation Council. A circular table sits in the centre of the room, overhead is a crystal chandelier containing 350,000 crystals weighing 12 tonnes (Dennehy 2019a). According to the Qasr Al Watan website the chandelier symbolises the UAE's commitment to equality and illumination.

At the centre of Qasr Al Watan is the 'Great Hall' featuring a large thirty-seven-metre diameter dome, which is significantly larger than the main dome of the Sheikh Zayed Grand Mosque. It is in the 'Great Hall' that foreign dignitaries and members of state would be greeted. The hall features four mirrored cubes that provide visitors with information more about the architectural features. The hall's grand architectural style draws influence from the Mughal-era as well as classical regional motifs such as the arch, dome and ornate tile-work (*ibid.*). A replica of the Birmingham Quran 'was gifted from Prince Charles of the UK and Northern Ireland to Sheikh Mohamed bin Zayed Al-Nahyan, the Crown Prince of Abu Dhabi' (Qasr Al Watan n.d.[b]). The manuscript discovered by a student at Birmingham University is one of the earliest known surviving records of the Holy Quran. The placing of the Birmingham Quran in the palace rather than one of the new large-scale museums such as the Louvre Abu Dhabi serves to reinforce the power of the ruling elite, the seat of the government and Abu Dhabi's transnational identity. The palace also features a lattice-inspired contemporary art sculpture by Emirati artist, Mattar bin Lahej. The national visioning of the palace is further reinforced by an evening light and sound show that presents in three acts the past, present and future vision of the country.

In addition to the permanent displays, Qasr Al Watan also hosts temporary exhibitions. The first temporary exhibition, *Codices of Mexico: The Old Books of the New World*, displayed loaned works from the *Museo Nacional de Antropologia*, Mexico City, the National Library of France, Paris and Florence National Central Library, Florence. The exhibition featured a series of pre-Hispanic codices and ancient manuscripts dating from the third and sixteenth centuries (Gillett 2019). The exhibition had a distinctly diplomatic and transnational remit, 'Codices of Mexico is an excellent example of embracing and appreciating the culture and history of another country, as we are keen to display priceless treasures from around the world under one roof to the public' (*ibid.*). The development of Qasr Al Watan illustrates that new autochthonous institutions are also being employed within the political landscape of Abu Dhabi. Like the cultural heritage franchises Qasr Al Watan is clearly being used to further enhance Abu Dhabi's transnational identity and to further develop its diplomatic ties to selected nations abroad.

Cultural heritage tourism

Shifts in geopolitical power also have implications for the way in which tourist economies develop, and by extension how heritage develops as a tourism resource. Tourism in general is an important source of income for nations around the world. According to the United Nations World Tourism Organization (UNWTO) global tourism stood at '10.4% of global GDP in 2017' (World Travel & Tourism Council 2018). In 2017, 'the total contribution of travel and tourism to' Abu Dhabi's 'GDP was AED154.1bn (11.3% of GDP)' and was forecast to rise to 'AED234.2bn by 2028' (World Travel & Tourism Council 2018: 3). Abu Dhabi chamber suggests, based on World Travel and Tourism Council figures, that Abu Dhabi was the fastest growing tourist destination in the Middle East in the last ten years (Abu Dhabi Chamber 2018: 3). Tourism is therefore a significant market in the UAE, which has had an impact on how cultural heritage it produced and managed.

Increasing interest is being paid to tourism within emerging regions of the world, particularly Asia and the Middle East (Al-Hamarneh 2005; Hazbun 2009; Winter 2009a 2009b; Wong, McIntosh and Ryan 2013). These studies have made strides in examining the socio-cultural trends and counternarratives to the dominant Euro-centric approach to tourism studies. Winter has argued that we need to broaden our understanding of tourists and visitor patterns outside of the Western world as it is no longer the sole preserve of affluent Western tourists (2010: 117). He argues in his study of Pacific Asia that regional tourism is on the rise. In Cambodia he observed that regional tourists, from China, Taiwan and Korea dominated the sector (*ibid.*: 120–121). The potential of non-Western tourism markets is not exclusive to Pacific Asia. Davidson has noted that Chinese tourism has increased in the UAE as a result of a change in visa rules making it easier for Chinese businessmen to visit Abu Dhabi (2010: 39). He predicted that 'Abu Dhabi and eventually the rest of the UAE will begin to claim a greater share of outbound business tourism market, which is currently valued at \$15 billion per annum and is set to grow by 15% annually' (*ibid.*). Since Davidson's predictions Chinese tourism has continued to rise in the UAE. More broadly a report by Colliers International in 2018 suggested that 'the availability of disposable income and the relative stability of the Chinese Yen' had influenced China's growing economy, which had the knock-on effect of boosting the outbound travel market which continued to grow at a 'rate of 10.8%' (2018a: 2)

Colliers reported that 'between 2013-2017 there was a significant increase in Chinese tourists in the UAE, recording a CAGR [compound annual growth rate] of 45% between those years' (*ibid.*). In 2019, figures from the Department of Culture and Tourism – Abu Dhabi indicated that visits to cultural sites had risen with a '21.5 per cent growth at cultural and historical sites, and a 22 per cent increase at museums' (Gulf Today 2019). The cultural authority suggested that these figures were influenced by a 31 per cent increase [in visitors] from China' (*ibid.*). Furthermore, Colliers International have identified an increasing demand for Islamic tourism from China with an estimated '12,000 and 14,5000 Chinese Muslims visit the two Holy Cities to perform Hajj' as well as travelling to visit friends and family in the Gulf region (2018b: 3).

However even though the number of Chinese tourists has been increasing it was recorded that they only spend on average only one-and-a-half days in Abu Dhabi, the shortest stay among all major visitor nations; instead, travellers from Germany, the United States and the United Kingdom stayed the longest and remain in the top tier of tourism spend per nation (Abu Dhabi Chamber 2018: 8–9). However, predictions continue to suggest that the Gulf Cooperation Council (GCC) will receive an estimated '2.9 million Total Chinese tourists' by 2022 and that by 2030 'China will account for a quarter of international tourism' (Colliers International 2018a: 2). Abu Dhabi Chamber notes the future potential for increasing Chinese tourists based on the current status of passport holders in China, accordingly 'only 7% (approx. 99 million) of the total Chinese population possess a passport, compared to approximately 40% of Americans and 76% of British' (2018: 4).

In addition to China further emerging markets are being sought to enhance the tourism market in the UAE (*ibid.*: 9). In 2019, India, Saudi Arabia, United Kingdom, Russia, China, Oman, United States and Germany remained the UAE's largest tourist markets and Russia and China were expected to remain the largest growth sectors (Colliers International 2019a: 2). Notably, 'India is now the fastest growing outbound travel market in the world, second only to China'; this is largely due to the 'burgeoning middle class (350 million), with increasing amount of disposable income' (Colliers International 2019b: 2). This means that India offers a huge opportunity for the Emirates, which is in easy geographical reach. For example, in 2017 '2.3 million Indian tourists' visited the UAE, which accounts for '13% of its annual visitors' (*ibid.*: 2). Furthermore, the 'United Nations World Tourism Organization estimates that India will account for over 50 million outbound tourists by 2022, making India a USD 45 billion outbound spend market' (*ibid.*). In terms of Russian tourists there was a large drop in tourists to the region when the value of the rouble dropped significantly in 2015. Over the period 2013–2018 the total number of outbound tourisms decreased by 33 per cent. However, Russian tourism to the GCC actually rose during this period by 120 per cent; for the UAE this reflected 530,000 visitors (Colliers International 2019c: 2). This pattern was set to continue into 2018, with a further 69 per cent predicted increase in tourists to the UAE. According to Danielle Curtis, Exhibition Director Middle East for the Arabian Travel Market key reasons for rises in Russian tourist numbers to the UAE include 'the introduction of additional and direct airline routes…relaxed UAE visa regulations and rising oil prices are helping to strengthen the Russian rouble, making the UAE more affordable' (WAM Emirates News Agency 2019). Therefore, the Indian, Chinese and Russian markets, all considered emerging markets, are key sources of tourism for the UAE along with KSA, the UK and Germany. The development of cultural heritage tourism in Abu Dhabi offers the potential for increasing the Emirate's cultural tourism within affluent non-Western markets.

Trends in cultural heritage tourism supports the reported rises in the tourism sector. Al-Mubarak (2018) stated that the target for the Louvre Abu Dhabi's first year of operation had been one million visitors and that the actual recorded number of visitors surpassed this figure as over one million people had visited the museum.[4] He stated that fifty-five per cent of the Louvre Abu Dhabi's visitors were international visitors. The Guggenheim Abu Dhabi and Abu Dhabi's Arab cultural heritage – the planned Zayed National Museum, the Heritage Village, and the Sweihan Festival building 'are key future assets' along with future bids for designations on the World Heritage List (Abu Dhabi Chamber 2018: 9–10).

Hazbun (2006) has argued that tensions between the West and Muslims have affected attitudes towards international travel. He suggests that the increase in Arab and Muslim visitors to the Gulf occurred at the same time as Western tourists decreased. He attributes this shift in visitor patterns to the broader effects of the Iraq War and the events of 9/11 in the United States and the subsequent 'war on terror' rhetoric. It is possible then that this increase in regional tourism may have counteracted the possible negative effects that could have occurred from the drop in Western tourists (Hazbun 2006: 229; see also Al-Hamarneh and Steiner 2004). In fact domestic tourism has continued to rise. 2017 saw '1.5 million domestic tourists' in the UAE, which accounted for '31%—almost one third—of all tourists who were registered by the Abu Dhabi Department of Cultural & Tourism' (Colliers International 2018b: 5). This suggest that the UAE market is also a strong market for heritage tourism. However, these predictions are likely to be impacted by the 2020 Covid-19 global pandemic.

Ultimately tourism trends are creating new opportunities for cultural heritage development in the region. Rico has suggested in her analysis of Islamophobia and heritage in the Gulf that, 'Islamic beliefs are understood as predominantly destructive' (2014: 19). She argues that Islamophobia has affected the debates that have emerged in relation to heritage in the

Islamic world, and that these debates have centred on the destruction of cultural heritage sites such as the Bamiyan Buddha statues in Afghanistan, which have generated global mass media attention (*ibid*.: 20). The destruction of the large-scale Buddha statues at Bamiyan in March 2001 was broadcast to news outlets around the world as a result of an order issued by the Taliban leader Mullah Omar for military forces of Afghanistan's Taliban government to destroy all non-Islamic shrines and statues (Cuno 2008; Rico 2014). Rico goes on to argue that the destruction of Islamic heritage has been used to demarcate Western and non-Western heritage, ultimately setting international heritage processes, such as UNESCO, as a positive force focused on preservation and collaborative action, and non-Western processes as a destructive force (2014: 19–24).

In Abu Dhabi we can see how the rhetoric that surrounded the opening of the Louvre Abu Dhabi was used to promote and advocate for global museums to be seen as symbols of tolerance and understanding. As McClellan suggests museum partnerships between the West and the Middle East are being used in 'the rhetoric of bridge-building' (2012: 280–281). For example, at the inauguration of the Paris-Sorbonne Abu Dhabi the French Culture Minister Gilles de Robien is quoted as having stated that the Paris-Sorbonne Abu Dhabi and the Louvre Abu Dhabi 'were testimony to the wish to find a dialogue between East and West' (Chrisafis 2017). In doing so, '[m]useums in the Middle East are pressed into double service, asserting a new global status while countering incidents that feed negative impressions in the West of a regressive Islamic ideology in the region (McClellan 2012: 279; see also Ajana 2015). The French president, Emmanuel Macron, overtly utilised the opening of the Louvre Abu Dhabi to promote French foreign policy and national identity, at home and abroad. Macron argued that by providing links between Europe and the Arab World, the Louvre Abu Dhabi serves to challenge the 'idiocy' and the 'lies' of 'obscurantism' (Chrisafis 2017). Macron went onto present France as the 'saviour' of the Arab World by suggesting that the new museum 'defend[s] beauty, universality, creativity, reason and fraternity' (*ibid*.). More broadly this is suggestive of the way in which the discourse of 'cosmo-universalism' has been employed as a counter discourse to Islamophobia and fears of 'culture clashes' between the Muslim and Western worlds (Huntington 1993).

Branding: Abu Dhabi city

The process of city branding, which has important implications for cultural tourism development, is intimately linked to cultural heritage development (Hubbard and Hall 1998). For Riza, Doratli and Fasli (2012) city identity is central to city branding because a city's image is an indispensable part of both. Dicks has argued that places, since the nineteenth century, have become 'visitable' by placing an emphasis on cultural 'display' (2003: 1). She uses the example of the 19th Great Exhibition of 1851 to demonstrate how changes – economic, technological and social – reshaped the ways in which the past was recreated as a 'visitable' and 'visual' aspect of the city (*ibid.*: 8–13). For Dicks heritage is made 'visitable' through the production of 'visual' markers that can be 'visited' such as heritage sites, museums and architectural icons (*ibid.*: 8–13, 134). In this sense, Dicks illustrate the role of 'visibility' in creating early tourist destinations. This book builds on this work to show how Gulf cities are creating places that are both desirable to 'visit' and globally 'visible' through the production and presentation of heritage. In doing so, I further contribute to understandings of heritage development and transnational tourist economies in non-Western nations.

Within the growth of contemporary Gulf cities global identity development and regional competition have been high on the agenda (Elsheshtawy 2008, 2013; Foster and Golzari 2013; Alraouf 2014, 2016b, 2016b; Nakib 2016; Wakefield 2017a; Molotch and Ponzini 2019). As noted in chapter one large-scale transformations have taken place in the development of cities in Bahrain, Kuwait, Qatar, the UAE and Saudi Arabia; these developments have occurred over time at varying scales, and as such they do not reflect a homogenous blanket development. The result has been the emergence of rapid museumscapes that have captured academic and international media attention. Cultural developments that have thus far been completed include: in Abu Dhabi – the Louvre Abu Dhabi (2017), Qasr Al Hosn (2018); in Dahran – King Abdulla Aziz Center (2017); in Dubai – Etihad Museum (2017), Art Jameel; in Doha – Museum of Islamic Art (2008); Mathaf (2010), Qatar National Library (2019), Qatar National Museum (2019) and in Kuwait City – the Sheikh Abdulla Al Salem Cultural Center (2018). These museum developments have been part of large-scale national development frameworks such as the *Qatar National Vision 2030* the government's US\$15 billion master plan, which provides a framework for Qatar's development and outlines a number of significant high-profile projects, including the Qatar National Museum which opened in March 2019 (Ministry of Development Planning and Services n.d.). Similar plans exist in other Gulf States such as the *New Kuwait Masterplan* (New Kuwait n.d.). These development plans set out, in a similar way to Abu Dhabi's, *Plan Abu Dhabi 2030*, the national and global outlook for both Kuwait's and Qatar's futures (Abu Dhabi Urban Planning Council 2007).

Within the West, this move has largely been understood within the context of the development of entrepreneurial cities, which has been a significant feature of neoliberal capitalist societies (Harvey 1989; Hubbard and Hall 1998; Sassen 2001; Massey 2007). Within the literature surrounding cities it is argued that a shift in governmental focus from a largely public welfare centred system, to a more external focused corporate system, marks an entrepreneurial shift within cities. Harvey (1989) has argued that changes in city governance have led to a shift from an approach based on managerialism to one based on entrepreneurialism. Through the entrepreneurial approach cities strived to create an attractive environment to attract businesses, tourists in order to increase economic growth (*ibid.*). Hubbard and Hall suggest that 'the new urban entrepreneurialism typically rests, then, on public-private partnerships focusing on investment and economic development with the speculative construction of place rather than amelioration of conditions within a particular territory as its immediate (though by no means exclusive) political and economic goal' (1998: 8). Cities such as London and New York were considered entrepreneurial as they were supported and financed by private-sector agencies and institutions rather than public government institutions (*ibid.*). The result was that governments were increasingly developing 'characteristics once distinctive to businesses – risk taking, inventiveness, promotion and profit motivation', which are considered entrepreneurial in nature (*ibid.*: 2). Within this model the city becomes 'entrepreneurial' through urban development and city branding resulting in increased competitive advantage over less-entrepreneurial cities. The entrepreneurial city has been analysed as a response to industrial decline and investment in the West during the 1980s and 1990s (Zukin 1995: 8). However, the entrepreneurial city model has largely been explored within the context of the West (*ibid.*) and to a lesser extent Asia (Jessop and Sum 2001), and therefore cannot be automatically applied to developments within non-Western contexts. Further this model is suggestive uniform of patterns of development where local cities are spurred to change from global waves of investment. This does not account for the myriad of economic bases from which development begin, their political governance and historical background, and their pre-existing heritage landscapes.

In the case of Gulf cities, they are characterised by unique socio-cultural developments that have emerged from the development of vast amounts of oil wealth (Khalaf 2006: 245). They

> Show a very different progression to the entrepreneurial city, it is not about neo-liberalism, it is about the development of oil rich societies and the associated socio-cultural developments...it even differs to other oil producing Islamic Middle Eastern societies such as Iran, Iraq, Algeria, Nigeria and Venezuela in standards of wealth, income per capita, population size and particular developmental needs such as reliance on massive imported expatriate labor.
>
> (*ibid*)

Rapid development has characterised city development in many of the Gulf States (*ibid.*; Elsheshtawy 2008). This notion of speed is apparent in that these cities are often referred to as 'sudden cities, instant cities, and rapidly urbanizing cities' (Elsheshtawy 2008: 258–259). Furthermore, as I noted in chapter one, the role of tribal kinship structures, religion and economics are significant aspects of Gulf Society (Heard-Bey 2004; Fox, Moutada-Sabbah and Al-Mutawa 2006b; Khalaf 2006). Ponzini notes '[c]ompared to typical western democratic contexts, the separation between public and private sectors in Abu Dhabi is practically non-existent because the same actors have key positions in public decision making and in the management of private companies (2011: 254). As such the ruling elite have maintained complete control of the state and the development and dissemination of national identity narratives. The importance of this for heritage is that the narratives that are produced are connected to kinship and tribal structure and not public private relationships as would be expected in the entrepreneurial city. However, in contrast, emerging Gulf cities have materialised using large-scale iconic architecture and exclusive city zoning becoming showcases of modernity, progress and prestige (Khalaf 2002; Elsheshtawy 2008).

Integral to the cultural heritage franchise is the use of internationally renowned architects to develop buildings that become landmarks for the city (Jencks 2005). The importance of high-profile architecture for Abu Dhabi is apparent in the way that it is presented within the promotion of the project. Like Bilbao, Abu Dhabi wants to be seen by the world. In setting out the project details in chapter one I mentioned that the architects for the five cultural institutions were: Frank Gehry for the Guggenheim Abu Dhabi, Jean Nouvel for the Louvre Abu Dhabi, Foster + Partners for the Zayed National Museum, Tadao Ando for the Maritime Museum and the late Zaha Hadid for the Performing Arts Centre, all of whom are Pritzker Prize-winning architects.

The heritage discourse that surrounds the developments suggests that the cultural institutions on Saadiyat Island were being created specifically to be cultural icons, 'symbols', for Abu Dhabi. For example in the Guggenheim Abu Dhabi section of the *Cultural District* exhibition at Emirates Palace it specifically stated that '[a] primary objective of the Guggenheim program is to design and construct a public building for Abu Dhabi that will be of extraordinary architectural and historical significance'.[5] Architectural plans for the museum feature significantly within the exhibition at Emirates Palace and the *Saadiyat Story* exhibition at Manarat al Saadiyat. Both exhibitions featured panels explaining in detail the architectural vision and models of the proposed museum by stressing the incorporation of local elements. The *Saadiyat Story* exhibition drew further attention to the importance of the architecture of the museum as it presented the Guggenheim Abu Dhabi's plans to develop an architecture gallery within the museum.

The architectural design of the Louvre Abu Dhabi features a geometric lace dome that hovers above the museum's internal structures. The design for the museum draws on local elements, Nouvel's 'geometric lace dome was inspired by the interlaced palm leaves traditionally used as roofing material and resulting in an enchanting ray of light' (Tourism Development Investment Corporation n.d.[d]). The dome of the completed museum sits above fifty-five buildings that form the basis of the museum's internal structure. The design of the roof creates reflections of light within the museum's internal space, which really captivates the visitors' attention (Figure 4.1). The buildings are set out to symbolically resemble an old medina featuring

Figure 4.1 Interior view of the Louvre Abu Dhabi.
Source: Photograph by the Author, March 2018.

houses, streets and a square. Ultimately, Nouvel wanted to 'create a meeting place' (Somers Cocks 2017) and 'a neighbourhood of art, rather than a building' (Wainwright 2017). These observations suggest that Abu Dhabi is using physical architecture to establish the project's credentials globally. Elsheshtawy suggested that Saadiyat Island was 'trying to establish itself as a regional centre by using local and traditional architectural elements and establishing global techniques and processes (2011: Interview; See also Elsheshtawy 2008). The result of this is that, 'these two factors produce architecture that represents a fusion between East and West' (*ibid*.). Incorporating traditional aspects in to architecture is not a new phenomenon. The Burj Al Arab, which opened in 1999, was designed by architect Tom Wright when he was employed by Atkins Architects (WKK Architects n.d.). The architects 'design brief was to create an icon for Dubai, a building that would become synonymous with the place' (*ibid*.). In addition to its iconic design the hotel is also the tallest single structure hotel on a man-made island (*ibid*.). The design for the Burj Al Arab hotel draws its inspiration from the Arabian Dhow Sail, which is linked to the UAE's seafaring history.

The Burj Khalifa in the Emirate of Dubai was designed by Skidmore, Owings and Merrill and was completed in 2010. The design for the Burj Khalifa 'was inspired by the geometries of a regional desert flower and the patterning systems embodied in Islamic architecture' (Skidmore, Owings and Merrill n.d.). At the time of writing the Burj Khalifa was the world's tallest building standing at 828 metres, however, Saudi Arabia's proposed Kingdom Tower was slated to overtake this record. Competition for iconic architecture is so intense that Saudi Arabia has yet to announce the exact height of the new tower amidst fears of competition (Brass 2011). According to the architect's website 'the design for the 162-story tower combines local cultural influences with cutting edge technology' (Skidmore, Owings and Merrill n.d.). The importance of these examples is that while the UAE strives to modernise and to develop iconic structures they are heavily influenced by the heritage of the UAE; Islam; and contemporary, and arguably Western, architectural practice.

Architecture then, is considered important within the process of cultural heritage franchising as it is used to create a landmark (Jencks 2005), which becomes a central feature of the museum's brand (Caldwell 2000: 33). This has created new audiences for museums as the building itself attracts visitors, as well as the collection. Or in some cases it is the building alone that attracts the visitor. This trend has led to the use of high-profile 'star' architects to build a range of new museums such as Daniel Libeskind's Imperial War Museum, Manchester, United Kingdom; Daniel Libeskind's Jewish Museum, Berlin, Germany; Frank Gehry's Guggenheim Museum Bilbao, Spain; and Frank Lloyd Wright's Guggenheim, New York, United States to name just a few. Auge notes that, 'even if these projects refer, in principle, to the historical or geographical context, they are quickly captured by worldwide consumption: the influx of tourists who come from all over the world to sanction their success' (2009: xv). Nouvel, Gehry and Foster + Partners all insist on the local appropriateness of their designs but they are all still part of what Auge suggests is a 'dominant aesthetic', which marginalises local expressions (*ibid.*: xiv). The Guggenheim Abu Dhabi has been criticised locally for bringing 'striking cultural juxtapositions since the museum is named after a major Jewish American family and designed by a Jewish American architect that will rise in the capital of a country that does not recognise Israel as a nation' (Ameen 2006). This suggests that the physical elements of the museum are also an important element within the cultural heritage franchising but that regardless of the architects' attempts they are not always seen to be culturally appropriate.

Ultimately, Gulf cities are adopting elements of contemporary global city rhetoric and prioritising global branding, in this sense they are displaying competitive and entrepreneurial elements of development within distinctive Gulf development models. This concept is particularly relevant in Abu Dhabi, where 'traditional' tribal structure and 'global practices' work together, though not always in harmony, to shape the city's social, economic and political development (Davidson 2009). Fox, Moutada-Sabbah and Al-Mutawa illustrate how 'globalization meshes with traditionalism rather than being an imported total package of lifestyles and values' in the Gulf States (2006b: 9). The implications of this for heritage production is that global processes and categorisations are used in a way that is deemed to fit local social structures and norms; they are hybrid (Wakefield 2017b).

I noted in the previous section how during the nineteenth-century architecture was used to evoke national and civic pride. In Abu Dhabi global display is supported through the development of large-scale architectural projects that have increasingly been used to convey elite global status and the emergence of the UAE's international power. As such large-scale architectural developments are used to address the intensified competition between places. According to Auge, architecture has been used to connect places to the global system through celebrity architects who are commissioned to produced 'monuments' that symbolise a place's status within the global system (2009: xv). He notes that '[e]ven if these architectural projects refer, in principle, to the historical or geographical context, they are quickly captured by worldwide consumption' (*ibid.*). Evans has argued that by 'associating a place with a cultural icon works to brand and differentiate places in peoples' minds by establishing a place's 'creative character' (2003: 421). The idea of a symbolic economy was established by Zukin (1995) and considers the way in which culture is used within the development of entrepreneurial cities. As I have argued elsewhere, the idea of the symbolic economy is highly relevant within the context of Abu Dhabi (Wakefield 2017b). Zukin suggests 'that a significant number of new public spaces owe their particular shape and form to the intertwining of cultural symbols and economic capital' (1995: 3). She goes on to argue that this system is developed by 'officials and investors whose ability to deal with symbols of growth yields "real" results in real estate development, new businesses and jobs' (*ibid.*: 7). The symbolic role of cultural heritage franchising is therefore important.

Jencks (2005) discusses in his book, *The Iconic Building,* how architects who have developed global recognition and public acclaim have become synonymous with the development of iconic architecture. The architects involved in the development of Saadiyat Island's Cultural District are all important to the development project not just because of their architectural expertise but because of their established names, and their ability to attract global press attention and prizes. Alvarez Sainz (2012) has noted that building the Guggenheim Museum Bilbao as a landmark enables people to associate the museum and its architecture with Bilbao. Rauen has suggested that 'the GMB made Bilbao visible, and, in doing so, it also made visible a shift in the global organisation of production' (2001: 288), which follows Dick's (2003) notion of 'visitibility'. McNeill (2000) on the other hand argues that the Guggenheim Museum Bilbao was a political and economic project to not only boost tourism but to also reinforce Basque nationalism and Bilbao's political position in the region. The development of cultural heritage franchises can therefore be linked to the ambitions and interests of governments and elites in cities around the world, which is connected to the emergence of entrepreneurial activities and global display.

However Stephenson and Knight have suggested that architecture has been used in the UAE not only as an element of branding but to also 'celebrate political autonomy and self-governance' (2010: 282). Size also plays a significant role in the development of flagship museums. This is evident within the way in which the Saadiyat Cultural District project is promoted. It was reported in *The National* (2009) newspaper that the Cultural District on Saadiyat Island is 'planned to be the largest concentration of premier cultural institutions in the World'. One of the issues that this raises is that it tends to side-line the more everyday aspects of heritage in favour of larger high-profile global projects.

International mega-events

International events also contribute to the way in which cities make themselves globally visible (Dicks 2003: 17). Pratt has noted that '[i]n the past three decades, mega-events have reached a size that has made them transformative ventures for entire cities, regions, and sometimes whole countries. Mega-events leave a material legacy as large-scale infrastructure, which serve as a global landmark for the event and the physical location for the event' (2010: 17; see also Preuss 2007; Gratton and Preuss 2008). It is these physical traces of global events that become part of the national legacy of the hosting nation, which has come to symbolise aspects of national identity and place-making. Ren suggests that the Beijing Olympics bid and preparations were used as an opportunity to present 'China's rise as a new global power backed by a dynamic national economy and consolidated under the rule of the communist party' (2008: 179). However, the Olympics have created problems for host nations when they have to deal with 'the legacy effect[s]' of the events, especially in terms of unrealised income and over expenditure (Pratt 2010: 17). Furthermore, the effects of the 2018 global economic crisis has meant that interest and funding for mega-events had declined in Western nations (Russell *et al.* 2014: 197).

The relevance of hosting international mega-events in some countries may be declining, yet they continue to play an important role within the Gulf. In the past mega-events have also played a hegemonic role in continuing to reinforce the dominance of the West over non-Western countries (*ibid.*), especially through the allocation of events and the decision-making processes (Gupta 2009: 1779). Gupta argues that globalisation and the rise of wealthy non-Western nations have challenged the power relations of international events and provided increased opportunities for non-Western countries to bid and host mega-events (*ibid.*). Within the Gulf States of Bahrain, Qatar and the UAE we can see the emergence of this trend with both Bahrain and Abu Dhabi hosting the Grand Prix annually, Dubai hosting the Dubai Expo 2020 and Doha hosting the FIFA 2020 World Cup. Expo 2020 is estimated to attract around '25 million visitors between October 2020 and April 2021' (Colliers International 2019a: 2). In the UAE, a number of annual art events are held that include the: *Sharjah Biennial* in Sharjah, *Art Dubai* in Dubai, and *Abu Dhabi Art* in Abu Dhabi (Ali 2014). In July 2019 it was announced that the Abu

Dhabi Department of Culture and Tourism had established a 'mega events fund' of 'Dh600 million'. The fund is part of the 'Ghadan 21 programme, a Dh50bn package of reforms by the Abu Dhabi government to stimulate the local economy' and 'will focus on developing entertainment and business activities and festivals…aimed at attracting investors and top talent to work, invest, live and visit Abu Dhabi' (Kamel 2019). These examples illustrate the prominence placed on large-scale international events in the Gulf. The non-West has therefore emerged as a financially lucrative market for mega-events (Russell *et al.* 2014: 198). It is yet to be seen how the Covid-19 global pandemic will impact these large-scale global events in the Gulf.

International Touring Exhibitions work in a similar way to mega-events, however, generally on a smaller scale. Lai (2004) has argued that international touring exhibitions tend to attract the attention of the global media and international tourists. The success of the Tutankhamen travelling exhibitions and others, such as the *Picasso: Masterpieces from the Musée National Picasso, Paris* exhibition, which toured in Abu Dhabi, Canada, Helsinki, Madrid, Moscow, Richmond, San Francisco, Seattle, Sydney and Tokyo (Art Gallery of Ontario n.d.) has led to the global recognition by cultural institutions of the benefits of staging such exhibitions. The global appeal of Tutankhamen's history has been recognised by the Cairo government, which has seen a series of different international travelling exhibitions touring the world from 1972 to 2013. Since the discovery of Tutankhamen's tomb and vast grave goods in 1922 by the archaeologists' interest in Egyptian artefacts has gained in popularity (British Museum n.d.[a]). The first Tutankhamen exhibition, *Treasures of Tutankhamun*, was held at the British Museum in 1972 in partnership with the Cairo Museum in Egypt. According to the museum's website the exhibition was 'the most popular exhibition in the Museum's history' and attracted 'over 1,650,000 visitors', making it the most popular successful exhibition (British Museum n.d.[b]).

Due to the success of the Tutankhamen touring exhibitions, and the limited display space at the Egyptian Museum in Tahir Square, Cairo the Ministry of Culture has set out its plans for a new large-scale museum, the Grand Egyptian Museum (Grand Egyptian Museum n.d.). The proposed museum will be situated near the pyramids of Giza and will be designed by Heneghan Peng Architects, in Al-Remayah Square in Egypt. The museum is expected to 'contain 24,000m^2 of permanent exhibition space, almost four football fields in size, a children's museum, conference and education facilities, a conservation centre and extensive gardens on the 50ha site' (Heneghan Peng Architects n.d.). The reputation that the Tutankhamen exhibitions hold is likely to serve as an important aspect of the way the new museum brands itself. However, the protests in Tahir Square, Cairo have served as the focus of Cairo's political unrest during the Arab Spring. This has impacted Cairo's reputation as a safe place for tourism, which has dramatically affected the Egyptian Museum.

International touring exhibitions are often used to promote bilateral accord and cross-cultural co-operation. In 2007, during the time I was living in

Bahrain, the Bahrain National Museum hosted the Tutankhamen touring exhibition *Treasures of Egypt*. The exhibition ran from April 11, 2007 to July 31, 2007 and featured 122 objects from the Cairo Museum in Egypt (Torr 2007). Significantly it was the first time that an exhibition featuring Egyptian antiquities had toured in the Arabian Peninsula (*ibid.*; see also Bew 2007; Fibiger 2011: 193). Fibiger notes that the introduction to the exhibition catalogue draws attention to the political and cosmopolitan nature of the partnership between the Bahraini government and the National Museum in Cairo 'the civilization of Bahrain will meet with another civilization equal in years of history and significance to mankind', and that the museum was obliged to, 'foster bridges of heritage amidst global community through the dialogue of culture' (2011: 193). Fibiger goes on to note that '[t]his text is clearly phrased in UNESCO "universal" terminology with its emphasis on words such as "mankind", "dialogues of heritage", and "dialogue of culture"' (*ibid.*). The importance of these exhibitions is that they are promoted in such a way that highlights the necessity of global co-operation and exchange. Furthermore, Aubrey (Forthcoming) discusses Sheikha Mai's role in developing Bahrain's diplomatic links abroad through the processes of exhibition exchange.

The result is that cosmopolitanism emerges as the central tenet of global identity formation. Yet cultural heritage institutions are often the preserve of particular nations and as such are intricately linked to the political motivations and objectives of the nation. The importance of international touring exhibitions to some of the larger cultural heritage organisations is reflected in the existence of specific departments dedicated to this role. The British Museum, for example, has a dedicated international loans section. The museum's transnational focus is evident on its website which states, 'the international touring exhibition programme allows this rich and diverse collection and museum expertise to be brought to museums and galleries around the world' (The British Museum n.d.[c]). The website goes on to explicitly state that the museum is working to develop its image as a national museum to a global museum, in particular 'a museum of the world for the world' (*ibid.*). These statements are indicative of the way in which the museum is moving towards a more globally focused approach.

Similarly, the Louvre Museum has devised a series of high-profile touring exhibitions. The museum developed seven touring exhibitions for the High Museum of Art, Atlanta, in a partnership that ran between October 2006 and 2009. During the course of the partnership the touring exhibitions attracted 'over 1.3 million visitors' (Art Knowledge News 2010). The exhibitions series, *Louvre Atlanta*, represented at the time an unprecedented partnership, which took almost five-hundred items from the Louvre Museum in Paris to the High Museum of Art in Atlanta, many of which had never before been seen in the United States (*ibid.*). Yet international travelling exhibitions have been criticised by Kratz and Karp 'as they rarely, if ever, reach less developed countries, which from the organisers' viewpoint lack both funds that such exhibitions require and a sufficiently elaborate infrastructure to support them' (2007: 12). International touring exhibitions in this sense are elite cultural commodities, which are obtained for their short-term value and impact. As such the way in which goods and services are experienced is important (Pine and Gilmore 1999: ix). In the case of the international touring exhibition it is the experience and excitement that blockbuster exhibitions provide that taps in to this market. In a similar way the cultural heritage franchise offers the visitor the experience of visiting branded and globally visible museums. In the case of international partnerships these do not necessarily have to be permanent, rather the ability to trade in transient and mobile heritage has come to be a marker of prestige and global identification.

Within the current debates concerning the relationship between globalisation and cultural heritage two main arguments dominate. The first suggests that one consequence of globalisation is the homogenisation and Westernisation of culture (Featherstone 1990; Ritzer 2010). The second argues that globalisation leads to the strengthening of local heritage in response to the threatening forces of globalisation (Harvey 1989; Khalaf 2000; Fox, Moutada-Sabbah and Al-Mutawa 2006b). If we are to understand and explore the dynamics of transnational heritage production the discussion needs to be extended to analyse how heritage processes are put to use within transnational contexts and the broader circumstances – social, economic and political – that brought them in to being. I have shown how assumptions regarding the boundedness of national heritage are not helpful in illuminating our understanding of global heritage processes and the questions that I pose within this book. One way to address this is through a consideration of transnational heritage as a hybrid process.

Notes

1 *Splendours of Mesopotamia*, March 29–June 27, 2011; *Treasures of the World's Cultures*, April 18–July 17, 2012 and *A History of the World in 100 Objects*, April 23–August 1, 2014 Manarat Al Saadiyat, Abu Dhabi.
2 The choice to name the gallery after the late ruler was part of the 2018 *Year of Zayed* commemorative activities. 2018 was designed the *Year of Zayed* to commemorate 100 years since the birth of Sheikh Zayed I Ministry of Presidential Affairs.
3 Previously the Zayed National Museum came under the umbrella of the TDIC. After the merger the two departments became known as the Department for Culture and Tourism (DCT Abu Dhabi).
4 Al-Mubarak, 'Session 1'. *The World's in a Museum* symposium was organised by the Louvre Abu Dhabi to celebrate the museum's first year of operation. The symposium took place on the November 10–11, 2018.
5 Observation: November 11, 2010.

5 Cultural capacity and professional practice

Education has played a significant role in the development of museums and heritage institutions since the nineteenth century in European nations (Bennett 1995; Harrison 2013). However, the relationship between pedagogy and heritage, particularly in non-Western contexts where heritage as an industry is still an emerging phenomenon, has been lesser explored. What I mean here is the explicit move to institutionalise and professionalise heritage and its implications for the development of the cultural heritage industry in Abu Dhabi. The proliferation of government-funded museum and heritage developments in the UAE, and the broader Gulf States, have drawn on the expertise and knowledge of international museum and heritage practitioners to varying degrees in both the planning and delivery stages. Alongside these developments is a recognised need to 'transfer' international expertise to the Gulf, which connects with official mandates to develop knowledge-based economies in the region. The result has been the development of professional training by bringing international 'experts' to work alongside Gulf nationals in a process of knowledge transfer. This process of transfer has resulted in the development of bespoke in-house training and university-based museum and heritage- training. This chapter analyses how expertise is used to develop and 'institutionalise' museum and heritage practice in the Gulf and how these developments are linked to the politics of heritage. In doing so, this chapter argues, drawing on the work of Kreps (2003: 116) that the professionalisation of the heritage sector in the Gulf needs to develop an 'appropriate museology' that is sensitive to the unique local and regional context of the Gulf, and in doing so challenge the dominant heritage discourses of the West.

Building capacity: cultural heritage, Emiratization and knowledge development

Developing Abu Dhabi into a knowledge economy has been an essential aspect of the government's agenda, which was set out in *Plan Abu Dhabi 2030* (Abu

Dhabi Urban Planning Council 2007). As a part of this process, the government has placed emphasis on 'Emiratization' as a priority area for development (Abu Dhabi Education Council n.d.[a]). Emiratization is aimed at developing the skills and knowledge of Emirati nationals within targeted industry sectors through formal education and work-based training.[1] Emiratization is essentially a nationalisation scheme to replace expatriate workers. Capacity building is further linked to national identity and the nation-building process. For example the mission statement for the Abu Dhabi Education Council (ADEC) states:

> The Abu Dhabi government aspires to transform the Emirate into an innovation-based knowledge society. Its vision is to build an oasis for the pursuit of knowledge and discovery, strongly connected to the global society and economy and yet deeply rooted in the culture and heritage of the Emirate.
>
> (Abu Dhabi Education Council n.d.[b])

Statements such as this suggest that knowledge and cultural development are intimately linked to economic diversification in Abu Dhabi. Similar patterns can be observed in Qatar: for example the Qatar National Vision states, '[a] knowledge-based economy characterized by innovation; entrepreneurship; excellence in education; a world-class infrastructural backbone; the efficient delivery of public services; and transparent and accountable government' (Ministry of Development Planning and Services n.d.: 29). Al-Roubaie and Abdul-Wahab have highlighted the relationship between learning and knowledge societies. They suggest that '[i]n a knowledge society the attitude toward learning also has to change, i.e. a new culture needs to develop that exhibits learning as a priority for human advancement' (2009: 233–234). The process of knowledge translation is therefore connected to new priorities in terms of learning and development in the UAE. At a broad level then, capacity building is used in Abu Dhabi to support the creation of new industries and institutions through the development of training and technical assistance. A measured shift towards developing new programmes focusing on art, cultural heritage and museology is evident within the educational system in Abu Dhabi.[2]

Knowledge development and nationalisation

At the same time, that heritage is being developed and institutionalised, universities in the UAE are developing programmes to support the emerging industry. Both branch campuses, which have been set up in partnership with international branded universities, as well as national universities, have begun to develop programmes that focus on arts and cultural heritage. Nusseibeh explained from his knowledge and involvement of strategy development within Abu Dhabi, working with both the current and the former rulers, that a critical government directive was to create cultural opportunities and to build local capacity (2011: Interview).[3] Capacity building has become embedded within the globalising discourses of the United Nations. For example, the United Nations Development Programme (UNDP) has defined capacity as 'the ability of individuals, institutions, and societies to perform functions, solve problems, and set and achieve objectives in a sustainable manner' and capacity development is defined as 'the process through which the abilities to do so are, strengthened, adapted and maintained over time' (Balassanian and Colville 2006). Capacity development in this sense is people centred. For UNESCO capacity development 'is seen as a form of people-centred change that entails working with groups of individuals to achieve improvements in approaches to managing cultural and natural heritage' (UNESCO 1972: 4).

Education and cultural heritage development are, therefore, explicitly linked to economic growth and diversification in this context. As Nusseibeh states 'the basic strategy [for Abu Dhabi] is that culture is an essential part of education and education is complementary to culture' (2011: Interview). This focus on education and growth links to Florida's 'creative class' in which he argues that 'human capital, or talent, has become the key factor of production', which serves to bring competitive advantages 'to places that can quickly mobilize the talent, resources and capabilities' (2004: 49). Educational development features significantly within the discourses of heritage. The Emirate's focus on education has been particularly apparent within exhibitions relating to the developments on Saadiyat Island. For example, the introductory section of the *Saadiyat Cultural District* exhibition at Emirates Palace featured text panels providing evidence of how the government has linked development to education and knowledge. The following text was on display:

> The real wealth of a country is not its material wealth, it is its people. They are the real strength from which we draw pride and the trees from which we receive shade. It is our conviction in this reality that directs us to put all efforts in educating people.[4]

Furthermore official statements made by the government explicitly link educational development to Emirati national identity. One way that this is done is by linking statements that Sheikh Zayed I, made in the past with contemporary developments in Abu Dhabi. For example, 'Section One: The Story of Abu Dhabi' in the *Saadiyat Story* exhibition at Manarat Al Saadiyat, features a quotation by Sheikh Zayed I, which states, '[t]he prosperity that we have witnessed has taught us to build our country with education and knowledge and nurture generations of educated men and women'.[5] Capacity building in this sense is linked directly to nationalism and nation-building. National pride, patriotism and supporting the government's vision are all used to promote the importance of education, heritage and the UAE's overall development.

However this leads to the production of 'un-cosmopolitan values' (Nussbaum 1996) that are essentially attached to the process of knowledge transfer. The hybrid make-up of the workforce is resisted through the nationalisation project. The Emiratization process is in-effect a response to threatening powers of transnational actors in the UAE who are deemed a threat to nationalism and national identity (Starkey 2012: 25). The naturalisation project emerges as an un-cosmopolitan response to the problem of the dominant numbers of transnational actors in the workforce. As such, the power remains with the Emirati nation at all times. So much so that the transnational worker is constantly reminded that they are 'a temporary guest' in the service of the state.

Transplant universities

Within Abu Dhabi, and more broadly the UAE, several transplant (or franchise) universities have been developed that are modelled on education systems in the UK and the US (Table 5.1). Within Abu Dhabi, this has led to the establishment of several university courses on museums and heritage at the foundation, undergraduate and graduate levels. It has also resulted in

Table 5.1 List of Transplant Universities in the UAE

American University in Dubai
American University in The Emirates
American University of Ras Al Khaimah
American University of Sharjah
British University in Dubai
Canadian University Dubai
ENGECON Dubai
Heriot-Watt University
Insead – The Business School for The World, Abu Dhabi
London Business School
Middlesex University Dubai
Murdoch University Dubai
New York Institute of Technology Abu Dhabi
New York University, Abu Dhabi (NYU Abu Dhabi)
Paris-Sorbonne University, Abu Dhabi
Rochester Institute of Technology – Dubai (RIT Dubai)
Royal College of Surgeons in Ireland – Dubai (RCSI Dubai)
Saint Joseph University
The University of Manchester Middle East Center (Previously Manchester University Business School)
University of Atlanta Dubai
University of Balamand in Dubai
University of Strathclyde Business School – Dubai Campus
University of Wollongong – Dubai Campus

Source: Table compiled by the author.

a review of heritage education in tertiary schools. However, the spread of Western-style education within non-Western nations is not a neutral process. As Stevens, Miller-Idris and Shami note '[h]ow universities organize knowledge about the rest of the world' is important (2018: 1–2). Furthermore, how that knowledge is translated into new regions, especially non-Western regions is particularly problematic. As such, formal education has been used as a critical strategy for positioning Western knowledge processes as hegemonic (Said 1978) and universal (Tuhiwai-Smith 2012). Within Abu Dhabi, and the UAE, several transplant (or franchise) universities have been developed. These universities are similar to cultural heritage franchises as they are branded campuses set up by one nation in partnership with universities from abroad.

The development of transplant universities works within, and alongside, the processes of globalisation. Furthermore, transplant universities operate in a similar way to cultural heritage franchises. Global satellite campuses are generally set up as intergovernmental agreements, which are akin to cultural heritage franchises in terms of the exchange process. The transplant university is usually developed in response to a local need for specific industry training. In Abu Dhabi, one of the industries that transplant university education is addressing the need for trained Emirati heritage professionals and the over-reliance on international heritage professionals, as noted in the previous section. The need for cultural heritage and museum studies courses has led universities such as the New York University Abu Dhabi Institute (NYU Abu Dhabi) and the Paris-Sorbonne Abu Dhabi to offer postgraduate courses in museums and heritage training. Similarly, University College London (UCL) has set up a satellite campus in Qatar focusing on master's courses in archaeology, conservation and museum studies. UCL Qatar is based in Education City, which features several US satellite universities such as Georgetown, Northwestern and Texas A&M. The development of UCL was a direct response to Qatar's developing cultural heritage sector and the government's focus on Qatarization (for a discussions on Qatar see Exell 2013b, 2016b). However, UCL will be withdrawing its name from the Doha institution from 2020, which is reflective of a lack of support for certain branch institutions in the home nation.

In Abu Dhabi, the satellite campus of NYU Abu Dhabi and the Paris-Sorbonne Abu Dhabi are responding to the needs of the Saadiyat Island project by providing museums and heritage training explicitly based on established international models in New York and Paris. NYU Abu Dhabi's permanent campus is located on Saadiyat Island close to the planned museum developments. Press articles and course outlines from the Paris-Sorbonne Abu Dhabi Campus and NYU Abu Dhabi provide valuable information about the political positioning of these courses. The Paris-Sorbonne Abu Dhabi's website also describes how the institution's undergraduate course in Archaeology and the History of Art and the Master's in Art History and Museums are targeted at tackling the needs of local society and the developing arts and cultural heritage sector in Abu Dhabi (Paris-Sorbonne University Abu Dhabi n.d.). Newspaper coverage of the development of the Paris-Sorbonne Abu Dhabi has also focused on promoting the university's local role and global authority. For example, Jean Yvs De Cara, executive director of the Paris-Sorbonne Abu Dhabi, is cited in the press stating 'Paris-Sorbonne Abu Dhabi, as an institution, exerts cultural leadership by creating courses that cater to emerging needs and meets the region's cultural expectations'.[6] The overall aim of the Master's was to prepare students for careers at the Louvre Abu Dhabi, the Guggenheim Abu Dhabi and other cultural heritage institutions by providing both theoretical and practical tuition in Abu Dhabi and France.

NYU Abu Dhabi's website stated that 'the notion of an internationally and cross-culturally "shared heritage" of material culture is the central theme of the entire program' (NYU Abu Dhabi 2017a). The cultural heritage courses are aligned to the cosmopolitan and global outlook that Abu Dhabi wishes to present. Which also ties into the broader global aims of NYU, which has also resulted in a further branch campus opening in 2013 in Shanghai (Daley 2011). John Sexton, NYU's president, had plans to make NYU a global university by developing 'a worldwide network with NYU's name on it' (*ibid.*), which is arguably similar to Frank Gehry's global Guggenheim model. Like the Louvre Abu Dhabi and the Guggenheim Abu Dhabi, NYU Abu Dhabi is entirely funded by the Abu Dhabi government (Hamdan 2012a). Notably, NYU Abu Dhabi's permanent campus is located on Saadiyat Island close to the Cultural District. It is perhaps, therefore, no surprise that official statements from the university suggest that 'studying, discussing and visiting these institutions are an important element within the course' (NYU Abu Dhabi 2017a).

NYU Abu Dhabi's pre-professional and liberal arts courses incorporate modules on museums and cultural heritage issues. In 2012, the following models were being offered as part of NYU Abu Dhabi's Liberal Arts Programme and the Pre-Professional Course in Museums and Cultural Heritage.

* Heritage, History, and Memory in the Modern Middle East
* Introduction to Museum Studies
* Meaning of Museums
* Multiple Lives of the Work of Art
* Shared Cultural Heritage: Practices and Perspectives
* Museums, Communities, and Public Art
* Museum Collections and Exhibitions
* Cabinets of Wonder
* International Issues in Cultural Policy
* Sharing Heritage
* Exhibition Industry

(*ibid*)

By Spring 2018, the modules offered by NYU had changed considerably. Only two of the courses offered in 2012 remained as indicated by the below list.

- Heritage, History, and Memory in the Modern Middle East
- Anthropology of Indigenous Australia: Art, Politics and Cultural Futures
- Museums in a Global Context
- Introduction to Museum Studies
- World Heritage Sites and Universal Collections
- Places of Suffering as Global Heritage Sites
- Shipwrecks and Seascapes
- Sharing Heritage of the Arabian Trade Routes
- Museum History, Theory and Practice: Case Study, Berlin

The changes at NYU Abu Dhabi indicate a shift towards a more heritage focused approach, which is further evident in the development of the 'Dhakira', Center for Emirati and Global Heritage Studies (NYU Abu Dhabi 2017b). This change is perhaps not surprising since cultural heritage is high on the national agenda of the Emirates.

NYU Abu Dhabi's website states that 'the notion of an internationally and cross-culturally "shared heritage" of material culture is the central theme of the entire program' (NYU Abu Dhabi 2017a). Illustrating that NYU Abu Dhabi's pre-professional course is aligned to the cosmopolitan and global outlook, which Abu Dhabi wishes to present. However, the university's website is telling of the predominance of interpretations of heritage as a tangible process. As the website goes on to state:

> The types of objects, and (museum) collections of objects, to which this notion relates, derive from, and belong to, all realms and ages of human productivity. The academic disciplines studying these objects and collections, such as anthropology, archaeology, history, art history, history of science, and modern media studies, inform the palette of heuristic perspectives from which students investigate processes and traditions of cultural heritage formation and preservation.

However, the museum and heritage courses have not run continuously due to insufficient student interest. A review of NYU Abu Dhabi's website in April 2017 indicated that the last time the course ran was Fall 2014 (*ibid.*). At the time of writing, NYU Abu Dhabi had plans to develop a Master of Fine Arts and a minor in heritage studies.

The presence of transplant educational institutions has been the subject of discussion within Abu Dhabi's national press. An article appeared in May 2010 in *The National* newspaper, which discussed the development of courses at the Paris-Sorbonne Abu Dhabi (Dajani 2010). The article suggested that the Paris-Sorbonne was developing courses in response to local needs and that transplant education in Abu Dhabi is viewed similarly to attending a university in France without the need for travel. A student from the Paris-Sorbonne Abu Dhabi is quoted as having said '[w]e were not able to travel ourselves to Paris to study, so the Sorbonne was brought to us'. The *New York Times* has also picked up on the trend for transplant education in the Gulf. It was reported that '43,000 students applied to the university (NYU Abu Dhabi) last year, 15,489 of whom expressed interest in studying at the Abu Dhabi campus, which offered 150 spots in 2012' (Hamdan 2012a). The interest shown by students illustrates the strength of NYU's reputation and brand strategy in the education sector. Culturally then there are benefits to be had by developing transplant, and national, university education since it is not always possible due to the religious and cultural nuances for Emiratis to travel and study abroad.

In a similar way to the cultural heritage franchise, the transplant university model is based on predominantly Western methods, mainly taught by Western-educated scholars, most of whom have little or no experience of cultural heritage within the region when first entering the country. The *New York Times* reported that NYU Abu Dhabi 'professors are from N.Y.U.'s New York Campus, as well as Harvard, Stanford, and the Paris School of Economics' (*ibid.*). No mention was made of regional scholars and the level of local expertise within the university, which led to the Paris-Sorbonne Abu Dhabi and NYU Abu Dhabi being criticised locally. This criticism has focused on the Western-centric nature of these courses and their inappropriateness for Abu Dhabi. A review of the Paris-Sorbonne Abu Dhabi's Master's in Art History and Museum Studies programme reveals the Western-centric nature of the course as it divides the discipline in to 'Western Art' and 'Non-Western Art' (Paris-Sorbonne Abu Dhabi n.d.). Suggesting that how cultural heritage is translated into the university system is far from problematic.

A further concern is a reliance on bringing faculty from abroad to Abu Dhabi for brief periods. This issue is not exclusive to the UAE as UCL Qatar has also relied heavily on visiting lecturers to deliver teaching, especially in terms of regional expertise. The main reason for this is that suitably qualified academics are not always available locally. However, it predominantly reinforces the power of Western academic institutions and their increasing presence in non-Western nations. A further issue, which I briefly touched on above, is that there are currently few academics that have significant knowledge, expertise and experience of Gulf museology and heritage. In particular, the brochure for the Paris-Sorbonne Abu Dhabi Master's course in Art History and Museum Studies refers to faculty of the Paris-Sorbonne and the Ecole du Louvre; however, no mention is made to the staff's experience or knowledge of the Gulf region (*ibid.*). The issue of staffing is not exclusive to the UAE as Qatar faced similar problems. UCL Qatar, for example, has sought to address this by relying heavily on 'visiting lecturers to deliver teaching' who have 'specialist knowledge', which is beneficial not just for the students but also for the development of UCL Qatar's staff development in terms of knowledge exchange (Exell 2013b: 548). However, it also shows the weakness of the UCL Qatar model. International faculty also have to adapt to their pedagogical approach and content when they enter the region. International faculty have to obey the norms and rules of the Gulf State, adapt to varying levels of educational attainment and language skills (see Harkness and Levitt 2017). Arguably these are issues in any global university, however, in the Gulf States the autocratic nature of society also impacts upon the teaching context.

A more general issue that arises from academia in the Gulf is the issue of academic freedom. In autocratic states, it is much more common for academics to be fired for speaking out about what are considered to be political topics. *The New York Times* has picked up on the political nature of transplant education. The newspaper recently published an article discussing the dismissal of an academic from Peking University after they publicly criticised the Chinese government (Lewin 2013). This issue has become arguably more problematic since the Arab Spring. Since the onset of the Arab Spring the 'United Arab Emirates has tightened its laws regarding dissent, imposing jail terms for anyone who derides or caricatures the Gulf Arab country's rulers or state institutions on the web' (Gulf Business 2012). Censorship, therefore, has important implications for academics and heritage practitioners, and the freedom that they have to debate and analyse contemporary issues affecting the Gulf States.

National university and heritage developments

At a national level, the UAE's universities are, perhaps not surprisingly, more focused on Emirati aspects of heritage. The primary focus for Zayed University (ZU),[7] as a Federal institution, is on educating Emirati nationals. International students are, however, allowed to enrol in the university's Master's course. In Abu Dhabi, the campus is segregated by gender. Male students are educated on one side of the campus and female students on the opposite side. In Dubai, the campus is for female students only. However, for one afternoon a week, male students are taught in one wing of the university after the female students have left. Students do not live on campus at ZU. National provision in this sense is tightly controlled and structured, which aligns with the authoritarian societal values and familial structures.

At an undergraduate level, students can opt to take a course on Emirati identity. The Emirati Studies course at ZU was developed by the College of Humanities and Social Sciences. Bristol-Rhys described the aims of the Emirati Studies programme at ZU. 'Our Emirati Studies programme is more about Emirati identity and basic history. It covers a lot of the things that these people should have been taught at school' (2011: Interview). When I reviewed the syllabus for the Emirati Studies course, I found that the course offered modules in history, heritage and the archaeology of the UAE. Based on the need for locally focused courses such as these, this course offers a welcome alternative to the transplant model. The course remained popular with undergraduate students at ZU until 2018 when the course was withdrawn. The Emirati Studies course was withdrawn from the syllabi as it was being replaced by a new BA in Heritage Studies. The new BA was proposed to focus on modules in archaeology, history and museum and heritage studies. The undergraduate course was developed to further fulfil the needs of the developing cultural industry in the UAE.

Again, mainly in response to the Saadiyat developments, ZU developed a minor in curatorial practices and a Master of Arts in Museum Studies. The MA course was developed in partnership with The University of St Andrews by the College of Humanities and Social Sciences (CHSS) at Zayed University. An essential element of the master's course was to provide 'a locally-tailored approach that emphasises the history and heritage of the UAE and to provide students with the knowledge and skills to design, develop and administer exhibitions in line with international standards and best practice' (*ibid.*). However, much like the courses at NYU Abu Dhabi and the Paris-Sorbonne Abu Dhabi, this course predominantly focused on established western European models of instruction. I reviewed the course outline for the Master's at ZU, which consisted of the following core modules:

- Theory and Practice of Museums, Galleries, and Associated Organizations
- Modern and Contemporary Art (post 1945)
- Islamic Design, Art, and Architecture
- The History and Heritage of the United Arab Emirates
- Projects and Development of Professional Portfolio

(Zayed University n.d.)

Only two of these modules were locally targeted, focusing on Islamic art and the history and heritage of the UAE. The remaining modules focused on heritage methods, which were based on practices that have primarily emerged from western Europe. What was lacking was a critical analysis of alternate ways of working with and presenting heritage in the UAE. The evidence, therefore, suggested that national university education, like transplant university education, also draws on the dominant global heritage processes that have emerged from the West that are developed through the authorized heritage discourse. More generally, it serves to reinforce the cosmopolitanism nature of the heritage industry by linking national university education to global heritage discourses.

However, the MA in Museum Studies was discontinued, and the Curatorial Studies Minor was moved to the College of Arts and Creative

Enterprises (CACE). The Curatorial Studies course has seen an increase in student numbers since its placement in CACE; however, this is perhaps unsurprising given the College is more arts-focused than CHSS. At the time of writing, CACE was undertaking a large-scale review of the MA in Museum Studies. Since the opening of the Louvre Abu Dhabi provision of museum studies courses has come to the fore.

However, the challenge as Kreps argues in her discussion of museum development in Indonesia is to develop a 'participatory approach', which takes account of the community that 'builds on people's own concepts and systems of cultural heritage management' (2003: 116). Krep's makes a vital observation, which is highly relevant to the development of cultural heritage pedagogy in the UAE. Essentially, the development of museum and heritage education in the Gulf needs to respond and engage with critical scholarship in the field, developments in Gulf museology and heritage, the expertise of faculty and the student experience.

Bridging the divide

An important theme that emerged from my discussions with academics and heritage practitioners in Abu Dhabi was that Emiratis lacked formal museum and heritage training. However, there have been barriers in place that have prevented regional actors from entering formal training. For example, entry-level requirements and degree recognition between universities in the West and Gulf universities are often different. For example, when UCL Qatar was first launched, it did not recognise degrees from Qatar University, which is the country's national university, which is an issue that has been identified in the national press. *The National* newspaper reported that Jean-Yves de Cara, executive director of the Paris-Sorbonne Abu Dhabi, had suggested that there are issues with the recognition of university admissions standards (Hamdan 2012a). A response to this has been the development of foundation and introductory courses in museums and heritage. As I noted in the previous section, NYU Abu Dhabi has offered a pre-professional course in Museums and Cultural Heritage, but due to insufficient student uptake in the 2013–2014 academic year, it was not running. These introductory or bridging courses are vital as they are used for promising students that fall below the minimum academic requirements (*ibid.*).

Language is also a problem within the university system. My analysis of taught university courses focused on museums and cultural heritage found that overall, they were predominantly delivered in English, even at Zayed University. It could be argued that this is perhaps the most practical approach as the majority of educators are expatriates and do not speak Arabic. The use of the Arabic language within higher education is an issue as Kharkhurin suggests, bilingualism can lead to undeveloped language skills, which can result in individuals having 'limited skills in each of their languages' (cited in Ismail 2012: 7). Language, therefore, may be having a detrimental effect on the educational attainment of Emirati's due to the pre-dominance of English within the system.

Heritage organisations in Abu Dhabi are aware of this issue and are re-sponding by trying to raise awareness through career days and outreach activities with schools and universities. A representative from ADACH sug-gested that knowledge of heritage careers is a crucial concern for Abu Dhabi (ADACH Representative 1 2011: Interview). One of the benefits of having well-known cultural heritage franchises is that the local and international attention that they can help to raise the profile of careers within the sector, making it more attractive to Emiratis. Besides, raising the profile of the cul-tural sector in general. The cultural heritage franchise can, therefore, be used to convey significant prestige and status on careers in the sector.

In addition to this, the Abu Dhabi government has recognised that cul-tural heritage needs to be introduced to the educational system at an earlier age. The response has been to launch a full review of tertiary education to incorporate heritage into the system at an earlier age. In 2011 ADEC announced a new model for schooling, which is reportedly bringing in a complete educational reform by revising and implementing primary and secondary education as part of its ten-year strategic plan. One of the prin-cipal targets of this model is to preserve UAE culture and heritage by en-hancing 'students' knowledge and pride of [their] own history and culture' (Abu Dhabi Education Council n.d.[b]). Hellyer argues that '[t]he treatment of UAE heritage in the schools is just awful. It is inaccurate and utterly un-satisfactory. Young Emiratis have been taught in school that there is no her-itage here, but that there are the glories of Egypt, or Babylon, or whatever' (2011: Interview). Describing the results of a survey among seventy-nine Emirati students in their first year at Zayed University Szuchman suggests that knowledge of local archaeology is limited. Less than twenty per cent of students interviewed could name an archaeological site, and forty-nine per cent could name a museum (Szuchman 2012: 41). Based on this evi-dence, although it is limited in scope, there is a need to develop more educa-tional awareness of cultural heritage in Emirati schools. More recently, the Louvre Abu Dhabi's has been working with the ministry of education to embed arts education, in particular, art history, within the school curricula (Somers Cocks 2017). As such these re-evaluations are being directed by expatriates, so the danger remains that the revised syllabus may still reflect a Western-centric approach.

Translating knowledge

I was particularly interested in unpacking how the process of knowledge transfer plays out with the development of official heritage processes and cultural heritage franchising in Abu Dhabi. Partnerships with museums, heritage institutions and international heritage consultants drawn from western European nations have been used as a method for setting standards, which are often promoted and sold overseas as international best practice. Cultural policy documents use the term 'best practice' as a catch-all 'fall back notion' (Pratt 2010: 14). Nusseibeh suggests that 'one of the benefits of cultural heritage franchising is that it can be used as a method for setting standards based on established international standards and best practice' (2011: Interview). The term 'best practice' is used within the cultural sector as part of the legitimising role of heritage standards and procedures, which is tied to Smith's (2006) authorizing role of heritage, which draws on ideas that emerged mostly from western Europe and worked to produce particular ideas and methods as universal, and often hegemonic. Similarly, Bennett (2013) has argued that culture continues to be employed as a means to govern societies through the power of knowledge and expertise, which has been used to 'order and transform' through the institutionalisation of culture.

The transfer of 'expertise', 'knowledge' and 'best practice' is particularly important for the transnational heritage economy. As Byrne notes 'heritage management "appears" in non-Western countries... as a response to an inherent, universal value', which 'is spread by a process of ideology transfer' (2008: 232). As such there is a growing trend for international heritage collaborations that extend beyond pre-designed exhibitions and events. These collaborations offer nations the opportunity to bring in experts to help develop museum and heritage projects. These projects are often developed in response to a local need that cannot be met using existing local capacity. The significance of these partnerships is that they are more focused on locally tailored heritage development.

The British Museum's *World Collections Programme* for example 'was formed in 2008 to establish a two-way partnership with institutions in Asia and Africa and increase their access to UK collections and expertise' (British Museum n.d.[a]). Partnerships such as these offer cultural heritage organisations the opportunity to increase their international reach by offering a range of services within the international cultural marketplace. In the case of the World Collections Programme, international services offered include:

- Developing new relationships
- Digitisation of Collections
- Professional development, training, skill sharing and staff exchange
- Non-English language access to the Collections (online, radio etc.)
- Public programme connected to exhibitions
- Overseas exhibitions and loans
- Joint research and conservation opportunities

(British Museum n.d.[d])

International collaborations operate in a similar way to cultural heritage franchising as they allow the cultural heritage organisation to extend their international profile and to reach new audiences. For the partner nation, it offers the opportunity to co-brand themselves with well-known Western heritage institutions, develop their international standing, attract tourists and local audiences, and perhaps most importantly build the capacity of the workforce. It is worth noting that the UK institutions that are involved in the World Collections programme are all based in London.[8] They are also considered to be national institutions and internationally renowned brands. Therefore, both the brand and the procedures and processes that they use are central to how they trade and operate as transnational actors.

Within the museums' sector, branded museums from western Europe, in particular, the Louvre and the British Museum, have partnered museums in regions that were looking to develop their heritage sectors. These partnerships are typically designed to develop knowledge and practical skills such as The British Museum's Africa Programme, which priorities the sharing of expertise, the development of skills and community partnerships (British Museum n.d.[e]). In addition to this programme, the British Museum has also been involved in a partnership, with the Ministry of Culture, Government of India National Culture Fund to train and support the future museum leaders in India (British Museum n.d.[f]). In 2012, it was reported in the media that the Dallas Museum of Art announced its global plans to establish international partnerships with institutions in India, Brazil, China, Russia and the African nations (Pes 2012). These examples illustrate the growing interest in more long-term, practically based, international cultural collaborations. Cultural heritage capacity-building incorporates training, technical assistance, mentoring and coaching aimed at the development goals of the partnering institution and the nation in which they are developing. The key objective is to bring about positive change by providing training and assistance relating to aspects of cultural heritage development and management. Again, these partnerships raise questions regarding the application of processes that have emerged mainly from western European museums (Kreps 2003; Smith 2006). These partnerships are advertised as collaborative ventures, but in reality, they are driven by the procedures and practices that have emerged and been applied within western European interpretations; interpretations that may well be very different to those that are held within non-Western contexts.

Heritage organisations are also operating transnationally as consultants on large-scale international heritage developments. Most notably for this study, as mentioned in the previous chapters, the British Museum was working as a consultant for the TDIC on the development of the Zayed National Museum. The Zayed National Museum project differs from the British Museum's previous international collaborations and projects as it is creating an entirely new national museum in a non-Western context. The British Museum was also involved in the development of the newly opened National Museum of Qatar, in Doha. International consultancy partnerships offer heritage organisations the opportunity to expand into other regions with significant input in the way that other nations produce and manage their heritage. Also, it brings considerable financial benefits without the adverse effects that are often attached to heritage franchising. However, what is interesting is that while these partnerships help to develop the transnational identity of the heritage organisation further, they are rarely actively promoted publicly. However the British Museum's website carried no mention of the museum's role as a consultant on the Zayed National Museum project. Conversely, the partnership with the British Museum offers Abu Dhabi the opportunity to construct a new national museum, develop the capacity of the local workforce, and bring significant media attention through the transfer of the museum's established brand name and established processes and procedures. The UAE has well-publicised the British Museum's involvement with the Zayed National Museum. International consultancy partnerships involve complex and politically loaded processes that have real consequences in terms of power, translation and representation.

Expertise and the cultural heritage franchise

The processes involved in cultural heritage franchising, therefore, plays a significant role in the ideological transfer of heritage 'values' and 'procedures'. The cultural heritage franchise is sold and operates globally on the basis that it embodies universal characteristics that are translatable globally. One of these characteristics is the 'expertise' that heritage practitioners employed by franchisee are perceived to hold. One of the benefits of temporary international partnerships is that they can be used to create an immediate heritage industry, which can then be used to train Emiratis. The partnership agreements between the Abu Dhabi Government and the museum partners – the Louvre Museum, the Guggenheim Foundation, and the British Museum – all feature Emiratization targets. The partnerships were therefore 'providing qualifications and on-the-job training for Emiratis' (Louvre Abu Dhabi Representative 2011: Interview). Knowledge transfer is, therefore, a significant aspect of the process of cultural heritage franchising in Abu Dhabi. As noted in chapter three, the process of cultural heritage franchising suggests a standardisation that has been critiqued for its homogenous implications. However, as Hooper-Greenhill observes '[t]here is no essential museum. The museum is not a pre-constituted entity that is produced in the same way at all times' (1992: 18). Therefore, regardless of whether a museum is franchised, or not, due to its inherent differences and historical developments.

International partnerships provide qualifications and on-the-job training for Emiratis in the field of cultural heritage. For example, Abu Dhabi's partnerships with the Louvre Museum, the Guggenheim Foundation and the British Museum were all being used to develop not only the Emirates identity and its cultural heritage holdings but also the cultural capacity of the local workforce. Knowledge transfer is, therefore, an essential element within the process of franchising cultural heritage in Abu Dhabi. What this suggests is that part of the desirability of the cultural heritage franchise comes from their established ways of doing things, their processes and procedures. However, how the museum partners and their employees may learn and develop from this process of knowledge transfer seemed to be completely absent. This was curious since practitioners in the region have acknowledged the hybrid nature of transnational professional practice. Underwood argues, 'staff can and do learn from outside the west' and that their 'experiences, conversations and museum visits' made them question both their own assumptions and their own prescribed ways of doing things (2013: 627).

This process of building capacity is similar to how the Sharjah Museums Department developed. Though it is important to note that cultural heritage franchising has not been a feature of Sharjah's approach to heritage development, rather autochthonous heritage and local audience development have taken precedence. As part of the Sharjah Museums Department's development consultants, advisors and temporary contractors were employed for short terms to meet specific needs. According to Al-Ataya:

> When the Sharjah Museums Department was established, the idea was that in the first two years there would be a larger expatriate group of workers. That was the duration that His Highness wanted them here in terms of training as well as carrying out particular projects. So there was a two-year deadline to move things up and to achieve specific goals. So once the two years were up, certain people had either completed their work and moved on, and others stayed for another two years. The idea was that those who had been trained would train others. Initially, we had about twenty expatriates, and now we have about three, so to me we achieved our objectives, and we can continue to develop in-house.
>
> (2011: Interview)

This approach has been practical since the Sharjah Museum Department has built the capacity of its local workforce and achieved its initial Emiratization goals. More broadly, this illustrates that alternatives to cultural heritage franchising do exist and have been successful in the UAE.

Furthermore, translation is not always an easy or straightforward process. A process for the Louvre Museum, which is easily understood, may not be so easily interpreted into the Louvre Abu Dhabi. For example, Barker Langham Recruitment was employed to revise the Louvre Abu Dhabi's Performance Plan into 'clearly defined technical competencies for all Louvre Abu Dhabi staff, to enable Line Managers and the HR Unit to adequately review and appraise employee performance against consistent and quantifiable standards' (Barker Langham 2017). The commissioning of a third party to help interpret and implement the performance plan suggests that the process of knowledge transfer is not as clear cut and easily defined as the cultural heritage franchise agreement sets out.

However, this assumes that cultural heritage education is a neutral and natural process which, as I established in the proceeding chapters, is rarely the case. I have illustrated thus far by drawing on the work of Smith, the central role that authorship and power play within the production of heritage. Smith argues that 'heritage expertise is based on the unequal distribution of power', which is based on the professionalisation of heritage as a specialist field that serves to place the management of the past in the hands of select groups of people (2006: 29). In this way, Smith has shown how power and knowledge are still very much implicated within the processes that surround contemporary museum and heritage practice. As such, the authorized heritage discourse works to represent the elite and marginalise alternative narratives. This problem is particularly acute within transnational settings where heritage is co-produced across boundaries. How official heritage processes are established and communicated through transnational pedagogical practices, therefore, requires more detailed and critical analysis.

The finite nature of the cultural heritage franchise contracts fits with the temporality of international practitioners in Abu Dhabi. The franchise serves a purpose for an agreed amount of time to develop the heritage industry to the point where international heritage practitioners are no longer required. It is through the process of cultural heritage franchising, and more broadly through the use of international practitioners on short contracts that the pace of change and development emerges as an important factor. Through the use of the franchise model, Abu Dhabi has created 'a culture accustomed to rapid delivery, which is the conjuring away the effort of development' (Tomlinson 2007: 72). The rapid and transitory process of development leads to a negative view of international heritage practitioners as dispensable. Once they serve their purpose, they are no longer considered useful. The franchise model, therefore, allows Emiratis to remain in control of these industries while importing best practices from abroad. The evidence suggests that the transfer of knowledge and skill-based training is a crucial factor in the development of cultural heritage franchises in Abu Dhabi. It will be interesting to observe how the power dynamics on these projects change over time in Abu Dhabi.

The expert as cultural commodity

The previous section has shown how cultural heritage franchising is being used to meet Emiratization goals and develop cultural expertise and knowledge in Abu Dhabi. An important aspect of franchising cultural heritage lies within what Bradach, writing about commercial franchising, has termed 'the *socialization process*, which involved using company people as franchisees' (1998: 7). What this suggests is that the cultural heritage franchising bases itself and its saleability on its distinctive heritage procedures and practices. The benefits of having well-known cultural heritage franchises is that they are staffed by international heritage specialists that otherwise may not be available in the local market.

Though it is important to note that many of the staff employed within the Louvre Abu Dhabi and the Guggenheim Abu Dhabi were recruited specifically for the new positions in Abu Dhabi, furthermore, staff employed in international settings may not be seen by employees 'at home' as full members of the organisation. Instead, they are seen as 'temporary' employees recruited for foreign projects that are far removed from the 'authentic' work of the parent museum. In the case of Abu Dhabi, cultural heritage franchises are, as I noted in chapter three, being developed using established processes that have emerged from western European nations. This process suggests that the 'positional superiority' (Said 1978) of the West is still implicated within the systems that drive the transnational heritage industry. Nardella and Mallinson have discussed the role of consultancy in cultural heritage preservation in Ethiopia for the World Bank-funded Ethiopia Cultural Heritage Project. They suggest that international development is explicitly connected to expertise and technical skill, which must be brought into nations with emerging heritage landscapes (2015: 188). In the case of Abu Dhabi, the cultural heritage franchise acts as the agent for distributing the processes of ordering, categorising and displaying, which are ultimately based on the European model of the museum. However these heritage processes may not be appropriate. This issue is compounded by the limited level of understanding that international heritage practitioners have of the local and regional contexts when they begin working on cross-cultural projects. According to Sheehan consultants, such as the Smithsonian Institute who were working in partnership with ADACH to develop its educational strategy and programmes, faced problems due to their lack of awareness of the region's history and heritage (2011: Interview). A broader but related issue 'is that most of the history has not been written down and so what gets displayed in the end is what these expats and outsider companies think it is all about' (Beech 2011: Interview).

What this suggests is that local knowledge and understanding is as vital as heritage 'expertise'. What we can observe, therefore, is that the process of producing heritage in the UAE is predominantly based on established international heritage methods. The issue with this is that international procedures and methods are bound up within Western terms of reference, which place the authority for producing and managing heritage in the hands of international heritage practitioners which results in the production of an 'authorized heritage discourse' (Smith 2006: 29).

Ultimately this serves to marginalise Emirati involvement through the introduction and establishment of new procedures and processes. In doing so, this creates a market for cultural heritage franchises because experts are needed to teach Emiratis how to produce and present heritage correctly. The franchisor's brand name and its associated expertise give the project the authority to produce and present transnational heritage. However, this is problematic as it suggests that Emiratis are not active agents in the production and representation of heritage. For example, it was reported in *The Art Newspaper* that a leaked letter from Sheikh Sultan to Agence France France-Muséums Museums suggested that the agency at the time was 'not sufficiently engaged with the reality in the Gulf: it should have more than two representatives in Abu Dhabi, it should already be training Emirati specialists for when the museum opens in 2016 and it should be liaising better with the authorities there' (Somers Cocks 2013). Through its established processes, the cultural heritage franchise reinforces the power of the West through the superior positioning of the expertise that is linked to the cultural heritage franchise. In terms of the Louvre Abu Dhabi, there needs to be a more critical examination of the role of French expertise within the project. The next generation of Emirati museum professionals need to be equipped with both the skills to continue to develop the new art historical discourses in Abu Dhabi and a critical concern and reflection of their role in the production of new global heritage discourses that are both connected and disconnected from the colonial past upon which critical heritage and new museological discourses are built upon. How the production of heritage relates to the 'production of knowledge' (Tuhiwai-Smith 2012) and 'ownership', and the discourses of the West (Said 1978) is important in the context of capacity building, particularly within non-Western nations. Knowledge and expertise are therefore explicitly linked to the processes that have emerged from western European nations. However, through the cultural heritage franchise, the dynamics of western European power is challenged through Abu Dhabi's power as the 'owner' of the brand and ultimately the new museum.

Interviews with Emirati residents also suggested that the international experts working on the new museum projects were seen positively for their general heritage skills but that they were viewed negatively in terms of their authority concerning Emirati heritage. Al-Gergawi, for example, argued that 'the staff at the British Museum lacks the local and historical knowledge of the UAE. The Zayed National Museum, all the foreign staff, are doing everything' (2011: Interview). A lack of consultation seemed to be exacerbating the issue, 'external expertise is needed, but the Emiratis know more about their culture than these external people. They need to consult Emirati people to make sure it fits with the local image' (Emirati Resident 1 2011: Interview).[9] While heritage practitioners may have expert knowledge of Western heritage processes, they were still viewed negatively in terms of their capability to translate their heritage expertise within the cultural context of Abu Dhabi. This issue has also been the subject of a published discussion by Aisha Deemas from the Museum of Islamic Art, Marjorie Schwarzer of the University of Florida and Leigh Markopoulos, California College of Arts in a conversation about museum values in the UAE. During this conversation, Deemas argues that 'the result is a lack of flexibility and tolerance towards existing local experiences and working practices' (Schwarzer, Deemas and Markopoulos 2013: 212). This disparity leads to two key issues. One is the applicability of the heritage methods that are being introduced, and two is the level of understanding of Emirati heritage.

The issue of local knowledge is also linked to the use of language. The primary language used within exhibitions and panel discussions was English, with Arabic translation available at most events. This has led to criticism from members of the Emirati community, '[h]ow can these things be for us when they do not even use or speak our language?...If it is Emirati, then the Emirati must come first surely? Something is wrong here' (Emirati Resident 2 2010: Interview). The use of English language in this way is perhaps not surprising given that only a small number of heritage practitioners were proficient in Arabic.

The issue of language is connected to how language translates across cultures. Blau has argued that 'as with the translations of popular novels are translated in to Arabic, a process of *ta'rib* (literally Arabisation) can occur with translation of archaeological interpretations' (1995: 122). More recently, Deemas has suggested concerning the production of museum text that non-Arabic speakers 'will write the text from his or her own perspective. But when translated into Arabic the text doesn't necessarily comply with the local perspective' (Schwarzer, Deemas and Markopoulos 2013: 225). She argues that the issue is not a matter of the text being right or wrong; instead, 'an Emirati or other Arab-Muslim will be coming to the museum with a certain level of background knowledge about the culture and such texts are not engaging in the right way' (*ibid.*: 225). Locally, international experts are viewed positively for their general heritage skills but negatively in terms of their authority on Emirati heritage. Ossewaarde has drawn on the work of Merton to suggest that knowledge of both the local and the cosmopolitan plays an essential role in transnational contexts (Merton 1968 cited in Ossewaarde 2007: 368–370). Arguing that cosmopolitans are valued for their knowledge and technical skills and that locals are valued for their local knowledge and understanding (*ibid.*: 371).

Similarly, cultural heritage franchising requires the international heritage practitioner and the resident to work together to co-produce new forms of heritage. The franchise process is, therefore, a hybrid heritage process. The way that heritage practitioners shape both the development of cultural heritage franchise organisations and the professionalisation of emerging heritage industries in non-Western contexts is, therefore, a crucial part of the process. The key issue that emerges is that the power relations underpinning the exchange are hidden through the cosmopolitan positioning of the process. Suggesting that while heritage practitioners may have expert knowledge of Western heritage processes, that they are still viewed negatively in terms of their capability to translate their heritage expertise within the cultural context of Abu Dhabi.

The franchise dialogue

As noted in chapter three, the importance of co-production is reflected within the franchise contract, which serves to benefit both parties. As part of their remits, the planned museums on Saadiyat Island promote the fact that they are engaged in local dialogues. Ultimately the franchise agreement is premised on cosmopolitanism, and that by sharing collections, expertise and cultural knowledge, a dialogue is created between cultures. The dialogic notion of the partnerships suggests an equal and value-free process, which I have already suggested does not exist. The selective nature of the dialogue is apparent in the choices that are made by the museum partners to gather information. The TDIC and the museum partners were engaging with Emirati residents and other external individuals through focus groups and other consultative channels. One way to address this is to see heritage production as 'hybrid forums' where 'experts and non-experts, ordinary citizens and politicians come together' (Harrison 2013: 230). Nardella and Mallinson have suggested that 'in a "learning process" approach, beneficiaries and international project staff share their knowledge and resources to create a fit between the needs and capabilities on both sides' (2015: 201). However, the early stages of development in Abu Dhabi served to exclude non-expert members of the local community who were not invited to be involved in this process (Beech 2011: Interview). When non-experts were consulted it was for acquiring information, ideas and developing networks to deliver the projects rather than community engagement and inclusion. These views further illustrate the political and cultural tensions that emerge through the processes of creating transnational heritage.

My findings are suggestive of the problems that emerge from using international expertise to develop projects in Abu Dhabi, particularly as they relate to issues of power and representation. Heritage practitioners, and in particular those practitioners working on the cultural heritage franchise projects, were seen to be imposing their views and values upon Emirati society (Emirati Resident 1 2011: Interview). This leads to 'a lack of fit' based on 'what development experts call "inappropriate ideology transfer"' (Byrne 2008: 232).

Heritage production in Abu Dhabi is based on a hegemonic system, whereby international heritage practitioners are brought in to develop the cultural heritage sector and to educate Emiratis' about the correct way of preserving and presenting cultural heritage. The hegemonic system operates based on the Authorized heritage discourse, which reinforces the role of Western-trained experts and Western knowledge. Also, it draws further attention to the flawed nature of cosmopolitanism, which is dominated by powerful nations who encourage and help nations elsewhere create heritage. However, as noted earlier, Abu Dhabi is an autocratic society. The expert may be responsible for producing official forms of heritage, but the processes used and the resultant heritage formations must receive official approval. The system in Abu Dhabi is top-down and allows very little if any, room for the production of alternative narratives. Interpretation in this sense remains the monopoly of the specialists and the ruling elite. It is only with the presence of the expert, and the development of an accepted, and approved, authorized heritage discourse that a dialogue can take place. One of the central issues that arise from cultural heritage franchising in Abu Dhabi is one of translation. The methods and processes that are used to produce heritage are bound up within the cultural assumptions of the heritage practitioner and the cultural heritage franchiser, which are not necessarily attuned to Emirati interpretations of heritage. The result is that the Emirati population has been marginalised from the official processes of producing heritage. The process of cultural heritage franchising and transnational heritage, in general, may well be established as a collaborative and dialogic process, but it fails to address and fully incorporate local knowledge and needs. Capacity building and knowledge transfer is, therefore, a political process, which is directly related to issues of power, representation and translation.

Within the UAE, capacity building has been used to support the creation of new industries and new institutions through the development of training and technical assistance. Capacity building in the cultural heritage sector faces two key challenges. First the applicability of international heritage methods, which are being translated into the region. Second the level of understanding of Emirati heritage and its incorporation into emerging knowledge systems in the UAE. Crucially, capacity development raises the issue of 'expertise' and 'knowledge claims', which are embedded to transnational heritage practices. The cultural heritage franchise works in a similar way as it works to establish the western European model of the museum as universal, which works to prioritise and authorise the processes and procedures that are translated within what are often markedly different non-Western contexts. However, the power of transnational 'expertise' is challenged through the process of translation. For example, the Emiratization nationalisation process serves to challenge and resist the authority of the transnational actor. Through their position as a guest, in service to the state, the transnational worker is reminded of their temporary and service driven role. This leads to a situation where 'ambivalence' (Bhabha 2010) and scepticism emerges within the processes of cross-cultural translation in Abu Dhabi.

Notes

1 Gulf nationalisation schemes also exist in: Bahrain – Bahrainization, Qatar – Qatarization, Kuwait – Kuwaitization, Oman – Omanization and Saudi Arabia – Saudization.
2 Similar trends can be observed in Doha. For example, UCL Qatar (a branch of UCL) was set up to provide courses in archaeology, conservation, library studies and museum and heritage studies.
3 Nusseibeh's support for educational development is also tied to his role on the administrative board of the Sorbonne University Abu Dhabi.
4 Observation *Saadiyat Cultural District* exhibition at Emirates Palace November 29, 2011.

5 Observation *Saadiyat Story* exhibition at Manarat Al Saadiyat October 11, 2010. The *Saadiyat Story* exhibition is a permanent exhibition at Manarat Al Saadiyat charting the development of the island.

6 The Ecole du Louvre, located in the Flora Wing of the Louvre Palace in Paris, provides courses in art history and museology, as well as archaeology, epigraphy and the history of civilisations (see Ecole du Louvre n.d.). During the symposium in December 2011 representatives from the Paris-Sorbonne Abu Dhabi, Agence France-Muséums and the Ecole du Louvre also presented a paper, *The Relation between Museum Study programmes in Universities and the Practical Needs of Museums* (AMEinfo 2011).

7 I taught for two years (2016–2018) within the College of Arts and Creative Enterprises at Zayed. I therefore have experience, as a transnational academic and heritage practitioner, of the very system that I describe. However, my analysis shall be based on the courses offered at Zayed University, rather than a critical reflection on teaching in the UAE, which is in-line with the aims of this book.

8 These institutions included the: British Museum, British Library, Natural History Museum, Royal Botanic Gardens (Kew), Tate and the Victoria and Albert Museum.

9 I chose to use the term Emirati Resident as it was important to distinguish between the views of Emirati residents and international residents.

6　Cross-border translations

Cultural translation plays a fundamental role in the transnational heritage economy, particularly in non-Western regions where new heritage industries are developing. This is because 'successful expansion needs transfer of quality and experience' (Adie 2017: 49). Audience development is a considerable facet of the emerging heritage industry in Abu Dhabi. A key directive for the planned institutions on Saadiyat Island is audience development and community engagement. For franchises, pre-opening events operate as promotional activities (Blair and Lafontaine 2005), which have the potential to reinforce brand identity and develop audiences. The Louvre Abu Dhabi, the Guggenheim Abu Dhabi and the Zayed National Museum have all organised and delivered a range of pre-opening exhibitions, events and performances. This chapter will provide an analysis of translation through an examination of these exhibitionary practices and their linkages to the transnational heritage economy. In addition, the chapter will analyse how cultural heritage institutions in Abu Dhabi are engaging with their audiences and how Emirati residents are responding to these initiatives.

I noted in the introduction to this volume that museums have existed in the Emirates since as early as the 1970s. Yet the idea of visiting museums as a social activity is still relatively new (Bull and Thani 2010; Al-Ali Forthcoming). This ties into the static nature of exhibitions within early ethnographic museums in the UAE, which did not feature temporary or changing exhibitions as part of their programming. The development of museums on Saadiyat Island has involved a process of transnational 'translation' and exchange. By providing pre-opening exhibitions, events and performances the institutions have sought to develop their audiences alongside the development of the physical buildings and collections. For example, it is stated in the TDIC's 2010 *Best Practice Report* that 'a strategy was created to increase the awareness of arts and culture in the region through conducting various exhibitions, symposiums and conferences' (Tourism Development Investment Corporation 2010). Kreps observed a similar process during her fieldwork in Indonesia where museum officials described 'how Indonesians are *belum* [not yet] museum-minded' (2003: 23). She describes how this term was used to explain how the museum is seen as an imported cultural form, and as such, the indigenous population had little awareness of its potential role in society. Kreps observed how museum officials recognised that to create 'museum mindedness' both 'museum infrastructure' and a 'museum mentality' must be developed (*ibid.*). More broadly, what this reflects is the introduction of new ideas about the museum as a public and social space.

Global ambitions

The name Manarat Al Saadiyat translates from Arabic to English as 'the place of enlightenment' (Tourism Development Investment Corporation n.d.[o]) and therefore overtly reflects its educative purpose. Within Manarat al Saadiyat is a permanent exhibition, which presents the Saadiyat Island project to the public. The *Saadiyat Story* exhibition provides visitors with an overview of the history of Saadiyat Island and sets out the details of the masterplan through a series of interactive exhibits and models. The exhibition is made up of nine chapters that narrate Saadiyat's development phases, past, present and future.

- Chapter One: The Story of Abu Dhabi.
- Chapter Two: The Vision for Saadiyat Island.
- Chapter Three: Saadiyat Island.
- Chapter Four: Saadiyat Cultural District.
- Chapter Five: Saadiyat Beach.
- Chapter Six: Saadiyat Marina.
- Chapter Seven: Saadiyat Living.
- Chapter Eight: Conserving Our Environment.
- Chapter Nine: Saadiyat Live.

In particular, chapters one to three pay particular attention to the modernisation project in Abu Dhabi and the role of the ruling elite within the city's development. *Chapter Three: Saadiyat Island* presents the masterplan for Saadiyat Island. *Chapter Four: Saadiyat Cultural District* then discusses each of the cultural institutions in detail, which includes information about the architect, the architectural plans and the different visions for each of the cultural institutions. Furthermore, the exhibition was used explicitly to develop Manarat's brand identity. According to Huijser the exhibition played an important role in making 'Manarat more like a brand' (2011: Interview). The permanent exhibition therefore served as the central feature of Manarat's visitor offer.

Similar patterns of using permanent and temporary exhibitions during the process of developing new large-scale cultural institutions and districts can be observed elsewhere. For example the visitor centre at the Oman Botanic Garden in Muscat was used to engage with audiences before it opened (Kneebone 2013: 351). Similarly, in Hong Kong a range of pre-opening exhibitions and events have been staged, such as the West Kowloon Bamboo

Theatre Festival and the Freespace Fest Outdoor Festival. Events such as these have been used to engage the public as part of the development of the West Kowloon Cultural District. Much like Manarat al Saadiyat, West Kowloon's M+ Pavilion, which opened in 2016, was being used to present pre-opening exhibitions in the lead up to the opening of the M+ Museum (West Kowloon Cultural District Authority 2018e). The actual process of creating cultural institutions, franchised or not, is used to develop the brand identity of the institution as it develops. More broadly, the cultural heritage franchise is utilised for communicating the potential of the role of the museum. In some respects, the process of engaging with the museum's future audience is almost as important as the end product.

I argue, however, that the *Saadiyat Story* exhibition plays a further political role. The development of the Cultural District, and the island more generally, is being used to produce an official discourse about the development of heritage and Abu Dhabi as a global city. The documentation and display of the actual process of producing cultural heritage franchises institutions, therefore, play a narrative role in the development of the 'official' heritage discourse. The process of development is used as part of the process of cultural branding and transnational identity-making before the opening of the planned institutions.

Observations of the *Saadiyat Story* exhibition illustrate how the visitors' experience of cultural heritage franchising in the development stage is predominantly visual. The use of pictorial representations offers a mode of communication that is less dependent on the audiences' ability to imagine how the projects will look from panel descriptions. The exhibitions allow the visitor to see and experience first-hand the development of heritage as it unfolds. Harvey has suggested that 'the World Expo constructs its own external reality to which the public is offered a number of guiding frameworks to the extent that it is not necessary actually to visit' (1996: 34). The way that cultural heritage franchising is promoted globally, especially through the use of iconic architecture, which is visibly reproduced, also enables people to see and connect with the museum without necessarily needing to visit. The performative nature of museum development is therefore significant.

Wallace noted in her discussion of museum branding that the way the museum operates through its acquisitions programme, management, programming, and merchandising shapes the development of the museum's brand identity (2006: 9–10). The Guggenheim Foundation has built its identity around its global art collection and its transportable brand. According to the Guggenheim Museum's website '[t]hrough its permanent collection, temporary exhibitions, and its educational programming the Guggenheim Abu Dhabi's will explore common themes and affinities among and between artists across time and geography' (Solomon R. Guggenheim Foundation n.d.[c]). The website goes on to suggest that it will focus on the 'interconnected dynamics of local, regional, and international art centres'. The way that the Guggenheim Foundation claims to be able to transcend boundaries through its global collection and global outposts feature heavily in how the Guggenheim Abu Dhabi presents itself as a transnational museum. Official statements from the Guggenheim Abu Dhabi section of the Saadiyat Island website stress the cosmopolitan nature of the museum and its programmes along with its linkages to the local context of Abu Dhabi, and the broader Gulf. How heritage crosses geographical boundaries, physically and ideologically, is an essential aspect of the transnational heritage process and is central to the way that heritage is being envisaged and developed in Abu Dhabi. It may be true that cultural heritage franchising can transcend geographical and cultural boundaries, but this fails to acknowledge alternative views of heritage that may not be based on museum and heritage models that have emerged from western European nations.

This transnational outlook features prominently in the way that the Cultural District and the proposed heritage institutions are presented to the public. The *Saadiyat Cultural District* brochure outlines the vision for the Guggenheim Abu Dhabi, which is based upon the idea of developing 'a contemporary global museum that reflects the cultural traditions of Abu Dhabi and the UAE with a strong focus on art from the Middle East' (Abu Dhabi Tourism Authority n.d.[b]: 22–23). The *Saadiyat Story* exhibition further reinforces this message by stressing the museum's role in the nation's emerging heritage industry. The development process was therefore being used to reinforce and legitimate the global role of the cultural heritage franchise.

Talking Art

The *Talking Art Series* was established to engage with audiences in Abu Dhabi, and the broader UAE, and to communicate the evolving role of the emerging cultural institutions (Tourism Development Investment Corporation n.d.[q]). The Louvre Abu Dhabi displayed its first public exhibition, *Talking Art: Louvre Abu Dhabi*, at Emirates Palace, Abu Dhabi (May 26–August 29, 2009). The exhibition presented a selection of nineteen artworks that had been acquired since 2007 by the Louvre Abu Dhabi. The artworks were displayed in an interactive video and included 'a 14th Century Mamluk holy Koran, the 5th-century Fibula from Domagnano, the Virgin and Child by Bellini, and Mondrian's Composition with blue, red, yellow, and black from 1922' (Vogel 2009). However, the high-profile nature of the exhibition opening, inaugurated by Abu Dhabi's Crown Prince Sheikh Mohammed bin Zayed al Nahyan and the French President at the time Nicolas Sarkozy, suggests that the show was as much about global recognition as it was audience development. The exhibition not only provided the public with its first view of the Louvre Abu Dhabi's developing collection, but it also set the transnational and elitist tone of the project.

The second exhibition, *The Louvre Abu Dhabi: Birth of a Museum* ran from April 21, 2013 to July 20, 2013 at Manarat al Saadiyat. This exhibition presented the public with a more in-depth look at the Louvre Abu Dhabi's developing collection. On view within the exhibition were 130 artworks from the Louvre Abu Dhabi's collection. The primary purpose of the exhibition was educative, to '...give an insight into the core principles that underpin the creation of the Louvre Abu Dhabi' (Louvre Abu Dhabi n.d.[b]). The exhibition was split in to six themes which included: *The Human Form, Ancient Worlds, The Sacred, Eastern Image, The Western Gaze, Cultures in Dialogue*, and the *Cy Twombly Cycle*.[1] Highlights from this exhibition included Paul Gaugin's *Breton Boys Wrestling* (1888) and a Bactrian Princess (or earth goddess) from the 3rd Millennium BCE, and Osman Hamdy Bey's *A Young Emir Studying* (1878).[2] In addition to presenting the selection of objects collected from the Louvre Abu Dhabi's permanent collection, the exhibition also included a section that was used to promote the future museum. This section, *Jean Nouvel's vision for a 21st Century universal museum in the Gulf*, focused on the architecture of the museum and how it linked to the architectural plans.[3] The focus of these early exhibitions was on developing a world-class collection, rather than accessible audience-driven exhibitions as the project rhetoric of the Louvre Abu Dhabi suggests.

The *Talking Art* activities, which included temporary exhibitions, events such as lectures, and panel discussions and performances, were aimed at developing the publics' awareness and knowledge of the social purpose of the museum and for the 'transmission' of skills and expertise prior to the museum's opening. In this sense, cosmopolitanism was also linked to proficiency, which reinforced the 'authorized heritage discourse'. However, this leads to questions regarding the social purpose of the museum in the Arabian Peninsula and its appropriateness for local audiences. As I noted earlier, Kreps has noted that in Indonesia 'Museum leaders and workers were responsible for cultivating a sense of museum-mindedness in the public, or rather, a particular way of thinking about museum's and their purposes' (2003: 23). She goes onto make argue that this process was based on 'a predetermined outcome based on their own perceptions of what it means to be museum-minded' (*ibid.*). Similarly in Abu Dhabi, the pre-opening events were being used to nurture a museum-minded public. However, this view is based on select ideas of what that 'public' should look like and how they should enact with cultural heritage. Staiff and Bushell have suggested that translation is not about producing an authentic copy. Instead, they argue that the process of translation 'is always a cultural, social and political intervention by the translator', therefore, 'who undertakes the translation and how it is undertaken are therefore critical issues' (2003: 117). Cultural heritage franchising then should be considered in relation to their distinct cultural settings and their responsiveness to their audiences – local, national and international.

Translating the transnational

The Louvre Abu Dhabi's transnational and 'cosmo-universal' aims were further embedded within the exhibitionary practices of the developing museum. As such, the pre-opening exhibition series also served to reinforce the projects transnational discourses. The museum's 'cosmo-universal' discourse was further evident within the rhetoric that surrounded the *Louvre Abu Dhabi: Talking Art Series* and the development of the museum's collection. According to the TDIC:

> The series engages with the heart of the museums and the concepts of discovery, convergence, and education that are deeply rooted in identity. They work as catalysts for progressive engagement on the overarching theme of universality on which the curation of the museum is based – drawing on the Middle East's role as a bridge between east and west, north and south, as a region at the crossroads of civilization.
> (Tourism Development Investment Corporation n.d.[q])

Statements such as 'ideas of sharing' and 'universal knowledge' have been explicitly used to reinforce the Louvre Abu Dhabi's 'cosmo-universal' approach.

The Guggenheim Abu Dhabi has also developed its own series, *Guggenheim Abu Dhabi: Talking Art Series,* similar in purpose to the Louvre Abu Dhabi series. The *Guggenheim Abu Dhabi: Talking Art Series* also featured exhibitions and events targeted at the museum's audiences. In addition, many of the events and exhibitions featured contemporary artists whose works were being incorporated into the museum's permanent collection.[4] Moreover, the series served to position the museum's narrative in transnational terms. In particular, it was stated on the Guggenheim Foundation's website that '[t]he artists selected for the series, reflect the fundamentally transnational perspective on art history being advanced by the Guggenheim Abu Dhabi, which acknowledges the dynamics of art-making across geographies and different moments in time' (Solomon R. Guggenheim Foundation n.d.[d]). The Guggenheim Abu Dhabi has also displayed highlights from its emerging collection in the exhibitions *Seeing Through Light: Selections from the Guggenheim Abu Dhabi Collection Guggenheim* (November 2014–March 2015), which 'introduced the future museum's curatorial vision through a theme-based collection presentation which examined the theme of light as a primary aesthetic principle in art', and *The Creative Act: Performance, Process, Presence* (March–July 2017), featuring more than twenty-five works exploring themes of performance, process and presence.[5] Embedded within this is a cosmopolitan ethic that sees the production of art as a cross-border phenomenon. However, this does not account for the political nature of cross-cultural exchange and interaction.

More broadly, these examples from the Louvre Abu Dhabi and the Guggenheim Abu Dhabi Talking Art Series' illustrate the political role that pre-opening exhibitions play within Abu Dhabi. Jessup and Smith have argued that exhibitions and curators have come to operate as 'diplomatic agents' (2016: 283). As such international temporary exhibitions serve as a collaborative form of public diplomacy with 'the power to engage foreign publics, shape new forms of association, and serve as a meeting ground for diverse communities' (*ibid.*). For example, in 2014, *The Birth of a Museum* exhibition was taken to France. The exhibition was held at the Louvre Museum in Paris from May 2 to July 28, 2014. The Louvre website stated that the purpose of taking the show to Paris was to introduce both the collection and project to French audiences (Louvre n.d.[b]). However, it was during this time that the project gained its nickname the 'Louvre in the Sands' as discussed in chapter four (Jones 2014: 51). Activities such as this in France remind us that the partnerships are not based solely on a one-way exchange. In this instance, the touring exhibition served to challenge French resistance by bringing to France the benefits of the partnership in terms of the emerging collection. Arguably, the pre-opening exhibitions on Saadiyat Island, and elsewhere, serve as forms of 'soft power' as a means of enticement and attraction (Nye 2004, 2011).

Narrating the transnational past

Similar patterns of pre-opening exhibitions can be observed in relation to the Zayed National Museum project. In 2011, the TDIC was working with the British Museum to create exhibitions to build support for the planned Zayed National Museum. The first exhibition to be produced was the *Splendours of Mesopotamia* which ran from March 29 to June 27, 2011. The exhibition, organised by the then TDIC and the British Museum, was shown at Manarat Al Saadiyat as part of a series of pre-opening exhibitions for the Zayed National Museum. The exhibition explored ancient Mesopotamian civilisation and included loans from the British Museum's Middle East Collection and UAE-based institutions, such as the Al Ain National Museum. According to the TDIC's Saadiyat Island website 'the story of the exhibition will be told through the three great centres of Mesopotamian civilization: Sumer, Assyria, and Babylon' (Tourism Development Investment Corporation n.d.[s]). *Splendours of Mesopotamia* made links through the Sumer section to the UAE through the inclusion of artefacts excavated from the archaeological sites of Hafeet and Umm Al Nar, which were on loan from the National Museum in Al Ain.[6]

> The first section on Sumer looks at the growth of society and its contact with the wider world in the 3rd Millennium BCE. Objects excavated from the Hafeet and Umm Al-Nar Cultures, based in modern day Abu

Dhabi and contemporaneous of Sumer, will demonstrate the close links between Sumer and the Gulf Region.

(Tourism Development Investment Corporation n.d.[s])

This extract is suggestive of the UAE's desire to illustrate that its role as a global city is not a purely modern phenomenon and to establish links to its history through these international connections.

National press coverage was also indicative of the way that heritage is being used to position Abu Dhabi's identity in the present. According to Neil MacGregor the British Museum was 'working together with our colleagues in the UAE on how to present the narrative of the national museum. Part of that is tying the achievement of the history and making of the UAE into the long history of the region' (Thomas 2011). The importance of this is that it illustrates the transnational and cosmopolitan agenda of the exhibition as it indicates how the *Splendours of Mesopotamia* exhibition attempted to place the history of the UAE within a regional and global context by illustrating the regions, and the ancient UAE's, role in trade and exchange with Sumerian, Assyrian, and Babylonian societies (Cited in Farah 2011). Furthermore the foreword to the *Splendours of Mesopotamia* exhibition brochure stated:

> It will explore how knowledge has been passed from the ancient to the modern world particularly in areas of science, communication, art and literature and will showcase objects drawn from the world famous British Museum along with objects from Al Ain National Museum treasures that link to the United Arab Emirates.
>
> (Tourism Development Investment Corporation 2011)

The *Splendours of Mesopotamia* exhibition was aimed at highlighting both Abu Dhabi's historical roots and its transnational past and at the same time challenging the Orientalist critiques and views of Abu Dhabi's historical past.

In 2012,[7] Manarat al Saadiyat hosted the *Treasures of the Worlds* international touring exhibition from the British Museum. *Treasures of the Worlds* was the second exhibition organised by the TDIC in collaboration with the British Museum. The exhibition featured works on loans from Al Ain National Museum, Sharjah Archaeology Museum and the private collection of H.E. Abdulrahem Al Sayed Al Hashemi (Tourism Development Investment Corporation 2011). The global and universal nature of the exhibition was emphasised by the British Museum who described the exhibition as '[c]omprising objects from the whole world, past and present, the exhibition allows us to consider the varied ways in which made things can embody ideas and concerns common to all humanity' (British Museum n.d.[g]). A significant critique of blockbuster exhibitions has been that they are based on pre-packaged curated shows that fail to take into account the knowledge, tastes or peculiarities of the regions in which they are sent (Lai 2004).

The *Treasures of the Worlds* exhibition in Abu Dhabi illustrates how the TDIC and the British Museum have tried to address this critique by incorporating autochthonous objects into international travelling exhibitions. The exhibition was described on the Cultural District website as:

> Bringing life to elements of human history dating back 2 million years, the exhibition addresses some universal themes, such as leadership, heritage and faith that will also be found in the Zayed National Museum where the galleries will tell the story of the region's history and the unification of the United Arab Emirates through the life of Sheikh Zayed bin Sultan Al Nahyan, father of the nation and continual source of inspiration.
>
> (Tourism Development Investment Corporation n.d.[t])

However, an analysis of the British Museum's website suggests the exhibition was still heavily framed within Eurocentric terms; '*Treasures of World's Cultures* offers visitors a sense of the British Museum collection as it can be experienced in London' (British Museum n.d.[g]). Extracts such as this suggest that the British Museum's aims were more focused on developing its international profile by touring its collection, rather than illustrating the subtle ways that the *Treasures of the Worlds* exhibition was tailored in specific localities. It also suggests that the value and interpretation process was drawn from the British Museum's definition of treasures.

The focus on 'made things', which are promoted as representing a global definition of 'treasure' (*ibid.*) is indicative of the authorized heritage discourse, which focuses on the primacy of objects as representative of the past. Middle East Online (2012) reported that these 'treasures' included 'paintings that reflect the rich and varied traditions of Islamic art and tools made in Eastern Africa during the Old Stone Age to masterpieces from Renaissance Europe'. These interpretations were predominantly based on artefacts and artworks drawn from the collections of the British Museum and interpretations of the British Museum staff in consultation with the TDIC. It can therefore be argued that the interpretations of treasures within this exhibition are based predominantly on the value systems of the British Museum curators. Autochthonous heritage is therefore put to use to connect with and reinforce the transnational narrative. In the political economy of heritage 'translation' is used as a means, a process, for creating a link in order for cross-cultural connections to occur, which is essentially a political strategy.

Translation and cultural capital

Translating the idea of the museum raises questions around the way that 'cultural capital' is gaining currency through transnational partnerships.

Furthermore, this relates to the idea of being 'museum-minded' (Kreps, 2003), which suggests that non-Western nations through their lack of 'cultural capital' are not able to produce or understand the rules of the game as set out by the West, who have traditionally been positioned as cultural carriers. Bennett, drawing on Bourdieu's 'cultural capital', has argued that nineteenth-century European museum collections functioned to reinforce the power of the elite as it was they who possessed 'the appropriate socially-coded ways of seeing – and in some cases, power to see' (1994: 35). In addition, through the 'exhibitionary complex' museums have traditionally set the rules of the game in terms of defining 'knowledge and expertise' (*ibid.*). As such while 'the gallery is theoretically a public institution open to all, it has typically been appropriated by ruling elites as a key symbolic site for those performances of "distinction"' (*ibid.*: 11). For Bourdieu (1984), cultural capital combines with economic, and social capital, which results in defining an individuals' cultural consumption, or ability to consume culture. Furthermore, he saw a correlation between education, cultural practice and museum visitors, which results in defining who can consume culture (Bennett 1994: 35; Fyfe 2004). What is particularly important within the context of cultural heritage franchising is that 'cultural assets are theorized not as merely derivative of other assets but as generative sources of power in their own right' (Fyfe 2004: 47; see also Ajana 2015), which leads to cultural hegemony.

In this sense, the cultural heritage franchises in Abu Dhabi could be seen as institutionalised forms of 'cultural capital'. According to Ajana Abu Dhabi is 'gaining legitimacy and symbolic power by proxy in the form of identification, brand association and acquisition of that which has already been labelled and established as world-famous high art' and that '[f]or France, it is a matter of converting the cultural capital embodied in the figure of the Louvre' (2005: 325). However, Ajana's analysis fails to account fully for the complexities of the partnerships or the processes of re-assembling the collections in Abu Dhabi. In doing so, she assumes that local knowledge carries no 'cultural capital'; instead, she argues that 'cultural capital' is produced purely by the Louvre Abu Dhabi. In doing so, she fails to acknowledge the power relations that exist within the partnership. For Ajana, cultural power comes from France and financial power from Abu Dhabi. Harrison has argued that we need to critically analyse the process of assembling and re-assembling collections, and how these processes are embedded within circuits of power, which serve to 'govern' and reproduce knowledge (2013: 27). The museum developments are engaged in more than an exercise in branding. Instead, they serve an educative role, not only is there a transference of power but there is also an active exchange of 'cultural competency' through the exchange network of the cultural heritage franchise, which embodies knowledge and expertise. Analyses must, therefore, serve to include both indigenous non-Western and Western knowledge systems in order to understand how they co-exist in hybridised heritage contexts. Translation serves to both establish 'cultural capital' through the appreciation of museum-going and works of art and as a means of encouraging and facilitating cosmopolitan encounters across borders through the exchange of 'dialogue'.

However, the statement '[w]e are the experts, and we will help the Emiratis choose' by the president and director of the Louvre Museum, Jean Martinez, during a panel discussion at the Guggenheim Museum in New York, suggests that the power-knowledge hierarchy is problematic and remains Euro-centric (Galet-Lalande 2014: 2). The cultural heritage franchise, in this sense, is used to convey French expertise to the inexperienced Emirati nation. However, this is problematic as it assumes that expertise and knowledge-transfer is a one-way process. Furthermore, instances of French superiority such as this are often subtly challenged. For example, during the opening remarks of the *Worlds in a Museums Symposium* at the Louvre Abu Dhabi, Mohammed Al-Mubarak (2018) stated in response to the Louvre Museum's opening remarks, which were dominated by French museological rhetoric, that '*we*...meaning all the people involved' created the Louvre Abu Dhabi. A dialogical knowledge-transfer would be based on a communicative strategy where both sides are acknowledged and given space within the hybridised experience, which is supposed to tie into the collaborative nature of the cultural heritage franchising process.

Further compounding the situation was the explicit link between the new museum projects and tourism, which were predominantly viewed as places for tourists and expatriate residents. Whereas national 'sites' of heritage such as Qasr Al Hosn and Sheikh Zayed Mosque and events such as heritage days were considered to be important sites and symbols of Emirati identity. The main reason cited for attending heritage events and places was 'to maintain traditions', which suggests that Emiratis are engaging with heritage events and places that are appropriate in terms of local and national identity and that imported heritage is given less precedence.

Developing and engaging visitors

As noted throughout this book, the cultural heritage franchise is being developed using display methods that have predominantly emerged from western Europe and are therefore assumed to be globally translatable. Public response and engagement with these exhibitions and events have been mixed. Members of the Emirati community have been especially critical of these events, suggesting that the events were not being tailored for the local community (Mushbarak 2011: Interview). Further, it was felt that these early events at Manarat al Saadiyat were failing to engage with Emirati audiences and that they were being presented at too high a level mainly due to the reliance on established practices that were not necessarily seen as appropriate or desirable by Emirati audiences (Emirati Resident 2 2011: Interview). The issue that then emerges is that communities with different traditions of display become alienated through the translation of new ideas and practices.

Developing audiences was therefore a significant challenge for museum and heritage practitioners in Abu Dhabi. A key challenge for museum and heritage professionals in Abu Dhabi was that at the time of this research there was no museum-going culture in the UAE; 'people do not know what museums do and why people visit them. There is no great tradition of museums; therefore, people need to learn what they are for' (British Museum Representative 2011: Interview). This is in line with Hooper-Greenhill's discussion of interpretive communities in museums. She suggests that 'the decision to visit a museum or to stay away is informed by the meaning constructed from an experience, or anticipation of such meaning' (2000: 20). For Falk and Dierking (1992) museum visitation is learned through a socialisation process, which involves active visitation often occurring through family networks. In Sharjah, the Sharjah Museums Department has been working towards addressing museum visitation and audience development for some time. Research conducted in Sharjah by the Sharjah Museums Department has suggested that 'there is not a culture of going to museums, people are not reading enough; people are not interested enough. If the parents are not going the children are not going' (Al-Ataya 2011: Interview).

Huijser suggested that the family was an important motivator for museum visitation at Manarat Al Saadiyat, which was reflected in the popularity of family programmes (2011: Interview). Therefore the museum must offer an experience that aligns with the individuals' interests as well as their financial and leisure time opportunities (Falk and Dierking 1992, 2000). Bull and Al-Thani found in their study of visitor figures in Qatar that, 'families... are much more likely to put social motivations ahead of other reasons for a visit to a museum (or other leisure activity)' (2013: 332). In this sense, we can see how the museum is experienced as part of an interpretive community, as defined by Hooper-Greenhill, by 'sharing it with those who share the same strategies for reading texts and assigning meaning' (Fish cited by Hooper-Greenhill 2000: 25). As Erskine-Loftus has argued 'unquestioned assumptions about how museum communicate and how visitors understand have been built on Western cultural and social understandings, which are not universal' (2013b: 471). Therefore social factors and kinship connections primarily motivate attendance.

Overall, residents felt that there was a general lack of awareness about museums and that this was harming museum visitation; 'If you are sixty years old, and you have never seen these things and never visited you have no experience of these things' (Al-Rahman 2011: Interview). Perhaps not surprisingly, then, observations at events and exhibitions in Abu Dhabi during the period of data collection were indicative of large numbers of international audience members. The evidence also suggested that when Emiratis do engage with heritage, they favour autochthonous exhibitions and events over ones organised by the cultural heritage franchise institutions.

Narrating the nation

The presentation of the national past has also been critiqued as top-down and state driven (Al-Mulla 2013: 160–162). The result has been the production of static displays (Prager 2015; Thabiti-Willis 2016) that communities do not relate to (Teskey and Alkhamis 2016: 110). Many early museums feature dioramas with limited or no interpretation (Blau 1995: 124; Langham and Barker 2014). The Al Ain Museum is located next to the Al Ain Oasis.[8] The Museum was developed at the request of Sheikh Zayed I. Through the 'invention of tradition' (Hobsbawm 2010) the nation was put on display by exhibiting ethnographic and archaeological collections. On entering the museum visitors encounter the first national symbol in the museum, a large-scale family tree[9] detailing the al-Nahyan family lineage. The museum features both ethnographic and archaeological collections, which are used to narrate the UAE's development. The first room the visitor enters is focused on the museum's ethnographic collection, which is used to narrate the story of pre-oil life in the UAE using objects from across the UAE. Dioramas depict aspects of life in the UAE and stress the desert and oases, which is not entirely unexpected given the location of the museum. Items in the collection include: women's clothing, jewellery, cooking implements, maritime objects, items relating to Quranic learning,[10] and weapons. The museum also features a *majlis* area, which is common in the early museums of the region. Then the museum moves onto the archaeological past, which is given precedence in the museum's collection. Representations of the UAE's archaeological past are set within transnational terms. For example, traded items such as coins and pottery are used to connect the UAE to the ancient civilisations of Sumer, Dilmun and further afield in Asia. In addition, items linking to the maritime trade further reinforce the transnational imagining of the past. Arguably, the transnational narrative has been present from the earliest museums, which demonstrate aspects of transnational imagining. The museum ends with a video installation that describes the Emirates development and the emergence of the oil economy. While this video is now dated it further illustrated the role that heritage has played in presenting the emergence of Abu Dhabi's contemporary identity, and that this is not a development that has emerged recently with the proposed new heritage developments. Furthermore, the video serves to reinforce the role of the UAE ruling elite in the development of the story. The exhibitions within both The Heritage Village and the Al Ain National Museum downplay the hardship and poverty of the past. The presentation of heritage in Abu Dhabi is selective and avoids explicit references to differences within the nation. Instead what is presented is a romanticised static image of the transnational past, which supports contemporary nation building.

   Audience research by consultants Barker and Langham has shown that when Emirati visitors engage with cultural heritage that they experience the past in a social and performative way. As such they stress the need for 'dynamic and sensory exhibits' with robust emotive storytelling that engages in multi-generational work through activities and performances (Langham and Barker 2014: 88). Festivals, heritage days and re-enactments are therefore particularly pertinent methods of audience engagement in the UAE. They differ from the events delivered on Saadiyat Island as they link into the emotional and generational aspects of community in the UAE.

The Heritage Village

I carried out observations at the Heritage Village (*qariya turāthiyya*) in Abu Dhabi, which is located on the cornice and consists of a reconstruction of a traditional oasis village. The Heritage Village also displays artefacts that relate to aspects of the Bedouin way of life in the desert, campfire coffee pots, *falaj*[11] irrigation system and workshops demonstrating traditional skills such as metalworking and pottery, weaving and spinning. I suggest that an Emirati heritage village is a form of living museum (see also Khalaf 2002: 23; Prager 2015: 31). According to Young:

> Villages of relocated [or reconstructed] buildings now constitute a phenomenon of the world's repertoire of heritage. They go by a multitude of names depending on their particular inflection: open air museum, folk museum, living history museum, heritage village, museum village and so forth.
>
> (2006: 321)

Heritage villages in the UAE follow a similar form as they generally consist of large-scale housing that has been recreated from the past accompanied by individuals, who are often Emiratis, re-enacting traditional practices such as weaving and metalworking. The performative and emotive aspects of these sites are therefore highly relevant, especially in terms of preserving traditional practices (Kirshenblatt-Gimblett 1998: 45; Rojek 1999; Prager 2015: 31).

Khalaf has argued that heritage villages are 'cultural representations where displays are organized, themized and presented to viewers as discourses of national heritage' (2002: 19). Young argues that the museum village 'draws their authority from the collections or in the case of re-creations the authenticity of their interpretations' (2006: 323). One way that this is achieved is through the staging of heritage days.[12] A central feature of the Heritage Day[13] is the practice of traditional activities. Commenting on the annual Heritage Day held at the Heritage Village in Abu Dhabi Al-Hamroudi explained how visitors to the centre are given an '*Emirati experience*' (2010: Interview), which suggests that heritage performances carry messages relating to '*authenticity*', which serve to legitimate the village as a site of learning and exchange. In this sense, the heritage village becomes a hybrid site of activity where Emirati's lead and shape the 'educative apparatus' of the state.

For some Emiratis, the connection of the local communities, heritage villages serve as important sites of local identity. These connections have led to members of the local community to set up their heritage villages, which act as forms of grounded bottom-up heritage practices (Samuel 1994). In 2012, Emirati residents in Ras Al Khaimah started a locally led heritage initiative to restore Jazirat Al Hamra,[14] 'a pearling town of the *za'ab* family (or tribe) that was abandoned after the modernization of the Emirates' (Zacharias 2012). Thompson (2011) digitally mapped the site of Jazirat Al Hamra and produced a 3D model of the village noting key features such as the *hisn* (fort), several mosques, a *Souq* (market) and over one-hundred houses. Since then Sheikh Saud bin Saqr Al Qasimi, Supreme Council Member and Ruler of Ras Al Khaimah ordered further work to be undertaken to restore the site and for it to be developed into a tourist attraction (Gulf News 2012). Numerous heritage villages exist throughout the Emirates, such as the Heritage Village on the Abu Dhabi Cornice, the Hatta Heritage Village and the Dubai Heritage and Diving Village, to name but a few. However, not all heritage villages in the Emirates have emerged from a community-led grass-roots movement, but rather the State officially sanctions most.

However, the act of actually visiting heritage villages as part of everyday leisure, however, does not seem to be that popular with Emiratis but is instead an activity reserved for the tourist and school groups. Interviews with older members of the Emirati community suggested that heritage places, such as heritage villages, were not meant for them as they were already familiar with their past through their knowledge of Emirati culture and their use of traditional objects and artefacts.[15] The older generation therefore did not see cultural heritage institutions engaging with them as users. Furthermore, several Emirati residents described the Al Ain National Museum and the Emirates Heritage Village as '*dead*', '*boring*', '*dusty*', '*smelly*', '*old*', '*past*' and '*outdated*', and suggested a static view of autochthonous heritage in the Emirates (see Blau 2003 for a discussion of archaeology).

Heritage organisations such as museums were seen as essential institutions for educating Emirati school children about the history and heritage of Abu Dhabi. Al-Hamroudi suggests that it was important for the younger generation to be educated formally about the past because 'the older generation is dying out and with it so too is a lot of our history and heritage. We need to address this before it is too late' (2011: Interview). More broadly, this focus on education is suggestive of the 'educative' role of the heritage village (Harrison 2013; Bennett 1995). This suggests an explicit policy to educate school children drawing on heritage. Set within this is the assumption that school children no longer live or have a connection with traditional Emirati life, that it is something which is no longer alive in the present.

Within the Gulf States, the role of education within museums is still a relatively new and emergent process. Whereas in the West the museum's educative role has emerged as an integral element of the museum activity. The Sharjah Museums Department, for example, has recognised the importance of community engagement and its potential to attract visitors. One way that the Sharjah Museums Department has responded to this issue is by developing educator training days in response to feedback from teachers. These teacher days are used to both strengthen the museums' outreach activities and to illustrate how the collections can be linked and utilised within the delivery of school and university curricula (Sharjah Museums Department Representative 2011: Interview). It will be worth exploring how these changes affect the awareness of heritage within the education system in future heritage research within the region. There is a clear drive to combine cultural development with educational development to create a collective memory and a viable cultural heritage industry.

Furthermore, heritage villages, through their use of specialist Emirati craftspeople and oral historians, challenged the knowledge-power dynamics (Prager 2015: 32). At the heritage village, it is the older Emirati generation that is seen to be the carrier of cultural capital. What seems to be of most important concerning the heritage village is the role they play in the cultural and emotional act of preserving heritage, which does not necessarily have to culminate in visitation to a heritage organisation or place.

Brand name awareness

The franchiser's brand name is a crucial element within the process of cultural heritage franchising. In Abu Dhabi, the use of brand name partnerships is a strategic and measured move. Nusseibeh[16] argued that cultural heritage franchises were being used to create museums of 'international stand from day one' by 'bringing the best of what is internationally available' (2011: Interview). Cultural development, as I noted in chapter four, is not just about establishing new cultural institutions, but it is about establishing world-class institutions, which place Abu Dhabi on the global map of culturally significant cities. This ties into the franchising process as, tourists tend to favour well-known franchises when travelling to new places (Lin, Lin and Ryan 2014). Interviews with Emirati residents indicated that the museums were primarily perceived as being developed for tourism and image enhancement and not the local community. For example, an Emirati resident and ADACH representative stated that 'with the Guggenheim and Louvre brands everyone is listening as the Guggenheim has that power' (2011: Interview). The large-scale media attention that was generated from the Guggenheim Museum Bilbao has shown that in some instances, franchising can lead to increased global image and tourism (Evans 2003). Obtaining one of the most exclusive franchise brands, carrying the Louvre name, was of paramount importance to Abu Dhabi. In addition, Emirati residents have connected positively to the exclusive and elite nature of this partnership. Thirty-nine of the forty-nine online survey respondents stated that they thought the heritage developments were primarily targeted at raising Abu Dhabi's profile. Notably, the aim for Abu Dhabi is not to merely obtain heritage franchises; the aim is to obtain what is arguably some of the world's best heritage brand names and to generate instant global awareness.

The literature on the Guggenheim Museum Bilbao has suggested that opinion on the development of cultural heritage franchises is often divided due to fears around loss of control and cultural homogeneity (MacClancy 1997; Baniotopoulou 2000; Gomez and Gonzalel 2001). Interviews with residents in Abu Dhabi showed that the general opinion was that cultural heritage franchising was beneficial for Emiratis, especially in terms of tourism and image enhancement. However, concern remained regarding the motives behind the projects. In particular, residents were concerned about how the cultural heritage franchises will fit within the local context, and the amount of public money being spent on them. For example, twenty of the survey respondents thought that the development of the cultural heritage franchises was a positive move, while fifteen thought it was detrimental to Abu Dhabi and Emirati identity. However, thirty of the forty-nine respondents stated that too much focus was being placed on the branded franchise museums and not enough focus on autochthonous heritage institutions. Berman observes that '[e]very culture resists translation, even if it has an essential need for it' (1992: 4; see also Bielsa 2016: 10–11). MacClancy (1997) has noted how the Guggenheim Museum Bilbao was opposed by artists, media, government officials and members of the local community. The amount of money invested in cultural heritage franchising, the emphasis placed on them rather than local projects and the political and economic motivations for doing so are key critiques of cultural heritage franchising (Plaza 2007). Resistance to cultural heritage franchising is not purely an Abu Dhabi problem; on the contrary, as I discussed in chapter four, both French and Emirati forms of resistance have developed from the franchising of the Louvre Museum.

The issue that emerges is that autochthonous heritage is seen to be marginalised. Elsheshtawy argued that the projects were 'imposing western aesthetic and western culture with no regard for local talent or a vibrant local arts culture' (2011: Interview). These interpretations of cultural heritage franchising are linked to the associations that people have with well-known museum brands. The cultural heritage franchise brand is, therefore, explicitly connected to its national origin. UAE identity was seen as suffering at the expense of the exporting culture.

The announcement of the Zayed National Museum project has helped to balance the way that residents and heritage practitioners perceive the Cultural District developments in Abu Dhabi. At the start of the fieldwork, which was before the in-depth details of the Zayed National Museum project were announced, people gave more sceptical views of the project. Once the Zayed

National Museum was announced publicly, I noticed a subtle shift in opinion whereby they could recognise that there was more being spent on autochthonous heritage and therefore more relevance to Abu Dhabi and the UAE. The notion of balancing both the local and the imported heritage was a key theme within my discussions with Emiratis. Emirati members of the community recognise that Arab art should be supported and in particular Emirati art. However, due to the vast size of the proposed cultural heritage franchises, they may well be less accommodating towards smaller, local, experimental and non-profit exhibitions and events. The idea of balancing autochthonous and franchised heritage, regardless of cultural context, is therefore an important issue. Primarily the collaborative and dialogic aims of the cosmopolitan project fail to transgress the power relations and politics that are bound up in the translation of cultural heritage across borders. This section has illustrated the complexities and fears that surround the development of hybrid heritage processes. Essentially these debates highlight how the issue of ownership is politically and culturally charged (Harrison 2013).

How heritage is translated and authored has significant implications in the Gulf region. Transnational heritage is therefore set up as a means of producing dialogical cross-cultural communication through the sharing and exchange of cultural heritage across borders. The political nature of heritage comes to the fore as the dominant model of development is based on established processes and practices, which may not necessarily translate in to non-Western contexts. The transnational procedures and processes that are used to create exhibitions and engage with audiences are therefore culturally specific and as such politically loaded. The evidence collected suggests that Emiratis are less interested in 'official' transnational forms of heritage provided by exhibitions and lecture series, such as the Louvre Abu Dhabi and the Guggenheim Abu Dhabi, and are more interested in autochthonous experiences. However, detailed audience research will be needed as the heritage landscape in Abu Dhabi emerges and evolves over the time. This chapter has merely served to offer some initial insights on audiences during the early stages of the developing projects in Abu Dhabi.

Museums have traditionally materialised the past by emphasising the visual and material presence of things. Whereas in the Islamic system, the transmission of knowledge has been based on oral intangible systems of communication (Burke 2009: 86). The focus on material culture and collecting through museums is, therefore, introducing newer ideas about how the past might be remembered and reproduced within the present. Furthermore we must recognise how local conditions, institutions and actors are affected and implicated in the development of hybrid heritage contexts. Instead, a hybrid and postcolonial approach must account for the conflictual, transient and variant negotiations that are involved in the process of cross-border work. The transnational museum needs to move away from curatorial 'authority', which has been increasingly challenged in non-Western nations, towards community dialogue and multi-vocality (Clifford 1997).

Notes

1 Observation, Manarat Al Saadiyat: April 22, 2013; see also Louvre Abu Dhabi (n.d.[b]).
2 See further examples at Agence France-Muséums (2014).
3 Observation, *The Louvre Abu Dhabi: Birth of a Museum*, Manarat Al Saadiyat, Abu Dhabi, April 22, 2013.
4 For further details on past exhibitions see the website for the Tourism Development Investment Corporation (n.d.[r]).
5 For an overview of past exhibitions see Abu Dhabi Culture and Tourism (2019).
6 Observation, Manarat Al Saadiyat: April 11, 2011.
7 *Treasures of the Worlds* ran from April 18 to July 17, 2012.
8 The museum was expanded in 1974.
9 Created in 1996.
10 Learning in the pre-oil period was based on memorisation of the Quran.
11 A *falaj* is an irrigation system based on a series of water channels. See for example (Environment Agency Abu Dhabi 2011).
12 Heritage days are held at a wide variety of institutions across the UAE including, and not limited to, museums, heritage villages, shopping centres, schools and universities.
13 Other annual events that are focused on national identity in the UAE includes events such as the: Abu Dhabi International Hunting and Equestrian Exhibition; Mazayina Dhafra Camel Festival; Liwa Date Festival; Mother of the Nation Festival and National Day.
14 The area is believed to have been occupied since the sixteenth century but was abandoned before the formation of the Federation (Gulf News 2012).
15 Interviews with Emirati Resident 3 2011; Emirati Resident 4 2011 and Emirati Resident 5 2011.
16 Zaki Anwar Nusseibeh was appointed Minister of State for the United Arab Emirates in October 2017.

7 Autochthonous heritage

I have argued throughout this book that the current drive to document and express heritage by the Abu Dhabi government is a deliberate move towards constructing official heritage narratives. As part of this process the government has taken measured moves to preserve, produce and promote autochthonous cultural heritage, tangible and intangible, that has resulted in several developments focused on autochthonous heritage. It is therefore essential to understand how autochthonous heritage is preserved and presented, how it relates to Emirati identity, and how it is embedded within hybrid heritage processes in Abu Dhabi. This chapter examines the processes that are used to define and present autochthonous heritage and how they are used in the construction of transnational identity in Abu Dhabi. In addition, it explores grass-roots responses to cultural heritage developments through a consideration of Emirati residents' attitudes and opinions. In particular, the chapter will interrogate the meanings and values that are placed on autochthonous heritage in Abu Dhabi, and how they are being used to institutionalise and govern heritage.

National cultural heritage policies

Official government strategies, like cultural heritage franchise contracts, can tell us a lot about the way that national heritage is preserved and presented in Abu Dhabi. These strategies take the form of official government plans and policies. Baba has argued that the UAE's government strategy documents, *2011–2013 UAE Government Strategy* and the *UAE Vision 2021*, target heritage preservation and development to reinforce local identity in response to the threatening forces of globalisation (2011: 7–8). This view is in-line with Khalaf's argument that heritage revival (*ihya'al turath*) has emerged as a direct result of globalisation and modernisation (2000, 2002). However, taking such a view sees heritage as embedded within debates that see heritage purely as a response to a threat of loss (Hewison 1987; Lowenthal 1998), globalisation and a perceived weakening of the nation state (Hobsbawm 2010). I have shown in my discussions thus far that taking such a view would present only a partial view of heritage in Abu Dhabi.

In my analysis of the *2011-2013 UAE Government Strategy* and the *UAE Vision 2021*, I found that cultural heritage does indeed feature as a significant aspect of how national identity is produced and presented. The *2011-2013 UAE Government Strategy* identifies several elements of identity that are linked to national identity. In particular, it states that:

> The government will promote community cohesion, preserve the UAE national identity, and encourage an inclusive environment that integrates all segments of society while upholding the unique culture, heritage and traditions of the UAE.
>
> (UAE Cabinet 2010a: 9)

The strategy goes on to discuss UAE heritage in more detail, suggesting that it aims to meet these strategic priorities, in part, by prioritising selected aspects of UAE national identity. It states:

> Emphasize the National Identity by spreading the core pillars of National Identity, preserving and propagating the use of the Arabic language, promoting the UAE's culture, heritage and tradition, embedding values of religious moderation, and encouraging and promoting authentic UAE principals.
>
> (*ibid.*)

Issues around the preservation of the Arabic language are also present in the global heritage discourses of UNESCO. For example, the threat of 'loss' concerning autochthonous languages has led to the establishment of UNESCO's programme for the Safeguarding of Endangered Languages in 2000 (Donnachie 2010: 135). UNESCO has defined endangered languages as those that are 'on a path toward extinction', more specifically, 'when its speakers cease to use it, use it in an increasingly reduced number of communicative domains, and cease to pass it on from one generation to the next' (UNESCO 2003b). In the UAE, English is used as the primary language, which has implications for the Arabic language and for the heritage sector as English is the dominant language used to communicate and present heritage, particularly in relation to policy documents, exhibitionary practices and pedagogical developments.

In addition, the *UAE Vision 2021* stresses the importance of national markers of Emirati identity and cultural heritage. Section 1.4 of the document sets out the role that cultural heritage plays within the development of the UAE's national identity. The document states:

> Our nation will celebrate its wealth of heritage and its deep-rooted ancestry. Emiratis will maintain a living link with the past by preserving and celebrating cultural anchors such as literature, traditional arts and poetry as beacons of a modern UAE.
>
> (UAE Cabinet 2010b: 7)

The UAE Vision suggests that heritage is positioned as a central aspect of national identity. Particular emphasis is placed on the importance of preserving autochthonous heritage and emphasising Arab and Islamic characteristics at a national level. However, the narrative is not defined solely in terms of national identity.

Furthermore, the document provides further evidence of how transnational identity has been used to construct and strengthen national identity in the UAE. Section 2.3 of the Vision states:

> We want the nation to draw strength from its traditions of openness, peaceful coexistence and understanding. In this way Emiratis will always resist the value-flattening effects of globalization and will always be enriched rather than threatened by their nation's openness to the world.
>
> *(ibid.*: 12)

The document goes on to explicitly link cultural exchange and cosmopolitanism with the national agenda by suggesting that:

> The UAE is also emerging as a point of reference in the cultural sphere. Sustained interaction between Emirati and other cultures has fostered mutual understanding and enrichment. Local traditions of literature, art and poetry will be promoted as international ambassadors for UAE culture.
>
> *(ibid.)*

The importance of preserving national identity within the process of cosmopolitan identity-making is, therefore, a central theme within the official heritage discourse in Abu Dhabi, and the broader UAE. National identity is produced and presented as part of a global re-imagining of the past and the present. National identity is therefore not at odds with contemporary cosmopolitan identity-making but rather continues to influence, and be influenced by, transnational heritage processes such as UNESCO's global classificatory system (Kirshenblatt-Gimblett 2007; Askew 2010; Long and Labadi 2010). As we saw in the discussion of the Zayed National Museum project in chapter four, national heritage operates within and alongside the transnational heritage. National identity is, therefore, a foundational element of the transnational heritage discourse in Abu Dhabi.

Heritage 'Values' and the preservation ethic

The accelerated demand for modernisation in the Gulf States since the 1970s has had a profound impact on built heritage in the region (Alraouf 2014: 174). In Abu Dhabi many of the city's earliest buildings have been demolished since the 1990s, largely due to the poor quality of the buildings.

Traditional Gulf urbanism was based on socio-cultural values, which produced organic patterns of development and an 'authentic' and 'distinctive' architectural aesthetic (*ibid.*: 174). Traditional architecture in the Gulf has focused on 'simplicity, functionality and robustness', which were designed in response to the desert environment and socio-cultural aspects of community life of the Gulf (Scharfenort 2014: 191). Whereas, within the contemporary urban landscape, neoliberal policies (*ibid.*: 192) and Western planning processes have resulted in standardised urban plans and dedicated spatial zoning (Elsheshtawy 2004). Place-making, according to Harvey, is connected to capitalism, which is 'growth orientated, technologically dynamic and crisis prone' (1996: 6). In the pursuit of the modern 'old' places have to be devalued, destroyed and redeveloped while new places are constructed. Within Abu Dhabi, the community is rooted in a Nomadic Bedouin past in which people did not form attachments to places, building or things due to their transitory existence. We can see this trend continuing in the contemporary project where the urban fabric is continually renewed when needs or attitudes change.

The conflicting goals of modernisation and preservation were evident within heritage developments in Abu Dhabi. Saving modern heritage buildings from falling into decline or saving them out of a decline phase are the aims of the strategies proposed by the Modern Heritage Preservation Initiative. Encouraging people and businesses to adapt and reuse buildings is a crucial aim of this initiative (ADACH Representative 2 2011: Interview). Sheehan suggested that a tendency exists to 'see old buildings as empty and of little value' but that 'this view is slowly changing as they are starting to be seen as important symbols (2011: Interview)'. As such, building specialists in Abu Dhabi are creating counterarguments for the preservation of modern heritage buildings by arguing that 'the UAE offers a unique opportunity to study urban development and heritage buildings', which 'reflect the changing symbolism between different groups' (ADACH Representative 3 2011: Interview). Yet, there have been in-roads in terms of regional conversations and developments to address some of the emerging issues surrounding identity formation and the role of cultural heritage preservation. This has resulted in the further institutionalisation of heritage through the development of new transnational centres such as the establishment of the ICCROM-ATHAR regional Conservation Center in Sharjah in 2004.

There has been a growing recognition that remaining tangible aspects from the past are being identified and preserved as aspects of Abu Dhabi's history and heritage. The result is that we are beginning to see much more debate around what should be preserved and by whom. This was most evident in a campaign to raise awareness about the Abu Dhabi Bus Station, which was scheduled for demolition. In 2011, the Historic Buildings and Conservation Department at ADACH were lobbying the Department of Transport to preserve the building as it was one of the last remaining well-known landmarks in the city. The campaign was aimed at 'creating a new collective memory for a new generation' (ADACH Representative 3 2011: Interview). More recently, the closure of Zaab *souq*, a small mall in Khalidiyah, which dates to the around late 1970s – early 1980s has led to community reaction on social media (Dennehy 2019b). One twitter user commented:

> Why have they just never let one single old landmark in the city? Other cities around the world have these really old landmarks that shape the culture of it. We no longer have these anymore! What are we going to show our children in the future?
>
> (Aroundme13 2019)

Community responses have focused on nostalgic feelings of loss and the destruction of historical landmarks in the city and their connection to attachments to place, which is indicative of the memories that certain buildings and places hold within the national imagination and shifting attitudes to the preservation of the past at a local level.

A further problem is that the city's early infrastructure was associated with the poverty of the past[1]; as such, 'you do not pay much attention if you knock it down because the differences were so enormous' (ADACH Representative 1 2011: Interview). Exhibitions within both national museums and heritage villages downplay the hardship and poverty of the past. Instead, what is presented are romanticised static images of pre-oil existence (Penziner-Hightower 2014; Thabiti-Willis, 2016; Prager, 2005). These negative perceptions also relate to how the Gulf States are typically viewed from the outside as oil wealthy but culture poor. This is distinctly different from developing (poor) nations who are typically viewed as culturally rich but impoverished (Radcliffe 2006). However, through the development process scales of power, local, national and global, are often challenged and reconfigured (*ibid.*: 18). The act of acquiring cultural franchises serves as a counterdiscourse as 'they show the world that we have our own heritage and that we can also have other peoples too' (Emirati Resident 2 2011: Interview). It also points to the dominance of tangible heritage over intangible heritage, which presents nations lacking intangible heritage as 'culture poor'. Hellyer argues that:

> The difficulty is going to be to present the UAE's heritage because it is mostly unbuilt and unwritten, to present it in such way that it appears to hold its own in relation to what is being imported...It is not easy to present what was effectively the heritage of a fairly poor trading community on the coast and a nomadic community inland.
>
> (2010: Interview)

The lack of physical traces from the past further reinforces the negative view of Abu Dhabi as culture poor. This idea that Abu Dhabi is perceived as having no heritage is prevalent within expatriate communities in

Abu Dhabi. According to long-term expatriate resident Jocelyn Henderson 'they (Emiratis) do not have any heritage, what will they put in these museums' (2011: Interview). My own experience within the region over the past thirteen years supports this as it is common to hear expatriates say there is no history or heritage in Abu Dhabi, or the other Gulf countries (see Exell and Rico 2013 on Qatar). The problem is compounded by the dominance of Eurocentric museum and heritage models (Wakefield 2013, 2014) and Orientalist discourses (Exell and Rico 2013, 2014; Wakefield Forthcoming).

One solution to the problem in Abu Dhabi is to import culture through the acquisition of objects from abroad. Emirati residents indicated that the development of heritage – both autochthonous and franchised – was therefore an essential means of demonstrating 'that Abu Dhabi has a heritage too' and more broadly countering Orientalist attitudes and assumptions. This idea is connected to the hegemonic power of heritage globally and the consequent transfer of 'values' regarding preservation and presentation. The burgeoning global heritage industry draws on emotions of 'loss', 'threat' and nostalgia as a call to arms for the categorisation and management of heritage. It does so by creating standardised criteria and processes based on hegemonic practices drawn from Western European nations. This process of standardisation and listing is then presented as a global and cosmopolitan concern for all (see also Harrison 2013: 63). In reality, this process serves to reinforce the dominant preservationist agendas of international policies such as UNESCO rather than a global humanity (Kirshenblatt-Gimblett 2007: 182). As such museums are 'one of the institutions and practices that are associated with modernity, part of a checklist for being a nation' (Kratz and Karp 2007: 3; see also McClellan 2012). Heritage is given what I term 'transnational currency', which is suggestive of the power and identity relations that come from combining autochthonous and franchised heritage, it in effect colonises.

National heritage museums: Qasr Al Hosn

In parallel to the issues of preserving modern heritage, historic buildings with clear links to the national story have become recognised as heritage resources. Especially, historic buildings that have a direct link to the ruling elite. In contrast to the high-profile global museum developments on Saadiyat Island is Qasr Al Hosn, which has undergone a large-scale renovation. The development of Qasr Al Hosn Fort into a national heritage museum is not an entirely new phenomenon within the UAE. As I noted in chapter one, historic fort sites have become emblematic symbols of the nation's past and popular tourist imagery (Baba 2011; Prager 2015). Qasr Al Hosn, which translates to 'palace fort' re-opened in 2018 after more than a decade of conservation and restoration work.[2] Qasr Al Hosn's watchtower was the city's first permanent structure, which served to monitor and defend coastal trade routes and the new settlement. As such, Qasr Al Hosn's watchtower is the oldest surviving building in Abu Dhabi city. Over time the site expanded into two key buildings, which consisted of an Inner Fort (1795) and an Outer Palace (c.1939–1945) (Qasr Al Hosn 2018a). In addition, Qasr Al Hosn has served several purposes; it has been the home of the Al Nahyan ruling family, the seat of governance and a military headquarters (*ibid.*, 2018b). The fort was later (c.1968–1970) utilised as the seat of the consultative council and a national archive (Qasr Al Hosn 2018c). The National Consultative Council[3] hosted Federal and National debates up until the late 1990s. The building was, therefore, the site of 'the development of new modern governmental systems, which has its roots in the traditional concepts of *Majlis* and *Shura*' (*ibid.*). The site is therefore attached to the national narrative through the historical debates, discussions and decisions that took place within it.

The Cultural Foundation was opened on the site in 1981 and was used as a community space comprising a library, a theatre and an exhibition hall, which Power (2018) suggests set the initial framework for Qasr Al Hosn's emergence as a heritage monument. Qasr Al Hosn in its contemporary form has been recognised for its potential as both a heritage symbolism and tourism potential. Qasr Al Hosn served as a symbol of the political and communal identity of Abu Dhabi. The positioning of this heritage site is indicative of the precedence that national identity takes over any form of transnational cultural formations. Qasr Al Hosn plays a leading role in narrating Abu Dhabi's development from Bedouin origins to a contemporary global city (Qasr Al Hosn 2018d). Qasr Al Hosn firmly places Abu Dhabi, the royal elite and national identity as the primary indices of Emirati identity. For example, the heritage discourses used to promote the site focus on the role of the fort as 'the ancestral home of Al Nahyan and the symbolic heart of Abu Dhabi' (Qasr Al Hosn 2018a) and 'the nation's living memorial and the narrator of Abu Dhabi's history' (Qasr Al Hosn 2018d). In doing so, the site is used to reinforce national tribal identity and the role of the ruling elite. In this sense, the site is presented as an active site that is entwined not only with the city's past but also its future. Qasr Al Hosn has essentially become a monument of Emirati heritage and national pride. As such, the fort is considered to be one of the most important national heritage symbols in the city.

I have argued elsewhere that Emirati heritage has primarily been dominated by intangible representations and re-interpretations of the past (Wakefield 2012). As Picton (2010) has noted, oral traditions have been the dominant mode of cultural transfer across generations. What is different today is that oral traditions have been reproduced as cultural heritage performances. Intangible heritage in the UAE and the border Gulf States takes many forms such as sporting events – falconry, camel racing, Saluki hunting, heritage festivals, oral traditions, poetry and Arabic coffee (Khalaf 1999; Khalaf 2000; Wakefield 2012; Koch 2015; Prager 2015). These intangible aspects of heritage have been incorporated into heritage events and performances that are enacted at festivals and within heritage villages.

Qasr Al Hosn's role as a national site is further exemplified through its engagement with intangible heritage. As such Qasr Al Hosn acts as a site of 'active' heritage, which is exemplified within the 'House of Artisans'. The House of Artisans is located adjacent to the fort within the heritage museum's grounds. The House of Artisans is focused on preserving and presenting intangible aspects of the nation's heritage in the form of traditional crafts. Traditional crafts are defined as those that are '[s]hared from generation to generation, they preserve not only the practical skills but also the shared social values associated with Emirati identity' (Qasr Al Hosn 2018b). The House of Artisans presents crafts – *al sadu*, *khoos*,[4] *talli*[5] and seacrafts[6] – as a form of living heritage. Emirati artisans are employed onsite to actively engage visitors using performative elements of heritage using oral histories and traditional techniques. For example, *Al-Sadu*, is a form of weaving, using wool from sheep, camels and goats, traditionally practised by Bedouin women to produce Bedouin *bait al-shaar* (the tent), interior items such as rugs and seating, and camel accessories. Inspiration for the geometric designs was often drawn 'from social identity and the surrounding environment' (Qasr Al Hosn 2018e). As noted in chapter two, *Al Sadu* had taken on global aspects of heritage identification through its inscription to UNESCO's List of Intangible Cultural Heritage in Need of Urgent Safeguarding in 2011. Again, this demonstrates the interconnections between transnational and autochthonous heritage in Abu Dhabi.

Qasr Al Hosn Festival

Qasr Al Hosn hosts the state-sanctioned annual *Qasr Al Hosn Festival*, which is organised by the Abu Dhabi Tourism & Culture Authority (TCA Abu Dhabi). In general, festivals are large-scale events 'that have national and international significance' and as such 'their primary focus cultural expression, and are locally based' (Pratt 2010: 16). In Abu Dhabi, the Qasr Al Hosn Festival is an autochthonous heritage event that has a strong national identity and community focus. The national significance of the Qasr Al Hosn Festival was displayed during the opening procession of the inaugural festival in 2013 (February 28–March 9), which coincided with the 250th anniversary of the Qasr Al Hosn (Qasr Al Hosn Festival 2014a). The procession, which went from Al Manhal Palace to Qasr Al Hosn in Abu Dhabi, was led by key members of state – Sheikh Mohammed bin Rashid, Vice President and Ruler of Dubai and Sheikh Mohammed bin Zayed, Crown Prince of Abu Dhabi and Deputy Supreme Commander of the Armed Forces. Marching alongside the Emirate's rulers were other members of the ruling elite and government officials, along with hundreds of Emiratis dressed in the traditional national dress. 'Upon their arrival, Sheikh Mohammed bin Rashid and Sheikh Mohamed bin Zayed were greeted with folklore songs glorifying the country and its leadership' (Khaleej Times 2016). The procession represented a large-scale heritage spectacle that was aimed at reinforcing national identity. Widely publicised in the local media, the symbolic act served to reinforce national group identity by re-connecting Emirati residents with the historic centre and reinforcing the role of Qasr Al Hosn as a national symbol and iconic landmark. The opening event ultimately served to reinforce the fort's role in the national imaginary as a centre of participatory practice and a forum for heritage performance. Through the reanimation of the site, the national community was 'reimagined' (Anderson 2006).

Qasr Al Hosn Festival has become established as an annual event, which is reflected in the festival's popularity. Importantly, events such as heritage festivals can become 'permanent' features of a city's cultural landscape, producing long-term benefits in terms of image, tourism and support for local cultural production (Bianchini 1993b: 204). In 2013, the festival attracted over 30,000 visitors (Qasr Al Hosn Festival 2014b) and by 2016 visitor figures had risen to over 140,000 (TCA Abu Dhabi 2016). The rising visitor figures serve to demonstrate how autochthonous heritage is further linked to the tourism economy (Kirshenblatt-Gimblett 1998; Lyon and Wells 2012; Prager 2015).

Festivals serve through their contemporaneous and transient nature as performative and ritual aspects of the past. Each year both tangible and intangible aspects of the nation's heritage are displayed using a range of 'exhibitionary' and 'performative' processes. These processes have included temporary exhibitions, traditional performances, contemporary performances, smartphone QR trails, conservation tours and workshops. The festival features five zones Desert, Oasis, Marine, Abu Dhabi Island and Qasr Al Hosn.[7] Each features artefacts and performances that represent the socio-cultural environment of each zone, which include material objects, traditional practices and Emirati cuisine. In addition, buildings and *dhows* are often built and replicated as part of the festival spectacle. These zones represent the historical development of Abu Dhabi, which is seen as beginning 'with Bedouin desert and oases culture and culminating in the contemporary hyper modern oil metropolis' (Prager 2015: 37). Prager argues that the Qasr Al Hosn Festival fails to engage with tribal differences due to tighter control of the national narrative, which is reflected in the festival's exhibitionary and performative practices (*ibid.*: 36). However, this is not particularly surprising given the role Qasr Al Hosn, and the Qasr Al Hosn Festival play in producing and reproducing national identity and Abu Dhabi's central role as the seat of power. Missing from this imaginary is the UAE's prehistoric past, which dates back millennia. Instead, the past is linked purely to the recent past and the Emirati national narrative, which serves to support the nation-building and the emergence of the modern nation state.

Intangible heritage performances are particularly important during the Qasr Al Hosn Festival. Each year the festival features traditional performances, such as *Al-Taghrooda* (poetry) – traditional Bedouin chanted poetry, storytelling, oral narratives and poetry readings derived from the UAE's collective memories by leading UAE poets[8]; *Al-Ayyala* (dance); music; and falconry. Further cultural activities have included the process of making coffee, cooking and the inclusion of animals – horses, camels and falconry. These activities represent a performative heritage-arts programme, which serves to reinforce Qasr Al Hosn Festival role as a community space and national symbol. As I noted above, many of the Emirates intangible heritage practices have become increasingly globalised through their inscription on UNESCO's World Heritage List (UNESCO 2003a). In this sense, intangible representations of national heritage are not set apart from the transnational heritage economy. Instead, national identity remains central to the emerging transnational identity that is being shaped to both reinforce and promote the Emirates identity locally, regionally and internationally.

The Story of a Fort theatre performance was shown at Qasr Al Hosn Festival in 2013. The show featured a fusion of Emirati traditional performances incorporating dance, music and poetry recital and contemporary acrobatics and visual and light projections. The global dimensions of the show were linked to the credentials of the globally renowned director, Franco Dragone, who was one of the founders of Cirque du Soleil. The show had a clear national message, which was used to reinforce the development narrative that has been woven into the story of Qasr Al Hosn. As such, the show attempted to further historicise Abu Dhabi's emergence as the capital of the UAE and the development of the nation. The spoken narrative was presented as a particular form of community engagement as it was provided in Arabic with no English translation. While the festival may be aimed at both Emirati and national audiences and connected to the global discourse of performing arts, the theatre show suggests that certain performative aspects of the event served the Emirati group exclusively.

Each year, the theme for Qasr Al Hosn Festival changes, however, a common trend throughout the festival's programming has been developing the Fort's role as a national symbol and as a community space. Before the re-opening of Qasr Al Hosn, the Qasr Al Hosn Festival was further utilised as a site of 'performative' conservation. Each year visitors were able to 'witness' the re-emergence of the fort as they observed conservation work during the Qasr Al Hosn Festival. For example, in 2014, visitors were able to take a guided tour of the courtyard area of the palace and former inner fort.[9] The festival also served as a 'stage' for the conservation of the fort. During the 2015 festival, a recording booth was installed where visitors were asked to provide feedback on the best ways to restore the fort (Rizvi 2015). In doing so, the festival provided a consultative space for heritage practitioners to engage and consult with Emiratis through the process of conservation. In this sense, the festival became a space for 'exchanging stories' and 'celebrating our heritage' (Emirati Resident 44 2015: Interview). This suggests a 'dialogical approach' (Harrison 2013: 51) to conservation and community engagement.

Temporary exhibitions supported the Qasr Al Hosn Festival's role in supporting and developing the national story. For example, the 2016 exhibition, *The Story of Abu Dhabi & its People*, focused on the development of the Fort, its connection to the Abu Dhabi ruling family and their role in developing the nation and the role of the contemporary conservation and redevelopment of the site.[10] Again these exhibitionary practices demonstrate the co-produced nature of these exhibitions, and as such, they are hybrid in the sense that they are not produced in a vacuum of local and national interpretative strategies but produced in a consultative environment using both local and international actors and practitioners.

However, the performative and highly specialised nature of the festival challenges the dominance of international practitioners as the Emirati – professional heritage practitioners, and amateur members of the community become the authorised practitioners holding the 'cultural capital' (Bourdieu 1984) to produce the 'authorized heritage discourse' (Smith 2006) at Qasr Al Hosn and the Qasr Al Hosn Festival. Similarly, heritage facilitators at Heritage Villages in the UAE were considered to have specialised expertise and knowledge, which in turn are seen as having more 'authenticity' than other forms of heritage (Prager 2015: 32). In this setting, the power dynamics between international heritage practitioners and Emirati's shifts towards the national. The result is that the international practitioner plays a supporting role in constructing the story using the techniques and processes of heritage.

Heritage, commemoration and the ruling elite

As mentioned in the previous chapter, Sheikh Zayed I plays a central role within the memory and identity of the nation as he is considered to be the father of the nation. The importance of the role of the rulers within Emirati identity and official heritage narratives is further indicated within exhibitionary practices. Within the *Saadiyat Story* exhibition at Manarat al Saadiyat, on Saadiyat Island and the *Cultural District* exhibition at Emirates Palace quotes by Sheikh Zayed I are used to promote and endorse the heritage developments. In the *Cultural District* exhibition, Sheikh Zayed I was cited as having said, '[h]istory is a continuous chain of events. The present is only an extension of the past'.[11] These displays seek to compress time by seeking to show that development is part of the natural progression of time, where the past and the present co-exist and co-create the present. It also serves to establish Abu Dhabi's place in the centre further reminding both nationals and visitors of the centrality of the ruler's contribution to modernisation and the cosmopolitan nature of Abu Dhabi, which serves to link cultural development and modernity explicitly. As Davidson notes 'his statements are highly valued currency' (2009: 29). This is most evident in the following phrase, which has been attributed to the Sheikh Zayed I, 'he who has no past, has no future'. This phrase has become so embedded within the national rhetoric that all the interviewees, Emirati and expatriate, mentioned this phrase when asked about the role that Sheikh Zayed I is given within the heritage project. The phrase also appears regularly in exhibitions, government statements and in publications. However, it is important to remember that these words have most likely been altered to fit current needs. According to Nusseibeh '[h]e would have said something similar to this, but these are really marketing words. Sheikh Zayed was a Bedouin man whose language was not as precise as this' (2011: Interview).

The official opening ceremony for the Founder's Memorial took place on February 26, 2018. However, the memorial opened to the public later on April 22, 2018 in Abu Dhabi. The opening of the permanent national memorial coincided with the Year of Zayed. The Year of Zayed served to commemorate one hundred years since the birth of Sheikh Zayed I. The Founder's Memorial, located near Abu Dhabi's Corniche and Emirate Palace, is a monumental public artwork entitled, *The Constellation*. The artwork features a three-dimensional portrait of the late Sheikh by American public artist Ralph Helmick. The work weighs 250 tonnes and consists of an installation of 1,327 geometric shapes suspended from a thirty-metre-tall cube (Zacharias 2018). The Ministry of Presidential Affairs developed the Founder's Memorial as a 'permanent national tribute that commemorates and celebrates the timeless legacy of the late Sheikh Zayed bin Sultan Al Nahyan, his visionary leadership and his vast influence on the UAE and the wider world' (The Founder's Memorial n.d.). The late Sheikh is presented using a familiar narrative, which focuses on 'a personal story of Sheikh Zayed, the man; the qualities that defined his character, his interests and pastimes; the causes he championed; and the beliefs he held dear' (Barker Langham n.d.). The memorial is explicitly linked to both the commemoration of the former leader and the heritage of the UAE. At the opening ceremony in February 2018, Sheikh Mohammed bin Rashid stated that the memorial conveyed an 'important message that links future generations to the memory of the leader who laid the foundations of the nation' (Zacharias 2018), which further demonstrates the nationalist undertones of the project.

Members of the Emirati community expressed their concerns about profound social changes and the diminishment of traditions, but stated that they trusted the big heritage projects because of the late ruler's desire and faith in the process of modernisation. Furthermore, connections to the past and heritage were expressed as personal and were often described via familial links with their direct descendants, the tribe, and the nation through personal connection and recollections that individuals had of the late ruler. This is indicative of the trust that Emiratis have in the autocratic rule of the ruling elite. The act of preserving heritage is linked metaphorically to Sheikh Zayed I, who is seen as the 'father of the nation', the head of the family/tribe, the ruler of the nation. Through this linkage, heritage is not just an act of preservation, but the very process of heritage comes to be seen as a cultural tradition. As Findlow has noted 'the more ancient heritage of political hegemony, loyalty to their particular ruler, is expected to hold more sway than Arab patriotism generally' (2000: 27). The central metaphor is that of the family, with the President referred to as the father of the nation. The implication of this for heritage is that inclusion is based on being born into Emirati society.

Animated heritage

One way that intangible heritage is gaining popular appeal is through the production of animated heritage. ADACH has developed an animated cartoon character called *Hamdoon* to promote and educate children about national identity (Middle East Online 2009). As Seaman (2009) argues, '[t]he series follows the life of Hamdoon who grew up abroad due to his father's job and who has since returned to the UAE with his sister to live with his grandparents'. The intended heritage message is the importance of exploring and maintaining Emirati identity, which is used to 'reinforce the importance of respect for the older generations as well as instilling a sense of national identity' (*ibid.*). ADACH aims to engage with the younger generation within the national discourse by making *Hamdoon* a popular national figure and at the same time highlighting the importance of preserving the national identity (Middle East Online 2009). Importantly it enables ADACH to connect with the younger generation about heritage in a way that is relevant and entertaining.

Similarly, *Freej* is a three-dimensional animated television series that was launched in 2006. The word *Freej* translates from Arabic to English as 'neighbourhood' (Petrys 2007). The name, *Freej*, reflects the importance of community connection in the globalised city of Dubai, which is also a theme of the show (The Economist 2011). In an interview with *The Economist,* the show's creator Mohammed Saeed Harib described the series as 'the tale of four old national women living in a secluded neighbourhood in modern day Dubai' (*ibid.*). According to the *Freej* website 'the shows main characters, Um Saeed, Um Saloom, Um Allawi and Um Khammis try to live a peaceful life in the midst of the ever-expanding city around them, but the city's boom unveils new social issues every-day that they would have to tackle in their own simple way' (Freej n.d.). The New York Times produced a story about *Freej*, which highlighted how the programme tries to explore 'the tension between old and new Dubai' (Stelter 2009). These animations tie in to the national narrative as they address the UAE government's drive to preserve Emirati culture within the context of living with cosmopolitanism. In this sense, as Smith has argued more recently, 'heritage is a cultural performance, in which the meaning of the past for the present is continually recreated and reinterpreted to address the political and social problems of the present' (2017: 16). Heritage is put to work then, not only to capture and recreate the past but also to help make sense of the present through residents 'cosmopolitan outlook' (Beck 1999: 391), in which they are emotionally connected to entanglements between the past and the present, which is embedded with feelings of loss and nostalgia as the contemporary world is seen as both 'threatening' and historically located. They also represent aspects of social commentary that have become part of the national identity. Animated cartoons provide evidence to suggest that Emirati residents are engaging with and discussing how issues such as globalisation and the pace of social change are affecting Emirati national identity.

Heritage initiatives such as these are indicative not only of their popularity but also how oral narratives and contemporary media are engaging with Emiratis in innovative ways. These animations connect to Emiratis and the broader Arab public in a way that other forms arguably do not. The cultural heritage franchises could do well to take note of these successes and consider what they could learn from them.

Oral histories

One of the challenges in Abu Dhabi and the UAE is that history has largely not been written down. Ong has noted that many cultures, such as those in the Arab World, 'have practiced and been familiar with writing for centuries but have never fully adopted it as a dominant mode of production' (2007: 26; see also Erskine-Loftus 2013b). The *Qur'an*, for example, is a symbol of both Arab religion and identity, and literally means the spoken word, which is further evidence of the centrality of oral traditions to Arab societies. Maitha Salman Al-Zaabi (2011: Interview), archivist at the National Center for Documentation and Research, argued that the histories that have been written down are those that have been written by other (mainly Western) people. More recently, the value of collecting oral histories has grown in importance within the UAE. This has seen the implementation of a large-scale oral history project by the National Center for Documentation and Research (National Center for Documentation and Research Representative 2011: Interview).[12] The importance of this and other oral history projects is not only to capture aspects of heritage but also to serve as an alternative source of history as a great deal of the documented histories have been recorded by international observers (Heard-Bey 2004).

Articles in the UAE's national press illustrate the vital role that poetry plays within Emirati society (see for example Ghazal 2011; Leech 2013). According to Sharar, director of the Sharjah Nabati Poetry Centre and well-known Emirati poet, poetry traditions have evolved but also provide important historical information:

> Before a poet would limit his poetry to the area where he lived and the stories that happened there. That way we can trace back what happened where and when. You can find old poems, some pre-Islamic, that comment on every aspect of life, from the most mundane like complaints about lack of water - to irresponsible youth, to tribal marriages and battles that help us trace our own history.
>
> (Ghazal 2011)

Sharar also goes on to note that there has been a transformation from more localised poems to ones that address more global concerns and events (*ibid.*). The role of poetry as an expression of heritage should therefore not be underestimated due to its central role within Islamic culture. *Millions Poet* and *Prince of Poets* are televised poetry competitions. *Million's Poet* was established by ADACH and is broadcast on both Abu Dhabi TV and the dedicated Million's Poet channel. Both shows are extremely popular, attracting millions of viewers. *Million's Poet* is based on Nabati poetry, which is a form of poetry that emerged from 'popular' culture, and Prince of Poets is based on Classical Arabic poetry (Holes and Abu Athera 2011; see also Langham and Barker 2014: 92). These autochthonous transformations represent a continuous and evolving process of hybridisation. Seen in this way heritage performances such as poetry combine with other factors such as globalisation, intangible practices and transnational heritage discourses.

Oral history holds the potential for furthering and supporting the interpretation and preservation of cultural heritage in Abu Dhabi. In a panel discussion at Manarat al Saadiyat on January 30, 2012, entitled *Heritage and Antiquity through Modern Eyes*,[13] Hossam Mahdy, Building Conservation Supervisor at ADACH, gave a presentation in which he illustrated how the loss of heritage is inscribed within poetry traditions. He suggested during his presentation that 'in classical Arabic poetry the poems generally start with a few sad lines about how the built heritage is changing as the world changes, they also refer to the standing remains of ancient sites and so on' (Mahdy 2012). In 2011, ADACH had begun to respond to the need for intangible heritage infrastructures through the development of initiatives such as the Al Ain Centre for Music in the World of Islam and the Bait al Oud, which translates from Arabic into English as the house of Oud (ADACH Representative 3 2011: Interview). These initiatives aim to encourage Emiratis to learn to play traditional musical instruments and to promote them as aspects of Emirati heritage.

However, while all of these initiatives seem to be moving in the right direction, a fundamental problem remains, which is that there are very few specialists who can record and interpret oral history and other aspects of intangible heritage. The problem then comes back to the reliance on expatriate workers who, as we have seen, do not always have the cultural knowledge or language skills to support their professional skills set. Priority needs to be given to developing intangible heritage by encouraging Emiratis to contribute both their existing knowledge and to develop careers within the sector.

Interpreting and defining heritage

I wanted to find out how the concept of heritage (*turath*) was understood and interpreted locally, and how this aligned with official understandings of heritage in Abu Dhabi. The purpose of asking this question was to first gain a better understanding of the local community's understanding of the term, to consider descriptions of what Emirati heritage is (or could be) and, to assess the appropriateness of the term and its use within the heritage sector in Abu Dhabi. I asked interview and survey respondents to describe what heritage (*turath*) meant to them and to pick one word that they felt could best describe what they consider to be their heritage.

Due to the hybrid processes that are at play within Abu Dhabi, it was vital to explore whether different concepts and understanding of heritage existed. The interview and survey data collected from Emirati respondents suggested that heritage (*turath*) was connected to national identity and kinship in the UAE. Survey responses indicated that Emirati understandings of heritage was directly connected to national identity and kinship; in particular heritage was associated with the 'past', 'traditions', 'national identity' and the 'family/tribe'[14] through an active process of performing heritage in both informal everyday settings; language (spoken and written); food; manners; dress; and formal settings, such as weddings and religious observances. Through the performative process, heritage was connected to the past, present and the future in an active cycle of renewal and reproduction; 'Heritage, to me, is carrying the past into the future. It is the customs, practices, ideals and values that have been part of our society for many years and still are' (Survey Respondent 23).

Heritage was also associated with the practices and ways of doing things that connect individuals to the Emirati group. National dress was important as it was used to distinguish Emirati nationals. Khalaf in his ethnographic study of UAE dress suggests that 'Emiratis (both men and women) use their national dress as a significant boundary marker for maintaining their distinct national identity within their highly globalized multi-ethnic urban contexts' (2005: 265). In other words, dress was used as a marker of belonging to the Emirati group. National identity was therefore linked to common traits that are associated with 'being Emirati', which are based on shared values that are attached to identity discourses both past and the present.

Langham and Barker suggested within their discussion of heritage terminology that *turath* is explicitly linked within the Arabic use 'to encompass all cultural patterns and habits that are passed from one generation to the next' and that this use suggests that a 'much greater emphasis is placed on the generational transmission of culture in the Gulf' (2014: 90). Partrick has observed similar trends from his analysis of nationalism in the Gulf States. He notes drawing on the results from a government survey that around half of those Emirati's surveyed said that 'common cultural values and traditions' were central to national identities (2009: 18). Therefore, as Miller argues 'a nationality exists when its members believe that it does and that this belief is historically grounded' (2000: 28). These traits then are used to establish who is included and who is excluded from the nation.

Interrogating this further, Emiratis saw their identity as linked to specific aspects of the past, which were particularly illuminating in their connections to intangible heritage and the active nature of producing heritage in Abu Dhabi, through heritage performances such as national day, poetry, the practice of the Islamic faith and familial activities across generations,[15] all of which were connected to the family and broader tribal relations through the positioning of Sheikh Zayed I as the 'father of the nation'. Heritage was seen as important not only for presenting the past but also for keeping heritage traditions alive, as Emirati resident Al-Rumaithi stated:

> For us, Arab heritage is different from the way you westerners see it. If you go to an old hut that used to be a traditional house they (the interviewee was referring to foreign heritage practitioners) see this building as heritage. This is not heritage; this is history. Things you do not use anymore you put in the museum. Things you still use: poems, manners, behaviours, music, dances, this is the heritage. This is what is still used. If they (the interviewee is referring to Emiratis) talk about the past, it is history; if they talk about heritage, it is the traditions.
>
> (2011: Interview)

The performative and emotive aspects of heritage were therefore given primacy over tangible interpretations. Heritage, in this sense, is an active part of identity-making. Seen in this way as Kirshenblatt-Gimblett argues in relation to intangible heritage, 'people are not only objects of cultural preservation but also subjects. They are not only cultural carriers and transmitters but also agents in the heritage enterprise itself' (2007: 179). In other words, performing heritage through the act of transmission situates heritage in the present, it is not purely heritage of the past, but the heritage of the past, present and the future (Picton 2010; Forero 2012; Langham and Barker 2014).

Heritage in Abu Dhabi is primarily an aspect of identity; for example, *turathi huwaiti* is a common saying meaning 'my heritage is my identity' (Emirati Resident 1 2011: Interview). It was suggested that 'keeping it [heritage] alive and practising it is what identifies' Emirati and in particular Abu Dhabians.[16] This relates to what Partrick has observed is a 'sense of a *Shakseeya Khaleeji* (Gulf personality, i.e. common cultural traits)', which is based on a 'manifestation of shared history' reflected in shared cultural and familial experiences' (2009: 31). My findings also suggest that *turath* is used as a way for Emiratis to distinguish themselves from outsiders and that group belonging comes from significant meanings that are attached to Emirati identity, which is connected to tribal and familial ties.

However, I argue that these aspects of heritage are based on an 'essentialist' view, which is problematic as it suggests that heritage is based on a set of unchanging characteristics that are passed from one generation to another. While traditions of performance may evolve, their role in the national imagination is directly connected to a 'pure' notion of Emirati origins. A pure origins approach allows no room for alternative readings. As such, it does not account for Emiratis of mixed descent to be given space within the national imagination. Postcolonial discourses have challenged essentialist identities based on 'pure', 'essentialised' or undisputed notions (Ashcroft, Griffiths, Tiffen and Tiffin 1995). The hybrid role of heritage is challenged as national heritage becomes associated with a 'pure' Emirati identity.

Far from being separate to the developments on Saadiyat Island, autochthonous heritage is used to develop further and consolidate the Emirate's transnational identity. Cosmopolitanism is activated through linkages to trade and cross-cultural relations, which is historicised through the strategic deployment of heritage. However, producing cosmopolitan identities is problematic as there is reluctance by the state to publicly recognise and explore aspects of the nation's past that do not fit with official state-sanctioned accounts and interpretations of the past. This illustrates the problem of developing cosmopolitan identities within autocratic nation states, where the public representation of alternative identities and traditions are marginalised and tightly controlled. I have demonstrated through my analysis of modern heritage, attitudes towards the material past are changing, which is largely the result of the introduction of international standards and procedures. However, this process is problematic as it serves to colonise more autochthonous forms of heritage, which results in global processes being given primacy over autochthonous processes.

Furthermore, as I have shown, neither autochthonous nor global heritage operate in a vacuum. Instead, both operate within a hybridised system where the power knowledge-networks are activated continuously. Instead, there are a series of emergent heritage processes that are developing alongside the planned institutions on Saadiyat Island, and it is essential to understand how both autochthonous and franchised heritage work together as a hybrid process.

Notes

1 Similar patterns have been observed in other Gulf cities such as Muhrraq in Bahrain, see for example Alraouf (2014: 177).
2 The programme of conservation and restoration at Qasr Al Hosn began due to the discovery of trapped moisture on the fort's walls, which was causing corrosion (Qasr Al Hosn 2018d).
3 The National Consultative Council was founded by Sheikh Zayed I between 1968 and 1970 (Qasr Al Hosn 2018c).
4 *Khoos* is the process of weaving date palm fronds together to form an object such as buildings and everyday objects such as food covers. Both men and women practise *Khoos*.
5 *Talli* is a traditional form of decorative embroidery practised by Emirati women.
6 Seacrafts included boat (*dhow*) building and the manufacturing of fishing nets and traps.
7 The Qasr Al Hosn zone was introduced in 2016 to develop the festivals further focus on the fort's links to the conservation, modern architectural heritage and archaeology (Khaleej Times 2016).

8 The 2014 Qasr Al Hosn Festival featured poetry readings by Saood Al Messabi, Hadi Al Mansoori, Hamdan Al Samahi, Ibrahim Al Shami, Rashid Al Mansoori and Hamdan Al Mahrami (TCA Abu Dhabi 2016).
9 Observation, Qasr Al Hosn Festival, Qasr Al Hosn, Abu Dhabi, February 22, 2014.
10 Observation, *The Story of Abu Dhabi & Its People* exhibition, Qasr Al Hosn, Abu Dhabi, February 11, 2016.
11 Observation, *Cultural District* Exhibition, Emirates Palace, October 11, 2010.
12 The NCDR was set up in 1968 and was the first of its kind in the region. The NCDR's remit focuses on 'collecting documents and information relating to the history, politics, social life and culture of the gulf region and Arabian Peninsula'. See the website for the National Archives (n.d.).
13 The panel discussion *Heritage and Antiquity through Modern Eyes* was held at Manarat al Saadiyat, Abu Dhabi on January 30, 2013. The purpose of the panel discussion was to discuss the similarities and differences between Western and non-Western approaches to heritage. The speakers on the panel included Hossam Mahmoud Mahdy, Building Conservation Supervisor, Abu Dhabi Tourism & Culture Authority; Daniel Roger, Curator, Etruscan and Roman Antiquities department, Louvre, Paris; and Jean-François Charnier, Curator of Heritage, Agence France-Muséums.
14 Survey Respondent 1; Survey Respondent 9; Survey Respondent 17; Survey Respondent 30; Survey Respondent 31.
15 There were differences between how older and younger members of society made connections to heritage. Younger Emiratis tended to place primacy on familial activities and exchanges over other forms of intangible aspects of heritage.
16 Survey Respondent 28.

8 New light
The Louvre Abu Dhabi

The opening of the Louvre Abu Dhabi on November 11, 2017 attracted widespread media coverage as the world's international press descended on the Emirate. Leaders of state, politicians, high-profile arts personnel and celebrities were invited to the museum as part of the opening ceremonies and events. The result was considerable fan-fare and column inches in global news outlets. The agreement between the UAE and France included, as noted in chapter three, the development of a permanent collection, the loaning of artworks from thirteen French institutions and the circulation of temporary exhibitions. This chapter examines how the cultural heritage franchise, in its final form, has been shaped by the cultural partnership between the United Arab Emirates and France. It examines how the discourse of 'cosmo-universalism' has been translated into the Louvre Abu Dhabi and the impact of this approach on the museum's collection and exhibitionary practices. The chapter then goes on to examine how travelling exhibitions and object loans serve to further develop the franchise relationship and by extension, the development of transnational identities across borders.

A 'cosmo-universal' project

As argued throughout this book, the Louvre Abu Dhabi has attempted to develop what I term a discourse of cosmo-universalism. In doing so, I suggest that the Louvre Museum through the franchise partnership is attempting to move away from its dominant past and its direct connection to nineteenth-century colonialism and imperialism (see Shelton 2000; Boast 2011 for further discussions around postcolonial museum legacies). The partnership offered the Louvre Museum in Paris, and more broadly the French Government, an unprecedented opportunity to re-position its contemporary identity within postcolonial terms through the development of a discourse that claims to be both globally inclusive and challenges the global art historical canon. I argued in chapter four that the partnership is as much about developing France's national identity in the Middle East as it is about the UAE developing its identity on the global stage, particularly in western

European nations. For Abu Dhabi, the partnership offers the opportunity to not only represent its power as an emerging global nation but also its ability to exert that power over the French nation, which arguably represents Abu Dhabi's neo-colonial power.

France's intentions are overtly positioned within the rhetoric around the new museum. For example, in the foreword of the Louvre Abu Dhabi's catalogue, it states that the museum 'offers an unprecedented opportunity to provide an interdisciplinary presentation of France's public collections, to show them to new people in new ways' (Al-Mubarak and Martinez 2017: 5). In addition, the rhetoric serves to re-position the Louvre within postcolonial terms, stating that:

> The discovery – or rediscovery – of the works exhibited in the Louvre Abu Dhabi is a unique experience: on the one hand because they are seen in a new light, that of Abu Dhabi filtered through the dome designed by Jean Nouvel, and on the other because of their dialogue with the works with which they are not usually presented increases their polysemy'.
>
> (Ladreit de Lacharrière 2017a: 6)

In so doing, France is attempting to position itself, somewhat ironically, as a leader of postcolonial transnational cultural production.

I discussed in chapter two how the western European museum models that emerged during the nineteenth and early twentieth centuries were tied to colonial and imperial imperatives, which served to present and reinforce the superiority of the Western world (Young 1991, 2001; Harrison 1997; Hooper-Greenhill 2000, 2003; Bennett 2004; Boast 2011). These colonial projects resulted in the large-scale acquisition and removal of objects and artworks from the New World. These objects were then, through the museum, ordered and classified, which led to 'authorized' processes of collecting, conserving, education, research and exhibition. Western progress was displayed alongside the exoticised primitive 'Other' (Bennett 2004). The museum was, and arguably continues to be, explicitly used as a tool of the nation state (Anderson 2006; Harrison 2013; Knell 2016, 2018). This history of museum development has left a lasting legacy in the form of an arguably deeply contested and politicised heritage of museological practice and representation. Museums have sought to address these legacies by responding to postcolonial and post-modern critiques within what some authors have termed the 'new museology' (Vergo 1989). The idea of the nation as defined by the state, inside and outside of pre-defined borders, persists and has an impact on how the past is imagined and reproduced by contemporary nation states (Wakefield 2020).

The new museology served to shift the focus of the museum as primarily research and collecting institutions to emphasising the museum's role as an audience-driven institution in service to its multiple communities (Vergo 1989; Macdonald and Fyfe 1996; Macdonald 1998). This shift towards audiences brought issues of social inclusion, equality and consultation to the fore (Clifford 2001; Cooke and McLean 2002; Sandell 2002; Peers and Brown 2003; Mason 2004). As museums grappled with new ways of thinking about their role as collecting institutes and as 'collaborative' audience-driven spaces (MacDonald 1998; Peers and Brown 2003; Phillips 2007; Boast 2011). These changes led Bennett (2004) to argue that museums have become 'differencing machines'. In this sense, difference and multiplicity of understanding are emphasised.

Scholars have noted the deeply entrenched links between globalisation and postcolonial art; and the associated role of geography, economics and social and cultural history (De Angelis, Ianniciello, Orabona and Quadraro 2014). As is overtly evident, the foundation of the Louvre Abu Dhabi and its discourses are intimately connected to the legacy of the enlightenment and its connection to French museology and consequently European colonialism. Zuliani argues that the postcolonial museum is embedded within a 'complex network of relations (both conceptual and of power)' (2014: 175). And Hall (2013) has argued that although postcolonialism has brought new ways of thinking and doing cultural work, colonialism is still embedded within the contemporary world.

The cosmo-universal rhetoric can be further identified through the positioning of the curatorial project and the collection. The Louvre Abu Dhabi has attempted to rethink museological frameworks and position them within postcolonial thought, to present a 'transversal view of art history' (Noujaim 2018). The museum's discourse claims that the collection challenges and repositions artworks in a way that reveals 'shared symbols' (*ibid.*). However, the reliance on 'universal' and 'enlightenment' frames of reference serves to draw attention to the history and geography politics of the museum. The project's global rhetoric positions Abu Dhabi geographically at the centre. The universal rhetoric that surrounds the Louvre Abu Dhabi presents the museum as a 'meeting place' where humanity can be seen in a new light. 'See Humanity in New Light' was the slogan featured in the Louvre Abu Dhabi's advertising campaign that featured on billboards along the Abu Dhabi highway and other promotional literature. The reference to light links to how the Louvre Abu Dhabi's dome roof reflects light onto the galleries. The metaphorical role of light has been overtly linked to the exhibition of artworks in Abu Dhabi. The rhetoric is used to both justify the presence of French collections in Abu Dhabi and to reinforce the museum's cosmopolitan and dialogic approach. For example, Marc Ladreit de Lacharrière, President of the Agence France-Muséums, states in the Louvre Abu Dhabi catalogue that

> on the one hand because they [the artworks] are seen in a new light, that of Abu Dhabi filtered through the dome designed by Jean Nouvel, and on the other because of their dialogue with the works with which they are not usually presented increases their polysemy
>
> (Ladreit de Lacharrière 2017a: 6)

More broadly of course reference to light could also be linked to the Enlightenment traditions of the Louvre Museum. In this sense, the geographical circulation and display of artworks is a politically laden process.

What we see in Abu Dhabi is an international policy focused on reframing global heritage through the 'cosmo-universal' positioning of the Louvre Abu Dhabi. For example, the opening ceremony and related events celebrating the launch of the museum emphasised the role of the museum as an agent of cross-border diplomacy. According to Jean-François Charnier, scientific director of Agence France-Muséums '[t]he aim is to create a universal perspective on things, not from a western or an eastern perspective, but from Abu Dhabi's position as a crossroads' (cited in *The National* newspaper, Leech 2014b). The positioning of a new collection jointly created, albeit temporarily, by the Louvre and the Department of Culture in Abu Dhabi has been overtly linked to the goal of bridging East and West by creating a meeting point. As Jessup and Smith suggest '[t]he curatorial dimensions of cultural diplomacy initiatives...attest to the important role that exhibitions and museums play in the sphere of global relations' (2016: 286). In effect, the museum comes to operate as a 'cosmopolitan canopy' (Schorch, Waterton and Watson 2017), which is activated through the politics of state and bilateral relations.

Anderson coined the term 'cosmopolitan canopy' to define 'neutral social settings, which no one group expressly owns but all are encouraged to share, situated under a protective umbrella, a canopy' (2011: 275). The 'cosmopolitan canopy' for Anderson is a place where people from diverse backgrounds can come together. Schorch, Waterton, and Watson whose analysis of the Immigration Museum, Melbourne, and the Te Papa museum suggest that the two museums offer a spatial 'canopy', drawing on the work of Anderson, under which different cultural perspectives can interact across a common sphere (2017: 100). In a sense, the Louvre Abu Dhabi has attempted to create its own 'cosmopolitan canopy', which serves as a zone for cross-cultural contact and understanding. The positioning of the new collection has therefore been overtly linked to the goal of bridging East and West, and more specifically Western and Islamic worlds. The Louvre Abu Dhabi explicitly presents itself as a space of equality and neutrality. However, due to current political issues within the Gulf, in particular the ongoing Qatar Blockade and broader tensions in the region, the museum, regardless of its best intentions, is inevitably not able to operate as a globally inclusive space.

The idea of Abu Dhabi being a global space of contact and exchange is omni-present within the museum's interior. Before entering the first gallery, the visitor enters the Grand Vestibule where they encounter a map designed like a portolan chart, an ancient navigational map. The map features Abu Dhabi's shoreline etched with the names of all the places where the museum's objects are drawn from. According to the museum's catalogue, the presence of these names adds further weight to the universal positioning of the museum, giving the impression that, 'the world converges on Abu Dhabi or that the Louvre Abu Dhabi lies at the centre of the world' (Ladreit de Lacharrière 2017b: 22). In this sense, the postcolonial museum continues to take an inherently ideological' and 'strategic' approach (Cuno 2011: 44). Essentially, the partnership represents a shared politics of identity motivated by global and political interests.

Challenging the canon: a global collection?

As mentioned in the previous section, the Louvre Abu Dhabi's curatorial approach aims to cross-cut the cultural and geographical divides that have traditionally been at the centre of global art history. It is also an attempt to challenge the Western-centric nature of the art historical canon. Traditionally, the art historical canon has produced a narrative focused on the artists, events, ideas and movements, which emerged within and alongside developments in western European nations. Ultimately, it aims to challenge and re-position the approach to art history that emerged within and alongside the colonial and imperial directives of early nineteenth-century nationalism. National identity and difference were prioritised within the nineteenth-century Louvre Museum, whereas, in the twenty-first-century Louvre transnational identity and pluralism are stressed. Louvre Abu Dhabi is attempting to de-centre the art historical narrative. More recently, scholars have begun to argue for a more globally focused art historical narrative. Tomii (2018) for example, calls for an art historical narrative that can identify and link commonalities and difference across geographical boundaries and disciplinary boundaries. The rhetoric that surrounds the Louvre Abu Dhabi claims the museum has developed a collection that represents and presents a new global history of art. Prior to the museum's opening a representative from the Louvre Abu Dhabi suggested:

> Its unique museological approach – displaying objects together and arts of the same period but from geographical origins – will create a dialogue between artworks, sculptures and objects: visitors will discover shared influences and connections between different cultures around the globe – giving insight into the history of humankind since the beginning of time.
>
> (Louvre Abu Dhabi Representative 2011: Interview)

This approach was widely referenced during the museum's official opening. Charnier noted that '[i]t is the first time we not only have the decompartmentalization of museum departments but a means of reflecting on unexpected dialogues between artefacts' (cited in Wainwright 2017). Which means that rather than separating works by location or artistic movement, the museum has placed works from different cultures alongside each other in dialogue. Bourrat (2017) presented a paper at the 2018 *Museums in Arabia* Conference in Bahrain where she discussed the Louvre Abu Dhabi's approach to developing the collection. She suggested that the Louvre Abu Dhabi was attempting to shift the focus from 'a comparative or a hierarchy of civilizations' to one that prioritises global diversity and similarities. Bourrat went on to suggest that the artworks in the Louvre Abu Dhabi's collection were strategically chosen 'to foster dialogue between them, whether through their shape, their pattern, their material or anything else that could generate sense and highlight crossroad connections, and sometimes intercultural dialogues, through the aesthetical or semantic values of the artworks' (*ibid.*). The act of displaying artworks side by side has its antecedents in the early princely collections where private collections were hung in a way to compare and contrast works side-by-side, which was linked to 'cultural capital' (Bourdieu 1984) in the sense that the elite aristocratic classes had the knowledge to understand the works on display (Duncan 1995).

However, the Louvre Abu Dhabi's shift in categorisation was also down to necessity rather than a shift in the ideological approach. Charnier notes in the introduction of the Louvre Abu Dhabi museum catalogue the difficulties of developing a universal collection during:

> a time of increased sensitivity to the question of provenance, when items of ancient art and especially archaeology are regarded as part of the heritage and identity of the countries in which they are discovered.
>
> (2017: 11)

He goes onto to suggest that the dialogic approach of the curatorial team was needed 'to compensate for the paucity of works' (*ibid.*). Charnier's statements are telling of the constraints within which the Louvre Abu Dhabi team has had to rethink their approach to creating the twenty-first-century global collection.

Furthermore, the Louvre Abu Dhabi is not the first museum to attempt a more globally focused curatorial approach. De Angelis *et al.* note that the Museum of World Culture, which opened in Gothenburg, Sweden in 2004, was developed around the idea of 'world culture'. The Museum of World Culture is one of four museums that make up Stockholm's national museums body, National Museums of World Culture.[1] Bodenstien and Pagani note that the singular 'world culture' was a conscious choice 'to break with the ethnographic traditions of displaying multiple "cultures" side by side' (2014: 46). The Museum of World Culture was established with dialogic aims as suggested by the museum's website, which states that:

> The Museum of World Culture aims to function as a platform for *dialogues* and reflections, where many different *voices* can be heard and controversial and contentious topics discussed - a place where people can feel at home and reach *across borders* [current author's emphasis].
>
> (National Museums of World Culture n.d.[a])

The global and cosmopolitan approach of the museum body is also evident in the following quotation from the *Swedish Code of Statutes Instruction SFS 2007:1185 and Annual Appropriation Directions*:

> National Museums of World Culture is responsible for displaying and bringing to life the various cultures of our world, in particular cultures outside of Sweden. Furthermore, the agency is to document and illustrate different cultural manifestations and conditions as well as cultural encounters and variations from a historical, contemporary, national and international perspective.
>
> (*ibid.*)

The Museum of World Culture elaborates on its role by emphasising global representation and its desire for a dialogue with its visitors.

> The Museum of World Culture aim to help make today's world more understandable through the provision of knowledge and perspectives. The objects and artefacts that are kept at the Museums of World Culture come from every corner of the world and represent many thousand years of human creations and creativity. By maintaining a dialogue with our visitors, we hope to embrace the diversity of our world and thus, contribute to a sustainable global development.
>
> (National Museums of World Culture n.d.[b])

What we see is the emergence of 'new platforms for a neo-colonial positioning of the new museum in relation to the ex-colonial Other' (Boast 2011: 65). Global collections are being re-framed as dialogic and cosmopolitan with very little real evidence to suggest that they have become untangled from their essentialised and entrenched histories.

In the museum's highlights catalogue, Manuel Rabaté, director of the Louvre Abu Dhabi, suggests that '[t]he collection of the Louvre Abu Dhabi is universal in its scope: from prehistory to the latest contemporary commissions' (2017: 7). Rabaté goes on to state that the museum 'does not attempt to show all the artistic traditions of the world but the humanity that is common to us all'. According to Bourrat (2017), the Louvre Abu Dhabi '...has chosen to use its collection to emphasise the universal elements that unite humanity through its presentation of a global history of art'. French authorities claim that the Louvre Abu Dhabi's developing collection is 'the key to understanding the characteristics common to all humanity and the elements that constitute and form our distinct identity filtered through the prism of time, culture and history' (Ladreit de Lacharrière 2017a: 6). The focus on humanity draws attention back to the project's similarities to the universal and globalising discourses of UNESCO. Yet, who decides how and what is defined as 'common humanity' is left undefined. What is needed is a more critical and rigorous reflection on how and to what extent the Louvre Abu

Dhabi draws on and diverges from the parent museum's highly political colonial and imperial past. As discussed throughout this book the museum's self-proclaimed universality remains a problem. A truly postcolonial approach to the Louvre Abu Dhabi would surely have moved away from the French rhetoric of essentialised universal discourses. Furthermore, the museum has made little attempt to incorporate minority communities into the museum.

In the past, dominant heritage discourses have excluded individuals and groups such as indigenous groups, lower social classes, women, LGBT, the disabled and so on, through the presentation of selected aspects of the past to maintain both the boundaries and identities of the nation (Graham, Ashworth and Tunbridge 2000; Sandell 2002; Smith 2006; Harrison 2013). The use of transnational heritage processes has led to further questioning of these boundaries, both within and across borders, which has brought increased focus on postcolonial representation, the emergence of counter-narratives and co-production within national and transnational settings. Yet the Louvre Abu Dhabi has failed to explicitly engage with issues around inclusion and counter-narratives.

A transversal view: the Louvre Abu Dhabi galleries

The Louvre Abu Dhabi galleries are arranged chronologically and are divided into twelve chapters beginning with *Chapter 1: The First Villages* and ending with *Chapter 12: A Global Stage*,[2] indicating that the museum still draws on traditional French museology. This has led some to criticise the museum for being 'more like a history textbook describing a worldly narrative of civilization - a narrative largely diluted of its darkness and tragedies. In an attempt to marry large concepts like religion and culture across geographical barriers, a holistic view of humanity is actually lost' (Abrar and Sinha 2017). Question marks were raised during the museum's development regarding the inclusion of works that would reference religion and nudity.

In response to questions regarding the display of religious and nude subjects Mubarak al-Muhairi addressed the question of religion in an interview with the *New York Times* suggesting that 'in principle there are no restrictions'; he went on to stress the collaborative nature of the partnership by arguing that 'both sides will agree on what is shown' (Riding 2007a: 2). The Louvre Abu Dhabi has incorporated works that represent different faiths and beliefs. For example, in one display case a Quran, a gothic Bible and a Yemenite Torah are shown side by side in the World Religions Gallery in the museum. During the *Worlds in a Museums Symposium* al-Mubarak (2018) stated that the World Religions gallery was the most popular with visitors. In addition, there are numerous works on display that are representative of male and female nude forms.

Perhaps not surprisingly, the cultural heritage franchise agreement sets out a clear power dynamic in terms of the developing collection. Articles 7 and 10 stipulate that the Agency must submit to the UAE proposals for all acquisitions and loans for prior approval. Curiously a clause in Article 7 goes on to remove any French responsibility regarding future disputes stating that 'The French Party, the Agency or the members of the Commission proposed by the Agency cannot be held responsible for the acquisition decisions taken by the UAE, the Museum or its agent' (Poncelet 2007). The agreement is illuminating in that it demonstrates that ultimately, the decision-making process is taken by UAE officials and that the French Government, Agency France-Muséums and French curators play a fundamentally supportive role. The problem, of course, remains and relates to the highly political role that 'cultural capital' plays in shaping the partnership and the museum in Abu Dhabi.

As McClellan notes 'Western prototypes such as the British Museum (1753) and Louvre (1793) promoted the host nation's standing as "civilised" by displaying what coalesced during the early modern period as a European canon of cultural achievement in the forms of Greco Roman and Italian Renaissance art together with examples of native achievement' (2012: 278). An illuminating statement appears within the agreement for the Louvre Abu Dhabi. Article 1 states that the museum will display 'major objects in the fields of archaeology, fine arts and decorative arts, open to all periods including contemporary art, although focusing on the classical period' (Poncelet 2007). This is rather strange given the Louvre Abu Dhabi's claims to resisting art historical divides between East and West.

Bourrat (2017) has discussed the role of 'contact masterpieces' within the museum's collection, which she defines as 'a concept to define the status of productions produced in the particular period of direct encounter between two worlds and that by their nature testify of the issues (economical, political, or cultural) taking place, consciously or not'. She suggests that they are not so much 'hybrid or colonial' but rather that they are 'multicultural' and 'between disciplines', and as a result have been marginalised within art historical and museological approaches due to their categorisation into separate departments, such as art, archaeology, anthropology and so forth. According to Bourrat 'an artwork can be the testimony of the encounter between two cultures, whether through its iconography (the Benin artists of Nigeria representing a Portuguese soldier), through its technique (a European iconography reproduce in a feather work painting by Aztec artists) or through its material (as brass and glass pearls of European provenance appearing on African traditional artworks or chemical blue on Melanesian sculptures as the Uli)' (*ibid.*). Bourrat uses the acquisition of two namban screens produced by Japanese artists as an example of early contact between Asian and European peoples' in the sixteenth and seventeenth centuries as observed and commented on by far-eastern artists of the time (*ibid.*). However, the 'contact masterpiece' approach fails to adequately unpick how these works create tension and resistance either through their histories or through the histories in which they represent.

For example in Gallery Four, which is themed 'Universal Religions', a stained-glass window from a Gothic, French church and an Islamic mosque lamp are displayed side-by-side. The text panel for the Gallery suggests that the linkages between the objects is based on the symbolism of light, which is presented as a 'universal metaphor'.[3] As such the narrative places these objects together within a dehistoricised and neutral narrative. However, by doing so, the museum removes any room for discussion around the problematic histories of these objects, which would have been created during the time of the Crusades (the works province is set somewhere between the twelfth and fourteenth centuries) when political tensions between Christian and Muslim nations were problematical (DeTurk and Wakefield 2018).

It also fails to situate the production of non-Western artworks within the system of power and political influences under which they were produced and circulated. For example, Rabaté (2017) states in the Louvre Abu Dhabi highlights catalogue that the works in the collection were chosen as they 'demonstrate the interconnection of ideas and techniques that result from global networks of communication and exchange'. The discussion and representation of 'contact masterpieces' need to be able to critically engage with the broader art historical canon to ask how and why specific works were circulated at particular times, who controlled the agency of artworks and consequently circulation and representation. This approach fails to adequately account for and address the complex ways in which objects 'reflect or embody external realities' and 'exert their own influence and *enact* relationships' (Schorch, Waterton and Watson 2017: 94), especially in terms of their colonial legacies (Harrison 1997; Sandell 2002; Peers and Brown 2003; Boast 2011). By placing particular objects, side-by-side the curators are producing narratives on and between those pieces. Besides, the fact that these works need to be singled out as 'contact works' serves to illustrate the still dominant role of the canon. Also, the dominance of 'masterpieces' within the collection serves to illustrate that the art historical canon still drives representation in the Louvre Abu Dhabi. The works on display have been chosen due to their quality. Perhaps most importantly, the museum needs to exhibit and explore the 'intersectionality' between different sensitive topics; it is not enough to place objects side by side. At present, the displays seem to be policy-led, in that they are being used to reinforce the cosmo-universal aims of the project. How the museum diverges from this and tackles pressing social and political issues will be crucial to its role as a global museum. As Staiff and Bushell suggest by illustrating cross-cultural similarities, there is potential for conversations around difference (2003: 157; see also Schorch,

Waterton and Watson 2017: 94). What is crucial here is that the museum creates a space in which those questions and conversations can be facilitated,
and this is where access, interpretation and communication will be critical
to the developing role of the museum.

Furthermore, we see a process of attempting to de-politicise the artworks
within the collection. Limited details are provided concerning the biography and description of the works. Instead, the emphasis is placed on showing the works purely as 'art', art, which is in dialogue in a predominantly
artistic sense. Kirshenblatt-Gimblett's refers to this process as the 'art of
detachment' (1998: 25) whereby dominance is placed on 'aesthetics'. However, by doing so, the museum is attempting to mask the works' role in identity politics. The museum has and continues to have a central role in the
construction of meanings and values. As Hooper-Greenhill, argues, museums hold the power of representation (1992: 19). This power manifests itself
through the activities of the museum, which include 'the power of officiating
narratives, the power to define and categorise and the power to represent
the past and the present' (*ibid.*: 19). Who is and who is not included and/
or represented has become a central question within museum and heritage
studies (Sandell 2002). However, the issue of representation becomes highly
charged when claims are made to the 'universal' and the 'global'. Inevitably,
no museum can represent everybody, everywhere, at all times. This means
that the museum is always making value judgements about whom to include,
and what message it conveys.

Furthermore, meaning-making is a complex process. There is no singular
way of interpreting or positioning an object, which becomes apparent when we
consider the museum's audience. Hall (2013) in his seminal work *Representation*, discussed the role of the viewer in terms of how people see and understand.
Hall considers the image as a signifier of meaning; however, they argue that
meaning is subjective and that as such it is the viewer that controls meaning
that is conveyed from any given work. The biggest question remains: does placing objects from different cultures and geographical locations enable visitors
to make connections across boundaries? The visitor is expected to do the work
and make connections themselves. The problem here is that the viewer needs to
understand the history of the objects before connections can be made. Most visitors to the Louvre Abu Dhabi will not be trained art historians equipped to do
that kind of work themselves. Visitors are given very basic guiding frameworks
for the interpretation of the objects. In some galleries, the text accompanying
the artworks are displayed at floor level, making it near impossible for many to
read the labels. As Schorch, Waterton and Watson have argued 'there cannot
evolve a cross-cultural dialogue between totalised collective entities, but only
an interpersonal dialogue among cultural human beings (2017: 107). Therefore,
there will never be one grand narrative but rather narratives, interpretations
and re-interpretations.

Furthermore, since 'museum-going' in the UAE is still within its infancy,
this is highly problematic. As I discussed in chapter seven the low-level of

awareness of museums was having an impact on museum visitation (see Al-Mulla 2013; Bull and Al-Thani 2013 on Qatar). It cannot be underestimated how undeveloped the idea of museum visitation still is within the UAE, which is an opportunity for the Louvre Abu Dhabi to do things differently. They do not, however, seem to be genuinely pushing the boundaries on this front. Also, entrance fees and heavy security may well preclude lower-paid workers and those less familiar with museum visitation from visiting the museum. Issues around power, knowledge and inclusion still loom large within the new museum. It will be interesting to observe how the museum evolves and develops its exhibitionary practices as the museum matures.

Cultural heritage franchising and the circulation of artworks

On October 12, 2014, it was announced that the Louvre Abu Dhabi would receive three-hundred loans from French partner institutions in its first year of operation. One of the benefits of cultural heritage franchising is that the institutions in the network have access to artworks that they may otherwise not be able to obtain. A press release by Agence France-Muséums suggested that the initial loaned works will be displayed between 'three months to two years' (2014). The cultural heritage franchise agreement stipulates specific terms for the loan agreements during the contract period. Article 11 stipulates that at the time of the museum's opening that 'the French Party undertakes to provide, in the form of loans from French public collections works of comparable quality to that of works presented at the Louvre Museum and major French museums' (Poncelet 2007) and that a significant proportion of these loans come specifically from the Louvre Museum. Annex 1 details the schedule further stipulating that three hundred works will be on loan and shown in the Louvre Abu Dhabi's galleries from the initial opening, from the fourth year two-hundred and fifty works will be shown, and from the seventh year, two-hundred works will be shown (*ibid.*). From the eleventh year onwards all works in the main galleries will be from the museum's permanent collection.

When the museum opened in November 2017 loaned works were on display from the: Louvre Museum; Orsay and Orangery Museums; Centre Pompidou; Quai Branly Museum – Jacques Chirac; National Museum of Asian Arts – Guimet; Château, Castle, Museum and National Domain of Versailles; Rodin Museum; National Library of France; Cluny Museum – National Museum of the Middle Ages; City of Ceramics – Sèvres & Limoges; Museum of Decorative Arts; National Archaeological Museum of Saint-Germain-en-Laye; and Fountainbleu Castle. Many of these institutions are also stakeholders of Agence France-Muséums, the organisation established for the realisation of Louvre Abu Dhabi (Agence France-Muséums 2014). As mentioned in chapter four, as the Louvre Abu Dhabi develops its collection, the number of works loaned is set to decrease. The benefit of the franchise agreement is that it gives the Louvre Abu Dhabi time to build up a collection while still being able to display some of the most significant artworks from the collections held in France.

The announcement of the first artwork to be loaned to the Louvre Abu Dhabi was also strategic. Leonardo Da Vinci's Portrait of an *Unknown Woman* (c.1495), also known as La Belle Ferronnière, was the first to be loaned by the Musée du Louvre. The exclusivity of the loan was evident as it was the first time that the painting had left Europe. Perhaps more significantly, it is the first time that a painting by Da Vinci has been exhibited in the Middle East (Leech 2014b). The strategic nature of these loans was also apparent in a statement made by Sheikh Sultan bin Tahnoon Al Nahyan, Chairman of what was then the Abu Dhabi Tourism & Culture Authority.[4]

> These outstanding loans from our French partners represent the collaboration and exchange, symbolic of Louvre Abu Dhabi and its progress to date.

> This will be the first time many of these works will travel to Abu Dhabi or even the Middle East and are a rare opportunity to see important art from French museums in dialogue with the Louvre Abu Dhabi's collection.

> (Agence France-Muséums 2014)

Other works loaned included: from the Louvre Museum - Edouard Manet's *The Fife Player* (1866); *King Ramesses II*, Diorite, (c.1279–1213 BCE) (nineteenth dynasty) found at Tanis and a Statue of Gudea; *Prince of Lagash, Praying*, Circa 2120 BC (Neo-Sumerian period, Gudea reign, 2125–2110 BC), ancient Girsu (Iraq); from the *Self-portrait*, Vincent Van Gogh, 1887 and Claude Monet's *The Saint-Lazare Station* (1877) on loan from Orsay and Orangery Museums one of four surviving canvases painted that represents the interior of the Parisian railway station in 1877, a rare salt cellar in ivory from the Benin Kingdom on loan from the Quai Branly Museum; Henri Matisse's *Still Life with Magnolia* (1941) and *Number 26 A*, Black and White, 1948, Jackson Pollock on loan from Centre Pompidou; and Jacques-Louis David's *Napoleon Crossing the Alps*, one of five versions of a portrait of Napoleon Bonaparte painted by French artist between (c.1801–1805) from the Museum and National Domain of Versailles. One of the issues with the presence of so many loans from French institutions is that it gives the museum a distinctly Franco-European feel. The reason for this is due primarily to the presence of French museum collections, as at the time of the museum's opening three-hundred artworks in the permanent galleries were loaned from major French museums. As Bourrat (2017) notes, 'these artworks are the mirror of the European perception of the world along the centuries during which the collections were made'.

The loaned works will change over the ten years of loans. One benefit of this locally is that visitors will be encouraged to go on repeat visits to see the frequently changing displays. The long-term circulation of loans through the franchise partnership also represents a subtle shift in the idea of permanence. In 2014, Charnier referred to the flexibility of the Louvre Abu Dhabi approach to displaying works, '[w]e are not working on totally permanent galleries – they are semi-permanent galleries where the changes will be important year-on-year [and] this mobility, this flexibility, this volatility is a key element of the identity of Louvre Abu Dhabi' (Leech 2014b). Manuel Rabaté suggests that the aim is to 'create a new dialogue between its permanent collection and the three hundred works on loan from thirteen French museums, including the Louvre' (2017: 14). Museum displays are traditionally associated with a museum's permanent collection. Items from the permanent collection may be circulated in and out of the stores over time. However, the majority of works in a museum are generally owned by the organisation. Any additional loans would either be small scale or part of a touring exhibition. In the case of the Louvre Abu Dhabi, the loaning of works through the partnership is suggestive of how a long-term partnership can offer greater flexibility in the circulation of works outside traditional centres of art.

The permanent collection of the Louvre Abu Dhabi

The collection of the Louvre Abu Dhabi spans prehistory to contemporary works, following the traditional chronological approach that is favoured by the Louvre Museum. The acquisitions for the Louvre Abu Dhabi 'began two years after the agreement was signed between France and the UAE' (Charnier 2017: 11). As part of the franchise agreement, an acquisitions committee was set up to oversee the development of the museum's collection. Members of the committee included: Henri Loyrette (president of the Louvre and of the scientific committee of France-Museums); François Baratte, professor of archaeology and art history of late antiquity at Paris IV Sorbonne; Gilles Venstein, professor at the Collège de France; Marie-Claude Beaud, director of the Nouveau Musée National in Monaco; Peter Furhing, scientific adviser at the Custodia Foundation; Jean-François Jarrige, former director of the Musée Guimet and Pierre Rosenberg (Rykner 2009). Four further committee members were from the Emirate.

Between 2009 and 2017, the Louvre Abu Dhabi acquired over 620 works for its permanent collection (Charnier 2017: 11). The first acquisition made by the museum was Piet Mondrian's *Composition with Blue, Red, Yellow and Black* on February 23, 2009. The work is considered to be an excellent example of Modernist abstraction. The artwork was acquired from the sale of *Collection Yves Saint Laurent et Pierre Bergé* by Christie's auction house held at the Grand Palais in Paris from February 23–25, 2009. The artwork, lot 42, was initially listed with a price estimate of 'EUR 7,000,000 - EUR 10,000,000', however, the work sold for the significantly higher price of 'EUR 21,569,000' (Christies 2009) on February 23, 2009. Charnier has subsequently described the work in reference to the museum's identity and legacy, 'Like Jean Nouvel's dome, this masterpiece of abstract art from the Dutch master's *Trees* series is a meditation on light, which thus commenced the adventure under the most favourable of auspices' (2017: 11). The acquisition of this work was the indication of the Louvre Abu Dhabi's intentions to acquire the works no matter the cost. The Louvre Abu Dhabi has chosen to highlight works of 'high-art' that are available on the contemporary art market. Furthermore, the 'acquisitions policy has been informed by the pursuit of quality from the very outset' (*ibid.*). This is reflected in the masterpieces that were obtained for the collection, which include works by European masters Paul Gaughin, Pablo Picasso and Paul Klee, ancient artefacts such as a rare Bactrian Princess from the third millennium BCE and a monumental bronze lion from Andalusia dating from the eleventh to the twelfth century and key regional works such as Osman Hamdi Bey's *Young Emir Studying*.

Perhaps one of Abu Dhabi's most significant statements of intent was the acquisition of 'Salvador Mundi' by Leonardo da Vinci in December 2017. The painting initially sold at Sotheby's London in 1958 for £45.00 (Somers Cocks 2018). It was initially reported that the buyer was the Saudi crown prince, Mohammed bin Salman. However, the Department of Culture and Tourism - Abu Dhabi announced in a Tweet on December 8, 2017, that they had acquired the artwork for the Louvre Abu Dhabi. The painting was significant as it was the last privately owned Da Vinci painting and one of less than twenty known works by da Vinci in existence (Shaheen 2017). The artwork (c.1500 CE) consists of an oil on panel painting depicting a half-length figure of Christ as Saviour of the World, facing the viewer, and dressed in flowing robes of lapis and crimson. The figure holds a crystal orb in his left hand as he raises his right hand in benediction (Gulf News 2017). The painting sold for $450.3 million at a Christie's auction in New York on November 5, 2017, becoming the most expensive painting ever sold on the global art market (Carvalho 2017). Which also ties into the UAE's political desire to do things bigger and better than any other nation. However, the painting has since disappeared with speculation as to its whereabouts and provenance continuing.

Rabaté has drawn attention to the religious nature of the work, which is linked to the museum's cosmo-universal discourse. 'Leonardo da Vinci's masterpiece Salvator Mundi fits perfectly into the narrative of Louvre Abu Dhabi, the first universal museum to break down the barriers between the different civilisations' (Gulf News 2017). However, nation-building and politics have highlighted a flaw within the universal rhetoric when it comes to this particular work. In January 2018 a landmark exhibition opening in London at The Royal Academy of Arts. The exhibition *Charles I: King and Collector*, which ran from January 27 to April 15 brought together over 100 works from the original collection of Charles I. This was the first time since Charles I execution in 1649 that the masterpieces have been together through a series of loans from private individuals and museum institutions in the UK and abroad (Royal Academy n.d.). 'Leonardo's Salvator Mundi was part of Charles I's collection, valued after his death at £30, sold to John Stone, a mason, and returned to Charles II after the restoration of the monarchy in 1660 and was then dispersed again' (Somers Cocks 2018). However, it was reported in *The Art Newspaper* in January 2018 that the Louvre Abu Dhabi had declined a request by the Royal Academy to lend the painting to the show in London as Abu Dhabi wants the new museum to be the first to show the painting (*ibid.*).

The universal and dialogic theme that the museum wishes to promote is carried through to the works commissioned. For example, Charnier argued that '[i]t was important to find the right artists and to work with them in dialogue to create artworks that are meaningful in this context' (Leech 2014b). For the opening of the museum, artists Giuseppe Penone and Jenny Holzer were commissioned to develop a series of installations and sculptures that reflect the values of the museum and its architecture (Rabaté 2017: 7). The Italian artist Giuseppe Penone created an installation consisting of four parts, Germination, which explores interconnections between art, humanity and the natural world. Penone's *Leaves of Light – Tree* (2016, Italy, Turin) is a central feature of the museum's atrium. The bronze cast tree symbolised life and was designed to reflect and interact with the light streams through the museum's roof. *Propagation* cast in porcelain, which was developed in collaboration with the workshops of Sèvres – Cité de la céramique, focuses on a fingerprint of Sheikh Zayed I, which expands outwards in a series of intricate hand-drawn concentric circles.[5] The text panel describes the work as '[t]he germination of a line, which transforms into spreading ripples, represents how an infinite space can result from a simple action'. Holzer's commissioned work for the Louvre Abu Dhabi takes the form of three marble panels engraved with text. The work is located outside the exhibition galleries in the main atrium of the museum. The panels feature inscriptions from three historical texts: 'a reproduction of an Ancient Mesopotamian cuneiform tablet that bears a Sumerian-Akkadian creation myth', 'a quote from French Renaissance philosopher and essayist Michel de Montaigne' and 'a passage from Ibn Khaldun's fourteenth-century Muqaddimah'.[6] The curatorial strategy of placing works side-by-side from different eras and regions continues into the atrium space. The commissioned works were shown alongside historical works from the museum's collection, which included an eighteenth-century Ottoman fountain and pavement from Damascus, Syria.

Temporary exhibitions

A vital component of the cultural heritage franchise agreement is the delivery of several temporary exhibitions. As part of the Louvre Abu Dhabi agreement, Agence France-Muséums is contracted to organise four temporary exhibitions annually over fifteen years (Ladreit de Lacharrière 2017b: 13). The French rhetoric behind the temporary exhibitions is telling of Francophone cultural-politico interests.

> It clearly reinforces existing recognition of French expertise in cultural and museum matters on the one hand, and of the diversity of the collections of the cultural institutions gathered under the umbrella of Agence France-Muséums on the other.
>
> (*ibid*)

The museum's temporary exhibitions are central to the development of the franchise partnership as they serve to promote further and reinforce the dialogic positioning of the project. For example, Noujaim stated during her opening remarks at a Symposium celebrating the Louvre Abu Dhabi's first anniversary the temporary exhibitions 'reconfirms the transcultural approach of the Louvre Abu Dhabi'. In this sense, the museum is attempting to 'develop the narrative of the permanent galleries' into the temporary exhibition space (Noujaim 2018).

The first temporary exhibition to be shown at the Louvre Abu Dhabi was *From One Louvre to Another*, which was on show from December 21, 2017, to April 7, 2018. The exhibition, curated by Jean-Luc Martinez, President-Director, Louvre Museum and Juliette Trey, Curator, Prints and Drawings, Louvre Museum, aimed to link the narrative of the Louvre Abu Dhabi museum to the Louvre Museum in Paris. The exhibition traced the history and development of the Louvre Museum in Paris during the eighteenth century. The exhibition featured 150 artworks, which were loaned from the Château, Castle, Museum and National Domain of and the Louvre Museum (Louvre Abu Dhabi n.d.[c]). Items on display included ceramics, furniture, paintings and sculpture. The exhibition was divided into three sections: *Versailles: The Royal Collections Under King Louis XIV*; *A Palace for Artists: The Louvre*; and *The Birth of the Musée du Louvre: The Initial Idea for the Museum*.

The exhibition was overtly linked to French politics and power. The 'official' discourses relating to the exhibition indicate that French cultural interests are directly linked to a re-positioning and strengthening of French museums in the global cultural economy, which was evident in the exhibition brochure. According to Marc Ladriet de Lacharriè, Chairman of Agence France-Muséums

> 'From One Louvre to Another: Opening a Museum for Everyone' echoes the museum's universal message as well as the history of the Musée de Louvre. It also illustrates how the Louvre Abu Dhabi, while clearly establishing its own identity, adheres to the long-established tradition of creating museums to underpin society.
>
> (2017b: 13)

Manuel Rabaté, Director of the Louvre Abu Dhabi also states:

> Under the bright Abu Dhabi sky on Saadiyat Island, the name of the Louvre and its collection unfurl again, emerging like an oasis of ideas, shaped by its history and welcoming a future that the audiences of tomorrow are creating.
>
> (2017: 15)

The shift in French interests towards the Gulf States is part of a broader trend towards museum development in the region and the increasing transnationalisation of the sector (Mathur 2005). The increase in the number of new museums and cultural projects in the Gulf States brings with it, the need for new skills development and expertise as discussed in chapter five. Opportunities in the non-Western world are therefore increasingly appealing for globally recognised museum brands such as the Louvre Museum. As Mathur notes 'new global relationships have resulted in different kinds of configurations of power and new kinds of political challenges to such power, and this has changed the dynamics between centres and margins that previously structured our exhibitionary world' (*ibid.*: 701). The Louvre Abu Dhabi has 'the potential to shift the attention of the art world to a new continent and to institutionalize new global perspectives make them an object of great curiosity and advance speculation' (McClellan 2012: 272; see also Ajana 2015). At the same time, Asian involvement in exhibitions in Gulf museums and art fairs serves to demonstrate that it is not just relations between the Western world that are contributing to and shaping the heritage landscape (Ajana 2015: 328). The problem remains that the West is dominating developments within new territories, which reinforces neo-colonial power.

The exhibition, *From One Louvre to Another*, plays another important political role in positioning the newly established museum in Abu Dhabi. The exhibition is also being used to position the Louvre Abu Dhabi as the 'heir' to the Louvre Museum, as indicated in the accompanying exhibition brochure. According to Martinez and Trey

> The study of the origins of the Louvre aims to inform our understanding of the Louvre Abu Dhabi as heir to both the Louvre of the Enlightenment, with its desire to share and educate, and the universal Louvre of the nineteenth century, open to cultures from around the world.
>
> (2017: 17)

In a similar vein Mohammed Al-Mubarak suggests that the exhibition:

> 'From One Louvre to Another' – includes the Louvre Abu Dhabi as the latest chapter in a much longer history, one that stretches back to the very origins of the Louvre during the French Enlightenment.
>
> (2017: 11)

What is particularly interesting about these statements is that Abu Dhabi would want to link itself to the origins of the Louvre Museum, which was heavily invested in nineteenth-century colonial and imperial motives and French nationalism. The exhibition provides an interesting glimpse into the history of French nation-building and museum development. However, the exhibition fails to adequately illustrate how the Louvre Abu Dhabi has broken away from the traditional categorisations and collecting policies that were central to the development of the Louvre Museum.

Co-Lab: Contemporary Art and Savoir-faire was a smaller scale temporary exhibition that ran at the same time as the exhibition *From One Louvre to Another*. *Co-Lab: Contemporary Art and Savoir-faire* was a collaborative project between four UAE-based artists and four French manufacturers, which drew inspiration from the notion of time. Talin Hazbar worked on ceramics with the National Ceramics Museum, Khalid Shafar, around the art of weaving with Beauvais, Zeinab Alhashemi worked with luxury glassware firm of Saint-Just, and Vikram Divecha worked with MTX Broderie Architecturale. The exhibition was initially scheduled to run from December 21, 2017 to March 25, 2018. However, due to popular demand, the show was extended until May 6, 2018 (Louvre Abu Dhabi n.d.[d]). The artists worked with artisans in Paris using traditional techniques to produce contemporary works. *Co-Lab: Contemporary Art and Savoir-faire* is part of the Louvre Abu Dhabi's plans to work with UAE-based artists.

The Louvre Abu Dhabi's second temporary exhibition *Globes: Visions of the World* ran from March 23 to June 2, 2018. The exhibition was curated by Catherine Hofmann, chief curator and Francois Nawrocki, chief curator and deputy director at the National Library of France. The theme of the exhibition explored the historical representation of the world and its scientific instruments from antiquity to the present day. As is typical of the Louvre approach, the exhibition was chronological beginning in Antiquity and ending in the present day. The exhibition featured one-hundred and sixty artworks and artefacts, which included over forty globes and spheres drawn from the collections of a number of the French partner institutions including the National Library of France, Louvre Museum, the Château, Castle, Museum and National Domain of Versailles, the Centre Pompidou and the Museum of Arts and Crafts. Also on display also were archaeological artefacts, scripts, astrolabes and world maps (Gulf News 2018). Key works included globes by Vincenzo Coronelli's and Jerome Martinot's armillary sphere. In addition, artists Jean-Luc and Patricia Boivineau were also commissioned to create an artwork inspired by the constellations and stars that can be observed during the winter in Abu Dhabi.

The exhibition also works to position the museum's global centric narrative further. It does so by prioritising the links between cartography and globalisation, 'it will introduce our guests to historical artefacts, including some of the oldest globes and astrolabes from the Islamic world, that have interconnected the world from ancient times to the present day' (Rabaté in WAM Emirates News Agency 2018). The exhibition highlights links between developments in science that occurred in the Arab world, which were fundamental to the development of the discipline of science (Hofmann and Nawrocki cited in WAM Emirates News Agency 2018). The evidence suggests this temporary exhibition, much like the first, was a strategic choice, carefully curated to reinforce the global rhetoric of the museum.

Essentially UAE and French authorities have attempted to position the Louvre Abu Dhabi as a postcolonial universal museum. In doing so, they have stressed the museum's role as a space of openness, tolerance and acceptance. However, the museum's 'transversal' approach, based on displaying works side-by-side, fails to adequately engage with issues around inclusion and multivocality. In doing so, the museum overlooks the complex histories and difficult questions that remain behind many of the objects in the collection. As such the museum makes assumptions about the visitors reading of the collection and the way it is 'translated' into the museum landscape in Abu Dhabi. Furthermore, the power dynamics, at this stage in the partnership, are clearly skewed towards French expertise and collecting priorities. It will be interesting to observe how the museum's focus and interpretation strategies evolve as the Emirati expertise emerges and begins to take precedence over French expertise. It is only then that we will truly begin to see if, and how, the universal museum has been re-imagined within the Arab World.

Notes

1 National Museums of World Culture was formed by the Ministry of Culture as the governing body to oversee Stockholm's National Museums, which included the Museum of Far Eastern Antiquities, the Museum of Mediterranean and Near Eastern Antiquities and the Museum of Ethnography (see National Museums of World Culture n.d.[b]).
2 The Louvre Abu Dhabi Galleries consist of the following twelve chapters – Chapter 1: The First Villages, Chapter 2: The First Great Powers, Chapter 3: Civilisations and Empires; Chapter 4: Universal Religions; Chapter 5: Asian Trade Routes; Chapter 6: From the Mediterranean to the Atlantic; Chapter 7: The World in Perspective; Chapter 8: The Magnificence of the Court; Chapter 9: A New Art of Living; Chapter 10: A Modern World?; Chapter 11: Challenging Modernity and Chapter 12: A Global World.
3 Observation, Louvre Abu Dhabi, November 11, 2017.
4 Previously the TCA Abu Dhabi.
5 *Propagation* took 600 hours to paint using forty-two porcelain plates that weighs 400 kilograms.
6 Observation, Louvre Abu Dhabi, December 3, 2018.

9 Shifting dynamics

The contemporary heritage landscape in Abu Dhabi presented a unique context in which to explore the processes that are being used to produce and present heritage through the implementation of new structures and procedures in a transnational setting. However, these very conditions of rapid change and new transformation of the heritage landscape also mean that various developments have occurred since researching this book, which is also relevant to understanding the current direction of heritage in the region. Therefore, this book does not proffer the view that this is the entire story of heritage in Abu Dhabi. Instead, it provides a snap-shot view of the emergence of cultural heritage institutions at a particular moment in time.

The book challenges the dominant view of heritage as bounded by space and place by arguing that contemporary heritage processes, such as cultural heritage franchising, are increasingly bound up within transnational and cosmopolitan identity-making processes. As such, I argue that debates within critical museum and heritage studies need to be further expanded in order to understand the varied ways in which, heritage is translated across and within different cultural contexts. This book has attempted to connect and critically unpack the political, social and economic implications of how heritage is engaged and put to use in transnational contexts by both heritage practitioners and diverse communities.

I have argued throughout that autochthonous heritage, and franchised heritage does not operate in isolation. I have traced, using an analysis situated in hybrid thinking, how franchised and autochthonous heritage combine within complex transnational cultural landscapes; by doing so I have offered an 'enmeshed' view of cultural heritage development within Abu Dhabi and provided a detailed exploration of the processes involved in the construction of heritage and emerging community responses. I have unpacked and interrogated Abu Dhabi's role within the global systems of heritage and argued that this approach is situated within a transnational framing of heritage that draws on autochthonous and franchised heritage in the development of contemporary heritage identities. What is new within the transnational heritage economy is a strategic awareness of the potential of 'cosmo-universalism', which serves as a 'self-conscious political affirmation'

(Beck and Sznaider 2010: 390). As such, I have argued that debates within critical heritage studies need to be expanded in order to understand the varied ways heritage is translated and remade across and within different cultural contexts. I have provided a way to move past the dichotomies and understand how heritage is emerging as an institutionalised and political project in Abu Dhabi using varying scales of heritage production.

This research addresses the perceived opposition of autochthonous and franchised heritage by recognising that they are both part of the same process of identity-making within Abu Dhabi. Within Abu Dhabi, this process is bound up within the objectives of *Plan Abu Dhabi 2030* and the Emirate's vision for the future (Abu Dhabi Urban Planning Council 2007). Ultimately, I argue that the discourses of heritage – autochthonous and franchised – are combined to preserve and present heritage in Abu Dhabi, which results in varied connections and disjunctures. In particular, Abu Dhabi's heritage discourses draw on cosmopolitan ideologies to position the Emirate's national, regional and international identity. Critical heritage studies allow us to examine in detail how individuals, institutions and communities grapple with moments of openness and exchange within and across borders. This book has begun to open up this area for examination through a detailed examination of cultural heritage franchising as a form of contemporary transnational heritage production.

A cohesive framework

Since undertaking the fieldwork for this project, there have been several re-evaluations of the way that heritage is structured and governed in Abu Dhabi. The first large-scale evaluation occurred in March 2012, when the Abu Dhabi Government conducted an audit of its planned infrastructure projects. This review included analysing the Emirate's cultural heritage sector. During this period many of the cultural heritage (autochthonous and franchised) projects were put on hold while the government reviewed the budgets, timelines and directives for each of the planned museums. A vital outcome of the review was the merger of the Abu Dhabi Tourism Authority (ADTA), the Cultural Department of Tourism Development & Investment Company (TDIC) and the Abu Dhabi Authority for Culture and Heritage (ADACH) into one cultural authority (Tourism Development Investment Corporation n.d.[v]). The new body was ordered by a Federal Decree issued by the UAE's current President Sheikh Khalifa, which formalised the newly merged institutions into the new entity – the Abu Dhabi Authority for Tourism and Culture (TCA Abu Dhabi). The newly formed TCA Abu Dhabi became the governing body for the management and development of all government-led cultural heritage initiatives in Abu Dhabi and as such all assets and staff from both ADACH and the TDIC were incorporated into the TCA Abu Dhabi.[1] This move was important locally as it meant that the perceived divide between autochthonous and franchised heritage had begun to be addressed. More broadly, it meant that cultural heritage practitioners could increasingly work together in a more cohesive strategic framework. The downside of this was that cultural heritage became increasingly tourism-focused as the sector was now under the direct umbrella of the tourism authority.

Also, in 2012, the National Council of Tourism and Archaeology was established (UAE Interact 2012). This development was indicative of a growing recognition of the importance of a national strategy for the care, collection and research of archaeological antiquities at a Federal level. The objectives of the council are archaeological preservation, tourism development and international co-operation and the development of global partnerships (UAE Cabinet n.d.). Mostly the National Council of Tourism and Archaeology will work on drafting national cultural heritage policies and overseeing their implementation within the seven Emirates. The establishment of the National Council of Tourism and Archaeology provides evidence of a broader shift towards a more centralised national strategy for the archaeological past. I suggest that more prominence is now being given to preserving the ancient past and its tourism potential. Evidence for this can be seen in several archaeological projects in Abu Dhabi.

Archaeological heritage

Excavations have been conducted on Marwah Island[2] since 1992 which have provided evidence of Stone Age activity (Beech 2011: Interview; Hellyer 2011: Interview). Radiocarbon dating of finds suggest that the site dates to the Neolithic period, which positions Marwah Island as the earliest known settlement in Abu Dhabi (Beech 2006). Ongoing excavations at the site have provided evidence of occupied buildings, ceramics and plaster vessels, arrowheads, jewellery and other bodily adornments, shells, human and animal bones. Key finds that have been incorporated into the Emirates new museums include an imported ceramic vase which is on display at Louvre Abu Dhabi and flint arrowheads and pearl oyster shell buttons on display at Qasr Al Hosn. This illustrates that both autochthonous and franchised heritage institutions are connecting to the activities of practitioners in the UAE to help build their future collections. Due to the success of the excavations on Marwah Island, and the growing recognition of the archaeological past, excavations have continued at the site. The site provides evidence about how we understand the Stone Age not just in Abu Dhabi but also the broader Gulf region.

Further archaeological context has been provided by the discovery of the late Miocene fossil trackway in Abu Dhabi, known as Mleisa 1, which is located in modern-day Al Gharbia is one of many fossil sites of the Baynunah Formation (Bibi *et al.* 2012; Beech and Hellyer 2015). Mleisa 1 is one of the largest trackway sites in the world, covering an area of five hectares. The trackway provides evidence of elephant herds crossing the area around seven million years ago and as such provides the known earliest evidence of prehistoric elephants interacting socially (Bibi *et al.* 2012; Beech and Hellyer 2015). Since then further trackways and partial fossilised elephant skeletons have also been discovered, which expands our understanding of ancient elephant behaviour (Beech and Hellyer 2015, 2018). The transnational past is further positioned within the national story. In an interview discussing the Mleisa 1 site, Saif Ghobash, director-general of the DCT, stated, '[a]s we look back on the history and archaeology of the UAE, we see the wealth of culture and heritage of Abu Dhabi. We look at the elements that are very local, such as the pearl industry, the creation of the falaj, the architecture that is symbolically Emirati and the ties to trade with the communities along the Arabian Gulf' (Dennehy 2018b). Again, official statements such as this, further reinforce the historical and transnational positioning of the past.

The Sir Bani Yas Monastery is the oldest Christian site discovered[3] in the UAE, dating back to the seventh century (Beech 2011: Interview). The seventh-century monastery (c. 600 CE) is located 200km west of Abu Dhabi city on Sir Bani Yas Island. Archaeological evidence from the site indicates that Islam and Christianity co-existed. Surviving elements of the monastery include a dormitory, nave, chapel, cooking areas, houses, bell tower and a burial area (Dennehy 2019d). The evidence suggests that the monastery belonged to the Nestorian order, which was also active in Saudi Arabia, Qatar and Kuwait. Also, the positioning of the monastery and its elaborate decoration suggest that it was meant to be seen (Elders 2003: 234). Artefacts found at the site suggest that the site was active in trade networks, both within the Arabian Peninsula and internationally, which include evidence of imported items, such as pottery and glassware. Finds from the site have now been incorporated into the collection at the Louvre Abu Dhabi. For example, a plaster relief from the site is on display within the Louvre Abu Dhabi. The incorporation of finds such as this into the Louvre Abu Dhabi serves to re-write the UAE, and the broader region, into the art historical canon. The Gulf region is notably absent from art historical survey textbooks despite the fact that increasing evidence is being collected.

The contemporary positioning of the monastery provides further evidence of the cosmopolitan positioning of Abu Dhabi using autochthonous heritage. The site has been open informally for many years. However, in 2019 there was a conscious shift to reorient the site as a tourist destination. The site opened officially to the public in 2019 after the construction of a new shelter, tourist information boards, lighting and new roads to improve access for tourists to the site (Hellyer 2019). The site's official opening coincided with the UAE's Year of tolerance in 2019. Sheikh Nahyan bin Mubarak, Minister of Tolerance, who opened the site to the public was cited in *The National* newspaper as having said that '[i]ts existence is proof of the long-standing values of tolerance and acceptance in our lands' (Dennehy 2019d). Further statements in the local media by government officials also highlight how the monastery is being used in the contemporary heritage economy. Mohammed Khalifa Al-Mubarak, chairman of Abu Dhabi Authority for Tourism and Culture, is cited as having said 'The archaeological finds [at the monastery] highlight the history of various religions and cultures that inhabited the island for thousands of years. It reflects the richness of the country's history' (*ibid.*). These examples add further weight to my argument that autochthonous and cultural heritage franchises are not opposed. As I have argued throughout this book, autochthonous and global heritage discourses operate side-by-side in the contemporary tourist economy.

An important issue that arose from the merger was that heritage then resides under the banner of the tourism sector. As I illustrated in chapter six, one of the issues for Emiratis concerning working in the cultural heritage sector is the negative image that is associated with the tourism sector. However, since the opening of Qasr al Hosn, the Louvre Abu Dhabi and other museum and heritage sites both within Abu Dhabi and the broader Emirates interest in and attitudes to the sector seem to be changing. It also serves to shed further light on the government's recognition of the economic potential of tourism. According to Mohammed al-Dhaheri, director of strategy and policy at the Abu Dhabi Tourism and Culture Authority:

The district's museums will attract culture seekers and art aficionados, as well as generic holidaymakers and visitors looking to twin leisure or business breaks with highbrow cultural adventures and excursions in an environment home to a host of world-class cultural institutions. In coming years, the museums will complement the island's leisure tourism credentials and enhance the emirate's wider appeal as a compelling and engaging, culturally-orientated destination for all.

(cited in Sinclair 2013)

The Saadiyat Island website also features reference to international visitors through the creation of 'world-class facilities' and 'cosmopolitan lifestyle' (Tourism Development Investment Corporation n.d.[w]). This tourism-centred approach has led to uncertainty and discontent for several employees in the sector who feel that the cultural objectives have become too focused on tourism. The reality, however, is that cultural heritage and tourism are intimately connected (see Kirshenblatt-Gimblett 1998; Lyon and Wells 2012; MacCannell 2013). The issue that emerges from this, which is in no way a new issue, is how to balance the commercial imperatives of the cultural heritage project with the cultural heritage processes.

Moving forward to 2017 the department was rebranded to the Department of Culture and Tourism – Abu Dhabi (DCT Abu Dhabi). The re-brand placed the emphasis back on culture as a priority area. The timelines for the projects on Saadiyat Island have evolved with the development of the cultural authority in Abu Dhabi. The international press was quick to dismiss the changing timeline as an indication of financial limitations. However, the

changing timelines have been closely connected to the continuing evaluation and streamlining of the projects in Abu Dhabi. For example, the review
in 2012 resulted in the development of a revised timeline that predicted the
Louvre Abu Dhabi would open in 2015, the Zayed National Museum in 2016,
and the Guggenheim Abu Dhabi in 2017.[4] However, no mention was made
of the timelines for the Phase Two institutions, the Maritime Museum and
the Performing Arts Center, which remain marginally represented within
official plans for the Cultural District. Then again in 2015, the deadline for
the Louvre Abu Dhabi was revised. The Louvre Abu Dhabi took a decade
of planning and development, opening five years later than the original estimate. Further factors that have inevitably affected the development of the
institutions on Saadiyat Island is the availability of artworks and artefacts
for the collections and a genuine desire to get things right.

These developments signal a positive step forward as this research has
shown that the absence of a cohesive heritage structure administratively and
ideologically in Abu Dhabi had initially led to disjointed accounts and representatives of the past. The fact that two separate heritage organisations
managed autochthonous and franchised heritage meant that they were seen
as symbolically and structurally separate. Autochthonous heritage was seen
as the preserve of local and national expressions of heritage, and franchised
cultural heritage was seen as the preserve of international expressions of
heritage primarily for tourism and economic development. This was evident
within the way both heritage practitioners and members of the local community viewed and spoke about the development of the cultural heritage
franchises. The processes of producing heritage are inherently value-laden,
and as such, they produce tensions that relate to ideas about defining and
presenting heritage within transnational settings.

Research during the period when the TDIC and ADACH were separate suggested that the division of cultural heritage in to autochthonous and franchised
heritage institutions served to reinforce the perceived global versus local divide
as ideologically and symbolically separate entities. Through the merger, the
government and heritage practitioners sought to neutralise this divide by developing a narrative that uses both autochthonous and franchised heritage to
position Abu Dhabi's place in the world in the past, present and the future. It is
only by recognising the need for different aspects of heritage to work together
towards the common goal that this will be achieved. The merger, therefore,
offered the potential to improve communication, understanding and exchange
between the different cultural heritage models, existing and developing within
Abu Dhabi. The balance of power within cultural heritage franchising is not
static and will continue to shift as different actors are engaging with the development process. It is anticipated that as heritage practitioners, responsible
for both autochthonous and franchised cultural heritage, work more closely
together that existing and new processes of heritage will adapt and emerge.

The continuing reassessment and realignment of the projects over time,
suggest three things. First, the government of Abu Dhabi recognised the

need for better integration between the processes that relate to both autochthonous and franchised heritage. By operating under the same governing body, a more cohesive heritage vision and operational strategy can emerge. The second was the re-affirmation of the economic potential of cultural heritage development in Abu Dhabi. Moreover, the third is a continuing process of evaluation, adaption and evolution of the work of the sector as it grows in the Emirate.

Process and effect

This book contributes to our understanding of the processes that surround cultural heritage franchising. It has sought to illustrate how these formations of heritage can be categorised and how they can be explored beyond the limitations of the well-studied Bilbao Effect (Giovanni 2001; Gomez and Gonzalez 2001; Azua 2005; Plaza 2007; Alvarez Sainz 2010). It has shown how this global phenomenon is bound up within the issues that surround the global translation of heritage, the development of hybrid heritage, and how heritage is engaged within transnational settings. Also, it picks up on new ways of understanding heritage, developed in the emerging field of interdisciplinary critical heritage studies, as a process (Harvey 2001, 2008; Smith 2006; Harrison 2013). I have shown how the dominant models of heritage, as bounded by national and local borders, are no longer the only means of exploring heritage processes. Instead, I have suggested that co-production and the translation of transnational forms of cultural heritage across borders require more in-depth research, particularly as new ideas and methods are introduced into regions where the idea of institutionalising heritage is relatively new. This is important because as globalisation continues to inform much of the way people live their lives in the contemporary world, so too will global heritage processes continue to increase.

I illustrated in chapter two how changes in the construction of heritage identities have shifted, and arguably intensified, alongside and within the processes of globalisation (Bennett 2007; Kirshenblatt-Gimblett 2007; Harrison 2013; Byrne 2011). Within the current debates concerning the relationship between globalisation and cultural heritage, two main arguments dominate. The first suggests that one consequence of globalisation is the homogenisation and Westernisation of culture (Featherstone 1990; Ritzer 2010). The second argues that globalisation leads to the strengthening of local heritage in response to the threatening forces of globalisation (Harvey 1989; Khalaf 2002; Fox, Moutada-Sabbah and Al-Mutawa 2006c). In chapter three, through my analysis of hybridity, I have shown how assumptions regarding the boundedness of national heritage do not help illuminate our understanding of global heritage processes and the issues described in this book. Instead, I argue that transnational heritage emerges and operates within specific politico-economic circumstances that often remain undiscussed.

In chapter four, I examined how cultural policy and international interests are shaping the way that heritage is being presented globally, which are directly related to the development of bilateral relations, trade and tourism. Global heritage, in this sense, as Long and Labadi note, is connected to soft power (2010: 6). In Abu Dhabi, the development of bilateral relations with other nations, as illustrated by the partnerships established between the UAE and France, represents a form of 'soft power' (Nye 2004: 5; Long and Labadi 2010: 6). In addition, cultural heritage franchising works to brand Abu Dhabi. In Abu Dhabi, the government has drawn inspiration from the Guggenheim Museum Bilbao and the potential of the 'Bilbao Effect' to establish Abu Dhabi as a global city (Giovanni 2001; Gomez and Gonzalez 2001; Plaza 2007; Plaza, Tironic and Haarichd 2009; Alvarez Sainz 2012). The rise of late capitalist economies and modernity has had a profound impact on the Emirate of Abu Dhabi (see Fox, Moutada and Al-Mutawa 2006a; Davidson 2007) and consequently the way that heritage is being developed and presented (Khalaf 2006). The development of heritage is therefore embedded within the societal changes that are taking place within Abu Dhabi. The interest in heritage, therefore, is linked to what Abu Dhabi wants to use it for in the context of modernity, and its potential for mapping out the future.

The transnational process

The new heritage industry has led to the development of new forms of heritage that are representative of transnational relationships and identities. I have suggested throughout this book that when cultural heritage is franchised, it is bound up within economic, political and social processes, which work within and alongside the processes of globalisation. I have considered the emerging consequences of developing heritage this way and questioned the cultural effects of cultural heritage franchising. Ultimately, I suggest that the process of cultural heritage franchising aims to connect diverse actors and nations around the world through the cosmopolitan call for collective, collaborative action and the sharing of global heritage. However, my findings suggest that cosmopolitan approaches to heritage create new inequalities and uneven distributions of power.

These heritage formations, and in particular the cultural heritage franchises, are connected to the production of universal ideas and global branding, which operate within an established global classificatory system, which is inherently hegemonic. Through the process of cultural heritage franchising, nations are using co-branding and co-production to develop their transnational image on a global scale. Through this process of transnational re-imagining Abu Dhabi seeks to establish the Emirate's credentials as a global and cosmopolitan centre in the Arab world. This has resulted in the proliferation of global expressions of heritage through the development of World Heritage Listing, international touring exhibitions, cultural heritage franchising, international heritage consultancy partnerships and so on.

Furthermore, this suggests that heritage has become globally mobile and translatable within non-Western contexts. I have argued that transnational heritage is produced and re-produced through a hybrid process involving the co-production of heritage across national borders by multiple actors whose goal is to both translate new ideas and processes, and to produce new formations of transnational heritage. The processes involved in transnational heritage production are far from static and as such are dependent upon the socio-political circumstances from which they emerge.

It is no longer acceptable to see heritage as a static homogeneous process, just as it is not acceptable to view cultural heritage franchises as pre-formed standardised products. Each cultural heritage franchise is different and responds to the unique socio-cultural circumstances in which it is developed. For example, I have shown how the Louvre Abu Dhabi and the Guggenheim Abu Dhabi are taking different approaches to the cultural heritage franchise process. The Guggenheim Abu Dhabi is taking a transnational approach that is based upon the Guggenheim Foundation's established model of franchising. This model utilises the franchise as a way of exhibiting the Foundation's collection around the world, which would not be possible without some form of transnational partnership. Furthermore, each Guggenheim museum serves to reinforce the potential of the Guggenheim Abu Dhabi franchise model, its collections and its brand globally. The Louvre Abu Dhabi, on the other hand, is using the process of cultural heritage franchising to re-imagine its universal model at a transnational level. By doing so, it is attempting to re-inscribe and translate the universal ideas and tendencies of the Enlightenment within Abu Dhabi under the guise of cosmopolitanism and collective dialogue, defined as 'cosmo-universal'. It, therefore, seeks to reinforce the museum's position as a global actor and retain its title as a world-renowned museum.

In addition, each cultural heritage franchise partnership responds to the needs and aspirations of both the franchisor – such as the Louvre and the Guggenheim Foundation – and the franchisee – in this case, the Abu Dhabi government. For the franchiser, namely the Guggenheim Abu Dhabi and the Louvre Abu Dhabi, it allows the cultural heritage organisation to access new audiences and develop its brand reach globally. For the franchisee, the cultural heritage franchise brings international exposure through the association with the brand name, expertise and introduces new methods and procedures. The use of branded museums is, therefore, an essential aspect of transnational identity formation. Therefore, the varied motivations and visions for different franchises affect how cultural heritage franchises are produced and translated across borders, and, in particular, in non-Western contexts. I have, therefore suggested that the key to understanding cultural heritage franchising as a process is to uncover and analyse the complex issues that arise within the hybrid heritage process. I have suggested that the hybrid heritage process that emerges through the co-production of heritage using autochthonous and franchised heritage processes does not produce non-Western heritage nor does it produce local heritage, on the contrary, it produces a new form of transnational heritage with its own dynamics.

This book has shed light on the issues that arise when heritage processes are translated globally. I have shown how cultural heritage franchising is used as a process for translating cultural heritage and cultural heritage processes. This represents a purposeful strategy based on methods and models that have emerged mainly from western European nations. I illustrated in chapters five and six how the principles and practices that have emerged from western Europe are playing a critical role in the development of museums in Abu Dhabi, and arguably other non-Western contexts. Ong has argued in her analysis of museums in non-Western contexts that 'western principles and practices play a critical role in the development of 'museum culture' – that is, a society's understanding, appreciation and use of museums to represent, locate and express their history, ideals and beliefs' (2007: 2). Understanding how transnational heritage processes are developed and implemented is crucial for our understanding of how the past and the present heritage processes are implicated in the construction of new institutions and the development of existing ones and by extension new identities globally. I also discussed how knowledge and cultural development are linked to economic diversification in Abu Dhabi. The importance of the franchise model is that it allowed the Abu Dhabi Government to remain in control of the project's vision while using international heritage processes from Western nations to create an immediate industry. This model of capacity building created an immediate brand for Abu Dhabi through the association with the Guggenheim Foundation and the Louvre Museum, and at the same time creating opportunities for the professionalisation of the cultural heritage sector. The cultural heritage franchise is therefore used as a means for developing both *infrastructure* and *knowledge*.

The development of heritage education at university level along with the use of experts is indicative of how heritage is being developed based on international policies and procedures. This is part of the 'socialization process' (Bradach 1998: 7), where cultural heritage practitioners form an essential part of the cultural heritage franchising process. This process is based on how the authorized heritage discourse works to professionalise cultural heritage as a global process. In this sense, heritage is produced and re-produced through a 'dominant Western discourse' (Smith 2006: 4), which is inherently political. Power and representation remain central issues. The findings from my field research in Abu Dhabi suggest that the methods and processes that are being used to create new forms of global heritage do not necessarily translate. This is mainly due to the 'experts' lack of cultural knowledge and their focus on tangible aspects of cultural heritage which is at odds with the predominance of intangible heritage as the dominant model of heritage production in Abu Dhabi. This process is also exclusionary as it marginalises more locally based, and alternative, expressions of heritage. A fundamental issue is how and in whose interest heritage 'knowledge' is constructed, which connects Said's (1978) observation that the 'west' is needed to 'educate' the 'rest'. As models of both heritage and education continue to be translated from western European nations, as part of the increasing globalisation of the sector, it is absolutely vital that we undertake more critical research into this area to explicitly understand how 'knowledge' is implicated within new forms of postcolonial power (see Tuhiwai-Smith 2012). As museums and heritage organisations become more and more global, the skills base from which they draw will also need to change. Employees with transnational knowledge and expertise are becoming more desirable as the industry continues to develop alongside the processes of globalisation. The presence of globally experienced staff makes it easier for institutions to justify their international reach, and in effect, position themselves as leading global cultural organisations.

Perhaps most importantly, in the case of developing nations, the process of cultural heritage franchising allows nations to work with well-known cultural heritage institutions to develop their collections and expertise. This is a crucial imperative for Abu Dhabi and one that is closely aligned to the process of Emiratization. For Abu Dhabi, as we have seen the ultimate aim is to use the expertise and the brand name of the Guggenheim Abu Dhabi and the Louvre Abu Dhabi over a set period to develop the sector. It is anticipated that once these periods of partnerships are over, the cultural heritage sector will have matured enough for the Emirates to be able to take the projects forward autonomously. It is perhaps at this point that we are likely to see shifts within the way that cultural heritage is produced and represented in Abu Dhabi. I have also illustrated how the educational system, through the Authorized Heritage Discourse, is being used to establish rules and standards for the future. I have argued that this system needs to recognise and engage with local and regional issues and debates. At the time of writing the College of Arts and Essentially, the development of museum and heritage education in the Gulf needs to respond and engage with critical scholarship in the field, developments in Gulf museology and heritage, the expertise of faculty and the student experience.

A discursive and adaptive process

The way that autochthonous and franchised heritage is balanced is essential. Abu Dhabi uses heritage to convey its image internationally, but at the same time, heritage is employed to reinforce and reconstruct local and national narratives. These developments are not merely the result of a threat to national identity (Khalaf 2000) instead, they are part of a conscious re-imagining of Abu Dhabi's identity. Cosmopolitanism was being used to reinforce and promote the nation's identity on a global scale through the development of its transnational heritage. Heritage is therefore employed to express Abu Dhabi's desire to be seen as both progressive and traditional by constructing a transnational and collaborative approach. One of the objectives of this, as I demonstrated in chapter four, was to develop Abu Dhabi's tourism sector. Cultural heritage development, in this sense, serves to make Abu Dhabi an attractive place for tourists. In this sense, it works to make Abu Dhabi 'visitable' (Dicks 2003: 1). One way to achieve this is through the exchange of established international heritage brands and processes.

The identity that Abu Dhabi is crafting for itself draws on cosmopolitan ideologies; by doing so, Abu Dhabi presents itself as an open and culturally diverse nation. Heritage is used to address the negative perception that people may have of the region, which stems from Orientalist and Islamophobic attitudes and the erroneous view that Abu Dhabi has no heritage of its own (Exell and Rico 2013). This was overtly apparent during the opening of the Louvre Abu Dhabi where the 'cosmo-universal' rhetoric was globally staged through the high-profile media campaign. In the case of the Louvre Abu Dhabi, we have seen how the curatorial approach and the collection is shaped by the franchise relationship, which is built around the rhetoric of 'cosmo-universalism'. Artworks in the galleries have been purposely placed in dialogue with one another. The curatorial approach attempts to re-shape the Louvre Museum's universal approach, with its roots in the Enlightenment, to instead stress the universal and cosmopolitan elements of the collection. However, the Louvre Abu Dhabi's 'transvocal' approach fails to adequately engage with alternative or conflicting versions of the past or marginalised audiences or identities. Furthermore, contemporary issues in the region, such as the Qatar Blockade, serve to highlight the challenges of creating a truly inclusive audience in the re-imagined universal museum.

I noted in chapter two that the promotion of cosmopolitanism as a global pursuit stresses the need for both national and global identities. These identities do not operate in isolation but rather work within and alongside each other. Autochthonous heritage is not isolated from global heritage discourses as is evidenced by the popularity of World Heritage Site Listing. Instead, it is used to reinforce the cosmopolitan project further, which is achieved by invoking both national and transnational solidarity through the use of local, national and global heritage narratives. Ong notes that 'the categorisation of the west and the non-west implies a duality and a double standard of measurement' (2007: 17). The development of the Zayed National Museum gives the projects on Saadiyat Island an increasingly transnational focus that is connected to the cosmopolitan project through the linkage to Sheikh Zayed I, the founder of the nation and the national story. The nation, as envisaged by the Zayed National Museum, is not opposed to the cosmopolitan project.

On the contrary, it expresses national identity through the context of globalism, thus not only providing a local justification for the project but also further establishing Abu Dhabi's global credentials by placing it within the centre of the Cultural District on Saadiyat Island. However, in utilising the brand association and expertise of the British Museum, Abu Dhabi's own position is marginalised in relation to the dominance of the Western museum partners. A further issue that arises is that it is the more every-day and contentious forms of heritage that are marginalised in favour of world heritage agendas and cosmopolitan identity-making. As we have seen Emirati heritage is very much based on intangible aspects of heritage that emphasise orality and performing heritage. Whereas, transnational heritage is understood more in terms of Western-focused terms of reference whereby the emphasis is placed on presenting heritage visually through specific heritage institutions and processes. Therefore, how the planned institutions engage with intangible aspects of identity and heritage is extremely important. This is suggestive of the tensions that emerge from transnational partnerships.

Transnational heritage processes are often challenged when they are applied in international contexts. I have demonstrated that when cultural heritage franchise projects are proposed and developed, mixed views emerge within the local community. The majority of residents felt that the projects were a good thing in terms of branding and tourism generation. Culturally, however, there were significant concerns. These concerns were related to questions about how the cultural heritage franchise would sit beside autochthonous heritage and whether they would be locally appropriate. When franchised heritage is seen to take precedence over autochthonous heritage, it leads to tension and resistance. Primarily cultural heritage franchising serves to exclude the community on an intellectual level due to the dominance of the authorized heritage discourse. One of the responses to this is to develop temporary exhibitions and events which can be used to engage with future audiences. However, I have demonstrated that there are issues in the way that audiences are engaged with during the development stage.

This is because there are significant differences between how heritage is developing in the Gulf States (and perhaps by extension, amongst some of the other emerging nations) and the old models of the development of heritage in the eighteenth and nineteenth centuries in western Europe. Grassroots' response to transnational heritage processes has been to produce and engage with alternative forms of unauthorised heritage which challenge the established discourses of heritage. In chapter seven, I demonstrated how unofficial heritage processes shed light on how heritage is valued by Emirati residents in Abu Dhabi, which is at odds with the global heritage processes that are being introduced. The findings from this study suggest that national identity in Abu Dhabi is based upon an active and shared cultural identity that is predominantly expressed through intangible cultural heritage, which is different from the idea that has been prevalent in western Europe, which sees heritage as being in the past and therefore, the preserve of museums. As Kirshenblatt-Gimblett argues, intangible heritage is not static but is often influenced by global processes (2007). I have suggested through an analysis of local attitudes that the dominant patterns of engaging with heritage are based on actively producing and performing heritage. In chapter six, I illustrated how alternative forms of heritage expression are emerging, such as the *Freej* animated series. These challenge the dominant approach, which has emerged from western Europe that places primacy on tangible heritage and traditional models of display. However, intangible heritage does not merely operate in opposition to transnational heritage. On the contrary, intangible heritage and the inscription of practices such as falconry onto UNESCO world heritage lists suggest that autochthonous heritage is also driven towards cosmopolitan agendas. I illustrate the discursive relationship between national and transnational processes and the construction and representation of cultural heritage.

Cultural heritage franchise organisations need to adapt their practices to incorporate better aspects of heritage that are not necessarily part of their standardised (Western) models. The challenge as Kreps argues in her discussion of museum development in Indonesia is to develop museums through a 'participatory approach', which takes account of the community that 'builds on people's own concepts and systems of cultural heritage management' (2003: 116). The heritage practitioner and the cultural heritage franchise organisation need to re-think and re-address how and in whose interests they are working to enable new methods and procedures to emerge in diverse transnational contexts.

Analyses need to recognise how local conditions, institutions and actors affect, and are affected by, and affect, the exchange of transnational culture. Harrison has proposed a 'dialogical model' where heritage is used to break down the 'bureaucratic divide between laypersons and experts, suggesting new models for decision-making processes in the future' (2013: 5). However, the process of heritage remains political and power-laden, even when suggesting a dialogical approach. Official heritage discourses in Abu Dhabi are still very much based on a community of acceptable inclusion. It is those individuals who are perceived to belong that are included collaborative practice in the collaborative heritage project. A dialogic understanding of heritage is not based on one system but instead is based on multiple interactions and practices, at different times and in different cultural settings (*ibid.*). Taking such a view suggests that in order to understand cultural heritage franchising as a hybrid heritage context, we need to see them less in terms of imported packages and more in terms of communicative practices. In doing so, it will then be possible to analyse the new intricacies and challenges that are created and occur within and alongside these hybrid heritage processes.

Reflections from the field

This book has shown that a useful way to explore transnational heritage is to talk to people and to experience the various ways that heritage is developed and co-produced by multiple organisations and multiple sites in specific settings. As mentioned in the *preface* to this volume in researching this book I took a qualitative approach, drawing on semi-structured interviews, participant observation and documentary and visual data collection allowed me to access and analyse the attitudes, meanings and experiences that are attached to heritage in Abu Dhabi. Since cultural heritage research in the Gulf States is still an emergent field it is useful to reflect on the methodology taken within this research. In doing so, I further elucidate the methodological approach taken and provide context to some of the issues and challenges that emerged during my time researching on-the-ground in Abu Dhabi.

An important aspect of accessibility within the Gulf is the notion of 'public loss of face' (Zaharna 1995: 249). In the Gulf speaking out publicly against the rulers, the government, an institution or an individual can be viewed negatively. In some cases, this is considered so serious that it leads to imprisonment. Zaharna has argued that the notion of 'public loss of face' therefore may impact requests for information, and responses to questions posed to participants (*ibid.*). Since heritage institutions in the UAE are government institutions this issue is further compounded. Some researchers in the Gulf such as Erskine-Loftus (2010) have argued against using interviews, questionnaires and so on for this reason. However I argue that spending time in the field was a major benefit in terms of cultivating relationships and generating data that would not have been available from other sources.

In the context of Abu Dhabi where respondents were few in number and trust is required to initiate contact, *snowball* sampling was invaluable in the process of referral (Atkinson and Flint 2001). Snowball sampling drew on the culturally specific process of *wasta* in order to gain access to individuals and organisations, and semi-structured interviews were used to access the opinions of both heritage practitioners and members of the local community. Observations were also carried out at 'sites' of heritage to explore how heritage is presented publicly and how, if at all, the local community is engaging with these representations. These were essential methods due to the lack of published research on heritage in the Gulf. Interviews and observations were therefore informative of new research sites and documentation that were not originally available outside of the field area. Furthermore, it was through sustained time and contact with participants in the field that I was able to gain more information and deeper insight.

In addition, since the topic of investigation was the development of heritage, and because the issue of heritage preservation is an issue that people often feel is of importance due to the rapid pace of change in Abu Dhabi, participants were more inclined to give opinions as they felt it was an important issue. The fact that individuals could remain anonymous meant that many people felt able to express their opinions without putting themselves 'at risk'. In addition, contributing to research enabled Emiratis to take an active role, to a limited extent, within discussions and debates about the production and presentation of heritage in Abu Dhabi. During the course of the research I had a strong sense that Emiratis are grappling with what their heritage is, what it means to them, and how it is being, and should be, displayed. While this provided invaluable data for the study it also made the interviews feel more loaded as the emotional aspects of heritage were omni-present.

What was particularly striking was that heritage practitioners seemed more concerned about giving their opinions than Emirati residents. In certain interviews expatriate workers spoke directly of their fears about speaking publicly about their opinions. As a result, many of the participants from heritage organisations opted to remain anonymous even though they were representing the views of their organisations. In this instance self-censorship provided valuable information about the level of dialogue that is possible between researchers and heritage practitioners, and between researchers and Emirati residents. It also illustrates the different dynamics and power relations that are at play for Emirati residents and expatriate workers. While the interview questions were generally unproblematic, one issue that did arise was related to the use of the word franchise as the TDIC, the Louvre Abu Dhabi and the Guggenheim Abu Dhabi did not want the heritage developments to be perceived or defined as franchises. This was quite difficult to negotiate due to the position that I take on cultural franchising within this study. However I was able to overcome this by simply referring to the franchises by their brand name or the franchise agreements as a partnership during these interviews.

In the Arab Gulf *wasta* is crucial and this is highly indicative of the way that I was able to gain access to certain sites and individuals. Cunningham and Sarayrah (1993) have discussed how *wasta* refers to the process of using a third party, such as a family member, associate, or friend to achieve certain goals. *Wasta* therefore has the potential to create in and out relationships and groupings. The impact of this for academic research is that in certain instances having the right connections and *wasta* is crucial in terms of gaining access. I was able to use the local system of *wasta* to access respondents that I may not have been able to access in different circumstances. For example, during my initial research stage it was extremely difficult to gain access to TDIC and staff working on the British Museum, Louvre Abu Dhabi and Guggenheim Abu Dhabi projects. I was able to generate interest within the office of Sheikh Sultan bin Tahnoon al-Nahyan for my research by calling and discussing my research. The next day I was given access to a heritage institution with whom numerous attempts to meet with had previously failed. This example illustrates the power and speed at which things move given the right connections and circumstances – *wasta*. Therefore an unexpected outcome of negotiating access was the insights that came with the difficulties of gaining access. The problems associated with gaining access can be used as an insightful part of the fieldwork process (*ibid.*). In this instance, the difficulties relating to access served to illustrate the complexity of the internal political landscape of heritage.

Overall, I suggest that using an ethnographic approach drawing on qualitative data sets is a useful way to approach research in the Gulf.

Contrary to negative media perceptions, conducting research on-the-ground in Gulf nations is both possible and enriching. This section has elucidated some of the unique specificities of research in the Gulf and I suggest that there is scope for further research into heritage methodologies and their application in the field, particularly in relation to hybrid non-Western contexts.

Conclusion

In this book, I have illustrated how the development of hybrid heritage processes in Abu Dhabi has led to the introduction of new transnational processes for developing and displaying cultural identity. Global heritage institutions were being employed to help develop the Emirate's transnational and cosmopolitan identity, at the same time it was making significant inroads within its development of autochthonous heritage by seeking to obtain World Heritage Listing for many of its cultural practices and sites. Establishing a visible past (locally and globally) and educating the public were central to the developing heritage industry. Therefore, the production of transnational heritage is a hybrid process that is deeply embedded within the state's agenda and identity concerns. The challenge is to identify and explore the varied dynamics that emerge through the co-production of heritage across borders. As the extent and reach of globalisation continue to grow so too will the transnational heritage economy. I have illustrated drawing on the academic debates within heritage that there is a need to explore the transnational dimensions of heritage and its 'globalising processes' (Harrison 2013). As we continue to experience the world in global terms this affects the way that heritage is perceived, constructed and mobilised globally. This is connected to the way that the global economy operates, the way that cities are using culture as a global symbols and the way that local and international actors co-exist and co-operate across borders. This book responds to this by providing a detailed consideration of the process of cultural heritage franchising. In doing so, I have examined some of the implications of these global economic power shifts and its effects on the mobilisation and development of cultural heritage in newly emerging global centres such as Abu Dhabi.

Furthermore, I have demonstrated how the concepts of universalism and cosmopolitanism are implicated in official heritage processes, which results in a discourse of 'cosmo-universalism'. In doing so, I argue that how cultural heritage franchises are put to use has important implications, which relates to the professionalisation of heritage within non-Western contexts through the training of staff, the use of franchise personnel (or heritage experts), the establishment of official heritage education, development of audiences and the development of collections. However, the evidence from my analysis suggests that the construction of cultural heritage franchises is an inherently political act, which is neither natural nor inclusive. This undermines the universalist assumptions about cultural heritage franchising, and its relevance for non-Western nations, which is positioned as universal, natural and globally translatable. Furthermore, the claim that the audiences for the cultural heritage franchise are global fails to acknowledge the fact that many individuals in the world still do not have the necessary means, resources and in some cases the desire, to engage with global systems, physically or virtually.

Perhaps most importantly, the museum as a form of heritage imagining is not a purely Western invention. Contemporary heritage is given 'currency' and 'legitimation' through its political positioning and attachment to the West, however, the process of developing museums in non-Western regions has been ongoing for centuries. Essentially, it is the political positioning of transnational heritage models, borne out of western European understandings, as the dominant and globally legitimate approach, which allows for the development of its transnational currency. The political and hegemonic processes that are imbued within the transnational project are masked through the 'cosmo-universal' discourse. The process of cultural heritage franchising is, therefore, as I have suggested throughout this book, connected to broader issues that relate to translation, hybridity, and our understanding of different relations of contact, exchange and collaboration. The result I argue is that 'cosmo-universalism' is implicated within the preservation and presentation of heritage, which plays an essential role in the way that Abu Dhabi imagines and represents itself through the heritage project. Therefore, we need to critically explore how cosmopolitan imagery is being used within the heritage industry in order to understand the dynamics of how it works within complex hybrid settings around the world. By doing so, it will be possible to identify and explore new forms of global heritage, which emerge from and alongside global identities.

Ultimately, I argue that the exchange and translation of heritage in diverse cross-cultural settings is a complex phenomenon that requires more in-depth interrogation. Suggesting that hybridity, translation and transnational contact zones are all central issues that arise from the process of cultural heritage franchising. I argue that places that accept cultural heritage franchises are marginalised from the dominant heritage discourse as transnational heritage takes precedence over autochthonous heritage, which serves to marginalise residents who may have alternative ideas about what constitutes heritage. Only time will tell how shifts in power will affect these dynamics within the Emirate of Abu Dhabi.

Notes

1 Organisations such as the Emirates Heritage Club, which operates the Heritage Village and the Zayed Centre in Abu Dhabi remained outside of the TCA Abu Dhabi's jurisdiction.

2 The Island is designated as a protected area for dugongs and hawksbill sea tur-
tles, known as the Marawah Marine Biosphere Reserve (Dennehy 2019c).
3 The site was discovered by archaeologists in 1992 during the Abu Dhabi Islands
Archaeological Survey (ADIAS)
4 The museums were originally scheduled to open in 2013 (Louvre Abu Dhabi),
2014 (Zayed National Museum) and 2015 (Guggenheim Abu Dhabi) (Tourism
Development Investment Corporation n.d.[n]).

References

Abdelhalim, J. (2010). 'Cosmopolitanism and the Right to Be Legal: The Practical Poverty of Concepts'. *Transience Journal*. 1(1), pp. 63–86.

Abrar, L. and Sinha, V. (2017). 'Female Representation at the Louvre Abu Dhabi Museum'. *The Gazelle*. [Online]. Available at: www.thegazelle.org/issue/126/features/representation-in-the-louvre-ad [Accessed 1 February 2018].

Abu Dhabi Authority for Culture and Heritage. (n.d.[a]). 'About'. [Online]. Available at: www.abudhabiclassics.com/en/about/adach [Accessed 15 June 2012].

Abu Dhabi Authority for Culture and Heritage. (n.d.[b]). 'Vision'. [Online]. Available at: www.adach.ae/en/portal/adach/mission.vision.aspx [Accessed 5 January 2010].

Abu Dhabi Authority for Culture and Heritage. (n.d.[c]). 'Abu Dhabi Classics'. [Online]. Available at: www.abudhabiclassics.com/en/about/adach [Accessed 6 January 2010].

Abu Dhabi Chamber. (2018). 'Tourism and the Private Sector in Abu Dhabi'. [pdf] October 2018. Available at: www.abudhabichamber.ae/OurDocuments/Tourism%20and%20the%20private%20sector%20in%20Abu%20Dhabi%20-%205099179c-5daf-4bd9-b82a-57d5c7004247/Tourism%20English%20lowl.pdf [Accessed 12 December 2018].

Abu Dhabi Culture and Tourism. (2019). 'Past Exhibitions'. [Online]. Available at: www.manaratalsaadiyat.ae/en/about/past.exhibitions.aspx [Accessed 17 July 2019].

Abu Dhabi Education Council. (n.d.[a]). 'Emiratization'. [Online]. Available at: www.adec.ac.ae/en/Education/KeyInitiatives/Pages/Emiratization.aspx [Accessed 30 May 2011].

Abu Dhabi Education Council. (n.d.[b]). 'Education History in Abu Dhabi'. [Online]. Available at: www.adec.ac.ae/en/ Education /Pages/Education-History-in-Abu-Dhabi.aspx [Accessed 30 May 2011].

Abu Dhabi Government. (n.d.). 'Al Hili Archaeological Park'. [Online]. Available at: www.abudhabi.ae/egovPoolPortal_WAR/appmanager/ADeGP/Citizen?_nfpb=true&_pageLabel=p584&lang=en&did=163136 [Accessed 15 June 2011].

Abu Dhabi Tourism Authority. (n.d.[a]). 'About'. [Online]. Available at: www.abudhabitourism.ae/en/portal/about-adta.aspx [Accessed 15 October 2011].

Abu Dhabi Tourism Authority. (n.d.[b]). *Saadiyat Cultural District Abu Dhabi*. Brochure. Abu Dhabi: Abu Dhabi Tourism Authority.

Abu Dhabi Urban Planning Council. (2007). *Plan Abu Dhabi 2030: Urban Structure Framework Plan*. [Online]. Available at: www.upc.gov.ae/en/MasterPlan/PlanAbuDhabi2030.aspx [Accessed 4 January 2010].

Abu-Lughord, I. (1998). 'Arab Culture Consolidation: A Response to European Colonialism'. In: Taher, M. (ed.) *Encyclopaedic Survey of Islamic Culture*. 15. New Delhi: Anmol Publication, pp. 243–257.

ADACH Representative 1. (2011). Interview at Abu Dhabi Authority for Culture and Heritage, Abu Dhabi. 15 November 2011.

ADACH Representative 2. (2011) Interview at Abu Dhabi Authority for Culture and Heritage Offices, Abu Dhabi. 17 November 2011.

ADACH Representative 3. (2011). Interview at Abu Dhabi Authority for Culture and Heritage Offices, Abu Dhabi. 29 March 2011.

Adie, B.A. (2017). 'Franchising Our Heritage: The UNESCO World Heritage Brand'. *Tourism Management Perspectives*. 24, pp. 48–53.

Agence France-Muséums. (2014). 'Louvre Abu Dhabi Reveals Loans from France for Opening Year'. [pdf]. Available at: www.agencefrancemuseums.fr/fichier/plug_news/5/news_file_en_pr.12.10.14.en.pdf [Accessed 17 April 2018].

Agence France-Muséums. (n.d.[a]). 'Our Mission'. [Online]. Available at: www.agencefrancemuseums.fr/en/l-agence-france-museums/l-agence-france-museums/ [Accessed 23 May 2003; 6 August 2019].

Agence France-Muséums. (n.d.[b]). 'The Board of Directors'. [Online]. Available at: www.agencefrancemuseums.fr/en/l-agence-france-museums/le-conseil-d-administration/ [Accessed 23 May 2003; 6 August 2019].

Agence France-Muséums. (n.d.[c]). 'The Scientific Council'. [Online]. Available at: www.agencefrancemuseums.fr/en/l-agence-france-museums/le-conseil-scientifique/ [Accessed 23 May 2003; 6 August 2019].

Ajana, B. (2015). 'Branding, Legitimation and the Power of Museums: The Case of the Louvre Abu Dhabi'. *Museum & Society*. 13(3), pp. 322–341.

Ali, A. (2014). 'The Rise of Art Institutions in the United Arab Emirates and Its Impact on Contemporary Art'. In: Exell, K. and Wakefield, S. (eds.) *Museums in Arabia: Transnational Practices and Regional Processes*. London and New York: Routledge, pp. 167–180.

Al-Ali, M. (2013). 'The Impact of Social Change on Museum Development'. In: Erskine-Loftus, P. (ed.) *Reimagining Museums: Practice in the Arabian Peninsula*. Edinburgh and Cambridge: MuseumsEtc, pp. 130–145.

Al-Ali, M. (Forthcoming). 'Motivations of Museum Visitors: A Case Study of Sharjah'. In: Wakefield, S. (ed.) *Museums of the Arabian Peninsula: Historical Developments and Contemporary Discourses*. Abingdon and New York: Routledge.

Al-Ataya, M. (2011). Interview at Sharjah Museums Department, Sharjah. 5 April 2011.

Alraouf, A.A. (2010). 'Regenerating Urban Traditions in Bahrain: Learning from Bab Al Bahrain: The Authentic Fake'. *Journal of Tourism and Cultural Change*. 8(1–2), pp. 50–68.

Alraouf, A.A. (2014). 'The Rehabilitation of the Muharraq Historical Center, Bahrain: A Critical Narrative'. In: Exell, K. and Rico, T. (eds.) *Cultural Heritage in the Arabian Peninsula: Debates, Discourses and Practices*. Farnham: Ashgate, pp. 173–188.

Alraouf, A.A. (2016a). 'Museums as a Catalyst for a New Urban and Cultural Identity in Qatar: Interrogating the Case of the Museum of Islamic Art'. In: Exell, K. and Wakefield, S. (eds.) *Museums in Arabia: Transnational Practices and Regional Processes*. London and New York: Routledge, pp. 151–166.

Alraouf, A.A. (2016b). 'One Nation, One Myth and Two Museums: Heritage, Architecture and Culture as Tools for Assembling Identity in Qatar'. In: Erskine-Loftus, P.; Penziner-Hightower, V. and Al Mulla, M. (eds.) *Representing the Nation: The*

Use of Museums and Heritage to Create National Narratives and Identity in the Arabian Peninsula. Abingdon and New York: Routledge, pp. 79–94.

Alvarez Sainz, M. (2012). '(Re)Building an Image for a City: Is A Landmark Enough? Bilbao and the Guggenheim Museum, 10 Years Together'. *Journal of Applied Social Psychology.* 42(1), pp. 100–132.

Ameen, A. (2006). 'Frank Gehry to Design Guggenheim Museum'. *Gulf News.* [Online]. Available at: http://gulfnews.com/news/gulf/uae/leisure/frank-gehry-to-design-guggenheim-museum-1.243948 [Accessed 12 July 2006].

AMEinfo. (2011). 'Paris-Sorbonne University Abu Dhabi Participates in Museum Symposium in Sharjah'. [Online]. Available at: http://ameinfo.com/blog/environment,-recycling-&-waste-management/psuad/paris-sorbonne-university-abu-dhabi-participates-in-museum-symposium-in-sharjah/ [Accessed 21 December 2011].

Anderson, B. (2006). *Imagined Communities*, 3rd ed. London and New York: Verso.

Anderson, E. (2011). *The Cosmopolitan Canopy: Race and Civility in Everyday Life.* New York: W.W. Norton & Company Inc.

Ang, I.; Isar, Y.R. and Mar, P. (2015). 'Cultural Diplomacy: Beyond the National Interest?' *International Journal of Cultural Policy.* 21(4), pp. 365–381.

Ansari, G. (1987). 'Urbanization and Cultural Equilibrium in the Arabian Gulf States'. *Bulletin of the International Committee on Urgent Anthropological and Ethnographical Research.* 28, pp. 19–24.

Appadurai, A. (1986). 'Introduction: Commodities and the Politics of Value'. In: Appadurai, A. (ed.) *The Social Life of Things: Commodities in Cultural Perspective.* Cambridge: Cambridge University Press, pp. 3–63.

Appadurai, A. (1990). 'Disjuncture and Difference in the Global Cultural Economy'. In: Featherstone, M. (ed.) *Global Culture: Nationalism, Globalization and Modernity.* London: Sage, pp. 295–310.

Appadurai, A. (1996). *Modernity at Large: Cultural Aspects of Globalization.* Minneapolis: University of Minnesota Press.

Appiah, K.A. (2007). *Cosmopolitanism: Ethics in a World of Strangers.* London: Penguin Books.

Appiah, K.A. (2009). 'Whose Culture Is It?' In Cuno, J. (ed.) *Whose Culture? The Promise of Museums and the Debate over Antiquities.* Princeton and Oxford: Princeton University Press, pp. 71–86.

Aroundme13. (Aroundme13). (2019). 'Why Have They Just Never Let One Single Old Landmark in the City? Other Cities Around the World Have These Really Old Landmarks that Shape the Culture of It. We No Longer Have These Anymore! What Are We Going to Show Our Children in the Future?' 15 August 2019. [Twitter Post]. Available at: https://twitter.com/aroundme13/status/1161966953650708480 [Accessed 19 August 2019].

Art Agency Partners. (2017). 'In Other Words #4 Globalization and Its Discontents'. [Podcast]. Available at: www.artagencypartners.com/podcast/episode-4-globalization-and-its-discontents-with-tom-krens/ [Accessed 28 April 2019]. Charlotte Burns (Executive Editor), Thomas Krens, the former director of the Solomon R. Guggenheim Foundation, and Eric Shiner, senior vice president of Contemporary art at Sotheby's and former director of The Andy Warhol Museum.

Art Gallery of Ontario. (n.d.). 'Art Gallery of Ontario'. [Online]. Available at: www.ago.net/picasso-masterpieces-from-the-musee-national-picasso-paris7 [Accessed 12 September 2012].

Art Knowledge News. (2010). 'Louvre Atlanta Partnership Brings in Over 1.3 Million Visitors to the High Museum of Art'. *Art Knowledge News.* [Online]. Available at:

http://artknowledgenews.com/201010068663/2009-09-19-23-56-37-louvre-atlanta-partnership-brings-in-over-1-3-million-visitors-to-the-high-museum-of-art.html [Accessed 1 July 2010].

Ashcroft, B.; Griffiths, G.; and Tiffin, H. (ed.) (1995). *The Post-Colonial Studies Reader*. Abingdon and New York: Routledge.

Askew, M. (2010). 'The Magic List of Global Status: UNESCO, World Heritage and the Agendas of States'. In: Labadi, S. and Long, C. (eds.) *Heritage and Globalisation*. Abingdon and New York: Routledge, pp. 19–44.

Atkinson, R. and Flint, J. (2001). 'Accessing Hidden and Hard-to-Reach Populations: Snowball Research Strategies'. *Social Research Update*. 33. [Online]. Available at: http://sru.soc.surrey.ac.uk/SRU33.html (Accessed 1 June 2010).

Aubry, A. (2014). 'Preserving Heritage: The Development of Costume Collections in the Gulf'. In: Erskine-Loftus, P. (ed.) *Museums and the Material World: Collecting the Arabian Peninsula*. Edinburgh and Cambridge: MuseumsEtc, pp. 116–189.

Aubry, A. (Forthcoming). 'Beyond Museum Walls: Envisioning a Role for Gulf Institutions as Instigators of Cross-Cultural Diplomacy'. In: Wakefield, S. *Museums of the Arabian Peninsula: Historical Developments and Contemporary Discourses*. Abingdon and New York: Routledge.

Auge, M. (2009). *Non-Places: An Introduction to Supermodernity*, 2nd ed. London and New York: Verso.

'Autochthonous'. (n.d.) In: Merriam Webster. [Online]. Springfield: Merriam-Webster, Inc. Available at: www.merriam-webster.com/dictionary/autochthonous [Accessed 3 February 2016].

Azua, J. (2005). 'Guggenheim Bilbao: "Coopetitive" Strategies for the New Culture-Economy Spaces'. In: Guash, A.M. and Zulaika, J. (eds.) *Learning from the Bilbao Guggenheim*. Reno: University of Nevada, pp. 73–96.

Baba, H. (2011). *Identity Traits in UAE Fort Museums*. Masters in Museums Studies. School of Museum Studies, University of Leicester.

Balassanian, D. and Colville, J. (2006). *UNDP and Capacity Development*. Presentation at the 9th JPO Workshop – Tbilisi, 25–29 September 2006 Capacity Development. United Nations Development Program. [Online]. Available at: www.jposc.org/documents/workshop_georgia_UNDP_and_CD.ppt [Accessed 13 March 2016].

Balkany, P. (2007). 'Report No. 239 on the Draft Law, Adopted By the Senate, Authorizing Approval of Agreements Between the Government of the French Republic and the United Arab Emirates Government Relating to the Universal Museum of Abu Dhabi. Commission on Foreign Affairs, National Assembly, 2 October 2007, Paris, October'. Available at: www.assemblee-nationale.fr/13/rapports/r0239.asp [Accessed 1 May 2008].

Baniotopoulou, E. (2000). 'Art for Whose Sake? Modern Art Museums and Their Role in Transforming Societies: The Case of the Guggenheim Bilbao'. *Journal of Conservation and Museum Studies*. 7, pp. 1–15.

Bardsley, D. (2011). 'Number of Tourists Surges After UAE Gets Seal of Approval'. *The National*, p. 7.

Barker Langham. (n.d.). 'The Founder's Memorial'. [Online]. Available at: http://barkerlangham.co.uk/projects/the-founder-s-memorial [Accessed 14 January 2019].

Barker Langham. (2017). 'Enhancing Staff Performance at Abu Dhabi's Newest Icon'. [Online]. Available at: http://barkerlangham.co.uk/projects/louvre-abu-dhabi [Accessed 18 July 2019].

Basu, P. and Modest, W. (2015). *Museums, Heritage and International Development*. Abingdon and New York: Routledge.

Beck, U. (1999). *World Risk Society*. London: Polity Press.

Beck, U. (2006). *The Cosmopolitan Vision*. Cambridge: Polity.

Beck, U. and Sznaider, N. (2010). 'Unpacking Cosmopolitanism for the Social Sciences: A Research Agenda'. *The British Journal of Sociology*. 61(1), pp. 382–403.

Beech, M. (2006). *Proceedings of the Arabia Peninsula through the Ages*. 7–9 May 2006, pp. 111–141.

Beech, M. (2011). Interview at Abu Dhabi Authority for Culture and Heritage Offices, Abu Dhabi. 29 November 2011.

Beech, M. and Peter Hellyer, P. (2015). *Abu Dhabi – 8 Million Years Ago Late Miocene Fossils from the Western Region*. Abu Dhabi: Abu Dhabi Islands Archaeological Survey (ADIAS).

Beech, M.; Beech, M.; Bibi, F.; Kraatz, B.; Omar, W.; Al Faki, A. and Al Mazrouei, M. (2018). *When Elephants Walked in Abu Dhabi's Al Dhafra Region: New Evidence for a Series of Late Miocene Proboscidean Trackways*. Unpublished Conference Paper. Archaeology 2018 Conference – Danat Al Ain Resort – 26–29 March 2018.

Bendix, R. (1997). *Authenticity: The Formation of Folklore Studies*. Madison: University of Wisconsin Press.

Benjamin, W. (1999). *The Arcades Project*. Cambridge: Harvard University Press.

Bennett, T. (1995). *The Birth of the Museum: History, Theory, Politics*. London: Routledge.

Bennett, T. (2004). *Pasts beyond Memory: Evolution, Museums, Colonialism*. London and New York: Routledge.

Bennett, T. (2007). 'Exhibition, Difference and the Logic of Culture'. In: Karp, I.; Krantz, C.; Szwaja, L. and Ybarra-Frausto, T. (eds.) *Museum Frictions: Public Cultures/Global Transformations*, 2nd Printing. Durham and London: Duke University Press, pp. 46–69.

Bennett, T. (2013). *Making Culture, Changing Society*. Abingdon and New York: Routledge.

Bennett, T. (2017). *Museums, Power, Knowledge*. Abingdon and New York: Routledge.

Berman, A. (1992). *The Experience of the Foreign: Culture and Translation in Romantic Germany*. Translated by S. Heyvaert. Albany: State University of New York Press.

Bew, G. (2007). 'Treasures of Ancient Egypt Draw 15000'. *Gulf Daily News*. [Online]. Available at: www.gulf-daily-news.com/NewsDetails.aspx?storyid=185342 [Accessed 18 May 2011].

Bhabha, H. (2010). *The Location of Culture*. Reprinted. London: Routledge.

Bianchini, F. (1993a). 'Remaking European Cities: The Role of Cultural Policies'. In: Bianchini, F. and Parkinson, M. (eds.) *Cultural Policy and Urban Regeneration*. Manchester: Manchester University Press, pp. 1–20.

Bianchini, F. (1993b). 'Culture, Conflict and Cities: Issues and Prospects for the 1990s'. In: Bianchini, F. and Parkinson, M. *Cultural Policy and Urban Regeneration*. Manchester: Manchester University Press, pp. 199–213.

Bibi, F.; Brian Kraatz, B.; Craig, N.; Beech, M.; Schuster, M. and Hill, A. (2012). 'Early Evidence for Complex Social Structure in Proboscidea from a Late Miocene Trackway Site in the United Arab Emirates'. *Biology Letters*. 8(4). DOI: 10.1098/rsbl.2011.1185.

Bielsa, E. (2016). *Cosmopolitanism and Translation*. Abingdon and New York: Routledge.

Blair, R.D. and Lafontaine, F. (2005). *The Economics of Franchising*. New York: Cambridge University Press.

Blau, S. (1995). 'Observing the Present – Reflecting the Past: Attitudes towards Archaeology in the United Arab Emirates'. *Arabian Archaeology and Epigraphy*. 6(2), pp. 116–128.

Blau, S. (2003). 'Conscious Receivers: A Discussion of Museums and the Construction of National Identity in the United Arab Emirates'. In: Potts, D. and Al-Naboodah, H. (eds.) *The Archaeology of the United Arab Emirates: Proceedings of the First International Conference on the Archaeology of the UAE*. London: Trident, pp. 23–30.

Boast, R. (2011). 'Neocolonial Collaboration: Museum as Contact Zone Revisited'. *Museum Anthropology*. 34(10), pp. 56–70

Bodenstien, F. and Pagani, C. (2014). 'Decolonising National Museums of Ethnography in Europe: Exposing and Reshaping Colonial Heritage (2000–2012)'. In: Chambers, I.; De Angelis, A.; Ianniciello, C.; Orabona, M. and Quadraro, M. (eds.) *The Postcolonial Museum: The Arts of Memory and the Pressures of History*. Abingdon and New York: Routledge, pp. 39–49.

Bouchenaki, M. (2011). The Extraordinary Development of Museums in the Gulf States.' *Museum International*. 63(3–4), pp. 93–104.

Bouchenaki, M. and Kreps, C. (2016). 'Part 1: Bouchenaki, M. – Making Sense of the Arabian Peninsula Museums'. In: Exell, K. and Wakefield, S. (eds.) *Museums in Arabia: Transnational Practices and Regional Processes*. London and New York: Routledge, pp. xv–xvii.

Bourdieu, P. (1984). *Distinction: A Social Critique of the Judgement of Taste*. London: Routledge and Kegan Paul.

Bourrat, O. (2017). 'Contact Masterpieces? Rethinking Concepts for a Global Art History'. Paper presented at Museums in Arabia 2017, Bahrain National Museum, Manama, Bahrain. October 11–13, 2017.

Bradach, J.L. (1998). *Franchise Organizations*. Boston, MA: Harvard Business School Press.

Bradley, K. (1997). 'The Deal of the Century – Opening of the Guggenheim Museum. Bilbao, Spain – Includes Interview with Thomas Kens – Cover Story'. *Art in America*. 85(7), pp. 48–55.

Brass, K. (2011). 'Saudi Signs Dh4bn Deal to Build 1km Tallest Tower'. *The National*. [Online]. Available at: www.thenational.ae/business/property/saudi-signs-dh4bn-deal-to-build-1km-tallest-tower [Accessed 3 August 2011].

Bristol-Rhys, J. (2011). Interview at Zayed University, Abu Dhabi. 8 December 2011.

British Museum. (n.d.[a]). 'Tutankhamun's Tomb'. [Online]. Available at: www.britishmuseum.org/whats_on/past_exhibitions/1972/archive_tutankhamun/tomb_of_tutankhamun.aspx [Accessed 2 June 2013].

British Museum. (n.d[b]). 'Treasures of Tutankhamun.' [Online]. Available at: www.britishmuseum.org/whats_on/past_exhibitions/1972/archive_tutankhamun.aspx [Accessed 2 June 2013].

British Museum. (n.d.[c]). 'International Touring Exhibitions: A Museum of the World'. [Online]. Available at: www.britishmuseum.org/about_us/tours_and_loans/international_exhibitions.aspx [Accessed 15 June 2013].

British Museum. (n.d.[d]). 'World Collections Programme'. [Online]. Available at: www. britishmuseum.org/about_us/skills-sharing/world_collections_programme.aspx [Accessed 4 February 2013].

British Museum. (n.d.[e]). 'Africa Programme'. [Online]. Available at: www.brit-ishmuseum.org/about_us/skills-sharing/africa_programme.aspx [Accessed 4 February 2013].

British Museum. (n.d.[f]). 'Leadership Training Programme'. [Online]. Available at: www.britishmuseum.org/about_us/skills-sharing/leadership_training_programme. aspx [Accessed 4 February 2013].

British Museum. (n.d.[g]). 'Treasures of the World's Cultures'. [Online]. Available at: www.britishmuseum.org/about_us/tours_and_loans/international_exhibitions/ treasures.aspx [Accessed 15 June 2013].

British Museum Representative. (2011). Interview at Café Arabia, Abu Dhabi. 16 October 2011.

Bull, J. and Al-Thani, S.H. (2013). 'Six Things We Didn't Know: Researching the Needs of Family Audiences in Qatar'. In: Erskine-Loftus, P. (ed.) *Reimagining Museums: Practice in the Arabian Peninsula*. Edinburgh and Cambridge: Muse-umsEtc, pp. 322–345.

Burgess, R.G. (1984). *In the Field: A Sourcebook and Field Manual*. London: Allen & Unwin.

Burke, P. (2009). *Cultural Hybridity*. Cambridge: Polity Press.

Byrne, D. (1991). 'Western Hegemony in Archaeological Heritage Management'. *History and Archaeology*. 5, pp. 269–276.

Byrne, D. (2008) 'Heritage as Social Action'. In: Fairclough, G.; Harrison, R.; Schofield, J. and Jameson J.H. (eds.) *The Heritage Reader*. London: Routledge, pp. 149–173.

Byrne, D. (2011). 'Archaeological Heritage and Cultural Intimacy: An interview with Michael Herzfeld'. *Journal of Social Archaeology*. 11(2), pp. 144–157.

Byrne, T. (2013). *Cultural Policy and the Creative City: Legitimation Discourses, Culture and the State*. [pdf]. Doctoral Thesis, Dublin Institute of Technology. DOI: 10.21427/D7G88B.

Cachin, F.; Clair, J. and Recht, R. (2006). 'Museums Are Not for Sale'. *Le Monde*. [Online]. Available at: www.bpe.europresse.com [Accessed 5 February 2010].

Caldwell, N.G. (2000). 'The Emergence of Museum Brands'. *International Journal of Arts Management*. 2(3), pp. 28–34.

Carmen, J. (2005). *Against Cultural Property: Archaeology, Heritage and Ownership*. London: Duckworth.

Carvalho, S. (2017). 'Louvre Abu Dhabi to Display Leonardo's "Salvator Mundi"'. *Reuters*. [Online]. Available at: www.reuters.com/article/us-emirates-louvre/louvre-abu-dhabi-to-display-leonardos-salvator-mundi-idUSKBN1E11IO [Accessed 8 December 2017].

Carroll, L. (2014). 'Saadiyat Beach Club Puts on a Fresh Face for the World. The National. 3 September 2014'. [Online]. Available at: www.thenational.ae/uae/ tourism/saadiyat-beach-clubputs-on-a-fresh-face-for-the-world [Accessed 27 December 2014].

Castells, M. (2009). *The Rise of Network Society: The Information Age: Economy Society and Culture*, 2nd ed., vol. 1. Oxford: Blackwell.

Cerisier-ben Guiga, M. (2007). 'Bill Authorizing the Approval of Agreements between the Government of the French Republic and the Government of the United Arab Emirates Concerning the Universal Museum of Abu Dhabi. Commission on Foreign Affairs and Defence, Senate, Paris, 19 September 2007'. [Online]. Available at: www.senat.fr/rap/l06-451/l06-4510.html [Accessed 10 January 2019].

Charnier, J-F. (2017). 'Louvre Abu Dhabi: Universal Collection'. In: *Louvre Abu Dhabi: Masterpieces of the Collection*. Exhibition Catalogue. Paris: Skira, p. 11.

Château de Fontainebleau. (n.d.[a]). 'History'. [Online]. Available at: www.chateaudefontainebleau.fr/History?lang=en [Accessed 10 July 2019].

Château de Fontainebleau. (n.d.[b]). 'The Imperial Theatre – Sheikh Khalifa bin Zayed Al Nahyan'. [Online]. Available at: www.chateaudefontainebleau.fr/The-Imperial-Theater?lang=en [Accessed 10 July 2019].

Chi, J.L. (2013). 'Network Societies and Internet Studies: Rethinking Time, Space, and Class'. In: Dutton, W.H. (ed.) *The Oxford Handbook of Internet Studies*. Oxford: Oxford University Press, pp. 109–128.

Chirac, M.J. (2007). 'Message from M. Jacques Chirac, President of the Republic, to Sheikh Khalifa Bin Zayed Al-Nahyan, President of the United Arab Emirates, during the Signing of the Intergovernmental Agreement Creating the Louvre Abu Dhabi Universal Museum. Speeches and Documents'. *Presidency of the Republic*. [Online]. Available at: www.jacqueschirac-asso.fr/archives-elysee.fr/elysee/elysee.fr/anglais/speeches_and_documents/2007/fi001286.html [Accessed 1 March 2019].

Chrisafis, A. (2017). 'Macron Hails Power of Beauty as Louvre Opens in Abu Dhabi'. *The Guardian*. [Online]. Available at: www.theguardian.com/world/2017/nov/08/macron-hails-louvre-abu-dhabi-as-example-beauty-fighting-discourses-of-hatred [Accessed 9 November 2017].

Christies. (2009). 'Lot 42: PIET MONDRIAN (1872–1944). Sale 1209 Collection Yves Saint Laurent et Pierre Bergé 23–25 February 2009, Paris'. [Online]. Available at: www.christies.com/lotfinder/paintings/piet-mondrian-composition-avec-bleu-rouge-j-5157367-details.aspx?from=salesummery&intObjectID=5157367&sid=-26ecd206-e786-453d-a8f8-96ff0b02cb19 [Accessed 15 March 2018].

Clair, J. (2007). *Malaise dans les Musées*. Café Voltaire, Flammarion: Paris.

Clifford, J. (1997). *Routes: Travel and Translation in the Late Twentieth Century*. Cambridge and London: Harvard University Press.

Clifford, J. (2001). 'Indigenous Articulations'. *The Contemporary Pacific*. 13(2), pp. 468–490.

Cody, E. (2009). 'First French Military Base Opens in the Persian Gulf'. *Washington Post*. [Online]. Available at: http://articles.washingtonpost.com/2009-05-27/world/36882134_1_rafale-french-soldiers-first-military-base [Accessed 27 May 2009].

Colliers International. (2018a). *GCC Source Market: China*. Research Paper. Arabian Travel Market Series. MENA | Hotels December 2018. [pdf]. Available at: https://arabiantravelmarket.wtm.com/RXUK/RXUK_ArabianTravelMarket/2019/PDF/Colliers/ATM%20Series%20-%20China-%202018.pdf?v=636916081301862639 [Accessed 6 January 2019].

Colliers International. (2018b). *GCC Source Market: China*. Research Paper. Arabian Travel Market Series. MENA | Hotels January 2018. [pdf]. Available at: www2.colliers.com/en-AE/Research#sort=%40fdatez32xpublished55910%20descending&f:_ED35CCC7-C1A3–48D6–86A5–4266613BA960=[2018] [Accessed 6 January 2019].

Colliers International. (2019a). *Arabian Travel Market: UAE Hospitality Market.* Report March 2019.[pdf]. Available at: https://arabiantravelmarket.wtm.com/RXUK/RXUK_ArabianTravelMarket/2019/PDF/Colliers/2019%20-%20ATM%20-%20UAE%20Hospitality%20Market%20ENG.pdf?v=636916075294823776 [Accessed 5 August 2019].

Colliers International. (2019b). *Arabian Travel Market Series: GCC Source Market: India.* Research Paper. MENA | Hotels October 2018. [pdf]. Available at: https://arabiantravelmarket.wtm.com/RXUK/RXUK_ArabianTravelMarket/2019/PDF/Colliers/ATM%20Series%20-%20India-%202018%20ENG.pdf?v=636916080941388193 [Accessed 5 August 2019].

Colliers International. (2019c). *Arabian Travel Market Series: GCC Source Market: Russia.* Research Paper. MENA | Hotels October 2018. [pdf]. Available at: https://arabiantravelmarket.wtm.com/RXUK/RXUK_ArabianTravelMarket/2019/PDF/Colliers/ATM%20Series%20-%20GCC%20Source%20Market%20-%20Russia.pdf?v=636916080604188834 [Accessed 5 August 2019].

Combs, J.G. and Micheal, S.C. (2004). 'Franchising: A Review and Avenues to Greater Theoretical Diversity'. *Journal of Management.* 30(6), pp. 907–931.

Cooke, S, and McLean, F. (2002) 'Our Common Inheritance? Narratives of Self and Other in the Museum of Scotland'. In: Harvey, D.C.; Jones, R.; McInroy, R. and Milligan, C. (eds.) *Celtic Geographies: Old Culture, New Times.* London: Routledge, pp. 109–122.

Coombes, A.E. and Brah, A. (2000). 'Introduction: The Conundrum of "Mixing"'. In: Brah, A. and Coombes, A.E. (eds.) *Hybridity and Its Discontent: Politics, Science, Culture.* Abingdon and New York: Routledge, pp. 1–16.

Cornejo Polar, A. (1997). *"Mestizaje e Hibridez: Los Riesgos de las Metáforas".* Revistas Iberoamericana. 63, p. 180.

Cronin, A.M. and Hetherington, K. 'Introduction'. In: Cronin, A.M. and Hetherington, K. *Consuming the Entreprenurial City: Image, Memory, Spectacle.* Abingdon and New York: Routledge, pp. 1–17.

Cunningham, R.B. and Sarayrah, Y. (1993). *Wasta: The Hidden Force in Middle Eastern Society.* Santa Barbara, CA: Praeger.

Cuno, J. (2008). *Who Owns Antiquity? Museums and the Battle over Our Ancient Heritage.* Princeton, NJ: Princeton University Press.

Cuno, J. (2011). *Museums Matter: In Praise of the Encyclopedic Museum.* Chicago: University of Chicago Press.

Curtis, N.G.W. (2005). 'A Continuous Process of Reinterpretation: The Challenge of the Universal and Rational Museum'. *Public Archaeology.* 4(1), pp. 50–56.

Curtis, N.G.W. (2006). 'Universal museums, museum objects and Repatriation: The Tangled Stories of Things'. *Museum Management and Curatorship.* 21(2), pp. 117–127.

Dajani, H. (2010). 'Sorbonne to Reflect UAE Needs'. *The National.* [Online]. Available at: www.thenational.ae/news/uae-news/education/sorbonne-to-reflect-uae-needs [Accessed 1 May 2012].

Daley, S. (2011). 'N.Y.U. in the U.A.E.' *The New York Times.* [Online]. Available at: www.nytimes.com/2011/04/17/education/edlife/edl-17abudhabi-t.html?pagewanted=print [Accessed 1 June 2012].

Davidson, C. (2007). 'The Emirates of Abu Dhabi and Dubai: Contrasting Roles in the International System'. *Asian Affairs.* 38(1), pp. 33–48.

Davidson, C. (2009). *Abu Dhabi: Oil and Beyond*. London: C. Hurst & Co.

Davidson, C. (2010). *The Persian Gulf and Pacific Asia: From Indifference to Interdependence*. London: C. Hurst & Co.

De Angelis, A.; Ianniciello, C.; Orabona, M. and Quadraro, M. (2014). 'Introduction: Distruptive Encounters – Museums, Arts and Postcoloniality'. In: Chambers, I.; De Angelis, A.; Ianniciello, C.; Orabona, M. and Quadraro, M. (eds.) *The Postcolonial Museum: The Arts of Memory and the Pressures of History*. Abingdon and New York: Routledge, pp. 1–21.

Delanty, G. (2006). 'The Cosmopolitan Imagination: Critical Cosmopolitanism and Social Theory'. *The British Journal of Sociology*. 51 (1), pp. 25–47.

Dennehy, J. (2018a). 'British Museum Renames Gallery after Sheikh Zayed'. *The National*. [Online]. Available at: www.thenational.ae/uae/heritage/british-museum-renames-gallery-after-sheikh-zayed-1.742467 [Accessed 31 July 2019].

Dennehy, J. (2018b). 'Three New Elephant Trackways Discovered in Abu Dhabi, Archaeological Conference Reveals.' *The National*. [Online]. Available at: www.thenational.ae/uae/heritage/three-new-elephant-trackways-discovered-in-abu-dhabi-archaeological-conference-reveals-1.716347?unique_ID=636576876118209028&videoId=5753639305001 [Accessed 26 March 2018].

Dennehy, J. (2019a). 'Abu Dhabi's Presidential Palace Opens to the Public for the First Time'. *The National*. 11 March 2019. Available at: www.thenational.ae/uae/abu-dhabi-s-presidential-palace-opens-to-the-public-for-the-first-time-1.835696 [Accessed 11 March 2019].

Dennehy, J. (2019b). 'Landmark Abu Dhabi souq set to be demolished'. *The National*. [Online]. Available at: www.thenational.ae/uae/heritage/landmark-abu-dhabi-souq-set-to-be-demolished-1.898495 [Accessed 19 August 2019].

Dennehy, J. (2019c). 'New Archaeological Discoveries at Abu Dhabi's Earliest Village'. *The National*. 3 April. Available at: www.thenational.ae/uae/heritage/new-archaeological-discoveries-at-abu-dhabi-s-earliest-village-1.844130 [Accessed 3 April 2019].

Dennehy, J. (2019d). 'Oldest Christian Site Discovered in UAE Reopens to Public'. *The National*. Available at: www.thenational.ae/uae/heritage/oldest-christian-site-discovered-in-uae-reopens-to-public-1.873973 [Accessed 13 June 2019].

Department of Culture and Tourism. (2017). 'The Restoration of Château de Fontainebleau's Imperial Theatre – The Sheikh Khalifa bin Zayed Al Nahyan Theatre – enters its final phase'. [Online]. Available at: https://tcaabudhabi.ae/en/media.centre/news/the.restoration.of.chateau.de.fontainebleaus.imperial.theatre.the.sheikh.khalifa.bin.zayed.al.nahyan.theatre.enters.its.final.phase.aspx [Accessed 30 July 2019].

Department of Culture and Tourism. (2018). 'Louvre Abu Dhabi'. [Online]. Available at: tcaabudhabi.ae/en/what.we.do/culture/museums/louvre.abu.dhabi.aspx [Accessed 17 April 2018].

DeTurk, S. and Wakefield, S. (2018). 'Material Culture in the Louvre Abu Dhabi: Museological and Art Historical Perspectives'. Paper presented at the Royal Anthropological Institute Conference: Art, Materiality and Representation. British Museum. June 3, 2018.

Di Giovine, M. (2015). 'The Ethics of Participation, Community Formation, and Governmentality in UNESCO's World Heritage Program'. In: Adell, N.; Bendix, R.F.; Bortolotto, C. and Tauschek, M. (eds.) *Between Imagined Communities of Practice: Participation, Territory and the Making of Heritage*. Göttingen: Göttingen University Press, pp. 83–108.

Dicks, B. (2003). *Culture on Display*. Maidenhead: Open University Press.

Dicks, B. (2015). 'Heritage and Social Class'. In: Waterton, E. and Watson, S. (eds.) *The Palgrave Handbook of Contemporary Heritage Research*. Basingstoke and New York: Palgrave Macmillan, pp. 366–381.

Donnachie, I. (2010). 'World Heritage'. In: Harrison, R. (ed.) *Understanding the Politics of Heritage*. Manchester: Manchester University Press, pp. 115–153.

Duncan. C. (1995). *Civilizing Rituals: Inside Public Art Museums*. Abingdon and New York: Routledge.

Duncan, C. and Wallach, A. (1980) 'The Universal Survey Museum'. *Art History: Journal of The Association of Art Historians*. 3(4), 448–469.

Duncan, G. (2019). 'Everything You Need to Know about Visiting Abu Dhabi's Presidential Palace'. *The National*. [Online]. Available at: www.thenational.ae/uae/heritage/everything-you-need-to-know-about-visiting-abu-dhabi-s-presidential-palace-1.833252 [Accessed 5 March 2019].

Ecole du Louvre. (n.d.). 'Ecole du Louvre'. [Online]. Available at: www.ecoledulouvre.fr/en/ecole-louvre [Accessed 23 February 2016].

Elango, B. and Fried, V.H. (1997). 'Franchising Research: A Literature Review and Synthesis'. *Journal of Small Business Management*. 35(3), pp. 68–81.

Elders, J. (2003). 'The Nestorians in the Gulf: Just Passing Through? Recent Discoveries on the Island of Sir Bani Yas, Abu Dhabi Emirate, U.A.E.' In: Potts, D.T.; Al Naboodah, H.; Nabudah, H.M. and Hallyer, P. *Archaeology of the United Arab Emirates. Proceeding of the First International Conference on Archaeology of the U.A.E.* London: Trident, pp. 230–236.

Elsheshtawy, Y. (2004). *Planning Middle Eastern Cities*. Abingdon and New York: Routledge.

Elsheshtawy, Y. (2008). 'Cities of Sand and Fog: Abu Dhabi's Global Ambitions'. In: Y. Elsheshtawy (ed.) *The Evolving Arab City: Tradition, Modernity, and Urban Development*. London: Routledge, pp. 248–304.

Elsheshtawy, Y. (2011). Interview at UAE University. 5 December 2011.

Elsheshtawy, Y. (2013). *Dubai: Behind an Urban Spectacle*. Abingdon and New York: Routledge.

Elsheshtawy, Y. (2019). *Temporary Cities: Resisting Transience in Arabia*. Abingdon and New York: Routledge.

Emirati Resident 1. (2011). Interview at Place of Business, Abu Dhabi. 8 March 2011.

Emirati Resident 2. (2011). Interview at Café Arabia, Abu Dhabi. 15 December 2010.

Emirati Resident 3. (2011). Interview at the Heritage Village, Abu Dhabi. 2 December 2011.

Emirati Resident 4. (2011). Interview at Al Fanr, Manarat Al Saadiyat, Abu Dhabi. 20 November 2011.

Emirati Resident 5. (2011). Interview at Ajman Museum, Ajman. 12 November 2011.

Emirati Resident 44. (2015). Interview at Qasr Al Hosn Fort, Abu Dhabi. 16 February 2015.

Emirati Resident and ADACH Representative. (2011). Interview at Abu Dhabi Authority for Culture and Heritage Offices. Abu Dhabi. 1 December 2011.

Environment Agency Abu Dhabi. (2011). 'Water Now and Then: A Falaj.' *Environmental Atlas of Abu Dhabi Emirate*. [Online]. Available at: www.environmentalatlas.ae/resourceOfLife/waterThenAndNow [Accessed 1 May 2013].

Erskine-Loftus, P. (2010). What is the Relationship Between Western Museological Practice and Philosophy and Display in the Sharjah Art Museum, United Arab Emirates? Unpublished Ph.D. Thesis. Submitted for the Doctor of Philosophy. International Centre for Culture and Heritage Studies, School of Arts and Cultures. Newcastle University, United Kingdom.

Erskine-Loftus, P. (2010). 'A Brief Look at the History of Museums in the Region and Wider Middle East.' *Art & Architecture.* Special Edition: Museums in the Middle East. 13, pp. 18–20.

Erskine-Loftus, P. (2013a). (ed.) *Reimagining Museums: Practice in the Arabian Peninsula.* Edinburgh and Boston, MA: MuseumsEtc.

Erskine-Loftus, P. (2013b). 'What Are We Silently Saying?' In: Erskine-Loftus, P. (ed.) *Reimagining Museums: Practice in the Arabian Peninsula.* Edinburgh and Boston, MA: MuseumsEtc, pp. 470–519.

Erskine-Loftus, P. (2014). (ed.) *Museums and the Material World: Collecting the Arabian Peninsula.* Edinburgh and Cambridge: MuseumsEtc.

Erskine-Loftus, P.; Penziner-Hightower, V. and Al-Mulla, M. (2016). (eds.) *Representing the Nation: The Use of Museums and Heritage to Create National Narratives and Identity in the Arabian Peninsula.* London and New York: Routledge.

Euronews. (2019). 'The Latest on Guggenheim Abu Dhabi: An Interview with Richard Armstrong'. *Euronews.* Available at: www.euronews.com/2019/04/19/the-latest-on-guggenheim-abu-dhabi-an-interview-with-richard-armstrong [Accessed 26 April 2019].

Evans, G. (2003). 'Hard-Branding the Cultural City – From Prado to Prada'. *International Journal of Urban and Regional Research.* 27(2), pp. 417–440.

Evans, G. (2005). 'Measure for Measure: Evaluating the Evidence of Culture's Contribution to Regeneration'. *Urban Studies.* 42(5–6), pp. 959–983.

Exell, K. (2013a). 'Lost in Translation: Private Collections in Qatar'. In: Erskine-Loftus, P. *Museums and the Material World: Collecting the Arabian Peninsula.* Edinburgh and Boston, MA: MuseumsEtc, pp. 258–294.

Exell, K. (2013b). 'Teaching as Learning: UCL Qatar's Museum Studies Masters Programme'. In: Erskine-Loftus, P. (ed.) *Reimagining Museums: Practice in the Arabian Peninsula.* Edinburgh and Cambridge: MuseumsEtc, pp. 538–569.

Exell, K. (2014). 'Collecting an Alternative World: The Sheikh Faisal Bin Qassim Al Thani Museum in Qatar'. In: Exell, K. and Rico, T. (2014). *Cultural Heritage in the Arabian Peninsula: Debates, Discourses and Practices.* Farnham: Ashgate, pp. 51–70.

Exell, K. (2016a). *Modernity and the Museum in the Arabian Peninsula.* Abingdon and New York: Routledge.

Exell, K. (2016b). 'Locating Qatar on the World Stage'. In: Erskine-Loftus, P.; Penziner-Hightower, V. and Al Mulla, M. (2016). *Representing the Nation: The Use of Museums and Heritage to Create National Narratives and Identity in the Arabian Peninsula.* London and New York: Routledge, pp. 27–42.

Exell, K. and Rico, T. (2013). '"There is No Heritage in Qatar": Orientalism, Colonialism and Other Problematic Histories'. *World Archaeology.* 45(4), pp. 670–685.

Exell, K. and Rico, T. (2014). *Cultural Heritage in the Arabian Peninsula: Debates, Discourses and Practices.* Farnham: Ashgate.

Exell, K. and Wakefield, S. (2016) (eds.) *Museums in Arabia: Transnational Practices and Regional Processes.* London and New York: Routledge.

Al-Fahim, M. (1995). *From Rags to Riches: Story of Abu Dhabi.* Ontario: IB Taurus.

Falk, J.H. and Dierking, L.D. (1992). *The Museum Experience.* Washington, DC: Whalesback Books.

Falk, J.H. and Dierking, L.D. (2000). 'The Contextual Model of Learning'. In Anderson, G. (ed.) *Reinventing the Museum.* New York: AltaMira Press, pp. 143–149.

Farah, N. (2011). 'Splendours of Mesopotamia'. [Online]. Available at: https://gulfnews.com/uae/environment/splendours-of-mesopotamia-1.783226 [Accessed 27 March 2011].

Featherstone, M. (1990). 'Global Culture: An Introduction'. In: Featherstone, M. (ed.) *Global Culture: Nationalism, Globalization and Modernity: A Theory Culture and Society Special Issue.* London: Sage, pp. 1–14.

Fibiger, T. (2011). 'Global Display – Local Dismay: Debating "Globalized Heritage" in Bahrain'. *History and Anthropology.* 22(2), pp. 187–202.

Findlow, S. (2000). *The United Arab Emirates: Nationalism and Arab Islamic Identity.* Abu Dhabi: ECSSR.

Fiskesjö, M. (2010). 'Global Repatriation and "Universal" Museums'. *Anthropology News,* 51(3), pp. 10–12.

Flessas, T. (2013). 'The Ends of the Museum'. LSE Legal Studies Working Paper No. 14/2013. [Online]. DOI: 10.2139/ssrn.2271501.

Florida, R. (2004). *Cities and the Creative Class.* Abingdon and New York: Routledge.

Forero, J. (2012). 'Where is Culture? Cultural Heritage Trends and Challenges'. International Conference on Humanity, History and Society. *International Proceedings of Economics Development and Research.* 34, pp. 96–98.

Foster, M. and Golzari, N. (2013). *Architecture and Globalisation in the Persian Gulf.* Abingdon and New York: Routledge.

Fox, J.W.; Moutada-Sabbah, N. and Al-Mutawa, M. (eds.) (2006a). *Globalization and the Gulf.* Abingdon and New York: Routledge.

Fox, J.W., Moutada-Sabbah, N. and Al-Mutawa, M. (2006b). 'The Arab Gulf Region: Traditionalism Globalized or Globalization Traditionalized?' In Fox, J.W.; Moutada-Sabbah, N. and Al-Mutawa, M. (eds.) *Globalization and the Gulf.* Abingdon and New York: Routledge, pp. 3–59.

Fox, J.W.; Moutada-Sabbah, N. and Al-Mutawa, M. (2006c). 'Heritage Revivalism in Sharjah'. In: Fox, J.W.; Moutada-Sabbah, N. and Al-Mutawa, M. (eds.) *Globalization and the Gulf.* Abingdon and New York: Routledge, pp. 266–287.

'Franchise'. (n.d.). In: Merriam Webster. Springfield: Merriam-Webster, Inc. [Online]. Available at: www.merriam-webster.com/dictionary/franchise [Accessed 8 February 2018].

Freej. (n.d.). 'About Freej'. [Online]. Available at: http://freej.ae/EN/AboutFreej.aspx [Accessed 16 June 2012].

Friedman, J. (2002). 'From Roots to Routes: Tropes for Trippers.' *Anthropological Theory.* 2(1), pp. 21–36.

Fyfe, G. (2004). 'Reproductions, Cultural Capital and Museums: Aspects of the Culture of Copies'. *Museum and Society,* 2(1), pp. 47–67.

Galet-Lalande. (2014). 'Lost in Translation: The Challenging Future of Satellite Museums'. Available at: www.thegazelle.org/issue/39/opinion/opinion_galet-lalande/ [Accessed 10 May 2014].

Garcia Canclini, N. (2005). *Hybrid Cultures: Strategies for Entering and Leaving Modernity.* (Chiappari, C.L. and Lopez, S.L., Trans), Expanded Edition. Minneapolis: Minnesota Press. (Original Work Published 1989 under the title *Culturas Hibridas: Estrategias Para Entrar Y Salir de la Modernidad*).

Gausset, Q.; Kenrick, J. and Gibb, R. (2011). 'Indigeneity and Autochthony'. *Social Anthropology.* 19(2), pp. 135–142.

Gell, A. (1986). 'Newcomers to the World of Goods: Consumption Among the Muria Gonds'. In Appadurai, A. (ed.) *The Social Life of Things: Commodities in Cultural Perspective.* Cambridge: Cambridge University Press, pp. 110–140.

Al-Gergawi, M. (2011). Interview at The Capital Club, Dubai. 28 November 2011.

Ghazal, R. (2011). 'Poems Can Trace the History of Arabic life and Global Events'. *The National.* [Online]. Available at: www.thenational.ae/news/uae-news/heritage/poems-can-trace-the-history-of-arabic-life-and-global-events [Accessed 5 December 2011].

Giddens, A. (1990). *The Consequences of Modernity.* Stanford: Stanford University Press.

Gillett, K. (2019). 'Ancient Mexican Artefacts on Show at Qasr Al Watan in Abu Dhabi'. *The National.* 14 May 2019. [Online]. Available at: www.thenational.ae/arts-culture/ancient-mexican-artefacts-on-show-at-qasr-al-watan-in-abu-dhabi-in-pictures-1.861481 [Accessed 18 May 2019].

Giovanni, J. (2001). 'The Bilbao Effect: Moving Beyond National Borders, City-States are Emerging on the Global Map, Powered by World-Class Architecture'. *Red Herring Magazine.* [Online]. Available at: www.acturban.org/biennial/doc_net_cities/the_bilbao_effect.htm [Accessed 12 June 2011].

Gomez, M.A. and Gonzalez, S. (2001). 'A Reply to Beatriz Plaza's "The Guggenheim-Bilbao Museum Effect"'. *International Journal of Urban and Regional Research.* 25(4), pp. 888–900.

Gonzalez-Ruibal, A. (2009). 'Vernacular Cosmopolitanism: An Archaeological Critique of Universalistic Reason'. In: Meskell, L. (ed.) *Cosmopolitan Archaeologies.* Durham, NC and London: Duke University Press, pp. 113–139.

Graham, B.; Ashworth, G.J. and Tunbridge, J.E. (2000). *A Geography of Heritage: Power, Culture & Economy.* London: Hodder.

Grand Egyptian Museum. (n.d.). 'Historical Background'. [Online]. Available at: www.gem.gov.eg/index/AboutGEM%20-Historical%20Background.htm [Accessed 2 June 2013].

Gratton, C. and Preuss, H. (2008). 'Maximizing Olympic Impacts by Building Up Legacies'. *The International Journal of the History of Sport.* 25(14), pp. 1922–1938.

Gulf Business. (2012). 'UAE Toughens Law on Internet Dissent'. *Gulf Business.* [Online]. Available at: http://gulfbusiness.com/2012/11/uae-toughens-law-on-internet-dissent/#.Uix4z8Zmim4 [Accessed 13 February 2013].

Gulf Labor Artist Coalition. (2019). 'Gulf Labor Statement April 28, 2019'. [Online]. Available at: https://gulflabor.org/2019/gulf-labor-statement-april-28-2019/ [Accessed 15 May 2019].

Gulf News. (2012). 'Restored Ancient Ras Al Khaimah Village Opens to Public'. [Online]. Available at: http://gulfnews.com/news/gulf/uae/heritage-culture/restored-ancient-ras-al-khaimah-village-opens-to-public-1.986066 [Accessed 26 February 2012].

Gulf News. (2017). 'Louvre Abu Dhabi Acquires "Salvatore Mundi"'. [Online]. Available at: http://gulfnews.com/news/uae/culture/louvre-abu-dhabi-acquires-salvatore-mundi-1.2137671 [Accessed 8 December 2017].

Gulf News. (2018). 'Louvre Abu Dhabi's Second Exhibition to Focus on Globes'. [Online]. Available at: http://gulfnews.com/news/uae/culture/louvre-abu-dhabi-s-second-exhibition-to-focus-on-globes-1.2186696 [Accessed 14 March 2018].

Gulf Today. (2019). 'Abu Dhabi's Hotel Guest Numbers Hit 1.2m Mark in Second Quarter'. Available at: www.gulftoday.ae/business/2019/08/04/abu-dhabis-hotel-guest-numbers-hit-1-2m-mark-in-second-quarter [Accessed 5 August 2019].

Gupta, A. (2009). 'The Globalization of Sports, the Rise of Non-Western Nations, and the Impact on International Sporting Events'. *International Journal of the History of Sport.* 26(12), pp. 1779–1790.

Habboush, M. (2009a). 'Sarkozy: We'll Take Risks for our Friends'. *The National.* [Online]. Available at: www.thenational.ae/news/uae-news/sarkozy-well-take-risks-for-our-friends [Accessed 27 September 2012].

Hall, P. (1998) *Cities in Civilization: Culture, Technology and Urban Order.* London: Weidenfeld and Nicolson.

Hall, P. (2000). 'Creative Cities and Economic Development'. *Urban Studies.* 37(4), pp. 639–649.

Hall, S. (2008). 'Whose Heritage? Un-settling 'The Heritage', Re-imaging the Post-Nation'. In: Fairclough, G.; Harrison, R.; Jameson, J.H. and Schofield, J. (eds.) *The Heritage Reader.* London: Routledge, pp. 219–228.

Hall, S. (2013). 'Introduction'. In: Hall, S.; Evans, J. and Nixon, S. (eds.) *Representation*, 2nd ed. Milton Keynes: Sage/The Open University, pp. xvii–xxvi.

Al-Hamarneh, A. (2005). 'New Tourism Trends in the Arab World'. *Islamic Tourism.* 16, pp. 50–54.

Al-Hamarneh, A. and Steiner, C. (2004). 'Islamic Tourism: Rethinking the Strategies of Tourism Development in the Arab World after September 11, 2001'. *Comparative Studies of South Asia, Africa and the Middle East.* 24(1), pp. 173–182.

Hamdan, S. (2012a). 'Elite Schools Find New Base in Emirates'. *The New York Times.* [Online]. Available at: www.nytimes.com/2012/03/28/world/middleeast/iht-elite-schools-find-new-base-in-emirates.html?pagewanted=all [Accessed 1 May 2012].

Hamdan, S. (2012b). 'After a Spluttering Start, the Louvre Abu Dhabi Project Gathers Pace'. *The New York Times.* [Online]. Available at: www.nytimes. com/2012/09/27/world/middleeast/27iht-m27-gulf-louvre.html [Accessed 26 September 2012].

Al-Hamroudi, I. (2011). Interview at Heritage Village: Abu Dhabi. 10 November 2010.

Hannerz, U. (1996). *Transnational Connections: Culture, People, Places.* Abingdon and New York: Routledge.

Harkness, G. and Levitt, P. (2017). 'Professional Dissonance: Reconciling Occupational Culture and Authoritarianism in Qatar's Universities and Museums. Sociology of Development, 3,(3), pp. 232–251.

Harris, G. (2018). 'British Museum Rekindles Relationship with Zayed National Museum after Loan Deal Ended Last Year'. *The National.* [Online]. Available at: www.theartnewspaper.com/news/british-museum-rekindles-relationship-with-zayed-national-museum-after-loan-deal-floundered-last-year [Accessed 2 August 2019].

Harrison, J. (1997). 'Museums as Agencies of Neo-Colonialism in a Postmodern World'. *Studies in Cultures, Organisational and Societies.* 3, pp. 41–65.

Harrison, R. (2010a). 'Introduction'. In: Harrison, R. (ed.) *Understanding the Politics of Heritage.* Manchester: Manchester University Press, pp. 1–4.

Harrison, R. (2010b). 'What is Heritage?' In: Harrison, R. (ed.) *Understanding the Politics of Heritage.* Manchester: Manchester University Press, pp. 5–42.

Harrison, R. (2013). *Heritage: Critical Approaches.* Abingdon and New York: Routledge.

Harvey, D.C. (1989). *The Condition of Post-modernity: An Enquiry into the Origins of Cultural Change.* Oxford: Blackwell.

Harvey, D.C. (1996). *Justice, Nature and the Geography of Difference.* Oxford: Blackwell.

Harvey, D.C. (2001). 'Heritage Pasts and Heritage Presents: Temporality, Meaning and the Scope of Heritage Studies'. *International Journal of Heritage Studies.* 7(4), pp. 319–338.

Harvey, D.C. (2008) 'The History of Heritage'. In: Graham, B. and Howard, P. (eds.) *The Ashgate Research Companion to Heritage and Identity.* Aldershot: Ashgate, pp. 19–36.

Hazbun, W. (2006). 'Explaining the Middle East Tourism Paradox'. *The Arab World Geographer.* 9(3), pp. 201–214.

Hazbun, W. (2009). 'Modernity at the Beach: A Postcolonial Reading from Southern Shores'. *Tourist Studies.* 9(3), pp. 203–222.

Heard-Bey, F. (2004). *From Trucial States to United Arab Emirates,* 2nd ed. Dubai/Abu Dhabi/London: Motivate Publishing.

Hein, H.S. (2000). *The Museum in Transition: A Philosophical Perspective.* Washington, DC: Smithsonian.

Hellyer, P. (2011). Interview at United Arab Emirates Media Council, Abu Dhabi. 28 February 2011.

Hellyer, P. (2019). 'Pope's Visit Speaks to a 1,400-Year-Old Tradition of Christianity in the Gulf'. *The National.* [Online]. Available at: www.thenational.ae/uae/the-pope-in-the-uae/pope-s-visit-speaks-to-a-1-400-year-old-tradition-of-christianity-in-the-gulf-1.819072 [Accessed 28 January 2019].

Henderson, J. (2011). Expatriate: Interview at Residential Home, Abu Dhabi. 20 March 2011.

Heneghan Peng Architects. (n.d.). 'The Grand Egyptian Museum'. [Online]. Available at: www.hparc.com/work/the-grand-egyptian-museum/ [Accessed 2 June 2013].

Herlory, J. (2008). *The Louvre Abu Dhabi Project: A New Arm for France's Cultural Diplomacy in the Persian Gulf Region?* Unpublished Masters Thesis, Aalborg University, Denmark.

Hewison, R. (1987). *The Heritage Industry: Britain in a Climate of Decline.* London: Methuen Publishing.

Herzfeld, M. (2004). *The Body Impolitic: Artisans and Artifice in the Global Hierarchy of Value.* Chicago: University of Chicago Press.

Hirst, A. (2012). 'Museum Development in the GCC: 55 Years and Counting'. Unpublished Conference Paper. Museums in Arabia Sessions, Seminar for Arabian Studies Annual Conference. The British Museum, London. July 14, 2012.

Hobsbawm, E. (2010). 'Introduction: Inventing Tradition'. In: Hobsbawm, E. and Ranger, T. (eds.) *The Invention of Tradition,* 18th ed. London: Cambridge University Press, pp. 1–14.

Hobsbawm, E. and Ranger, T. (2010). *The Invention of Tradition,* 18th ed. London: Cambridge University Press.

Holes, C. and Abu Athera, S.S. (2011). 'Introduction: Nabati Poetry – The Colloquial Poetry of the United Arab Emirates'. In: Holes, C. and Abu Athera, S.S. (eds.) *The Nabati Poetry of the United Arab Emirates,* Ithaca, NY: Reading, pp. 1–40.

Honigsbaum, M. (2001). 'McGuggenheim?' *The Guardian.* [Online]. Available at: www.theguardian.com/books/2001/jan/27/books.guardianreview2 [Accessed 15 September 2010].

Hooper-Greenhill, E. (1992). *Museums and the Shaping of Knowledge.* Abingdon and New York: Routledge.

Hooper-Greenhill, E. (2000). 'Changing Values in the Art Museum: Rethinking Communication and Learning'. *International Journal of Heritage Studies.* 6(1), pp. 9–31.

Hooper-Greenhill, E. (2003). *Museums and the Shaping of Knowledge.* Abingdon and New York: Routledge.

Hubbard, P. and Hall, T. (1998). *The Entrepreneurial City: Geographies of Politics, Regime and Representation.* Chichester: John Wiley and Sons.

Huijser, M. (2011). Interview at Manarat al Saadiyat, Abu Dhabi. 15 March 2011.

Human Rights Watch. (2009). 'The Island of Happiness: Exploitation of Migrant Workers on Saadiyat Island, Abu Dhabi'. [Online]. Available at: www.hrw.org/sites/default/files/reports/uae0509webwcover_4.pdf (Accessed 23 March 2013).

Human Rights Watch. (2012a). 'The Island of Happiness Revisited: A Progress Report on Institutional Commitments to Address Abuses of Migrant Workers on Abu Dhabi's Saadiyat Island'. [Online]. Available at: www.hrw.org/sites/default/files/reports/uae0312webwcover_0.pdf [Accessed 23 March 2013].

Human Rights Watch. (2012b). 'UAE: Saadiyat Workers Better Protected but Gaps Remain'. Available at: www.hrw.org/news/2012/03/21/uaesaadiyat-workers-better-protected-gaps-remain [Accessed 23 March 2013].

Huntington, S. (1993). 'The Clash of Civilizations?' *Foreign Affairs.* 72, pp. 22–49.

ICCROM. (2016). 'Conservation of Cultural Heritage in the Arab Region: Issues in the Conservation and Management of Heritage Sites'. Italy: ICCROM. [pdf]. Available at: http://athar-centre.org/wp-content/uploads/2013/02/1st-series.pdf [Accessed 15 August 2018].

ICOM. (n.d.). 'History of ICOM'. [Online]. Available at: https://icom.museum/en/about-us/history-of-icom/ [Accessed 14 July 2019].

ICOM. (2007). 'Museum Definition'. *International Council of Museums.* [Online]. Available at: http://icom.museum/the-vision/museum-definition/ [Accessed 4 January 2011].

ICOM. (2019). 'Museum Definition'. [Online]. Available at: https://icom.museum/en/resources/standards-guidelines/museum-definition/ [Accessed 21 July 2020]

ICOMOS. (2015). 'The Venice Charter'. [Online]. Available at: www.icomos.org/venicecharter2004/ [Accessed 14 July 2019].

ICOMOS. (2019). 'The Athens Charter for the Restoration of Historic Monuments – 1931'. [Online]. Available at: www.icomos.org/en/167-the-athens-charter-for-the-restoration-of-historic-monuments [Accessed 14 July 2019].

Ijjasz-Vasquez, E. and Licciardi, G. (2016). 'Why Cultural Diversity Matters to Development'. [Online]. Available at: https://blogs.worldbank.org/voices/why-cultural-diversity-matters-development [Accessed 11 April 2019].

'Indigenous'. (n.d.). In: Merriam Webster. [Online]. Springfield: Merriam-Webster, Inc. Available at: www.merriam-webster.com/dictionary/indigenous [Accessed 3 February 2016].

Internet World Stats. (n.d.). 'Middle East Usage and Population Statistics: Internet World Stats'. [Online]. Available at: http://internetworldstats.com/middle.htm#ae [Accessed 10 September 2012].

Isin, E.F. and Turner, B.S. (2010). 'Citizenship, Cosmopolitanism and Human Rights'. In: Elliot, T. (ed.) *The Routledge Companion to Social Theory.* Abingdon and New York: Routledge, pp. 173–187.

Ismail, M. (2012). 'Professor's Plan for Bilingual Education'. *The National.* 8 January 2012, p. 7.

Jencks, C. (2005). *The Iconic Building: The Power of Enigma.* London: Frances Lincoln London.

Jessup, L. and Smith, S.E.K. (2016). 'Guest Editors Introduction: Curating Cultural Diplomacy'. *Journal of Curatorial Studies*. 5(3), pp. 283–288.

Jessop, B. and Sum, N-L. (2001). 'An Entrepreneurial City in Action: Hong Kong's Emerging Strategies in and for (Inter-)Urban Competition'. *Urban Studies*. 37(12), pp. 2287–2313.

Johnson, D. (2013). *Media Franchising*. New York and London: New York University Press.

Jones, K. (2014). 'Shifting Sands'. *ArtAsiaPacific Magazine*. Issue 91. Nov/Dec. [Online]. Available at: http://artasiapacific.com/Magazine/91/ShiftingSands [Accessed 11 November 2018].

Kamel, D. (2019). 'Abu Dhabi launches Dh600m Fund to Attract Entertainment and Business Events'. *The National*. 30 July 2019. [Online]. Available at: www.thenational.ae/business/economy/abu-dhabi-launches-dh600m-fund-to-attract-entertainment-and-business-events-1.892470 [Accessed 31 July 2019].

Kapoor, I. (2003). 'Acting in a Tight Spot: Homi Bhabha's Postcolonial Politics'. *New Political Science*, 25(4) pp. 561–577.

Kendall, G., Skrbis, Z. and Woodward, I. (2008). 'Cosmoscapes and the Promotion of Uncosmopolitan Values'. [pdf]. Available at: https://research-repository.griffith.edu.au/bitstream/handle/10072/24325/53072_1.pdf?sequence=1 [Accessed 15 August 2013], pp. 1–14.

Kelly, M. (2016). 'Kuwait's Museums: For local's Only?' In: Exell, K. and Wakefield, S. (eds.) *Museums in Arabia: Transnational Practices and Regional Processes*. Abingdon and New York: Routledge, pp. 137–150.

Kersel, M.M. (2009). 'Walking a Fine Line: Obtaining Sensitive Information Using a Valid Methodology'. In: Sorenson, M.L.S. and Carmen, J. (eds.) *Heritage Studies: Methods and Approaches*. London: Routledge, pp. 178–200.

Khalaf, S. (1999). 'Camel Racing in the Gulf: Notes on the Evolution of a Traditional Cultural Sport'. *Anthropos*. 94, pp. 85–106.

Khalaf, S. (2000). 'Poetics and Politics of Newly Invented Traditions in the Gulf: Camel Racing in the United Arab Emirates'. *Ethnology*. XXXIX (3), pp. 243–261.

Khalaf, S. (2002). 'Globalization and Heritage Revival in the Gulf: An Anthropological Look at Dubai Heritage Village'. *Journal of Heritage Affairs*. 19(75), pp. 13–42.

Khalaf, S. (2005). 'National Dress and the Construction of Emirati Cultural Identity'. *Journal of Human Sciences*. 11, pp. 230–267.

Khalaf, S. (2006). 'The Evolution of the Gulf City Type, Oil and Globalization'. In: Fox J.W.; Mourtarda-Sabbah, N. and Al-Mutawa, M. (eds.) *Globalization and the Gulf*. London: Routledge, pp. 244–265.

Khaleej Times. (2016). 'Abu Dhabi to Celebrate Qasr Al Hosn Festival'. [Online]. Available at: www.khaleejtimes.com/nation/abu-dhabi/abu-dhabi-to-celebrate-qasr-al-hosn-festival [Accessed 16 May 2019].

Khaleej Times. (2007). 'Khalifa Gives 10m Euros to Restore French Palace'. *Khaleej Times*. [Online]. Available at: www.khaleejtimes.com/DisplayArticle09.asp?xfile=data/theuae/2007/April/theuae_April818.xml&section=theuae [Accessed 15 March 2010].

Kirshenblatt-Gimblett, B. (1998). *Destination Culture: Tourism, Museums, and Heritage*, Berkeley/Los Angeles: University of California Press.

Kirshenblatt-Gimblett, B. (2007). 'World Heritage and Cultural Economics'. In: Karp, I.; Kratz, C.A.; Szwaja, L. and Ybarra-Frausto, T. (eds.) *Museum Frictions: Public Cultures/Global Transformations*, 2nd printing. Durham, NC: Duke University Press, pp. 161–202.

Klebnikov, P. (2001). 'Museums Inc.' *Forbes Magazine*. [Online]. Available at: www. forbes.com/forbes/2001/0108/068.html [Accessed 16 June 2011].

Kluijver, R. (2013). *Contemporary Art in the Gulf: Context and Perspectives*. Gulf Art Guide. [Online]. Available at: http://gulfartguide.com/g/GAG-Essay.pdf [Accessed 8 June 2015].

Kneebone, S. (2013). 'Engaging Visitors, Without an Attraction!' In: Erskine-Loftus, P. (ed.) *Reimagining Museums: Practice in the Arabian Peninsula*. Edinburgh and Cambridge: MuseumsEtc, pp. 346–391.

Knell, S. (2016). *National Galleries*. Abingdon and New York: Routledge.

Knell, S. (2018). *The Contemporary Museum: Shaping Museums for the Global Now*. Abingdon and New York: Routledge.

Koch, N. (2015). Gulf nationalism and the Geopolitics of Constructing Falconry as a 'Heritage Sport.' *Studies in Ethnicity and Nationalism*. 15(3), pp. 522–539.

Kopytoff, I. (1986). 'The Cultural Biography of Things: Commoditization as a Process'. In: Appadurai, A. (ed.) *The Social Life of Things: Commodities in Cultural Perspective*. Cambridge: Cambridge University Press, pp. 64–91.

Kraidy, M.M. (2005). *Hybridity, or the Cultural Logic of Globalization*. Philadelphia, PA: Temple University Press.

Kratz, C.A. and Karp. I. (2007). 'Introduction'. In: Karp, I.; Kratz, C.A.; Szwaja, L. and Ybarra-Frausto. T. (eds.) *Museum Frictions: Public Cultures/Global Transformations*, 2nd Printing. Durham, NC: Duke University Press, pp. 1–31.

Kreps, C.F. (2003). *Liberating Culture: Cross-Cultural Perspectives on Museums, Curation and Heritage Preservation*. Abingdon and New York: Routledge.

Ladreit de Lacharrière, M. (2017a). *Louvre Abu Dhabi: Masterpieces of the Collection*. Paris: Skira, p. 6.

Ladreit de Lacharrière, M. (2017b). 'Preface'. *From One Louvre to Another: Opening a Museum for Everyone*. Paris: Xavier Barral, p. 13.

Lai C.L. (2004). 'Art Exhibitions Travel the World'. In: Sheller, M. and Urry, J. (eds.) *Tourism Mobilities: Places to Play, Places to Play*. Abingdon and New York: Routledge, pp. 90–102.

Langham, E. and Barker, D. (2014). 'Spectacle and Participation: A New Heritage Model for the UAE'. In: Exell, K. and Rico, T. (eds.) *Cultural Heritage in the Arabian Peninsula: Debates, Discourses and Practices*. Farnham and Burlington: Ashgate, pp. 85–98.

Leech, N. (2013). 'Ancient Bedouin Verse, the "People's Poetry", has Found a New Audience'. *The National*. [Online]. Available at: www.thenational.ae/arts-lifestyle/the-review/ancient-bedouin-verse-the-peoples-poetry-has-found-a-new-audience#full [Accessed 7 November 2012].

Leech, N. (2014a). 'Historic French Theatre Restored and Renamed in Honour of Sheikh Khalifa'. *The National*. [Online]. Available at: www.thenational.ae/uae/historic-french-theatre-restored-and-renamed-in-honour-of-sheikh-khalifa-1.245854 [Accessed 31 July 2019].

Leech, N. (2014b). 'Louvre Abu Dhabi to Be First Museum in Middle East to Show a Leonardo da Vinci Painting'. *The National*. [Online]. Available at: www. thenational.ae/arts-culture/louvre-abu-dhabi-to-be-first-museum-in-middle-east-to-show-a-leonardo-da-vinci-painting-1.480196 [Accessed 10 January 2018].

Leech, N. (2017a). 'Louvre Abu Dhabi: The Museum of Then, Now and the Future'. *The National*. [Online]. Available at: https://insidethelouvreabudhabi.thenational. ae/ [Accessed 6 September 2017].

Leech, N. (2017b). 'The Louvre is also a work of art'. *The National*. [Online]. Available at: www.thenational.ae/arts-culture/the-louvre-is-also-a-work-of-art-1.53128 [Accessed 30 July 2019].

Lewin, T. (2013). 'U.S. Colleges Finding Ideals Tested Abroad'. *The New York Times*. [Online]. Available at: www.nytimes.com/2013/12/12/education/american-colleges-finding-ideals-are-tested-abroad.html?pagewanted=all&_r=0 [Accessed 13 December 2013].

Lewis, G. (2004). 'The Universal Museum: A Special Case?' *ICOM News*. 1(3). [pdf]. Available at: http://icom.museum/fileadmin/user_upload/pdf/ICOM_News/2004-1/ENG/p3_2004-1.pdf [Accessed 1 February 2011].

Lidchi, H. (1997). 'The Spectacle of the "Other"'. In: Hall, S. (ed.) *Representation: Cultural Representations and Signifying Practices*. London. Thousand Oaks, CA and New Delhi/Milton Keynes: Sage/Open University, pp. 190–223.

Lin, Y.H.; Lin, J.L. and Ryan, C. (2014). 'Tourists' Purchase Intentions: Impact of Franchise Brand Awareness'. *The Service Industries Journal*. 34, pp. 811–827.

Logan, W.S. (2001). 'Globalising Heritage: World Heritage as a Manifestation of Modernism, and Challenges from the Periphery'. In: Jones, D. (ed.) *Twentieth Century Heritage: Our Recent Cultural Legacy: Proceedings of the Australia ICOMOS National Conference 2001*. 28 November–1 December 2001. [pdf] Adelaide: University of Adelaide and Australia. Available at: http://dro.deakin.edu.au/eserv/DU:30004820/logan-globalizingheritageworld-2001.pdf [Accessed 12 March 2013].

Long, C. and Labadi, S. (2010). 'Introduction'. In: Labadi, S. and Long, C. (eds.) *Heritage and Globalisation*. Abingdon and New York: Routledge, pp. 1–16.

Louvre Abu Dhabi. (n.d.[a]). 'Our Story'. [Online]. Available at: www.louvreabudhabi.ae/en/about-us/our-story [Accessed April 2017].

Louvre Abu Dhabi. (n.d.[b]). 'Birth of a Museum: Discover the World of Louvre Abu Dhabi'. [Online]. Available at: http://louvreabudhabi.ae/en/exhibitionsandevents/birthofamuseum/Pages/birth-of-a-museum.aspx [Accessed 19 April 2013].

Louvre Abu Dhabi. (n.d.[c]). 'From One Louvre to Another'. [Online]. Available at: https://louvreabudhabi.ae/en/art/exhibitions/1st-exhibition-from-one-louvre-to-another [Accessed 12 January 2018].

Louvre Abu Dhabi. (n.d.[d]). 'Co-Lab: Contemporary Art and Savoir-fair'. [Online]. Available at: www.louvreabudhabi.ae/en/art/exhibitions/co-lab-contemporary-art-and-savoir-faire [Accessed 12 January 2018].

Louvre. (n.d.[a]). '*Louvre Abu Dhabi*'. [Online]. Available at: www.louvre.fr/en/louvre-abu-dhabi [Accessed 10 February 2012].

Louvre. (n.d.[b]). 'Exhibition: Louvre Abu Dhabi'. [Online]. Available at: www.louvre.fr/en/expositions/birth-museumlouvre-abu-dhabi [Accessed 18 April 2018].

Louvre Abu Dhabi Representative. (2011). Interview at Manarat al Saadiyat. 9 December 2011.

Lowenthal, D. (1998). *The Heritage Crusade and the Spoils of History*. Cambridge: Cambridge University Press.

Lowry, G.D. (2004). 'A Deontological Approach'. In: Cuno, J.B. (ed.) *Whose Muse? Art Museums and the Public Trust*. Princeton, NJ: Princeton University Press, pp. 129–150.

Loyrette, H. (n.d.). 'Missions and Projects: The Louvre: An Age Old Institution Looks to the Future'. *Louvre*. [Online]. Available at: www.louvre.fr/en/missions-projects [Accessed 15 September 2012].

Lyon, S. and Wells, E.C. (eds.) (2012). *Global Tourism: Cultural Heritage and Economic Encounters*. Lanham, MD: Altamira Press.

MacCannell, D. (2013). *The Tourist: A New Theory of the Leisure Class*, Revised ed. Berkeley, Los Angeles and London: University of California Press.

MacClancy, J. (1997). 'The Museum as a Site of Contest: The Bilbao Guggenheim'. *Focaal Journal of Anthropology*. 27, pp. 91–100.

Macdonald, S. (ed.) (1998). *The Politics of Display: Museums, Science, Culture.* Abingdon and New York: Routledge.

Macdonald, S. and Fyfe, G. (eds.) (1996). *Theorizing Museums: Representing Identity and Diversity in a Changing World.* Oxford: Blackwell.

Macgregor, N. (2011). 'The National Museum: A Symbolic Identity?' Panel Discussion. Manarat al Saadiyat, Abu Dhabi.

Mahdy, H. (2012). 'Heritage and Antiquity through Modern Eyes.' Manarat al Saadiyat, Saadiyat Island, Abu Dhabi.

Markusen, A. (2006). 'Urban Development and the Politics of a Creative Class: Evidence from a Study of Artists'. *Environment and Planning A*. 38, pp. 1921–1940.

Martinez, J-L. and Trey, J. (2017). 'Foreword'. In: Martinez, J-L. and Trey, J. (eds.) *From One Louvre to Another: Opening a Museum for Everyone*. Paris: Xavier Barrel, p. 17.

Massey, D. (2007). *World City*. Cambridge: Polity.

Mason, R. (2004). 'Conflict and Complement: An Exploration of the Discourses Informing the Concept of the Socially Inclusive Museum in Contemporary Britain'. *International Journal of Heritage Studies*. 10(1), 49–73.

Mathur, S. (2005). 'Museums and Globalization'. *Anthropological Quarterly*. 78(3), pp. 697–708.

McClellan, A. (2012). 'Museum Expansion in the Twenty-First Century: Abu Dhabi'. *Journal of Curatorial Studies*. 1(3), pp. 271–293.

McNeill, D. (2000). 'McGuggenisation? National Identity and Globalisation in the Basque Country'. *Political Geography*. 19(4), pp. 473–494.

Meethan, K. (2001). *Tourism in Global Society*. Basingstoke and New York: Palgrave MacMillan.

Mejcher-Atassi, S. and Schwartz, J.P. (eds.) (2012). *Archives, Museums and Collecting Practices in the Modern Arab World*. Farnham, Surrey and Burlington, VT: Ashgate.

Meridiam. (2017). 'Our Firm'. [Online]. Available at: www.meridiam.com/en/about/company [Accessed 10 August 2018].

Merton, R.K. (1968). *Social Theory and Social Structure*. New York: The Free Press.

Meskell, L. (2009). 'Introduction'. *Cosmopolitan Archaeologies (Material Worlds)*. Durham, NC and London: Duke University Press, pp. 1–27.

Meskell, L. and Brumann, C. (2015). 'UNESCO and New World Orders'. In: Meskell, L. (ed.) *Global Heritage: A Reader*. Maldon, Oxford and Chicester: Wiley Blackwell, pp. 22–42.

Middle East Online. (2009). 'Abu Dhabi Launches New TV Cartoon Series to Promote Culture'. [Online]. Available at: www.middle-east-online.com/english/?id=33178 [Accessed 15 July 2009].

Middle East Online. (2012). 'Abu Dhabi Exhibition Features World's Most Magnificent Objects. Middle East Online'. [Online]. Available at: www.middle-eastonline.com/english/?id=51711 (Accessed 20 April 2012).

Mignolo, W.D. (2002). 'The Many Faces of Cosmo-polis: Border Thinking and Critical Cosmopolitanism'. In: Breckenridge, C.A.; Pollock, S.; Bhabha, H.K. and Chakrabarty, D. (eds.) *Cosmopolitanism*. Durham, NC and London: Duke University Press, pp. 157–187.

Miller, D. (2000). *Citizenship and National Identity*. Cambridge: Polity Press.

Ministry of Development Planning and Services. (n.d.). *Qatar National Vision 2030*. [Online]. Available at: www.gsdp.gov.qa/portal/page/portal/gsdp_en/qatar_national_vision/qnv_2030_document/QNV2030_English_v2.pdf [Accessed 12 November 2013].

Ministry of Presidential Affairs. (2018). 'Year of Zayed'. [Online]. Available at: www.zayed.ae/en/year-of-zayed/about/ [Accessed 12 December 2018].

Mitchell, K. (1997). "Different Diasporas and the Hype of Hybridity." *Environment and Planning: Society and Space*. 15, pp. 533–553.

Mitchell, W.J.T. (1995). 'Interview with Cultural Theorist Homi Bhabha'. *Artforum*. 33(7), pp. 80–84. Available at: https://prelectur.stanford.edu/lecturers/bhabha/interview.html [Accessed 12 September 2018].

Mohammad, F. (2011). Interview at Sheikh Saeed Al-Maktoum House, Bastakiya, Dubai. 22 March 2011.

Molotch, H. and Ponzini, D. (2019). *The New Arab Urban: Gulf Cities of Wealth, Ambition, and Distress*. New York: New York University Press.

Morris, L. (2009). 'UNESCO Lists Has Few Arab Entries'. *The National*. [Online]. Available at: www.thenational.ae/news/uae-news/unesco-list-has-few-arab-entries [Accessed 15 March 2012].

Al-Mubarak, H.K. and Martinez, J-L. (2017). 'Foreword'. *Louvre Abu Dhabi: Masterpieces from the Collection*. Paris: Skira, pp. 4–5.

Al-Mubarak, M.K. (2017). 'Preface'. In: Martinez, J.L. and Trey, J. (eds.) *From One Louvre to Another: Opening a Museum for Everyone*. Paris: Xavier Barrel, p. 11.

Al-Mubarak, M.K. (2018). 'Session 1: Museums and Globalisation I'. *Worlds in a Museums Symposium*. Louvre Abu Dhabi, 10–11 November 2018.

Al-Mulla, M. (2013). 'Museums in Qatar: Creating Museums in a Time of Global Unease'. In: Erskine-Loftus. P. (ed.) *Reimagining Museums: Practice in the Arabian Peninsula*. Edinburgh: MuseumsEtc, pp. 160–203.

Al-Mulla, M. (2014). 'The Development of the First Qatar National Museum'. In: Exell, K. and Rico, T. (eds.) *Cultural Heritage in the Arabian Peninsula: Debates, Discourses and Practices*. Farnham: Ashgate, pp. 117–128.

Al-Mulla, M. (2017). 'History of Slaves in Qatar: Social Reality and Contemporary Political Vision'. *Journal of History Culture and Art Research*, 6(4), pp. 85–111.

Mullin, S. (2009). 'Would You Like Fries with that Picasso? The International Franchising of World Class Museums'. *Art Law Gallery*. [Online]. Available at: www.artlawgallery.com/2009/01/articles/museums-private-collectors/would-you-like-fries-with-that-picasso-the-international-franchising-of-world-class-museums/print.html [Accessed 8 June 2010].

Mushbarak, F. (2011). Education Specialist, Sharjah Museums Department, Sharjah. 30 November 2011.

Nakib, F. (2016). *A City Transformed*. Stanford, CA: Stanford University Press.

Nardella, B.M. and Mallinson, M. (2015). "Only Foreigners Can Do It'? Technical Assistance, Advocacy and Brokerage at Aksum, Ethiopia'. In: Basu, P. and Modest, W. *Museums, Heritage and International Development*. Abingdon and New York: Routledge, pp. 188–210.

Nash, K. (2009). 'Between Citizenship and Human Rights'. *Sociology*. 43(6). 1067–1083

Nashashibi, R. (2007). 'The Blackstone Legacy, Islam, and the Rise of Ghetto Cosmopolitanism'. *Souls*. 9(2), pp. 123–131.

National Archives. (n.d.). 'About Us'. [Online]. Available at: www.na.ae/en/aboutus/aboutna.aspx [Accessed 19 January 2015].

National Center for Documentation and Research. (n.d.[a]) 'British Era'. [Online]. Available at: www.cdr.gov.ae/ncdr/English/uaeGuide/hisBritish.aspx [Accessed 19 November 2013].

National Center for Documentation and Research. (n.d.[b]) 'The UAE: A Federation'. [Online]. Available at: www.cdr.gov.ae/ncdr/English/uaeGuide/PrintFederation.aspx [Accessed 19 November 2013].

National Museums of World Culture. (n.d.[a]). 'National Museums of World Culture'. [Online]. Available at: www.varldskulturmuseerna.se/en/the-government/the-national-museum-of-world-cultures/ [Accessed 25 April 2018].

National Museums of World Culture. (n.d.[b]). 'Museum of World Culture: Organization'. [Online]. Available at: www.varldskulturmuseerna.se/en/varldskulturmuseet/about-the-museum/organisation/ [Accessed 25 April 2018].

NCDR Representative. 2011 at the National Center for Documentation and Research, Abu Dhabi, 30 March 2011.

Nederveen Pieterse, J. (2009). *Globalization and Culture: Global Mélange*, 2nd ed. Lanham, MD: Rowman & Littlefield.

New Kuwait. (n.d.).' New Kuwait'. [Online]. Available at: www.newkuwait.gov.kw/ [Accessed 15 February 2019].

Noujaim, S. (2018). 'Opening Remarks'. *Worlds in a Museums Symposium*. Louvre Abu Dhabi, 10–11 November 2018.

Nusseibeh, Z. (2011). Interview at The Royal Court Abu Dhabi. 11 April 2011.

Nussbaum, M.C. (1996). 'Patriotism and Cosmopolitanism'. In: Nussbaum, M.C. (ed.) *For Love of Country: Debating Limits of Patriotism*. Boston, MA: Beacon, pp. 3–20.

Nyadzayo, M.W.; Matanda, M.J. and Ewing, M.T. (2011). 'Brand Relationships and Brand Equity in Franchising'. *Industrial Marketing Management*. 40, pp. 1103–1115.

Nye, J. (2004). *Soft Power: The Means to Success in World Politics*. New York: Public Affairs.

Nye, J. (2011). *The Future of Power*. New York: Public Affairs.

NYU Abu Dhabi. (2017a). 'Museums and Cultural Heritage Studies'. [Online]. Available at: http://nyuad.nyu.edu./en/academics/undergraduate/pre-professional-courses/museum-and-cultural-heritage-studies.html [Accessed 15 April 2018].

NYU Abu Dhabi. (2017b). 'Dhakira Center for Heritage Studies in the UAE'. [Online]. Available at: http://nyuad.nyu.edu./en/research/centers-labs-and-projects/dhakira-center-for-heritage-studies-in-the-uae.html [Accessed 15 April 2018].

O'Neill, M. (2004). 'Enlightenment Museums: Universal or Merely Global?' *Museum and Society*. (3), pp. 190–202.

Ong, A. (2007). *Museums in Non-Western Contexts: Challenging the Popular Paradigm*. Masters. Colombian College of Arts & Sciences. [Online]. Available at: http://programs.columbian.gwu.edu/museumstudies/sites/default/files/u9/museumsinnon-westerncontexts.pdf [Accessed 1 October 2012].

Onley, J. (2009). *Britain and the Gulf Shaikhdoms, 1820–1971: The Politics of Protection*. Doha: Georgetown University Center for International and Regional Studies of Foreign Service in Qatar.

Ossewaarde, M. (2007). 'Cosmopolitanism and the Society of Strangers'. *Current Sociology*. 55, pp. 367–388.

Ostling, S. (2007). 'The Global Museum and the Orbit of the Solomon R. Guggenheim Museum New York'. *The International Journal of Humanities*. 5, pp. 87–97.

Oxford Dictionaries. (2014). 'Franchised'. [Online]. Available at: www.oxford dictionaries.com/definition/english/franchise?q=franchised#franchise__19 (Accessed 14 January 2014).

Palmer, C. (2009). 'Reflections on the Practice of Ethnography within Heritage Tourism'. In: Sorenson, M.L.S. and Carmen, J. (eds.) *Heritage Studies: Methods and Approaches*. London: Routledge, pp. 123–139.

Paris-Sorbonne University Abu Dhabi. (n.d.). 'Master of Arts and Museum Studies'. [Online]. Available at: www.sorbonne.ae/EN/Documents/Paris%20Sorbonne_History%20of%20Art.pdf [Accessed 17 October 2011].

Parry, B. (1996). 'Problems in Current Theories of Colonial Discourse'. In: Ashcroft, B.; Griffiths, G. and Tiffin, H. *The Postcolonial Studies Reader*. Abingdon and New York, Routledge: 36–44.

Partrick, N. (2009). 'Nationalism in the Gulf States'. *The Centre for the Study of Global Economics*. London: London School of Economics. [Online]. Available at: http://webfirstlive.lse.ac.uk/government/research/resgroups/kuwait/documents/NeilPartrick.pdf [Accessed 5 October 2011].

Peers, L. and Brown, A. (2003). 'Introduction'. In: Peers, L. and Brown, A. (eds.) *Museums and Source Communities*. London: Routledge, pp. 3–16.

Penziner-Hightower, V. (2011). *In the Time Before Oil: A History and Heritage of Pearling in the United Arab Emirates*. PhD. History Department, Florida State University.

Penziner-Hightower, V. (2014). 'Purposeful Ambiguity: The Pearl Trade and Heritage Construction in the United Arab Emirates'. In: Exell, K. and Rico, T. (eds.) *Cultural Heritage in the Arabian Peninsula: Debates, Discourses and Practices*. Farnham: Ashgate, pp. 71–84.

Pes, J. (2012). 'Dallas Launches International Programme'. *The Art Newspaper*. [Online]. Available at: www.theartnewspaper.com/articles/Dallas-launches-international-programme/26631 [Accessed 7 June 2012].

Petrys, L. (2007). 'Freej'. *Society Dubai*. [pdf]. Available at: http://freej.ae/uploads/Media/English/6-4-10-73media41b.jpg [Accessed 16 June 2012].

Phillips, R.B. (2007). 'The Museum of Art-Thropology: Twenty-First Century Imbroglios'. *Research*. 52, pp. 9–19.

Pianese, C. (2018). *Museum Approaches and Models of Practice: A Comparative Investigation of the Current Cultural Paradigm in Dubai, Sharjah and Abu Dhabi*. Unpublished Masters Dissertation. London: University College London.

Picton, O.J. (2010). 'Usage of the Concept of Culture and Heritage in the United Arab Emirates – An Analysis of Sharjah Heritage Area'. *Journal of Heritage Tourism*. 5(1), pp. 69–84.

Pine, J.B. and Gilmore, J.H. (1999). *The Experience Economy: Work is Theatre and Every Business a Stage*. Harvard: Harvard Business Press.

Plaza, B. (2007). 'The Bilbao Effect (Guggenheim Museum Bilbao)'. *Museum News*. 86(5), pp. 13–16, 68.

Plaza, B.; Tironic, M. and Haarichd, S.N. (2009). 'Bilbao's Art Scene and the "Guggenheim Effect" Revisited'. *European Planning Studies*. 17(11), pp. 1711–1729.

Poncelet, C. (2007). 'Bill 180: Law Project, Adopted by the Senate, Authorizing the Approval of Agreements between the Government of the French Republic and the United Arab Emirates Government Relating to the Universal Museum of Abu Dhabi. Commission on Foreign Affairs, National Assembly, 26 September 2007, Paris'. [Online]. Available at: www.assemblee-nationale.fr/13/projets/pl0180.asp [Accessed 1 May 2008].

Ponzini, D. (2011). 'Large Scale Development Projects and Star Architecture in the Absence of Democratic Politics: The Case of Abu Dhabi, UAE'. *Cities.* 28, pp. 251–259.

Power, T. (2018). 'Qasr Al Hosn: From Residential Palace to Living Monument, Its Transformation is Complete'. *The National.* [Online]. Available at: www. thenational.ae/opinion/comment/qasr-al-hosn-from-residential-palace-to-living-monument-its-transformation-is-complete-1.799901 [Accessed 6 December 2018].

Prager, L. (2015). 'Displaying Origins: Heritage Museums, Cultural Festivals, and National Imageries in the UAE'. *Horizons in Humanities and Social Sciences.* 1(1), pp. 22–46.

Pratt, A.C. (2010). 'Creative Cities: Tensions within and between Social, Cultural and Economic Development a Critical Reading of the UK Experience'. *City, Culture and Society.* 1, pp. 13–20.

Preuss, H. (2007). 'The Conceptualisation of Measurement of Mega Sport Event Legacies'. *Journal of Sport Tourism.* 12(3), pp. 207–228.

Prior, N. (2009). 'The Slug and the Juggernaught? Museums, Cities, Rhythms'. [pdf]. *Edinburgh Working Papers.* 38, pp. 1–39. Available at: www.sociology.ed.ac. uk/__data/assets/pdf_file/0009/55899/WP38Slug_Juggernaut_Nick_Prior.pdf [Accessed 13 June 2012].

Qasr Al Hosn. (2018a). 'Qasr Al Hosn'. [Online]. Available at: https://qasralhosn.ae/ [Accessed 13 February 2019].

Qasr Al Hosn. (2018b). 'History'. [Online]. Available at: https://qasralhosn.ae/history/ [Accessed 13 February 2019].

Qasr Al Hosn. (2018c). 'Discover'. [Online]. Available at: https://qasralhosn.ae/discover/ [Accessed 13 February 2019].

Qasr Al Hosn. (2018d). 'Qasr Al Hosn an Historic Landmark'. [Online]. Available at: https://qasralhosn.ae/qasralhosn/ [Accessed 13 February 2019].

Qasr Al Hosn. (2018e). 'House of Artisans'. [Online]. Available at: https://qasralhosn.ae/house-of-artisans/ [Accessed 13 February 2019].

Qasr Al Hosn Festival. (2014a). 'A Celebration of over 250 Years History'. [Online]. Available at: http://archive.qasralhosnfestival.ae/ [Accessed 3 February 2019].

Qasr Al Hosn Festival. (2014b). Overview. [Online]. Available at: http://archive.qasralhosnfestival.ae/2013-festival-site/overview/ [Accessed 1 February 2019].

Qasr Al Watan. (n.d.[a]). Presidential Gifts. [Online]. Available at: www.qasralwatan.ae/explore-the-palace/presidential-gifts [Accessed 28 May 2019].

Qasr Al Watan. (n.d.[b]). House of Knowledge. [Online]. Available at: www.qasralwatan.ae/explore-the-palace/house-of-knowledge [Accessed 28 May 2019].

Quinn, B. (1999). 'Control and Support in International Franchise Network'. *International Marketing Review.* 16, pp. 345–362.

Rabaté, M. (2017). 'Preface'. In: Martinez, J.L. and Trey, J. (eds.) *From One Louvre to Another: Opening a Museum for Everyone.* Paris: Xavier Barrel, pp. 14–15.

Radcliffe, S.A. (2006). *Culture and Development in a Globalizing World: Geographies, Actors, and Paradigms.* Abingdon and New York: Routledge.

Al-Rahmah, M.A. (2011). Interview at Caribou Coffee, Dubai. 7 September 2011.

Al-Ragam, A. (2014). 'The Politics of Representation: The Kuwait National Museum and Processes of Cultural Production'. *International Journal of Heritage Studies.* 20(6), pp. 663–674.

Rauen, M. (2001). 'Reflections on the Space of Flows: The Guggenheim Bilbao'. *Journal of Arts Management.* 30(4), pp. 283–300.

Ren, X. (2008). 'Architecture and Nation Building in the Age of Globalization: Construction of the National Stadium of Beijing for the 2008 Olympics'. *Journal of Urban Affairs*. 30(2), pp. 175–190.

Rico, T. (2014). 'Islamaphobia and the Location of Heritage Debates in the Arabian Peninsula'. In: Exell K. and Rico T. (eds.) *Cultural Heritage in the Arabian Peninsula: Debates, Discourses and Practices*. Farnham: Ashgate, pp. 19–32.

Riding, A. (2007a). 'The Louvre's Art: Priceless. The Louvre's Name: Expensive'. *The New York Times*. March 7 2007, pp. 1–2. Available at: www.nytimes.com/2007/03/07/arts/design/07louv.html [Accessed 12 December 2018].

Riding, A. (2007b). 'France Frets as Louvre Looks Overseas'. *The New York Times*. [Online]. Available at: www.nytimes.com/2007/01/01/arts/design/01louv.html?fta=y&_r=0 [Accessed 15 August 2011].

Riding, A. (2007c). 'Abu Dhabi Is to Gain a Louvre of Its Own'. *The New York Times*. [Online]. Available at: http://query.nytimes.com/gst/fullpage.html?res=9E02E5D-A1330F930A25752C0A9619C8B63&sec=&spon=&pagewanted=2 [Accessed 15 August 2011].

Ritzer, G. (2010). 'An Introduction to McDonaldization'. In: Ritzer, G. (ed.) *McDonaldization*, 6th ed. London: Sage, pp. 3–25.

Rizvi, A. (2015). 'Procession Marks Opening of Annual Qasr Al Hosn Festival'. *The National*. [Online]. Available at: www.thenational.ae/uae/procession-marks-opening-of-annual-qasr-al-hosn-festival-1.38404 [Accessed 13 February 2015].

Riza, M.; Doratli, N. and Fasli, M. (2012). 'City Branding and Identity'. *Procedia – Social and Behavioural Sciences*. 35, pp. 293–300.

Robertson, C.J. and Al-Khatib, J.A. (2002). 'The Relationship between Arab Values and Work Beliefs: An Exploratory Examination'. *International Business Review*. 44(5), pp. 583–601.

Robertson, R. (1992). *Globalization: Social Theory and Global Culture*. London: Sage.

Robertson, R. (1995). 'Glocalization: Time-Space and Homogeneity-Heterogeneity'. In: Featherstone, M.; Lash, S. and Robertson, R. (eds.) *Global Modernities*. London: Sage, pp. 25–44.

Robbins, B. (1998). 'Introduction Part 1: Actually Existing Cosmopolitanism'. In: Pheang, C. and Robbins, B. (eds.) *Cosmopolitics: Thinking and Feeling beyond the Nation*. Minneapolis: University of Minnesota Press, pp. 1–19.

Rojek, C. (1999). 'Fatal Attractions'. In: Boswell, D. and Evans, J. (eds.) Representing the Nation: A Reader: Histories, Heritage and Museums. Abingdon and New York: Routledge, pp. 186–207.

Rosenbawm, L. (2009). 'Abu Dhabi Update: British Museum Participates in Saadiyat Island's Museum-Development Spree'. [Blog] *CultureGrrl*. Available at: www.artsjournal.com/culturegrrl/2009/07/british [Accessed 15 January 2012].

Al-Roubaie, A. and Abdul-Wahab, P.S. (2009). 'Building a Knowledge Society in the Arab World. In: C. Marcinkowski'. (ed.) *The Islamic World and the West: Managing Religious and Cultural Identities in the Age of Globalisation*. Berlin and Zurich: Lit Verlag, pp. 231–242.

Royal Academy. (n.d.). 'Charles I: King and Collector'. *Royal Academy of Arts*. [Online]. Available at: www.royalacademy.org.uk/exhibition/charles-i-king-and-collector

Ruiz, C. (2017). 'Guggenheim Abu Dhabi Should Be Postponed or Downsized, Says the Man Who Launched the Project.' *The Art Newspaper*. [Online]. Available at: www.theartnewspaper.com/news/guggenheim-abu-dhabi-should-be-postponed-or-downsized-says-the-man-who-launched-the-project [Accessed 26 March 2017].

Al-Rumaithi, M. (2011). Interview at Café Arabia, Abu Dhabi. 4 March 2011.

Russell, K.; O'Connor, N.; Dashper, K. and Fletcher, T. (2014). 'Sports Mega-Events and Islam: An introduction'. In Dashper, K.; Fletcher, T. and Mccullough, N. *Sports, Events, Society and Culture*. Abingdon and New York: Routledge, pp. 189–204.

Rutherford, J. (1990). 'The Third Space: Interview with Homi Bhabha'. *Identity, Community, Culture, Difference*. London, Lawrence and Wishart: 207–221.

Ryan, J. and Silvanto, S. (2011). 'A Brand for All the Nations: The Development of the World Heritage Brand in Emerging Markets'. *Marketing Intelligence & Planning*. 29(3), pp. 305–318.

Rykner, D. (2006). 'Petition'. *La Tribune de l'Art*. [Online]. Available at: www.latribunedelart.com/petition [Accessed 17 March 2010].

Rykner, D. (2007). 'The Flight Continues'. *La Tribune de l'Art*. [Online]. Available at: www.latribunedelart.com/le-combat-continue [Accessed 17 March 2010].

Rykner, D. (2009). 'First Acquisition Committee for the Louvre-Abu Dhabi'. [Online]. Available at: www.thearttribune.com/First-acquisition-committee-for.html [Accessed 16 October 2018].

Said, E. (1978). *Orientalism*. London: Vintage Books.

Salman, N. (2019). 'France's Imperial Theatre Reopens Following UAE Restoration Efforts. Emirates News Agency'. [Online]. Available at: http://wam.ae/en/details/1395302768883 [Accessed 19 June 2019].

Samuel, R. (1994). *Theatres of Memory: Past and Present in Popular Culture*. London and New York: Verso.

Sandell, R. (2002). *Museums, Society, Inequality*. Abingdon and New York: Routledge.

Sassen, S. (2001). *The Global City*. Princeton, NJ: Princeton University Press.

Al-Sayegh, F. (2011). Interview at UAE University, Al Ain. 21 March 2011.

Sayyid, S. (2000). 'Bad Faith: Anti-Essentialism, Universalism and Islamism'. In: Brah A. and Coombes, A. (eds.) *Hybridity and Its Discontents: Politics, Science, Culture*. Abingdon and New York: Routledge, pp. 257–271.

Schiller, N.G. and Irving, A. (2017). *What's in a Word? What's in a Question? Whose Cosmopolitanism?: Critical Perspectives, Relationalities and Discontents*. New York and Oxford: Berghahn Books, pp. 1–26.

Schofield, J. and Szymanski, R. (2011). 'Introduction'. In: Schofield, J. and Szymanski, R. (eds.) *Local Heritage, Global Context: Cultural Perspectives on Sense of Place*. Farnham and Burlington: Ashgate, pp. 1–12.

Schorch, P.; Waterton, E. and Watson, S. (2017). 'Museum Canopies and Effective Cosmopolitanism'. In: Tolia-Kelly, P.; Waterton, E. and Watson, S. (eds.) *Heritage, Affect and Emotion*. Abingdon and New York: Routledge, pp. 93–113.

Schuster, P.K. (2004). 'The Treasures of World Culture in the Public Museum'. *ICOM News*. 1, pp. 4–5. [pdf]. Available at: http://icom.museum/fileadmin/user_upload/pdf/ICOM_News/2004-1/ENG/p4_2004-1.pdf [Accessed 4 March 2011].

Scharfenort, N. (2014). 'The Sheered Project in Doha: The Heritage of the New Urban Design in Qatar'. In: Exell, K. and Rico, T. (eds.) *Cultural Heritage in the Arabian Peninsula: Debates, Discourses and Practices*. Farnham: Ashgate, pp. 189–204.

Schwarzer, M.; Deemas, A. and Markopoulos, L. (2013). 'Social Change and the Rules of the Game: A Conversation about Museum Values in the United Arab Emirates'. In: Erskine-Loftus, P. (ed.) *Reimagining Museums: Practice in the Arabian Peninsula*. Edinburgh and Cambridge: MuseumsEtc, pp. 204–237.

Seaman, A. (2009). 'TV Cartoon Hamdoon Explores UAE Identity'. *The National.* [Online]. Available at: www.thenational.ae/news/uae-news/tv-cartoon-hamdoon-explores-uae-identity [Accessed 4 July 2012].

Shaheen, K. (2017). 'Leonardo's Salvator Mundi: Abu Dhabi Bought World's Most Expensive Painting'. *The Guardian.* [Online]. Available at: www.theguardian.com/artanddesign/2017/dec/07/world-record-da-vinci-painting-to-be-exhibited-at-louvre-abu-dhabi [Accessed 8 December 2017].

Sharjah Museums Department Representative. (2011). Interview at Sharjah Museums Department, Sharjah. 27 November 2011.

Sheehan, P. (2011). Interview at Al Jahili Fort, Al Ain Abu Dhabi. 5 December 2011.

Shelton, A. (2000). 'Museum Ethnography: An Imperial Science'. In: Hallam, E. and Street, B. (eds.) *Cultural Encounters: Representing "Otherness".* London: Routledge, pp. 155–193.

Sherman, D.L. (2004). "Peoples Ethnographic": Objects, Museums, and the Colonial Inheritance of French Ethnology'. *French Historical Studies.* 27(3), pp. 669–703.

Simpfendorfer, B. (2009). *The New Silk Road: How a Rising Arab World if Turning Away from the West and Rediscovering China.* Basingstoke and New York: Palgrave Macmillan.

Simpson, I.R. (2014). 'Concern amid the Oysters as Pearling is Honoured: Nature and the Environment in Heritage Practice'. In: Exell, K. and Rico, T. (eds.) *Cultural Heritage in the Arabian Peninsula: Debates, Discourses and Practices.* Farnham: Ashgate, 33–50.

Sinclair, K. (2013). 'Art at the Heart of Plan for Cultural Travellers to Abu Dhabi'. *The National.* [Online]. Available at: www.thenational.ae/news/uae-news/tourism/art-at-the-heart-of-plan-for-cultural-travellers-to-abu-dhabi [Accessed 4 July 2013].

Skidmore, Owings and Merrill. (n.d.). 'Burj Khalifa'. [Online]. Available at: www.som.com/projects/burj_khalifa [Accessed 15 December 2012].

Skluzacek, C.R. (2010). *Universality and its Discontents: the Louvre and Guggenheim Abu Dhabi as a Case Study in the Future of Museums.* Masters Dissertation. [pdf]. Available at: http://digitalcommons.macalester.edu/art_honors/1 [Accessed 17 June 2018].

Smith, L-J. (2006). *Uses of Heritage.* Abingdon and New York: Routledge.

Smith, L-J. (2012). 'Editorial'. *International Journal of Heritage Studies.* 18(6), pp. 533–540.

Smith, L-J. (2017). 'Heritage, Identity and Power'. In: Hsiao, H.H.M.; Yew-Foong, H. and Peycam, P. *Citizens, Civil Society and Heritage-making in Asia.* Acadamia Sinica, pp. 15–39

Soderland, H.A. (2009). 'The History of Heritage: A Method in Analysing Legislative Historiography'. In: Sorensen, M.L.S. and Carman, J. (eds.) *Heritage Studies: Methods and Approaches.* London: Routledge, pp. 55–84.

Sokolovskiy, S. (2013). 'Rooted or Extinct? Post-Soviet Anthropology and the Construction of Indigenousness'. Vargas-Cetina, G. *Anthropology and the Politics of Representation.* Alabama: The University of Alabama Press, pp. 193–211.

Solomon R. Guggenheim Foundation. (n.d.[a]). 'History'. Guggenheim. [Online]. Available at: www.guggenheim.org/guggenheim-foundation/history [Accessed 20 April 2013].

Solomon R. Guggenheim Foundation. (n.d.[b]). 'Guggenheim Abu Dhabi: About'. Guggenheim. [Online]. Available at: www.guggenheim.org/abu-dhabi/about [Accessed 2 April 2012].

Solomon R. Guggenheim Foundation. (n.d.[c]) 'Guggenheim Abu Dhabi: Curatorial Concept'. [Online]. Available at: www.guggenheim.org/abu-dhabi/about/curatorial-concept [Accessed 2 April 2012].

Solomon R. Guggenheim Foundation. (n.d.[d]) 'Talking Art Series Shares Curatorial Vision of Guggenheim Abu Dhabi'. [Online]. Available at: www.guggenheim.org/guggenheim-foundation/news/5475-talking-art-series-shares-curatorial-vision-of-guggenheim-abu-dhabi- [Accessed 20 May 2013].

Solomon R. Guggenheim Foundation. (2007). 'Abu Dhabi and SRGF Announce New Guggenheim Abu Dhabi'. Guggenheim. [Online]. Available at: www.guggenheim.org/abu-dhabi/press-room/press-releases/1852-operating-framework-release [Accessed 10 December 2014].

Somers Cocks, A. (2013). 'Bad Feelings over Abu Dhabi's Unspent €25m Gift to the Louvre'. *The Art Newspaper*. [Online]. Available at: http://ec2-79-125-124-178.eu-west-1.compute.amazonaws.com/articles/Bad-feelings-over-Abu-Dhabis-unspent-m-gift-to-the-Louvre/29411 [Accessed 30 July 2019].

Somers Cocks, A. (2017). 'The Five Gifts Louvre Abu Dhabi Offers to the UAE and the World'. *The National*. [Online]. Available at: www.thenational.ae/opinion/comment/the-five-gifts-louvre-abu-dhabi-offers-to-the-uae-and-the-world-1.674392 [Accessed 9 November 2017].

Somers Cocks, A.S. (2018). 'Royal Academy of Arts Tried to Borrow $450m Salvator Mundi for its Charles I Exhibition'. *The Art Newspaper*. [Online]. Available at: www.theartnewspaper.com/news/royal-academy-of-arts-tried-to-borrow-usd450m-salvator-mundi-for-its-charles-i-exhibition [Accessed 28 January 2017].

Staiff, R. and Bushell, R. (2003). 'Heritage Interpretation and Cross-Cultural Translation in an Age of Global Travel: Some Issues'. *Journal of Park and Recreation Administration*. Special Places Issue. 21(4), pp. 105–123.

Starkey, H. (2012). 'Human Rights, Cosmopolitanism and Utopias: Implications for Citizenship Education'. *Cambridge Journal of Education*. 42(1), pp. 21–35.

Steger, M.B. (2009). *Globalization: A Very Short Introduction*. Oxford: Oxford University Press.

Stelter, B. (2009). 'Dubai Superheroes: Little Old Grannie Who Wear Veils'. *The New York Times*. [Online]. Available at: www.nytimes.com/2009/09/03/arts/television/03animated.html?pagewanted=all [Accessed 16 June 2012].

Stephenson, L.M. and Knight, J. (2010). Dubai's Tourism Industry and its Societal Impact: Social Implications and Sustainable Challenges. *Journal of Tourism and Cultural Change*. 8(4), pp. 278–292.

Stevens, M.L.; Miller-Idris, C. and Shami, S. (2018). *Seeing the World: How US Universities Make Knowledge in a Global Era*. Princeton, NJ and Oxford: Princeton University Press.

Stracke, N. (2008). 'A French Base in Gulf'. *Al Arabiya*. 27 January. Available at: www.alarabiya.net/views/2008/01/27/44773.html [Accessed 27 May 2009].

Szuchman, J. (2012). 'Archaeology, Identity, and Demographic Imbalance in the United Arab Emirates'. *Heritage and Society*. 5(1), pp. 35–52.

TCA Abu Dhabi. (2016). 'Qasr Al Hosn Festival Concludes with a Record Number of Visitors'. Available at: https://tcaabudhabi.ae/en/media.centre/news/2016.qasr.al.hosn.festival.concludes.with.a.record.number.of.visitors.aspx [Accessed 17 May 2019].

Teskey, R. and Alkhamis, N. (2016). 'Oral History and National Stories: Theory and Practice in the Gulf Cooperation Council'. In: Erskine-Loftus, P.;

Penziner-Hightower, V. and Al Mulla, M. (2016). *Representing the Nation: The Use of Museums and Heritage to Create National Narratives and Identity in the Arabian Peninsula*. London and New York: Routledge, pp. 109–122.

Thabiti-Willis, J. (2016). 'A Visible Silence: Africans in the History of Pearl Diving in Dubai, UAE'. In: Exell, K. and Wakefield, S. (eds.) *Museums in Arabia: Transnational Practices and Regional Processes*. London and New York: Routledge, pp. 34–50.

The Economist. (2011). 'Arab Television: The Q&A: Mohammed Saeed Harib, Animator'. [Online]. Available at: www/economist.com/blogs/prospero/2011/08/arab-television [Accessed 16 June 2012].

The Founder's Memorial. (n.d.). 'The Founder's Memorial'. [Online]. Available at: www.thefoundersmemorial.ae/en/ [Accessed 10 May 2019].

The National. (2009). 'Zayed and British Museums Collaborate'. [Online]. Available at: www.thenational.ae/news/uae-news/zayed-and-british-museums-collaborate [Accessed 16 November 2013].

Thomas, J. (2011). 'Mesopotamian Splendour on Saadiyat Island'. *The National*. [Online]. Available at: www.thenational.ae/news/uae-news/tourism/mesopotamiansplendour-on-saadiyat-island [Accessed 29 March 2011].

Thompson, S. (2011). 'Reclaiming Histories and the Virtual Museum: A Proposal to Preserve Al Jazeera Al Hamra'. *International Journal of Arts*. 6(2), pp. 127–138.

Thornley, A. (2002). 'Urban Regeneration and Sports Stadia'. *European Planning Studies*. 10(7), pp. 813–818.

Tibi, B. (1990). 'The Simultaneity of the Unsimultaneous: Old Tribes and Imposed Nation-States in the Modern Middle East'. In: Khoury, P. and Kostiner, J. (eds.) *Tribes and State Formation in the Middle East*. Berkeley: University of California Press, pp. 127–152.

Tomii, R. (2018). *Radicalism in the Wilderness: International Contemporaneity and 1960s Art in Japan*. Cambridge, MA and London: MIT Press.

Tomlinson, J. (2007). *The Culture of Speed: The Coming of Immediacy*. London: Sage.

Torr, R. (2007). 'Treasures of Egypt on Show'. *Gulf Daily News*. [Online]. Available at: www.gulf-daily-news.com/NewsDetails.aspx?storyid=178646 [Accessed 20 May 2011].

Tourism Development Investment Corporation. (2010). *Best Practice Report 2010*. [pdf] Abu Dhabi: Abu Dhabi Tourism Authority. Available at: www.tdic.ae/en/section/media/page/6?limit=170&view=full [Accessed 16 November 2010].

Tourism Development Investment Corporation. (2011). *Splendours of Mesopotamia: Exhibition Brochure*. Abu Dhabi: Abu Dhabi Tourism Authority.

Tourism Development Investment Corporation. (2012). *Treasures of the World's Cultures. Exhibition Leaflet*. Abu Dhabi: Abu Dhabi Tourism Authority.

Tourism Development Investment Corporation. (2013). 'Chairman'. [Online]. Available at: www.saadiyat.ae/en/about/about-our-management/chairman.html (Accessed 7 July 2013).

Tourism Development Investment Corporation. (n.d.[a]). 'About Saadiyat'. Saadiyat Cultural District. [Online]. Available at: www.saadiyat.ae/en/about/about-saadiyat-island.html [Accessed 19 May 2012].

Tourism Development Investment Corporation. (n.d.[b]). 'Saadiyat'. [Online]. Available at: www.tdic.ae/en/project/projects/master-developments/saadiyat-island.html [Accessed 11 October 2011].

Tourism Development Investment Corporation. (n.d.[c]). 'The Legacy'. Saadiyat Cultural District. [Online]. Available at: http://saadiyatculturaldistrict.ae/en/saadiyat-cultural-district/our-story/ [Accessed 19 May 2012].

Tourism Development Investment Corporation. (n.d.[d]). 'Outside the Museum'. Saadiyat Cultural District. [Online]. Available at: www.saadiyat.ae/en/cultural/louvre-abu-dhabi1/louvre-abu-dhabi-architecture-outside.html [Accessed 25 May 2012].

Tourism Development Investment Corporation. (n.d.[e]) 'Inside the Museum'. Saadiyat Cultural District. [Online]. Available at: http://saadiyat.ae/en/cultural/louvre-abu-dhabi1/architecture3.html [Accessed 25 May 2012].

Tourism Development Investment Corporation. (n.d.[f]) 'Outside the Museum'. [Online]. Available at: www.saadiyat.ae/en/cultural/guggenheim-abu-dhabi1/architecture-outside.html [Accessed 25 May 2012].

Tourism Development Investment Corporation. (n.d.[g]) 'Curatorial Concept'. Saadiyat Cultural District. [Online]. Available at: www.saadiyat.ae/en/cultural/guggenheim-abu-dhabi1/curatorial-concept.html [Accessed 25 May 2012].

Tourism Development Investment Corporation. (n.d.[h]) 'Inside the Museum'. Saadiyat Cultural District. [Online]. Available at: www.saadiyat.ae/en/cultural/guggenheim-abu-dhabi1/architecture2.html [Accessed 25 May 2012].

Tourism Development Investment Corporation. (n.d.[i]) 'Outside the Museum'. Saadiyat Cultural District. [Online]. Available at: www.saadiyat.ae/en/cultural/maritime-museum1/maritime-museum-architecture-outside.html [Accessed 25 May 2012].

Tourism Development Investment Corporation. (n.d.[j]) 'Inside the Museum'. Saadiyat Cultural District. [Online]. Available at: www.saadiyat.ae/en/cultural/maritime-museum1/architecture.html [Accessed 25 May 2012].

Tourism Development Investment Corporation. (n.d.[k]) 'Overview'. Saadiyat Cultural District. [Online]. Available at: www.saadiyat.ae/en/cultural/performing-arts-centre1/performing-arts-centre-overview.html [Accessed 25 May 2012].

Tourism Development Investment Corporation. (n.d.[l]) 'Inside the Centre'. Saadiyat Cultural District. [Online]. Available at: www.saadiyat.ae/en/cultural/performing-arts-centre1/architecture1.html [Accessed 25 May 2012].

Tourism Development Investment Corporation. (n.d.[m]) 'Outside the Centre'. Saadiyat Cultural District. [Online]. Available at: www.saadiyat.ae/en/cultural/performing-arts-centre1.html [Accessed 25 May 2012].

Tourism Development Investment Corporation. (n.d.[n]) 'TDIC Announces Opening Dates of Saadiyat Cultural District Museums'. [Online]. Available at: www.tdic.ae/en/news/media-center/news/tdic-announces-opening-dates-of-saadiyat-cultural-district-museums.html [Accessed 25 January 2012].

Tourism Development Investment Corporation. (n.d.[o]). 'Manarat Al Saadiyat: Overview'. [Online]. Available at: www.Saadiyatculturaldistrict.ae/en/Manarat-al-saadiyat/overview/ [Accessed 19 September 2012].

Tourism Development Investment Corporation. (n.d.[q]). 'Louvre Abu Dhabi Talking Art Series'. [Online]. Available at: http://saadiyatculturaldistrict.ae/en/cultural-programme/events/Louvre-Abu-Dhabi-Talking-Art-Series-/ [Accessed 5 February 2013].

Tourism Development Investment Corporation. (n.d.[r]). 'Guggenheim Abu Dhabi: Talking Art Series'. [Online]. Available at: http://saadiyatculturaldistrict.ae/en/cultural-programme/events/Guggenheim-Abu-Dhabi-Talking-Art-Series/ [Accessed 20 May 2013].

Tourism Development Investment Corporation. (n.d.[s]). 'News: TDIC Presents Splendours of Mesopotamia'. [Online]. Available at: www.saadiyat.ae/en/media-centre/news/splendours-of-mesopotamia-news.html [Accessed 31 March 2011].

Tourism Development Investment Corporation. (n.d.[t]). 'Treasures of the World's Cultures. Saadiyat Cultural District'. Available at: www.saadiyatculturaldistrict.ae/en/cultural-programme/exhibitions/Treasures-of-the-Worlds-Cultures/ [Accessed 20 April 2012].

Tourism Development Investment Corporation. (n.d.[u]). 'Louvre Abu Dhabi Overview'. [Online]. Available at: www.saadiyat.ae/en/cultural/louvre-abud-dhabi1/louvre-abu-dhabi-overview.html [Accessed 6 March 2012].

Tourism Development Investment Corporation. (n.d.[v]). 'TDIC Announces Opening Dates of Saadiyat Cultural District Museums'. [Online]. Available at: www.tdic.ae/en/news/media-center/news/tdic-announces-opening-dates-of-saadiyat-cultural-district-museums.html [Accessed 25 January 2012].

Tourism Development Investment Corporation. (n.d.[w]). 'Saadiyat'. [Online]. Available at: www.tdic.ae/en/project/projects/master-developments/saadiyat-island.html [Accessed 11 October 2011].

Tsing, A.L. (2005). *Friction: Ethnography of Global Connection*. Princeton, NJ and Oxford: Princeton University Press.

Tuhiwai-Smith, L. (2012) *Decolonizing Methodologies: Research and Indigenous Peoples*, 2nd ed. London and New York: Zed Books.

Turki, E.M. (2011). Interview at Abu Dhabi Authority for Culture and Heritage, Abu Dhabi. 16 March 2011.

Turner, B.S. and Khonder, H.H. (2010). *Globalization East and West*. London: Sage.

Tveit, E. (2007). 'Folklore on Display: The Authenticity Debate Revisited.' *Studia Ethnologica Croatica*. 19, pp. 293–302.

UAE Cabinet. (n.d.). 'The Established Councils'. [Online]. Available at: www.uae-cabinet.ae/English/The%20Cabinet/Pages/TheEstablishedCouncils.aspx [Accessed 5 January 2013].

UAE Cabinet. (2010a). *UAE Government Strategy 2011–2013*. [pdf]. Available at: www.abudhabi.ae/cs/groups/public/documents/publication/mjix/njq4/~edisp/adegp_nd_221648_en.pdf [Accessed 27 December 2012].

UAE Cabinet. (2010b) *UAE Vision 2021*. [pdf]. Available at: www.abudhabi.ae/cs/groups/public/documents/publication/mjix/njuw/~edisp/adegp_nd_221650_en.pdf [Accessed 27 December 2012].

UAE Interact. (2012). 'Cabinet Approves National Council for Tourism' & 'Antiquities' Board'. [Online]. Available at: www.uaeinteract.com/docs/Cabinet_approves_National_Council_for_Tourism_&_Antiquities%E2%80%99_board_/50747.htm [Accessed 5 January 2013].

Ulrichsen, K.C. (2010). *The GCC States and the Shifting Balance of Global Power*. Qatar: Georgetown University Qatar.

Underwood, S. (2013). 'Professional Reciprocity and its Opportunities'. In: Erskine-Loftus, P. (ed.) *Reimagining Museums: Practice in the Arabian Peninsula*. Edinburgh: MuseumsEtc, pp. 624–637.

UNESCO. (n.d.[a]). 'UNESCO in Brief – Mission and Mandate'. [Online]. Available at: https://en.unesco.org/about-us/introducing-unesco [Accessed 21 January 2019].

UNESCO. (n.d.[b]). 'The World Heritage Convention'. [Online]. Available at: https://whc.unesco.org/en/convention/ [Accessed 21 January 2019].

UNESCO. (n.d.[c]). 'World Heritage List'. [Online]. Available at: http://whc.unesco.org/en/list/ [Accessed 6 January 2019].

UNESCO. (n.d.[d]). 'World Heritage List. Cultural Sites of Al Ain (Hafit, Hili, Bidaa Bint Saud and Oases Areas)'. [Online]. Available at: http://whc.unesco.org/en/list/1343 [Accessed 21 July 2017].

UNESCO. (n.d.[e]). 'Browse the Lists of Intangible Cultural Heritage and the Register of Best Safeguarding: "United Arab Emirates"'. [Online]. Available at: www.unesco.org/culture/ich/en/lists?display=default&text=&inscription=0&country=00066&multinational=3&type=0&domain=0&display1=inscriptionID#tabs [Accessed 21 February 2016].

UNESCO. (n.d.[f]). 'Seven New Elements Inscribed on UNESCO's Representative List of the Intangible Cultural Heritage of Humanity'. [Online]. Available at: www.unesco.org/new/en/culture/themes/single-view/news/seven_new_elements_inscribed_on_unescos_representative_list_of_the_intangible_cultural_heritage_ of_humanity/#.UhHGMpIweSo [Accessed 13 November 2012 and 15 December 2014].

UNESCO. (n.d.[g]). 'Palace and Park of Fontainebleau'. [Online]. Available at: https://whc.unesco.org/en/list/160/ [Accessed 1 February 2019].

UNESCO. (1972). 'Convention Concerning the Protection of the World Cultural and Natural Heritage: Full Text'. [Online]. Available at: https://whc.unesco.org/en/conventiontext/ [Accessed 21 January 2019].

UNESCO. (2001) *Universal Declaration on Cultural Diversity.* [pdf]. Available at: http://unesdoc.unesco.org/images/0012/001271/127160m.pdf [Accessed 5 March 2012].

UNESCO. (2003a). '*Text of the Convention for the Safeguarding of the Intangible Cultural Heritage*'. Available at: https://ich.unesco.org/en/convention#art2 [Accessed 6 January 2019].

UNESCO. (2003b). *Language Vitality and Endangerment UNESCO Ad Hoc Expert Group on Endangered Languages Document submitted to the International Expert Meeting on UNESCO Programme Safeguarding of Endangered Languages Paris, 10–12 March 2003.* [pdf]. Available at: www.unesco.org/new/fileadmin/MULTIMEDIA/HQ/CLT/pdf/Language_vitality_and_endangerment_EN.pdf [Accessed 12 July 2018].

UNESCO. (2011). *Convention Concerning the Protection of the World Cultural and Natural Heritage World Heritage Committee.* Thirty-Fifth Session Paris, UNESCO Headquarters 19–29 June 2011. [pdf]. Available at: http://whc.unesco.org/archive/2011/whc11-35com-9Be.pdf [Accessed 7 February 2016].

UNESCO. (2019). 'World heritage List Statistics'. [Online]. Available at: http://whc.unesco.org/en/list/stat [Accessed 19 August 2019].

UNOG. (n.d.[a]). 'History of the League of Nations'. [Online]. Available at: www.unog.ch/80256EDD006B8954/(httpAssets)/36BC4F83BD9E4443C1257AF3004F-C0AE/%24file/Historical_overview_of_the_League_of_Nations.pdf [Accessed 11 July 2019].

UNOG. (n.d.[b]). 'League of Nations: Intellectual Cooperation'. United Nations Research Guides. [Online]. Available at: http://libraryresources.unog.ch/lonintellectualcooperation/ICIC [Accessed 11 July 2019].

Verbieren, S.; Cools, M.; and Van den Abbeele, A. (2008). 'Franchising: A Literature Review on Management and Control Issues'. *Review of Business and Economics.* 53(4), pp. 398–443.

Vergo, P. (1989). (ed.) *The New Museology*. London: Reaktion Books.

Vogel, C. (2009). 'Abu Dhabi Gets a Sampler of World Art'. *New York Times*. [Online]. Available at: www.nytimes.com/2009/05/27/arts/design/27louv.html [Accessed 8 August 2012].

Wakefield, S. (2011). 'Beyond Boundaries: Exploring Hybrid Heritage in Abu Dhabi'. Paper presented at the First International Conference on Emerging Research Paradigms in Business and Social Sciences. Middlesex University Dubai. November 22–24, 2011.

Wakefield, S. (2012). 'Falconry as Heritage in the United Arab Emirates'. *World Archaeology*. 44(2), pp. 280–290.

Wakefield, S. (2012). 'The Universal Museum: Towards a Critical Approach to the Museum Franchise'. Paper presented at the Special Session: Museums in Arabia, Arabian Seminar. The British Museum, London. July 14–16, 2012.

Wakefield, S. (2013). 'Hybrid Heritage and Cosmopolitanism in the Emirate of Abu Dhabi'. In: Erskine-Loftus, P. (ed.) *Reimagining Museums: Practice in the Arabian Peninsula*. Edinburgh: MuseumsEtc, pp. 98–129.

Wakefield, S. (2014). 'Heritage, Cosmopolitanism and Identity in Abu Dhabi'. In: Exell K. and Rico T. (eds.) *Cultural Heritage in the Arabian Peninsula: Debates, Discourses and Practices*. Farnham and Burlington: Ashgate, pp. 99–116.

Wakefield, S. (2015). 'Museum Development in the Gulf: Narrative and Architecture'. *Architecture and Urbanism Now*. Special Issue: UAE and The Gulf. 85(1), pp. 20–27.

Wakefield, S. (2017a). 'Contemporary Art and Migrant Identity "Construction" in the UAE and Qatar'. *Journal of Arabian Studies Arabia, the Gulf, and the Red Sea*. CIRS Special Issue: Art and Cultural Production in the GCC. 7(1), pp. 99–111.

Wakefield, S. (2017b). 'Transnational Heritage in Abu Dhabi: Power, Politics and Identity'. In: Stephenson, M. and Al-Hamarneh, A. (eds.) *International Tourism and the GCC States: Developments, Challenges and Opportunities*. Abingdon and New York: Routledge, pp. 235–244.

Wakefield, S. (2020). 'Museums, Migrant Labourers and Ethnic Spatiality in the United Arab Emirates'. In: Rey, V. (ed.) *The Art of Minorities: Cultural Representations in Museums of the Middle East and North Africa*. Edinburgh: Edinburgh University Press.

Wakefield, S. (ed.) (Forthcoming). *Museums of the Arabian Peninsula: Historical Developments and Contemporary Discourses*. Abingdon and New York: Routledge.

Wakefield, S. (ed.) (Forthcoming). 'Transnational Museologies in the UAE: New Models or Historicised Global Practice?' In: Wakefield, S. (ed.) *Museums of the Arabian Peninsula: Historical Developments and Contemporary Discourses*. Abingdon and New York: Routledge.

Wainwright, O. (2017). 'Louvre Abu Dhabi: Jean Nouvel's Spectacular Palace of Culture Shimmers in the Desert'. *The Guardian*. [Online]. Available at: www.theguardian.com/artanddesign/2017/nov/07/louvre-abu-dhabi-sheikh-chic-throws-controversial-construction-in-relief [Accessed 7 November 2017].

Walsh, K. (1992). *The Representation of the Past: Museums and Heritage in the Post Modern World*. London and New York: Routledge.

Wallace, M.A. (2006). *Museum Branding: How to Create and Maintain Image, Loyalty, and Support*. Oxford: Altamira Press.

WAM Emirates News Agency. (2018). 'Globes: Visions of the World' to Open at Louvre Abu Dhabi. *Emirates 24/7*. [Online]. Available at: www.emirates247.com/lifestyle/globes-visions-of-the-world-to-open-at-louvre-abu-dhabi-2018-03-13-1.666721 [Accessed 14 March 2018].

WAM Emirates News Agency. (2019). 'UAE to Welcome 8.92m Visitors from Top Five Source Markets by 2023'. *Emirates 24/7*. [Online]. 27 February. Available at: www.emirates247.com/business/uae-to-welcome-8-92m-visitors-from-top-five-source-markets-by-2023-says-atm-research-2019-02-27-1.680330 [Accessed 12 March 2019].

Waterton, E. and Watson, S. (2015a). 'Heritage as a Focus of Research: Past, Present and New Directions'. In: Waterton, E. and Watson, S. *The Palgrave Handbook of Contemporary Heritage Research*. Basingstoke and New York: Palgrave Macmillan, pp. 1–17.

Waterton, E. and Watson, S. (2015b). 'The Ontological Politics of Heritage; or How Research Can Spoil a Good Story'. In: Waterton, E. and Watson, S. *The Palgrave Handbook of Contemporary Heritage Research*. Basingstoke and New York: Palgrave Macmillan, pp. 21–36.

Waterton, E.; Watson, S. and Silverman, H. (2017). 'An Introduction to Heritage in Action'. In: Silverman, H.; Waterton, E. and Watson, S. (eds.) *Heritage in Action: Making the Past in the Present*. Switzerland: Springer, pp. 3–16

West Kowloon Cultural District Authority. (2018a). 'About the District'. [Online]. Available at: www.westkowloon.hk/en/the-district/about-the-district [Accessed 29 January 2018].

West Kowloon Cultural District Authority. (2018b). 'Authority: Vision and Objectives'. [Online]. Available at: www.westkowloon.hk/en/the-authority/vision-and-objectives [Accessed 29 January 2018].

West Kowloon Cultural District Authority. (2018c). 'The District: Development Plan'. [Online]. Available at: www.westkowloon.hk/en/the-district/development-plan [Accessed 29 January 2018].

West Kowloon Cultural District Authority. (2018d). 'Xiqu Centre'. [Online]. Available at: www.westkowloon.hk/en/the-district/architecture-facilities/xiqu-centre [Accessed 29 January 2018].

West Kowloon Cultural District Authority. (2018e). 'M+ Pavilion'. [Online]. Available at: www.westkowloon.hk/en/mplus/m-pavilion [Accessed 29 January 2018].

Winter, T. (2009a). 'Asian Tourism and the Retreat of Anglo-Western Centrism in Tourism Theory'. *Current Issues in Tourism*. 12(1), pp. 21–31.

Winter, T. (2009b). 'Conclusion: Recasting Tourism Theory towards an Asian Future'. In: Winter, T.; Teo, P. and Chang, T.C. (eds.), *Asia on Tour*. Abingdon and New York: Routledge, pp. 315–325.

Winter, T. (2010). 'Heritage Tourism: The Dawn of a New Era?' In: Labadi, S. and Long, C. (eds.) *Heritage and Globalization*. Abingdon and New York: Routledge, pp. 117–129.

Winter, T. and Daly, P. (2011). 'Heritage in Asia: Converging Forces, Conflicting Values'. In: Daly, P. and Winter, T. (eds.) *The Routledge Handbook of Heritage in Asia*. Abingdon: Routledge, pp. 1–35.

WKK Architects. (n.d.). *Burj Al Arab, Dubai*. [Online]. Available at: http://wkkarchitects.com/#/burj-al-arab/ [Accessed 15 December 2012].

Wong, C.U.I.; McIntosh, A. and Ryan, C. (2013). 'Buddhism and Tourism: Perceptions of the Monastic Community at Pu-Tuo-Shan, China'. *Annals of Tourism Research*. 40, pp. 213–234.

World Bank. (2017). 'UNESCO and World Bank Collaborate on Culture, Urban Development, and Resilience'. *Press Release*. [Online]. Available at: www.worldbank.org/en/news/press-release/2017/07/13/unesco-and-world-bank-collaborate-on-culture-urban-development-and-resilience [Accessed 11 April 2019].

World Travel & Tourism Council (2018). *Travel & Tourism Economic Impact 2018: United Arab Emirates.* Available at: www.wttc.org/-/media/files/reports/economic-impact-research/regions-2019/world2019.pdf [Accessed 6 January 2019].

Yee, A. (2011). 'An Increasingly Important Economic Partner for Abu Dhabi'. *The National*, p. 7.

Young, L. (2006). Villages that Never Were: The Museum Village as a Heritage Centre'. *International Journal of Heritage Studies.* 12(4), pp. 321–338.

Young, R. (1991). *White Mythologies: Writing History and the West.* London: Routledge.

Young, P. (2001). *Postcolonialism: An Historical Introduction.* Oxford: Blackwell Publishers.

Al-Zaabi, M. (2011). Interview at the National Center for Documentation and Research. 30 March 2011.

Zacharias, A. (2012). 'Ras al Khaimah Tribe Return to Abandoned Village'. *The National.* [Online]. Available at: www.thenational.ae/news/uae-news/ras-al-khaimah-tribe-return-to-abandoned-village [Accessed 26 February 2012].

Zacharias, A. (2018). 'Abu Dhabi's Founder's Memorial opens to the public'. *The National.* [Online]. Available at: www.thenational.ae/uae/abu-dhabi-s-founder-s-memorial-opens-to-the-public-1.723834 [Accessed 22 April 2018].

Zaharna, R.S. (1995). 'Understanding Cultural Preferences of Arab Communication Patterns'. *Public Relations Review.* 21(2), pp. 241–255.

Zayed National Museum. (n.d.[a]) 'The Vision: Biography'. [Online]. Available at: www.zayednationalmuseum.ae/the-vision/biography.html [Accessed 25 May 2013].

Zayed National Museum. (n.d.[b]) Galleries: Overview. [Online]. Available at: www.zayednationalmuseum.ae/galleries/sheikh-zayed-life-and-times.html [Accessed 25 May 2013].

Zayed University. (n.d.). 'Master of Arts (M.A.) in Museum Studies'. [Online]. Available at: www.zu.ac.ae/main/en/graduate_programs/Graduate_Programs_Folder/Masters_Degree_Prog/CSSH_Masters/intro_ma_museum_studies.aspx [Accessed 15 December 2011].

Zukin, S. (1995). *The Cultures of Cities.* Cambridge: Blackwell.

Zulaika, J. (1997). 'The Seduction of Bilbao'. *Architecture.* 86(12), pp. 59–62.

Zulaika, J. (2003). *Guggenheim Bilbao Museoa: Museums, Architecture, and City Renewal.* Nevada: Center for Basque Studies.

Zuliani, S. (2014). 'The Postcolonial "Exhibitionary Complex": The Role of the International Expo in Migrating and Multicultural Societies'. In: Chambers, I.; De Angelis, A.; Ianniciello, C.; Orabona, M. and Quadraro, M. (eds.) *The Postcolonial Museum: The Arts of Memory and the Pressures of History.* Abingdon and New York: Routledge, pp. 175–184.

Index

Note: **Bold** page numbers refer to tables; *Italic* page numbers refer to figures and page numbers followed by 'n' denote endnotes.

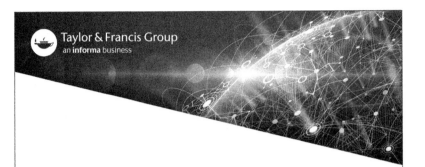

Printed in the United States
By Bookmasters